Victor Duruy

History of Rome and of the Roman people

From its origin to the Invasion of the Barbarians

Victor Duruy

History of Rome and of the Roman people
From its origin to the Invasion of the Barbarians

ISBN/EAN: 9783337046682

Printed in Europe, USA, Canada, Australia, Japan

Cover: Foto ©ninafisch / pixelio.de

More available books at **www.hansebooks.com**

BARBARIANS.

By VICTOR DURUY,

MEMBER OF THE INSTITUTE, EX-MINISTER OF PUBLIC INSTRUCTION, ETC.

TRANSLATED BY M. M. RIPLEY AND W. J. CLARKE.

EDITED BY

THE REV. J. P. MAHAFFY,

PROFESSOR OF ANCIENT HISTORY, TRINITY COLLEGE, DUBLIN.

Containing over Three Thousand Engravings, One Hundred Maps and Plans,

AND NUMEROUS CHROMO-LITHOGRAPHS.

VOLUME VI. — SECTION I.

PUBLISHED BY

C. F. JEWETT PUBLISHING COMPANY,

BOSTON.

TABLE OF CONTENTS.

VOLUME VI.

———•———

THE EMPIRE AND ROMAN SOCIETY IN THE FIRST TWO CENTURIES OF OUR ERA (*Continued*).

CHAPTER LXXXII. (*Continued.*)

THE FAMILY.

CHAPTER LXXXIII.

THE CITY.

CHAPTER LXXXIV.

THE PROVINCES.

CHAPTER LXXXV.

GOVERNMENT AND ADMINISTRATION.

CHAPTER LXXXVI.

MANNERS.

CHAPTER LXXXVII.

IDEAS.

ELEVENTH PERIOD.

THE AFRICAN AND SYRIAN PRINCES (180–235 A. D.).

CHAPTER LXXXVIII.

COMMODUS, PERTINAX, DIDIUS JULIANUS, AND THE WARS OF SEVERUS (180–211).

CHAPTER LXXXIX.

GOVERNMENT OF SEPTIMIUS SEVERUS (193–211).

CHAPTER XC.

THE CHURCH AT THE BEGINNING OF THE THIRD CENTURY.

LIST OF FULL-PAGE ENGRAVINGS.[1]

VOLUME VI.

[1] Facing the pages indicated.

ALPHABETICAL INDEX

TO

TEXT ILLUSTRATIONS, INCLUDING MAPS AND PLANS

VOLUME VI.

———

HISTORY OF ROME.

THE EMPIRE AND ROMAN SOCIETY

IN THE FIRST TWO CENTURIES OF OUR ERA

(CONTINUED).

CHAPTER LXXXII — (Continued).

THE FAMILY.

IV. — MASTER AND SLAVE; PATRONUS AND FREEDMAN.

HOMER shows us, in the palace of Ulysses, twelve women employed night and day in grinding corn for the house, *i. e.*, for perhaps two hundred persons. We now have flour-mills in which twenty-four workmen can grind every day by machinery as much corn as will furnish bread for a hundred thousand men. In ancient societies an enormous amount of manual labor was required to supply the simplest wants of life; so that slavery was then a necessity, as, for other reasons, it so long seemed to be in European colonies within the tropics.

In the Roman Empire a person was born a slave or became so; slavery was kept up by birth, commerce, and war. Anciently the creditor sold the insolvent debtor; magistrates, the citizen who refused military service; and the father, his own son. These sources of slavery became less abundant as manners became milder, but without entirely disappearing; not until the time of Caracalla and Diocletian do we find rescripts which protect the child and the insolvent debtor against servitude imposed by the father and the creditor.[1] Against piracy, another source of slavery, the Emperors

[1] *Code*, vii. 16, 1, and iv. 10, 12 (*anno* 294).

constantly strove, keeping careful watch along endangered coasts. Hadrian broke up the *ergastula*, where many persons of free birth were kept as slaves; and Trajan granted to children exposed or stolen a perpetual right of claiming their original free con-

dition. Lastly, by an interpretation favorable to liberty. Hadrian and the jurisconsults admit that if the slave-mother had been free for any period during her pregnancy her son should be born free.

According to the rigor of primitive law. the slave belonged to his master as a chattel; he had no will of his own. he was not a person. and consequently the protection of civil law did not extend to him. He did not contract marriage; his union was a mere physical fact (*contubernium*). and his children "were an increase" to the master's benefit. However, at the Saturnalia he enjoyed a short space of liberty; at the Compitalia

SLAVE CHILD (VILLA BORGHESE).

he offered sacrifices like the free-born; Minerva shielded his labor. and religion protected his tomb.

But absolute logic yielded by degrees to humanity; and the Emperors. without touching the actual principle of slavery. which was one of the bases of ancient society, progressively softened its rigor. "In civil law." said Ulpian. "the slave is nothing; in natural law. all men are equal." [1] It was impossible but that this philosophic doctrine held by the jurisconsults should penetrate

[1] *Digest*, l. 17. 32.

here and there into the laws when equity was entering into them from every side, and the interest of the master when properly understood counselled kindness towards his slaves.[1] Cato has no great reputation for mildness, yet he allowed his wife to give the breast to the children of their slaves, in order that with her milk they might imbibe affection for her own son.[2]

A Petronian law, which perhaps dates from Augustus, several senatus-consulta, and a rescript of Hadrian, prohibited the master

MINERVA OVERLOOKING SLAVES AT WORK.[3]

from delivering up his slaves or selling them to fight in the arena without some legitimate cause verified by public authority, and Marcus Aurelius nullified clauses in wills to the effect *ut cum bestiis pugnarent.*[4]

The slave incurably ill was turned out of doors. Claudius decided that if a master abandoned a slave suffering from serious infirmities, the latter should be free, and that if the master killed him he should be indicted for murder. Antoninus, plainly defining the penalty, punished the master as though he had slain the slave

---

[1] See the care that Columella took of his, even of those whom it was needful to keep in chains. In his house every slave woman who had three children was set free from labor, and she who had more was emancipated (*De Re rust.* i. 7-8).

[2] Plutarch, *Cato,* 20.

[3] Bas-relief found at Capua, bearing an inscription commemorative of the construction or restoration of the theatre of that city. Cf. Guhl and Koner, *Das Leben der Griechen und Römer,* p. 685.

[4] *Digest,* XVIII. i. 42.

of another man.[1] Now this penalty was for the *honestiores* banishment, for the *humiliores* death.[2] Antoninus even decided that if slaves who had fled to temples or to the statue of an Emperor could prove to the magistrates that they had been cruelly treated, the master should be compelled to sell them.[3] Hadrian had already taken away, in the most serious cases, the right of the master to cause his slave's death; domestic justice subordinated to public justice could carry out a capital sentence only after a magistrate's decision.[4]

We see then that under the Empire, and chiefly by the Antonines, the slave was protected against extreme violence; so was he also against bad treatment, and even as regards his honor. He was allowed to lodge a complaint against his master for cruelty, deprivation of food, attempts on modesty.[5] Hadrian condemned to five years' banishment a matron who for very slight reasons misused her slaves. In fact legislation came very near allowing the slave rights as a husband and father. He could not indeed contract a legitimate marriage, but the natural parentage which resulted from the union was considered after emancipation to constitute a new civil hindrance to marriage. Some regard was paid to the feelings and affections of slaves. At sales separation was interdicted of father and son, husband and wife, brother and brother; and the reason that Ulpian gives for this is implied in the word *pietas*, which contains the idea of religious justice and humanity.[6] Later it was established that the slave attached to farm labor and inscribed on the registers of the land tax could not be separated from the estate.[7] The law interposed even between him and his master to prevent the latter from compelling the slave to do work which was degrading to

[1] *Inst.* i. 8, sect. 2. See Vol. IV. p. 526.

[2] *Digest*, xlviii. 8, 5, sect. 5. Constantine, more indulgent towards the master, required for the application of this penalty that the slave should have been killed at one blow, which allowed the former in many instances to escape the rigor of the law (*Code*, ix. 14).

[3] Gaius, i. 53.

[4] See above, p. 397.

[5] Rescripts of Antoninus (in the *Digest*, i. 6, 2) and of Septimius Severus: . . . *Praefecto Urbi datum est ut mancipia tueatur ne prostituantur* (ibid. 12, 8).

[6] *Digest*, xxi. 1, 35, and xxxiii. 7, 12, sect. 7 : . . . *Neque duram separationem injunxisse credendus est.* Cf. Paulus, *ibid.* xxi. 1, 39; Scaevola, *ibid.* xxxii. 41, sect. 2 : *pietatis intuitu.*

[7] Valentinian and Valens, in the *Code*, xi. 47, 7. [He was in fact made a serf, as the Russian peasant was till lately.—Ed.]

him; for example, to make a handicraftsman of a literary man, or a porter of a musician. Cato would have felt indignant at this intermeddling of the magistrate with domestic discipline, and the intractable conservative would have been right. for it was nothing less than the beginning of a revolution. Humanity was then making one of its great social advances. These laws indeed were not devised by a few wise men in advance of their time; they were called for by the manners of the day, which in their turn were the result of the new modes of thought. feeling, and living which

AN EDUCATED SLAVE CALCULATING BEFORE HIS MASTER.[1]

prevailed in that immense Empire. Juvenal, so stern towards the noble and the rich, is full of sympathy for the slave. " whose body is made of the same clay as ours," full of anger against the master, " who delights to hear the crackling sound of the thong. —a music sweeter to him than the song of the Sirens." [2]

Thus the slave ceased to be a chattel, he became a person : and in teaching the equality of all before God, Christianity. now drawing near, was destined to introduce still more humanity into the relations of the master with his slaves. In respect to the legal condition of the latter it will do nothing more than the Antonines

[1] Sarcophagus in the Capitol, Museo Capit. vol. pl xx.   [2] Sat. iv. initio.

did. The Empire was rewarded for this solicitude: it had not one servile war, while republican Rome had had four.[1]

As regards third parties, the slave remained his master's tool. All harm done to him was damage done the master, and the latter sought reparation by special actions. Thus the Aquilian law gave the master whose slave had been killed the right of demanding from the perpetrator of the murder the highest value of the slave during the last year: an indemnity was also granted in the case of simple wounding. " The praetor," says Ulpian, " must punish an injury done to a slave." Doubtless it was the master's property which the law protected in the slave; at the same time, without effacing from him the stamp of servitude, it obliged the master and the rest of free men by degrees to recognize him as also a man.

The slave was unable to hold property; all that he gained was for his master's profit: that was the rule. But this rule was by degrees modified in practice. Most of the industrial population being in servitude, masters found it advantageous to interest the slave in the profits of their business by allowing him the free disposition of a *peculium*, which served as the capital employed in carrying on the work. In law, this *peculium* belonged to the master; but as a matter of fact he rarely took it. He even found it for his advantage to promise the slave his liberty when the latter should have saved up a certain sum, and the law gave the decision that in the absence of any expressed statement to the contrary, the gift of liberty should carry with it the gift of the *peculium*. Thus was brought about a situation which would have seemed most strange to an old Roman, — the master kept an account with his own slaves; and while the natural obligations created by these business relations were not legally protected, a civil security could be added to them.

In the employment of a *peculium* there was need to contract active or passive obligations, and the slave had neither the right of binding himself personally nor of binding his master. The praetor secured the new condition of the slave by creating the action *de peculio,* by means of which third parties might obtain their due from the master to the amount of the *peculium*. In

[1] See in Vol. II. the two servile wars in Sicily, that of the gladiators in Italy, and the war against the pirates.

this case the slave seemed to be acting in his own name; but when he was the mandatory of his master, the latter was put under obligation. The slave placed in charge of a business or a maritime expedition bound his master also for the fulfilment of all engagements made by him in the exercise of his functions. Lastly, if the master had not authorized the negotiation or the industrial undertaking of his slave, he could at least be sued to the amount of the profit he had derived therefrom. The state recognized in public slaves, who were very numerous and in a very easy condition, the right of disposing by will of the half of their *peculium*, and the younger Pliny allowed his slaves to dispose of the whole in favor of a fellow-slave. No doubt many masters did the same, and even better, by not requiring that the *peculium* should remain in the *familia*, where the master could always legally appropriate it.

A rescript of Caracalla runs thus: "The slave presented for enfranchisement must render an account of his management." That it was needful to make a general law on this subject proves that many slaves were intrusted by their masters with the conduct of industrial or commercial affairs.[1] History shows, in fact, a great number of persons of servile condition who were confidential advisers of their rich masters, *employés* of governors in the offices of the provincial administration, even of the Emperor in the innumerable *officia* of the palace,[2] and some enjoying large credit, or making display enough in their manner of living to cause envy even to the noblest of the patricians. Thus a slave belonging to Tiberius, imperial treasurer at Lyons, makes the journey to Rome with an escort suitable for a prince, — a physician, three secretaries, an agent, a treasurer, a servant, two cooks, two money-changers, and two lackeys. At Pompeii another acts as a banker, and on the receipts given in the name of the duumvirs he puts his seal by the side of that of the city magistrates.[3]

---

[1] . . . *Nisi prius administrationum rationes reddiderit quas, quum in servitute esset, gessisset* (*Digest.* xl. 12, 34).

[2] The *Digest* (xlix. 14, 30, and 46, 47) frequently mentions *actores*, slave administrators of properties lapsed to the treasury, and prohibits procurators from alienating them by sale or manumission without the Emperor's consent, because the treasury has need of slaves who are well acquainted with the management of estates. The researches made recently in an ancient cemetery in Carthage prove that the subordinate offices of the proconsulate were filled by slaves and freedmen who lived and died in them.

[3] Tablets found in 1875 (*Le Tavolete cerate di Pompei*, by De Petra).

All this was not yet for the slave the ownership of his own person and property, but it was the beginning of it; and if even under the Antonines he was still an instrument of labor, he was no longer treated as a thing which may be thrown away or broken at will: human personality was recognized in him. Marcus Aurelius went so far as to give him the right of prosecuting his master if the latter refused to grant the enfranchisement of which he had received the price, which he had been obliged to promise at the time of purchase, or which a testator had made obligatory upon him.[1]

As a conspicuous symbol of the protection accorded by the Empire to the most wretched, the Emperor's statue was an inviolable asylum for the suppliant slave who came and embraced its knees.

The more recent legislation, therefore, showed itself milder for the slave. It protected him against violence and allowed him to increase his *peculium*, it acknowledged his right to appeal against injustice, and it had dried up some of the sources of servitude; but it did not open to him a broader road to liberty. Of the two laws which till Justinian's time regulated enfranchisements, one of them, the *lex Junia Norbana*, had created a sort of half-servitude which facilitated the escape from slavery, though making the complete acquisition of liberty more rare;[2] the other, the *lex Aelia Sentia*, limited the number of those enfranchised by will. The tax of the twentieth on enfranchisements arrested the good-will of the master, who saw himself obliged to make a double sacrifice, since he had to give a sum of money to the treasury at the same time that he gave liberty to his slave. Finally, a council composed at Rome of five senators and five knights, and in the provinces of five *recuperatores*, all Roman citizens, were to examine into the reasons for the enfranchisement; so that the master might indeed by the act of setting free deprive himself of his property, but there remained to the civil power, as represented by the council, the right of deciding whether the new citizen was worthy to

[1] On the whole question of slavery, see M. Wallon's book. The print given on the next page represents a monument erected to Amemptus, a freedman of the Empress Livia: *Drea Aug*(ustae) *libertus*). We give one of the sides and the reverse of the monument, as well as the bas-relief which decorates the principal face,—a scene which to the ancients was a picture of future happiness (Museum of the Louvre, Frohner, *op. cit.* No. 373, pp. 312 *et seq.*).

[2] See Vol. IV. pp. 112, note 3; 113, note 4; 134, notes 3 and 4; and 371.

SEPULCHRAL CIPPUS OF A FREEDMAN (SEE P. 8, N. 1).

obtain citizenship.[1] In spite of these obstacles, many freedmen, escaping from servitude, obtained riches, but not honors.[2] Tacitus remarks with bitterness that the Germans knew how to keep in an inferior condition those parvenus who at Rome eclipsed the oldest families with their insulting luxury, or, like Narcissus and Pallas, took advantage of their master's vices to govern the Empire.[3]

The freedman became, according to circumstances — a *citizen*, without, however, possessing all the rights of the Roman by descent; a *Junian Latin*, whereby he lived as if free, but died a slave, his estate going to his patron, as the *peculium* did to the master;[4] a *peregrinus dediticius*, who was prohibited from approaching Rome. Sometimes, however, every trace of his former condition was obliterated, so that he could enjoy all the rights of citizenship and attain honors in general refused to the freedman. Caesar and Augustus, who created patricians, created also *ingenui*, — that is, recognized as born in liberty some who had been born in servitude; and the jurisconsults found a motive of humanity for this modification of the old law. They said: "In this case respect is paid to the state in which all men were at their origin, and not to that whence the freedman has come forth."[5]

The freedman was under the obligation of considering his former master as a father; he took his name and remained connected with his family. These relations, established by Roman manners, were embodied in a number of legal obligations. First of all was respect and deference towards the patron; who, in order to secure these from his freedmen, was armed with a right of correction, which the Emperors softened by requiring the intervention of the magistrate, but did not suppress entirely. Patrons might strike their freedmen, — as is shown in the case of the one whom

[1] Gaius, i. 20.

[2] The freedman was unable even to enter the curia of a provincial city, and in early times he was forbidden the army (*Code*, xi. 21, *ad leg. Visell.*).

[3] *Germ.* 25, and the famous passage (*Ann.* xiii. 27): . . . *late fusum id corpus [libertorum]; hinc plerumque tribus, decurias, ministeria magistratibus et sacerdotibus, cohortes etiam in urbe conscriptas et plurimis equitum, plerisque senatoribus, non aliunde originem trahi.*

[4] This condition of the Junian Latin was like that of those subject to mortmain in the Middle Ages.

[5] This was the *restitutio natalium*, which effaced all trace of servile birth, and the *jus aureorum annulorum*, which opened the path to honors.

the younger Pliny protected from his master's blows, — could have them exiled beyond the twentieth mile,[1] at a later period could have them sent to the quarries or subjected to a penalty fixed either by the prefect of the city or the governor of the province. Claudius had decided that a freedman bringing a suit which involved the status of his patron should lose his liberty. Commodus generalized the principle that ingratitude on the part of the freedman should cause his relapse into servitude.[2] Even in the case of actually proved adultery between the patron and the freedman's wife, the freedman must not kill his former master. "For," says Papinian, " if he is bound to spare his reputation, he is in greater reason bound to spare his life."[3] This obligation of respect was imposed on the freedman and his children even towards the children of the patron. Pliny, when soliciting from Trajan citizenship for several Junian freedmen, takes care to tell the Emperor that he has previously made sure of their patrons' consent.[4]

By an application of this principle the freedman needed the praetor's permission in order to sue the patron and his parents or children. He was forbidden to bring against them a suit involving infamy except for very grave reasons, and never one involving capital punishment. He owed them help in times of need, and could never refuse the administration of their property or the guardianship of their children: Vergil consigns to the infernal regions[5] the freedman who has betrayed his patron. Lastly, the

[1] According to the law *Aelia Sentia*, passed under Augustus.

[2] Tac., *Ann.* xiii. 26 and 27; *Digest*, xxxvii. 14 and 15. Cf. Accarias, *Précis de droit romain*, i. 74.

[3] *Digest*, xlviii. 5, 38, 69.

[4] *Epist.* x. 6.

[5] The print on the next page in the lower portion represents some of the legends relating to the infernal regions, — Sisyphus pushing the rock and urged by a Fury with her whip; Mercury, the messenger of the dead; Hercules chaining up Cerberus, while a Fury tries to repulse him with torches; Tantalus, the king of Phrygia, in Asiatic costume, trying to seize fruits which always escape his hand. In the upper part, in a magnificent temple, Dionysus Chthonios, the infernal Bacchus, to whom Ceres has come to ask back Proserpine, whom she has sought with a lighted torch throughout all the world. On the right the three judges in Hades, and above them perhaps Theseus and his friend Pirithous, delivered from their captivity in the infernal regions and protected by Minerva (?). To the left Orpheus playing the lyre, and two groups difficult to explain. The two young men with a star above their heads are perhaps the Dioscuri with their mother Leda, herself also become a divinity. Is the other group on the left, in contrast to the condemned of the lower part, a family of the blest making their way to the Elysian Fields across the kingdom of Hades? See Millin, *Les Tombeaux de Canosa*, pp. 5-23, folio.

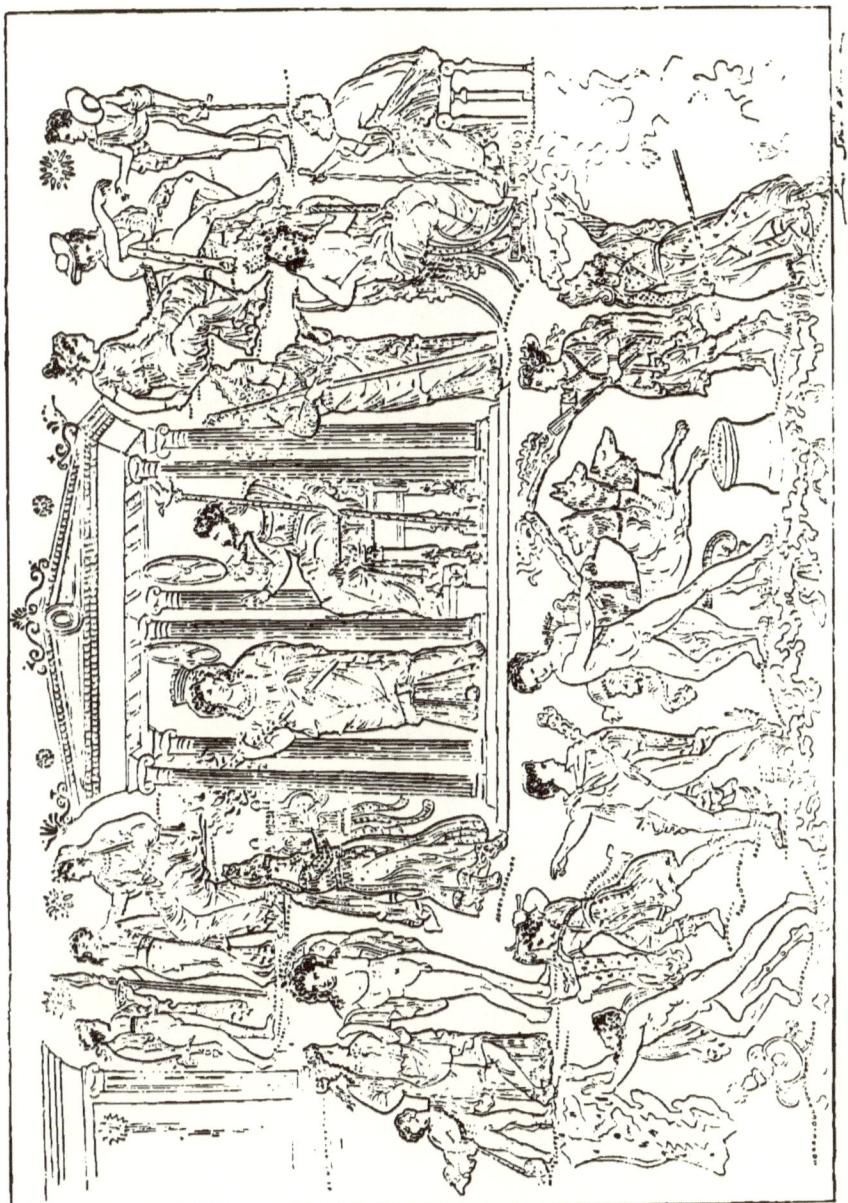

THE INFERNAL REGIONS, OR KINGDOM OF HADES (FROM A VASE OF CANOSA).

patron and his descendants were the legal guardians of the freedman, were even his heirs if the latter left no children, and were in
any case the heirs of the freedwoman. Marcus Aurelius abolished
this distinction; and since the passing of the Orphitian senatus-
consultum the children of a *libertina* inherited from their mother.

Enfranchisement was often accompanied by onerous conditions.
For example, the freedman engaged under oath, or in the form
of a written stipulation, to make presents in certain circumstances
and to render services either of respect (*officiales*), — which ceased
at the patron's death, unless it had been expressly stipulated that
they should be continued to the children — or of utility (*fabriles*),
which passed to the heirs of the patron along with the estate. A
special interdict, *de liberto homine exhibendo*, furnished sanction to
this obligation. The freedman's services then had a real value
for the patron; but they were not considered as commercial
transactions, and the law *Aelia Sentia* forbade setting on them
a value in money.

When the enfranchisement was not entirely free and sponta-
neous, the rights of patronage were considerably diminished. Thus
the heir who enfranchised a slave in fulfilment of a trust could
not accuse the freedman of ingratitude, or demand supplies from
him, or impose on him the obligation of services. He even lost
his right of patronage if he had set the slave free when compelled
by legal authority. The refusal of provisions[1] or the abuse of
authority on the part of the patron brought the loss of the right of
patronage. But these relations were as a rule marked by respect
on the one side and affection on the other. At the time of the
triumviral proscriptions the fidelity of slaves was remarked;
under the Empire, freedmen were the habitual confidants of their
patrons, and many in time of need their devoted servants, even to
death and dishonor. A senator kills a woman who refused to
marry him, and is accused of murder: his freedman assumes the
crime as his own, and exposes himself to a frightful punishment,
by declaring that it was he who struck the blow to avenge his
master.[2]

Thus they in fact formed a part of the family; often the patron
chose them to be his heirs.[3] At Nicomedeia and in many other

[1] *Digest*, xxxvii. 14, 5, sect. 1.   [2] Tac., *Ann.* xiii. 14.   [3] *C. I. L.* vol. iii. No. 328.

places the master builds a tomb to his "very faithful and very loving slave."[1] In an epitaph on the Appian Way a freedman of Cotta Messalinus relates that his patron gave him at different times to the amount of four hundred thousand sesterces, — i. e., sufficient to raise him to the rank of knight; that the patron undertook the education of his children; that he gave dowries to his daughters like a father, and aided his son to attain the rank of military tribune; and that, finally, he has at his own expense provided

SEPULCHRAL REMAINS, ON THE APPIAN WAY.

this funeral monument.[2] Many did even more, — they admitted their freedmen to lie beside them in the tombs they had built for themselves, so that even in death the *paterfamilias* was surrounded by all his household. This custom, which was general, shows how strongly the Roman family was constituted. Cotta was a friend of Tiberius. A century after, the younger Pliny inserted in his will a legacy of nearly two million sesterces, the interest of which was to be employed in the support of his hundred enfranchised slaves.[3] The provident solicitude of the master for those who

[1] *Inscr. de Lyon*, Nos. 113, 376, 505; Heuzey, *Mission de Macédoine*, p. 41.
[2] Henzen, *Annales de l'Instit.* 1865, p. 6.
[3] The legacy amounted to 1,866,666 sesterces, the annual interest of which at 6 per cent would amount to 111,999 sesterces, for each freedman 1,119 sesterces, or a maintenance of about

had served him was indeed one of the moral obligations which this society imposed. Is it as much observed in modern times?

We have seen that the Emperor's freedmen were very important personages; in due proportion it was also often the same in families and cities, and for this we have given the reason already.[1] Many slaves gained liberty by their vices; but many also by their ability, and some by their virtues. We know what Cicero thought of Tiro, his *libertinus*, or rather his friend. One of this class, on whom had rested the burden of two servitudes, since he was the freedman of a freedman of Augustus, had this inscribed on his tomb: "Religious and of pure morals, I have lived as much as possible without lawsuits, quarrels, or debts. I was faithful to my friends, poor in goods, but rich in heart."[2]

The relations between patron and freedman formed a clearly defined legal condition; it was by no means the same as regards the relations between clients and him whom they styled their lord and king (*dominum regemque*). Of this relation we shall therefore speak only in the chapter on the City.

V. Persons in Mancipio and the Coloni.

The father invested with the *potestas* could sell his child to a third person. This sale, which took place by mancipation, gave the purchaser a right called *mancipium*, which was nearly equivalent to the right of property. The person *in mancipio* was considered as a slave. Moreover, while the *patria potestas* and the *manus* ceased at the death of the father or the husband, the *mancipium*, or right of property, passed to the heirs of the purchaser. The person *in mancipio* had no longer any political rights, but preserved

$50. After the decease of the pensioners this revenue was to be used in defraying the cost of an annual banquet for the citizens of Como (Orelli, No. 1.172). See Vol. V. p. 566, a still more important foundation of Dasumius, and in the *Herodes Atticus* of Vidal Lablache (p. 52) the funeral inscriptions which witness so vividly to the affection of Atticus and his wife for their freedman Polydeucion.

[1] Vol. IV. p. 522.

[2] Wilmanns, 2,704. See, in Wallon, *Hist. de l'esclavage*, iii. 62-75, all the ameliorations introduced by jurisprudence into legislation relative to enfranchisements.

his condition of birth and could bring an action for damages against his master. His previous marriage remained good, and his children preserved their liberty. Like the slave, the person in *mancipio* made profit for his master, and the obligations contracted by him were legally payable only from the property which he would have possessed had he not fallen into that condition. Moreover, the usage of *mancipium*, like that of *manus*, became more and more rare, and was restricted to the case in which the son having caused an injury. the father gave him *in mancipio* to the injured person, by way of indemnity.

The insolvent debtor adjudged to his creditor, *addictus*, and working on behalf of the latter until he is indemnified ; the *auctoratus*, who was sold as a gladiator ; the Roman, a prisoner of war ransomed by another Roman. — were in a similar condition.

We find like relations of dependence in the colonial system, which made a beginning before the time of Constantine, being developed early as a social necessity in proportion as the class of small farmers diminished and large estates were formed.[1] To bring the *latifundia* into culture, from the failure of free labor the proprietor established slaves there whose interest he made it to draw the largest produce possible from the lands, and also free laborers, who were either farmers paying a money rent or *coloni* dividing the produce with the owner. We have nothing to say of this leasehold farmer except that the leases constantly were made longer, so as to become gradually changed into a perpetual rent-charge or long-term lease. " The cities," says Gaius, " never resume occupation of the land so long as the farmer or his heirs pay the rent."[2] and the colleges, corporations, etc., did as the cities. As for the slaves employed in the cultivation of the estate, while still chattels of which the master may dispose, they were in the interests of the domain left on the soil and customarily transferred with it. In order to determine at a census the value of a landed estate. the slaves " who stocked it " were reckoned in. The usage became established of considering them as attached to the soil. Marcus Aurelius confirmed that usage.[3] and the Emperors of the fourth century prohibited a sale of the slaves without the land.

[1] See what Columella (i. 3) and Appian (*Bell. civ.* i. 7) say of the *latifundia*.
[2] *Comm.* iii. 145.   [3] *Digest*, xxx. 112.

or of the land without the slaves.[1] Here we see the appearance of the serfs of the soil.

The metayer tenure also begins a new rural condition, which the Middle Ages were to inherit. "There shall be included," says a rescript of the Theodosian Code,[2] "in the survey of the estate the slaves and the domiciled peasants or *coloni*." Cato, Varro, and Tacitus make mention of these laborers; Columella gave to the proprietor of several estates this rule for good management, — that he should cultivate the land on which he resides by means of his slaves, but the rest of his land by the free *coloni*. He desired that the *coloni* should be hereditary. "The most prosperous domain," he says, "is that which the laborers till who are born on it."[3] This wish was fulfilled: there are inscriptions speaking of laborers who have been on the same land twenty, thirty, fifty years,[4] and Tacitus was already aware of the fact that these cultivators owed to the landlord a fixed quantity of corn, cattle, and clothing.[5]

Private individuals had *coloni*; the state and the emperor, represented by the two administrations of the treasury and the *res privata*, had many more. In the time of the Antonines the law was already concerned in the *coloni Caesaris*, and Hadrian made general regulations concerning them, — a fact which leads us to suppose that this rural class was very ancient.

There were several sorts of *coloni*, or farm laborers. Some, holders of a long term, or even hereditary, paid to the farmer a fixed rent or a part of the produce,[6] and owed the state the poll-tax and military service. Others, settled on a vast imperial domain (*saltus*), the greatest part of which was farmed out to one or more *conductores*, paid the usual rent in cash or in kind, but in addition furnished obligatory labor to secure a return from the land of the treasury. In a document recently discovered, the farm laborers

---

[1] Constantine and Valentinian I. in the *Code*, xi. 47, 2 and 7. [2] ix. 42, 7.

[3] *Felicissimus fundus qui colonos indigenas habet* (i. 7).

[4] Mommsen, *Inscr. Neap.* Nos. 2,572, 2,901, 5,501; Orelli, No. 4,644.

[5] *Frumenti modum dominus aut pecoris, aut vestis, ut colono, injungit* (*Germ.* 25). Cf. Pliny, *Epist.* iii. 19.

[6] *Colonus . . . qui ad pecuniam numeratam conducit . . . partiarius colonus [qui] quasi societatis jure et damnum et lucrum cum domino fundi partitur* (Gaius. in *Digest*, xix. 2. 25, sect. 6)

(*coloni*) of the *saltus Burunitanus* complain to Commodus that, contrary to Hadrian's law, the domain farmer (*conductor*), upheld by the procurator, exacts of them more than the regular obligations or labor-dues, which are, annually, two for digging, two for weeding, and two for harvesting. To their complaints, they say, the answer has been imprisonment, and in spite of their being Roman citizens blows of such severity that some have died under the rod. An imperial letter recalls the agents of the treasury to the observation of the ancient customs.[1] This condition of Roman farm laborers was the same with that of the Wallachian peasantry a few years ago in relation to the Boyards, and it would not be surprising if this kind of tenure were traceable back to Trajan's time.

To the free laborers who chose this life were added numerous Barbarian captives. Instead of selling them, the Emperors distributed them among the great land-owners. Thus did Marcus Aurelius, Claudius II., Aurelian, Probus, and many other Emperors. Augustus had shown them the example of transporting entire peoples into places where men were brought into the condition of serfs sold along with the land (*venalis cum agris suis populus*).[2] We read in an ordinance of the year 409, in the Theodosian Code, that after the conquest of the country of the Scyri the praetorian prefect was authorized to deliver those Barbarians to such persons as might ask them of him, to cultivate the fields, not as slaves, but under the name of *coloni*.

The obligations imposed on the *coloni* of the domain of Burunitanus were very mild; but the rents and obligatory services must have greatly varied, and were in many places very onerous. We have a proof of this in an ordinance of Constantine prohibiting the exaction of extraordinary labors in seed-time and harvest, in order that the *colonus* should not be prevented sowing his own land and reaping his corn at the fitting time.[3]

[1] See in the *Journal des Savants*, of November, 1880, the text of this inscription, found by M. Tissot in Tunis, and an interesting study by M. Esmein, who convincingly combats Mommsen's opinion on certain points. We were already acquainted with a similar, but less important, inscription for the imperial domain of Saepinum in Samnium (Wilmanns, 2,811).

[2] Pliny, *Hist. nat.* iii. 20. It was the lot, under Augustus, of the *triumpilini*. Elsewhere we shall speak of the *dediticii*, *foederati*, and *laeti*.

[3] *Code.* xi. 47, 1: *Numquam sationibus vel colligendis frugibus insistentes agricolae ad extraordinaria onera detrahantur.* These texts do not belong to the history of the Earlier Empire, but they illustrate it. Huschke (*Ueber den Census*, pp. 156 et seq.) believes that the

After the dues to the masters came those to the state, — the poll-tax, military service, the dues to be paid for the transport and sale of his produce at the neighboring market, taxes which were light in early times, but later became very heavy, especially when the master, legally responsible for the debts of his *coloni*, came to add to the demands of the treasury those of a proprietor growing more and more exacting as he became overburdened with debt.

These *coloni* were free, and their marriages were legal; they were able to acquire substance, and some of them reached such easy circumstances as, in spite of their condition, caused them to be called upon by the curia to aid the *possessores* in bearing the weight of the *munera*.[1] The law exempted them from this, in order to reserve all their resources for the improvement of their farming, from which the treasury benefited, *ut idoneiores praediis fiscalibus habeantur*.[2] In the end they owed only their rents and established labor-dues; if the farmer on his estate, or the *conductor* on the imperial domain, asked more, the judge or the Emperor interfered.

But one condition, which in time became more general, is to be set off against these advantages; namely, that the *colonus* was attached to the soil. He was transferred with it to the purchaser of the property,[3] and the proprietor had over him later, if he has not already, a right of correction: the *colonus* who abandons the land is treated as a runaway slave. Moreover, in the case of the *colonus* as of the slave, we must allow for arbitrary conduct,

colonal system was established by Augustus; this is to go very far back and to attribute to a man the accomplishment of one of those slow social revolutions which manners prepare and the law afterwards consecrates. Yet the mention of a regulation made by Hadrian proves that the colonal system was very old, since this intervention of the sovereign had been necessary to correct abuses which had had already time to arise.

[1] For the *Munera*, see the *cap. seq.*

[2] *Digest*, l. 6, 5, sect. ii., confirmed by three laws of Constantine, in the *Code*, xi. 67, 1–3.

[3] A rescript of Marcus Aurelius and Commodus (*Digest*, xxx. 112) says: *Si quis inquilinos sine praediis quibus adhaerent legaverit, inutile est legatum.* It may be that the *inquilinus* of this text is a *servus*; but the date when the slave might be fixed to the soil must have been very nearly the same with that on which the *colonus* was attached to it. Ulpian, at the beginning of the third century, confounds them in this respect: *Si quis inquilinum vel colonum non fuerit professus . . .* (*Digest*, l. 15, 4, sect. 9); and if the *coloni* of the *saltus Burunitanus*, some of whom died under the rod, had not all fled away, it was only because they were unable to do so. A law of Theodosius says (*Code*, xi. 51, 1): *Coloni . . . originario jure teneantur et licet conditione videantur ingenui, servi tamen terrae ipsius, cui nati sunt, existimentur.*

If the *colonus* had rights, the judge was far away, to enter a
complaint was dangerous and difficult; and when the recruiting
officer requires of the proprietor his contingent of soldiers, the
latter will select as he pleases from his *coloni*, and those with
whom he is dissatisfied will be sent "to bend the back under the
centurion's vine-rod."[1] Salvianus compares them to the victims
of Circe, the terrible magician who changed men into beasts; he
says, "The master receives them as voluntary residents, and keeps
them like serfs of his land."[2]

VI. — SUMMARY.

ALL the rights which have just been explained, except the
dominica potestas, an institution common both to the *jus civile* and
the *jus gentium*, were rights purely Roman. But local legislation
became constantly more and more assimilated to the laws of the
metropolis, and we have seen that[3] the Roman people already
formed three quarters of the population of the Empire, of
which it will soon form the whole; so that, while seemingly
engaged only with Romans, we have in reality exhibited the domestic organization of the greater part of the provincials. It will
be therefore legitimate to draw from this special study a general
conclusion.

And in the first place we can report a continuous progress in
equity and natural law. The strong organization of the Roman
family exists; the father maintains in its midst unity of worship,
inheritance, and authority; he is still priest, administrator, and
judge; the master obeyed by his son, his wife, his slaves, his *coloni*,
and those whom he holds *in mancipio*; and the patron honored
of his freedmen.[4] A part, however, of his ancient rights he
has lost, and the condition of all those around him has become
easier, even that of the slave. But in causing more justice and
a little liberty to enter into the family, the Emperors have not

[1] Eumenius, *Pan. Vet.* iv. 9.   [2] *De Gubern. Dei*, v. 8, 9.
[3] See Vol. V. p. 513, note 1.
[4] Tacitus proves that there existed in the family much of the ancient paternal authority,
and Gaius (i. 112-113) still speaks of the *manus* in the marriages by *confarreatio* and *coemptio*.

destroyed its primitive character, and this discreet liberty which has taken its place at the domestic hearth continues deferential and respectful towards paternal authority. The manners of the time as depicted by Apuleius, Juvenal, and Petronius will be brought up against us, and later we shall reply to this objection; meanwhile, it must be admitted that with existing laws the paternal home would in a great number of families maintain a severe rule, leaving its mark on the minds of men, and it will be concluded that children so disciplined were not likely to become turbulent citizens.

The family explains in advance the City, as the fortune of the City, in the first centuries of the Empire, will help us to understand that of the State at the same period.

Another point of resemblance, — public authority has already penetrated the family under the name of equity, as it will penetrate the City by the name of better justice. Inheriting the duty of the Republican censors, the Emperor or the Senate, his instrument, diminishes the rights of father and husband; represses unjust exheredation, and himself punishes the adulterer;[1] seeks also to check divorces,[2] and assures rewards to the conjugal virtues. In a word, the public judge is superseding the domestic judge, as in the City the Emperor's agent by degrees takes the place of the municipal magistrates. These encroachments of the public power, however profitable for the moment to those interested, announce the approach of a time when neither liberty nor law will stand in the presence of the sovereign master, the State.

The family is not the only thing modified: economic order is also changing, and the world of labor assumes new forms. We have not yet reached the time when industrial corporations will become hereditary; but in the social scale many of free birth go down, many slaves ascend, and they meet half-way between servitude and liberty, — a degradation for the former, a promotion for the latter. And since the future — even a remote future — always in its germ exists in the present, it is in the bosom of this

---

[1] *Lex fuit . . . ut adulterum cum adultera deprehensum marito liceret occidere. Haec lex abolita est lege Julia quae jussit adulterii cognitionem ad judices referri* (Schol. ad Horatii, Sat. II. vii. 63).

[2] *Divortiis modum imposuit* (Suet., Octav. 34).

great Roman commonwealth, where the citizen had been so proud and the slave so abject, that was making ready the formation of that innumerable class, the serfs of the Middle Ages, — a class whose condition was to be less wretched than had been that of the slaves of the earlier period.

¹ Large bronze.

PIETAS, AS REPRESENTED BY LIVIA.¹

CHAPTER LXXXIII.

THE CITY.

I. — Extent of the Municipal Liberties.

WHEN we consider, in its magnificent simplicity, the plan of creation, we may almost venture to say that God made use of but two or three ideas in constituting the endless variety of existences.

Humanity has needed also, in the course of its historic development, only three or four social principles to produce the most diverse forms, slowly elaborating out of the chaos of brute force the idea of justice and the theory of the duties and the rights pertaining to the individual, the family, the city, and the state. As regards the two extremes of this progression, the Romans fell short, since they preserved slavery, and in the midst of peoples accustomed to liberty, they ended by establishing despotism; but they ameliorated the constitution of the family, and they bequeathed to modern times the municipal system with the civil laws arising from it. By this one achievement they placed themselves almost on a level with the Greeks in the general work of civilization.

Bossuet has said respecting the early ages of the Republic: "The Roman state was at that time of the temperament most fruitful in heroes." The municipal system in its best days, during the Empire, had effects very different, and yet analogous, for this system gave Rome the period of the Antonines, — a period which was illustrious by its pacific greatness, its laws, and its monuments. only because it abounded in men who had been trained in the free administration of the cities. This is not only an important fact in the history of Rome; wherever municipal life has had this freedom we find the same results, whether in ancient Greece or mediæval Italy, in the Flemish communes and the Hanseatic cities or in the English boroughs. Under the Empire it had for three centuries the virtue of neutralizing the effect of bad political laws.

Rome, which had subdued the world by arms, secured to herself its peaceable possession by the municipal system. She carried it into all places where it did not as yet exist; and where it existed already, she brought it closer to her own ideal. In the Greek and Punic speaking countries, in Egypt, in Carthaginian Africa, the work had long ago been accomplished, and only slight

reforms were needed; but in Numidia, Mauretania, Spain, and Gaul, in the valleys of the Alps, of the Danube, and of the Rhine, nearly the entire work had to be done, and the Romans did it. They carefully obliterated the former divisions into peoples, tribes, or nations, and substituted instead the division of the country into urban districts. They compelled the sparse populations to gather about a centre where their civil and religious interests would be under the guardianship of magistrates elected by themselves, and also where their common life would be under the eye and hand of the governor of the province. In this way

ROMAN TOMB AT HAYDRA (ROMAN AFRICA).

the savage inhabitants of the Alpine valleys were attached to cities built at the foot of their mountains, — Luna, Ivrea, Cremona, Brescia, Trent, Verona, Trieste. There they were required to register their names for the census; thither they must bring the tribute due to the state and the recruits required for the army : there they must seek the judges who would settle their disputes. Rome compelled even the Lusitanians, in the Iberian peninsula, to leave the high districts and build cities in the plains.[1] In Dacia alone a hundred and twenty-two Roman colonies have been enumerated, and this province was under Roman sway only for a hundred and seventy years.[2]

Augustus spent much time in organizing according to these ideas the Gauls and those tribes who were established on the left bank of the Rhine and in the upper basin of the Danube. The

RUINS OF A ROMAN AQUEDUCT AT CHEMTOU (SIMITTU COLONIA).

elder Pliny found in his own days in Tarraconensis a hundred and fifty tribes living in scattered dwellings to a hundred and seventy-nine who had a capital; under the Antonines, Ptolemy enumerated there two hundred and forty-eight cities and only twenty-seven scattered tribes. This process of dividing into districts had therefore been so rapid that in less than a century the number of urban agglomerations had increased by sixty-nine, and that of tribes had diminished by eighty-seven. In all directions the

same change had taken place, — in the north, Germany, Rhaetia.
Vindelicia, the region of Noricum. Pannonia, and Moesia ; in the
south, Mauretania and Numidia had been covered with towns.
At every step in Algeria, to the very borders of the desert, the
French soldiers have discovered Roman ruins ; and often these
remains have aided their generals to discover hidden springs or
subterranean reservoirs which saved their regiments from thirst.[1]

The dominant idea in Roman municipal life is that of civic
duty. The citizen of a provincial town is called *municeps ; i. e.,* one
who takes his share of public duties.[2] This duty he cannot escape,
for no one has the right of deliberately renouncing his origin ;[3]
and he is bound to fulfil it in the spirit of concord and fraternity,
which seemed in the beginning to be the necessary rule of inter-
course between the inhabitants of the same city. This word
" fraternity " is thoroughly Roman. Cicero asks, " What is a city
if not an association founded on justice ? " and Ulpian, who styled
even the bonds of commerce " a sort of fraternal tie," certainly
regarded the city as the family enlarged.[4] The patrons of corporations often assumed the title of father or mother, the members
that of brothers, and of this they have left on their tombs touching evidence. Even as late as the fourth century we find expressions of love and pious affection as expressing a citizen's feelings
for his city.[5]

But how was this idea embodied ? He who by birth or adoption[6]

---

[1] Marshal Randon says : " Whenever in an expedition my regiments suffer from thirst,
I make inquiry of the inhabitants if there are Roman ruins in the neighborhood ; and when
I come upon them, I immediately order the ground to be bored : we always find water."

[2] *Municeps,* from *munus capessere* (Aulus Gellius, xvi. 13).

[3] *Origine proprin neminem posse voluntate sua eximi manifestum est* (*Code*, x. 38, 4).

[4] *Juris societas* (Cic., *De Rep.* i. 32). *Societas jus quodammodo fraternitatis in se habet*
(*Digest,* xvii. 2, 63).

[5] *Amor et religio erga cires universos . . . amor civicus* (Orelli, No. 4,360). The inscription is of the year 386, but pagan.

[6] The town was able to create, by the grant of citizenship (*allectio*), new families, — *Cives
origo, manumissio, allectio vel adoptio facit* (*Code,* x. 7, 39). We find even in Apuleius (*Met.*
iv.) : *Adulescens . . . quem filium publicum omnis sibi civitas cooptavit ;* and in Greek inscriptions the words *son of the senate, of the city, of the people,* etc., doubtless given as titles of
honor in order to recompense or evoke liberal acts, are very frequent (*C. I. G.* No. 3,570 ;
Waddington, *Voy. arch.* part v. 4,018, 4,019, 4,626, 4,630, and No. 53, 1,602a). Similarly
Venice adopted Bianca Capella, " the daughter of the Republic." The freedom of the city
was granted to women, *civis recepta* (*C. I. L.* vol. ii. No. 813). An imperial rescript could
also confer it. Cf. Pliny, *Epist.* x. 22, 23. Dion Chrysostom, *Orat.* xli. *ad Apam.* ii. 181
(edit. Reiske).

belonged to a municipal family, who within the walls or in the territory of the city had his domestic hearth, his Penates, and the sepulchre of his fathers ; he who performed the sacred rites at the public altars in honor of the guardian deities of the community, — this man, and at first this man only, was *municeps*. He voted in the Forum and could be elected to deliberate in the Senate, to exercise authority in public offices, and to judge in the tribunals. The stranger (*peregrinus*), the citizen of another town of the province, even though a dweller in the city (*incola*),[1] the freedman, who established a family only in the second generation, the slave, who was not taken at all into consideration, — all remained outside the municipium. This was composed therefore of families connected with each other by religious bonds, common memories, a community of duties, a solidarity of interests. Hence it is not to be wondered at that this city, so well united, finally obtained from Rome the character of a moral being, a living and legal personality.[2]

Old institutions, effaced at Rome by revolutions, continued in vigor in the provinces as a result of that conservative force natural to localities into which political agitations do not penetrate, and because the *formulae* given to the provincials at the time of conquest had been drawn up by men still lovers of municipal liberty. The scholars of the Palatine library would have found again in a crowd of municipalities the *populus*, or the dominant nobility, the *plebs*, or the disinherited multitude; the *curia*[3] and the *curio* of the royal period; the magistracies of republican times,[4] —

---

[1] Cicero well shows the spirit of ancient law in this respect: *Peregrini et incolae officium est nihil praeter suum negotium agere . . . minimeque esse in aliena republica curiosum* (*De Officiis*, i. 34). Later on the *incola* shared with the *civis* the onerous offices, *munera*, as the allies received as Roman citizens were obliged to accept its obligations. Ulpian (in the *Digest*, l. 1, 1, sect. 1) says: *Municipes appellati recepti in civitatem ut munera nobiscum facerent*, while adding: *Nunc abusive municipes dicimus suae cujusque civitatis cives*. The *incola* could not at first obtain posts of dignity, *honores* (*Code*, x. 39, 5 and 6); yet in the end he succeeded in obtaining them (Orelli, No. 2,725, and Agen. Urbicus, *In Gromat.* p. 81). Already the *lex Malac.* recognized his right of voting in the assembly if he had the *jus civitatis* or the *jus Latii*. On the *munera*, see *infra*, p. 67.

[2] *Personae vice fungitur municipium et decuria* (Florent., in *Digest*, xlvi. 22).

[3] For the division of the people into *curiae*, cf. Orelli, Nos. 3,727, 3,710, 3,771, and Henzen, Nos. 6,963 (note 2), 7,420f, 7,430fa; L. Renier, *Mél. d'épigr.* p. 220, and *Inscr. d'Algérie*, Nos. 91, 185, 1,525, 2,871 ; C. I. L. vol. ii. No. 1,346.

[4] There were still found in Hadrian's time praetors in Etruria, dictators in Latium (Spart., *Hadr.* 19; cf. Borghesi, i. 490, vi. 315), and the duumvirate recalled, by its prerogatives, the ancient consulate of Rome, before the creation of the censorship and praetorship.

tribunes of the people,[1] aediles, quaestors, censors, and public assemblies divided into tribes[2] and centuries,[3] with a forum, rostra, elections, and all the excitement of the comitia. Aulus Gellius, in the time of the Antonines, still calls the colonies "the diminished image, but the true likeness, of the Roman people."[4] A century later, Modestinus says, "The law against canvassing has no longer any validity at Rome, because the appointment to office there depends on the Emperor and not on popular favor;" and he considered it as still in full force in the municipalities.[5] In Africa, in the time of Constantine, the people still had elections.[6] The cause of this is that municipal life had been extinguished in Rome because there it would have been political life, while it still prevailed in the provinces because there it could raise no distrust. It is a common fact that the conqueror, from self-interest, respects for a long while the social customs of the conquered. Does not France act thus in her colony of Algeria, in spite of her tendencies to excessive centralization and extreme uniformity?

Occupied on the banks of the Tiber in consolidating their power and defending their lives against conspiracies of the nobles, the first Emperors did not trouble themselves about those obscure forms of liberty which were as dear to the half-savage natives of the West as their own had been to the inhabitants of the brilliant cities of the Hellenic East. Far from weakening these liberties, the Emperors favored their extension; and thanks to the order, the sound justice, which all the Emperors — except those who may be regarded as actually insane — strove to establish among their subjects, the municipal system, instead of disappearing with the Republic, prospered for nearly two centuries. These old customs of Italy, found by the conquerors or carried by them[7] to

[1] There were tribunes of the people at Teanum, at Venusia, and at Pisa (Or.-Henzen, Nos. 3,145, 5,985, 6,218, 7,143).

[2] As at Genetiva Colonia, cap. ci.

[3] C. I. L. vol. ii. No. 1,064. The division into centuries, which was fundamental in the army, had also been adopted by some industrial guilds. Cf. Orelli, Nos. 4,060, 4,071, 4,137, etc.

[4] Noct. Att. xvi. 13: Populi Romani . . . coloniae quasi effigies parvae simulacraque.

[5] Haec lex in urbe hodie cessat . . . Quod si in municipio contra hanc legem, magistratum aut sacerdotium quis petierit . . . (Digest, xlviii. 14, 1).

[6] Cod. Theod. xii. 5, 1.

[7] What we know of the provincial formulae and the municipal laws; regulations made for the Sicilians; the formula of Bithynia drawn up by Pompey; the Table of Heraclea and the Rubria for Italy; the laws of Salpensa, Malaga, and Osuna for Spain; the explanatory

provincial soil, were so tenacious of life that they for a long while existed there as mementos of the past which time in its work of levelling hesitated to touch. Many of these mementos have disappeared; what remain suffice to prove the existence in the early Empire of a municipal organization very different from that exhibited in the Theodosian Code. This latter system has been often described with its disastrous consequences; we ought also to be acquainted with the former and its happy results.

There was not for the cities, as has been thought, a general law which we have lost,[1] but all the questions relative to municipal organization had been long since settled. The great law of Caesar, or Table of Heracleia, for the Italian peninsula (45 B. C.), the *lex Rubria* for Cisalpine Gaul (49), a host of others with whose existence we are acquainted, may have served as models and constituted a common source whence materials could be derived by old cities desiring to put in writing or reform their custom, as well as by new ones to which a law must be given. In Domitian's time they were still frequently prepared,[2] and a learned man of the second century defined a municipium to be a city which has its own system

---

inscription of the organization of the census in the provinces, etc., — recalls institutions or customs of Rome, "the common native land," as say Modestinus (*Digest*, l. 1, 33) and Cicero (*De Leg.* ii. 2, 5). For example, there are found the prerogatives of the president of the comitia, the distinction between the senators inscribed in the white book and those who are so by virtue of their office, the rank assigned to each in the curia, the magistrates designate, the interval of several months between the election and entrance into office, the places of the magistrates and senators in the theatre, the regulations against faction, the right of intercession and delegation, the oath in the five days succeeding the election, the duality of the offices, the adjudication of public works and the farming of the revenues, the obligation on elected magistrates to provide games, etc. In drawing up a new statute, old statutes formed the basis, sometimes even they were copied; chapter civ. of the bronzes of Osuna is evidently borrowed from the *lex Manilia*; and how many others have been taken from the Julian laws!

[1] This is nevertheless the opinion of Mommsen (*C. I. L.* i. 123 *et seq.*) and of Rudorff (*Röm. Rechtsg.* i. 34). Marquardt (iv. 66) says even of the *lex Julia municipalis*: *Eine vollständige und allgemeine, sowohl für die Hauptstadt selbst als für die italischen und ausseritalischen Municipien geltende Communalordnung, welche in der Kaiserzeit fortbestand.* Were the cities able to modify their laws? The cities in alliance could, without any doubt, but the colonies and municipia which received these charters from Rome could only modify them in concert with the sovereign power. Thus Arpinum changed the mode of voting in the comitia (Cic., *De Leg.* iii. 16). We can see in the Verrine orations, on the subject of the laws made for the Sicilians, how Rome gave attention to consult the customs and desires of the people to whom she gave laws.

[2] Those of Salpensa and Malaga were drawn up between 81 and 84, that of Osuna from Caesar's time, but was published and perhaps corrected about the same time. After having received from Vespasian the *jus Latii*, Spain must have had to revise its municipal laws, making more or less changes in them.

of law and its special statutes.[1] Trajan forbade that it should be detracted from.[2] Under Hadrian and Antoninus, the great juris-consult Julianus, seeking how one ought in certain cases to supply the silence of the written law, made this rule: "Let custom be followed; that failing, what comes closest to it; lastly, if nothing can guide the judge, let him have recourse to Roman law."[3] Still later Ulpian asks: "What is to be done if the municipal law permits what a rescript of the Emperor forbids?"[4] Even in the fourth century Diocletian recognizes the authority of the munici-pal laws and does not permit the governor to break them.[5] No more than are the English of our own time were these Romans sub-missive to the tyranny of uniformity,[6] or possessed with the need of putting all their local institutions into perfect agreement. They allowed those laws to live on which pleased their subjects, or those which ceased to suit them to fall into disuse without being for-mally abolished; and they never aspired, as the French do, to break up the state every ten years in order to cast the fragments again in a new mould.

In the early Empire the laws differed therefore, as in ancient France, between one city and another, since each had its own. The municipia also differed from one another in their political condi-

---

[1] Aul. Gell., xvi. 13. A single city sometimes had two different constitutions, whether it had received two colonies, *cives novi et veteres*, or the ancient inhabitants, *municipes*, had kept their charter and the new comers, *coloni*, had brought another with them (Henzen, No. 6,962). Cf. *C. I. L.* ii. 501: *Duplicem ordinem, duplicemque omnino rem publicam fuisse scimus com-pluribus oppidis, ut Pompeiis, Arretio, Valentiae.*

[2] Pliny, *Epist.* x. 114.　　　　　　　　　　[3] *Digest*, i. 3, 32.

[4] *Digest*, xlvii. 12, 8, sect. 5. These special laws were still in force in the third century, even later. Yet before the end of the second century, Aulus Gellius said already: *Obscura, obliterataque sunt municipiorum jura quibus uti jam per innotitiam non queunt.* These words, *jam non queunt*, indicate that the movement which was about causing municipal laws to fall into disuse was only beginning.

[5] *Si lex municipii potestatem duumviris dedit ut . . . nihil contra hujus legis tenorem rector provinciae fieri patietur (Code*, viii. 49, 1, and xi. 29, 4). A law book drawn up in the fifth century shows that below Roman law there still existed local customs, not only for weights and measures, the calendar, etc., but also for juridical matters (Bruns, *Syrisches Rechtsbuch, passim*, and Esmein, in the *Journal des Savants* for May, 1880).

[6] The whole correspondence between Pliny and Trajan proves that, even at that period, the government did not yet like to adopt general measures of administration. For example, Pliny requests Trajan to draw up an ordinance for Pontus and Bithynia. The Emperor replies: . . . *In universum a me non potest statui . . . sequendam cujusque civitatis legem puto* (Pliny, *Epist.* x. 114). Respecting the Christians, he had replied to the same import: . . . *Neque enim in universum aliquid, quod quasi certam formam habeat constitui potest (ibid.* x. 98). Nero, when asked by the Senate to publish a regulation concerning the status of the freedmen, had refused and replied: "Each case must be examined as it presents itself" (Tac., *Ann.* xiii. 27).

tion. Viewed from without and in its relation to the sovereign power, the city is to be placed in one of those classes whose different modes of existence we have examined in the history of the Republic. In the second century of the Empire we see, as in the preceding age, tributary cities subject to the absolute power of the Roman governor, while yet preserving their own laws, their *curia*, their elective magistracies with a certain jurisdiction; and privileged cities, — colonies, municipia of Roman citizens, and Latin cities, allied, free, or with the *jus Italicum*. The former were the more numerous; but the number of the others would be very high if documents enabled us to count them wherever they existed, since they formed a third of the communities of Hither Spain, and after Vespasian's time covered the whole peninsula;[1] since Narbonensis had no other cities;[2] and since entire provinces, as Sicily, the Maritime Alps, and the Cottian Alps had obtained the *jus Latii*.

In relating Rome's conquest of the world, it was proper to note the different advantages granted to different peoples for the purpose of dividing the resistance and of deceiving the vanquished as to the extent of their defeat; but it would be useless to repeat this task in the case of the first century of the Empire. Political history is not required to take account of privileges which were no longer a means of domination, but it ought to study, if not in all its existing varieties, at least in its most complete form, the municipium, the one thing at that time alive in the Roman world outside of the Emperor's palace. The vitality of the municipal system at so many points of the Empire explains the marvellous prosperity of that epoch, as the decay of urban liberties in the third century will presage the approaching fall of the colossus, whose base was now insufficient.

But were these expressions, "allied peoples," "free cities," "autonomous cities," "Roman colonies," — which inscriptions, medals, texts, everywhere give us, — mere empty formulas, beneath which was hidden the real nothingness of urban liberties?

---

[1] Pliny, *Hist. nat.* iii. 5.

[2] Herzog (*Galliae Narb. prov. Rom. Historia*) reckons seven Roman colonies there, thirty-six Latin towns, and Marseilles, *civitas foederata, libera et immunis*. On the *jus Latii*, see Vol. II. pp. 242 *seq.* The *jus Italicum*, which is supposed to have been created by Augustus or Caesar, changed the provincial soil into Italian soil, which gave the inhabitants the Quiritarian domain and exemption from tribute.

We might believe so from certain passages in a writer of that time, Plutarch, who after having comprehended on the banks of the Tiber the true position of Rome, " that keystone of the universe," became again in his small Bœotian town, as it were, a contemporary of Philopœmen. He did not see that "the Roman peace," with which he was so delighted, could exist only on condition that municipal liberties should not mean independence. The archon of Chaeroneia, the high priest of Apollo, regrets on behalf of his municipality the loss of sovereign rights. I should regret them too if the situation could have been different, if even it had not been well that it should be as it was. "It is no longer the time," he says to an ambitious young man, " for entering on wars, concluding alliances, forming great enterprises. It is permitted you at your entrance into public life to examine before the tribunals some civil question,[1] to prosecute abuses, to defend the weak. You can still watch over the apportionment of the taxes, the care of harbors and markets, or fill some office of municipal police. The occasion will perhaps offer itself of carrying on a negotiation with a neighboring town or with a prince; finally, with the maturity of age, you may aspire to a mission to the Emperor and to the supreme magistracy of your country. But to whatever rank you are raised, remember it is not a time to say to yourself, as Pericles said when putting on his chlamys: ' Think of this, Pericles, those whom you command are free men, are Greeks, are Athenians !' Say to yourself rather : ' You command, but you are commanded; the city which you govern is a subject city, a city under the Emperor's lieutenants.' You must therefore wear a simpler chlamys; you must from the step on which you are seated have an eye to the tribunal of the proconsul, and not lose sight of the sandals which are above your head."[2] And in another place: " What authority is that which, on a word from the Roman governor, can be annihilated, or transferred to another?"[3] All this is true, but only of a part of the Empire. Plutarch even uses expressions which, coming from this passionate admirer of the old independence, become singularly significant. After saying that

---

[1] The text says more: δίκαι δημοσίαι (*Præc. polit.* 10).

[2] In this passage, which I borrow from M. Gréard, *Morale de Plutarque*, pp. 224-225, various passages from his *Political Precepts* are summarized.

[3] Plutarch, *Præc. polit.* 32.

among the most enviable blessings for a state are peace and
liberty. he adds: "As regards peace, there is no need to occupy
ourselves, for all war has ceased: as to liberty, we have that which
the government leaves us, and perhaps it would not be good that
we should possess more."[1] It was equivalent. or nearly so. to
saying that the nations were then in possession of all needful
liberties.

Under the Republic each city had, like Rome, a popular
assembly which was sovereign in making laws and creating magistrates. Only fourteen years before the battle of Actium, Caesar's
municipal law exhibits, throughout all Italy, the popular assembly
in full possession of its rights (*populus jubet*).[2] Till lately, moreover, it has been believed that Tiberius having in Rome committed
the elections to the Senate, a similar revolution had immediately
taken place in the provinces. It is true that the popular assembly,
without being formally abolished, was by degrees deprived of its
power, to the gain of the senate-house, and that the municipal
organization, originally democratic, became aristocratic, as the result
of a movement of concentration which from day to day became
more evident in the imperial administration, after having been the
policy of the republican Senate.[3] But this revolution, nearly completed in the third century, was by no means so in the first or
even in the second, at which time we still find public assemblies
in the cities. If at Rome a shadow of the comitia and of the popular
elections was preserved even to Trajan's time,[4] we have much more
reason to think that the reality in many cities took the place of
these empty forms, especially in those which, in their internal
administration, were legally withdrawn from the action of the
Roman magistrate, whether by treaties of alliance concluded at the
time of conquest, which were habitually respected, or by concessions

---

[1] . . . καὶ τὸ πλέον ἴσως οὐκ ἄμεινον (*ibid.* 32).

[2] Cap. xii. Cf. Or.-Henzen, Nos. 2.531, 3.701, 6.966, 7.227.

[3] Cf. Appian. *Mithrid.* 39: Pausanias, vii. 16, 6. Cicero has neatly formulated this
policy : . . . *Ut civitates optimatium consiliis administrentur* (*Ad Quint. fratr.* I. i. 8, 25); but
there was this difference between the Republic and the Middle Empire.—that the former
was satisfied with favoring the influence of the nobles in the cities, which was one form of
municipal life, while the other was by degrees led to suppress all life in them.

[4] Dion. lvii. 20, and Pliny, *Panegr.* 63, 64, 79. Cf. Vopiscus, *Tac.* 7. where he shows the
soldiers and people (*milites et Quirites*) ratifying the election made by the Senate; and later,
the election of Gordian III. made by the people and imposed by it on the Senate.

secured later. Pergamean Asia, Bithynia, Macedonia,[1] Africa, still made use, under the Antonines, of the laws which had been given them immediately upon their conquest. Respect for the terms made by the Republic with peoples and cities continued in the Early Empire the rule of government; the contrary was the exception. The inscriptions prove this beyond a doubt; and not the least of the services which they have rendered us is that by means of them we are aided in recovering at least two centuries of active, ardent municipal life in this Empire which has been described as an inexplicable solitude full of despotism and servility.

Before the third century of our era Graeco-Latin antiquity was not really acquainted with the official, — that new rank formed in modern monarchies by the centralization of powers, at once a cause of strength and of weakness to them. Offices were annual or temporary, even in the state, and much more so in the cities. At Rome, men came into office, nominally by the choice of the Senate, but in reality by the Emperor's selection, and in the provinces by popular election. The acts of liberality shown to the people by those who wished to secure the magistracies — acts which are referred to in a great number of inscriptions — form a presumption that the candidates had need of the people to obtain these offices. But we have direct proofs. Thus comitia of election are found in active operation at Bovillae, at the gates of Rome, in the year 157;[2] at Perusia, under Marcus Aurelius;[3] at Amisus, during Pliny's administration:[4] at Tralles, under Hadrian;[5] at Smyrna, about 211;[6] in Caesarian Mauretania, about Caracalla's time;[7] in

---

[1] In the second century of our era Justin (xxxiii. 2) says of Macedonia: . . . *Leges, quibus adhuc utitur, a Paullo accepit:* Appian, of the inhabitants of Brundusium, that Sylla gave them ἀτέλειαν, ἣν καὶ νῦν ἔχουσιν (*Bell. cir.* i. 79).

[2] Orelli, No. 3,701.   [3] *Id.*, No. 2,531.

[4] *Epist.* x. 110 : . . . *Dale et ecclesia consentiente.*

[5] . . . τοῖς ψηφίσμασι τῆς τε βουλῆς καὶ τοῦ δήμου (*C. I. G.* No. 2,927). Likewise at Tarsus, and in many other places are found ἡ βουλὴ καὶ ὁ δῆμος.

[6] *Ibid.* No. 3,161.

[7] At least this is what one may conclude from an inscription of Caracalla's time, recovered by M. L. Renier at Joumium (*Inscr. d'Alg.* No. 4,070), in which a duumvir mentions his election by the *Ordo,* which he would not have done had it been the custom. At Tergeste, under Antoninus, entrance to the senate-house was *per aedilitatis gradum* (Or.-Henzen, No. 7,168). The usage of the public assemblies was still so well preserved in the middle of the second century that Plutarch, in his advice to candidates, recommends presenting to the multitude only premeditated speech (*Praec. polit.* 6).

the whole province of Africa as late as the year 326;[1] and in every variety of circumstance the assent of the people is mentioned together with the decree returned by the decurions.[2] One of the streets of Pola leading to the forum of that ancient flourishing colony is still called the Street of the Comitia.

We know that Pompeii, at the moment of the catastrophe which destroyed it, was engaged in popular elections. Wall-posters have been found containing the political creed of the candidates, placards of supporters and of opponents, even the recommendations of the government — that is, of the Senate — in favor of an official candidate.[3] These notices were posted everywhere, even on the tombs, which, in Roman cities, were by the sides of the roads leading to the city; and in certain inscriptions the deceased defend their last resting-place against candidates by imprecations with which in advance they threaten those who affix electoral placards to their tombs (. . . *repulsam ferat*).[4] The law of Malaga,

---

[1] *Cod. Theod.* xii. 5, 1: . . . *nominatio candidatorum populi suffragiis.*

[2] Cf. Orelli-Henzen, No. 5,171 : *Ordo et universus populus ;* No. 5,185 : *Dec. aug. et plebs.* No. 7,170: *Consensu plebis ;* No. 1,779 : *Dec. et liberis eorum, ser. aug., plebei universae ;* at Gaëta, under Hadrian, . . . *Rogatus ab ordine, pariter et populo* . . . (No. 3,817). Cf. Nos. 3,882, 4,020, etc., etc. In the case of Ancyra and Pessinus, see Perrot, *De Galatie,* pp. 147 et seq.; for Palmyra: βουλὴ καὶ δῆμος; cf. Letronne, *Recherches sur l'admin. égyptienne,* p. 268, and De Vogüé, *Inscr. sémit.* p. 18.

[3] Subjoined are two electoral announcements in red letters on the walls of Pompeii (house of Vesonius Primus). E. Pressuhn, *op. cit.* p. 4.

C·GAVIVM RVFVM Ⅱ ᵛᶦᴿ

VTILEM·R·P·VESONIVS·PRIMVS·ROGAT

C(aium) GAVIVM RVFVM Ⅱvir. O. V. F. (oro vos facite) VTILEM R(ei) P(ublicae) VESONIVS PRIMVS ROGAT.

(Vesonius Primus recommends to your votes Caius Gavius Rufus, a man useful to your city, and I beseech you to elect him to the office of duumvir.)

CN·HELVIVM   AED·D·R·P VESONIVS. PRIMVS·ROG

CN. HELVIVM AED(ilem) D(ignum) R(ei) P(ublicae) VESONIVS PRIMVS ROG(at).

(Vesonius Primus recommends you to choose as aedile Cneius Helvius, a worthy man of our city.)

[4] Orelli-Henzen, Nos. 3,700, 6,966, 6,977, 7,227, 7,276, and all those to which Henzen refers in his *Index,* p. 169. When the news of Caesar's death (44 n. c.) reached Pisa, the colony,

drawn up under Domitian, details minutely the necessary formalities for the regular holding of the comitia,[1] and condemns to a penalty of ten thousand sesterces any one who hinders or disturbs the assembly. In the time of Alexander Severus, Paulus comments on the Julian law respecting bribery; he says: " The citizen who solicits a magistrateship or sacerdotal office in a province, and by giving bribes stirs up the crowd to obtain votes, is guilty of public violence and condemned to transportation." [2]

If Rome left to so many cities their electoral and legislative assemblies, she must have left their magistrates a considerable share of jurisdiction. But within what limits? On this question we have only the *Digest*, which exhibits the administrative law of the third century and not that of the first.[3] Now while at the two periods the civil law was nearly the same, the administrative law was not so. Moreover the great jurisconsults of the Republic and Early Empire, anterior to Salvius Julianus, have altogether furnished to the *Pandects* only a number of fragments equal to an eighth of the quotations from Ulpian and Paulus. The meaning of this inequality plainly is, that though admitted into the Justinian collection in order to confirm with their authority the civil law of the later age, a continuation of that which they had established, the old jurists had had very little material to furnish for the administrative law, for the reason that the law of their time no longer existed except as fundamentally modified.[4] We still possess the *Table of Heraclcia* and the *Lex Rubria*, drawn up for Italy, and not for the provinces, and the Spanish laws, which would remove every difficulty if they were complete. But the light shed by these laws on many points does not make clear the whole of the municipal system; and as they reveal very little respecting the civil jurisdiction of the magistrates, and

then in the full crisis of the elections, had no magistrates *propter contentiones candidatorum*. The details of the public mourning were determined *per consensum omnium ordinum* (Wilmanns, 883, and Lupi, *I Decreti della colonia Pisana*).

[1] *Lex Malacitana*, art. 51-59.

[2] . . . *Si turbam suffragiorum causa conduxerit* . . . [*Sent.* v. 30 (A).]

[3] The number of fragments of the older jurists inserted in the *Digest* is only 586 ; Ulpian furnished 2,462, Paulus, 2,084. Cf. Puchta, *Cursus der Institutionem*, i. 431–477.

[4] Another example of the silence of the *Corpus Juris* respecting an ancient institution ; it does not name the *Augustales* once, which the inscriptions prove to have occupied a considerable place in the society of the Early Empire, but which had disappeared two centuries before Justinian.

nothing respecting their competency in criminal matters, we have
been led to reduce the judicial authority of the duumvirs to the
proportions that it had in the Middle Empire, when the competence of the magistrate in civil suits was stopped, like that of the
French *juges de paix*, at a certain sum,[1] and in criminal cases
went only so far as to punish the man of free condition by a
fine, and the slave by a few strokes of the rod.[2] However, since
the Emperors had not yet covered the provinces with their functionaries, social life would have been as if suspended in those
immense territories, if from the Thames to the Euphrates, from
the mouths of the Rhine to the cataracts of Syene, there had
been need to await the arrival of the thirty governors to open
the assizes in order that all cases might be heard and all the
guilty punished.[3] Reason says that it must have been otherwise,
and history adds that what exists most largely in the present is
always an inheritance from the past ; now of this past Rome was
not at all disposed to make *tabula rasa*. The laws recently discovered and innumerable inscriptions prove this as regards political institutions, and certain facts indicate that it must have been
the same for judicial institutions.

The condition of certain cities in the middle of the first century is very succinctly portrayed by Strabo and the jurisconsult
Proculus. "Massilia," says the former, "is not in subjection,
either as regards herself or her subjects, to the governors of the
province."[4] The latter says : "Free is the people which is not
subjected to the power of any other ; federated is the one which
has concluded with another a treaty on equal conditions, or which,
in the treaty of alliance, has promised to respect the majesty of
another people. That does not imply that the first is not free,
but means that the second is superior ; thus our clients remain

---

[1] Paulus, *Sent.* v. 5a, 1.

[2] *Digest*, ii. 1, 12.

[3] In Spain in Pliny's time there were 513 cities and only fourteen *conventus juridici*,
one in thirty-seven, where the governor held his assizes for some days every year. In France,
where the tribunals are permanent, we have a *juge de paix* for each canton, a tribunal
of first instance to every *arrondissement*, tribunals of commerce, and one half more appeal-
courts (26) than Spain had of *conventus*.

[4] lib. iv. p. 181 : . . . ὥστε μὴ ὑπακούειν τῶν εἰς τὴν ἐπαρχίαν πεμπομένων στρατηγῶν.
Marseilles had with Rome a treaty of alliance, *foedus aequo jure percussum* (Justin, xliii. 5).
The *socii populi Rom.* were not dispensed from certain payments in kind stipulated in the
treaty, — soldiers, ships, sailors, etc., entertainment of Roman magistrates passing through

free men, while as regards authority and dignity they are inferior
to us. Yet inhabitants of federated towns can be accused before us,
and if they are condemned we punish them." [1] He says again:
"Doubtless the free and federated peoples are not within our
Empire." [2] Cicero before him, and Tacitus a little later, said the
same thing,[3] and the Senate of Tiberius had sanctioned this view
by a solemn decision.[4] Every federated or free city preserves
then the ownership of its soil, its whole jurisdiction, and its tolls;
only its inhabitants have the right of appealing to the tribunal of the governor of the province, as the Italians, according to
the *lex Julia*, could accept the decision of the municipal judge, or
could take their cause to Rome. There is no possession of the
Empire where cities of this kind are not found; and they were in
great number, since all the famous cities of Greece and Asia had
obtained this title, and there were as many as thirty in the province
of Africa alone.[5] Thus it is allowable to say that municipal life
in its plenitude had been in many points respected by the first
Emperors. In the second century Trajan wrote to Pliny: "I cannot

their cities, etc. Strabo (viii. 365) says of the Lacedaemonians : ἔμειναν ἐλεύθεροι, πλὴν τῶν
φιλικῶν λειτουργιῶν ἄλλο συντελοῦντες οὐδέν. The senatus-consultum in favor of the Chiotes
(*C. I. G.* No. 2,222), the plebiscitum of the year of Rome 682 for Termessus major, are
equally explicit. Cicero had said (*Verr.* ii. 66, 160): *Taurominitani . . . qui maxime ab
injuriis nostrarum magistratuum remoti consuerant esse praesidia foederis.* Cf. *Id., De Prov.
cons.* 3, 6: *. . . Omitto jurisdictionem in libera civitate contra leges senatusque consulta: Id.,
In Pison.* 16: *Lege Caesaris justissima atque optima* [*multis sen. cons.* in the *Pro Domo,* 9]
populi liberi plane et vere liberi. In the *Pro Balbo* (16, 35–36), speaking of Gades, which was
foedere inferior, he extols that policy which had known how to combine the rights of the
paramount people with the autonomy of the vassal people.

[1] *Ut fiunt apud nos rei ex civitatibus foederatis et in eos damnatos animadvertimus* (*Digest,*
xlix. 15, 7, sect 1). Cf. Cicero, *In Pison.* 16, 37.

[2] *Quin nobis externi sint* (*Digest, ibid.*). Suetonius (*Caesar,* 28) and Tacitus (*Ann.* xv.
45) speak similarly. Festus is still more explicit (p. 218): *Cum populis liberis et cum foederatis
et cum regibus postliminium nobis est ita, uti cum hostibus.* So an exile could be received into a
federated city. Cf. *Polyb.* vi. 14, 8: Tac., *Ann.* iv. 43. Nevertheless, this independence only
could extend to the internal administration. If the allied peoples did not form part of the
province, they did of the Empire, and from a political point of view they were in subjection to
the Emperor or his representatives. Kuhn (*Die städt. und bürgerl. Verfass. des röm. Reichs,*
ii. 26 and 290) compares the free and federated cities of the Empire to the Swiss cantons
and the States of the Rhine Confederation, the inhabitants of which Napoleon called his
subjects.

[3] Cic., *Pro Balbo,* 17, and Tac., *Ann.* iii. 55.

[4] Tac., *Ann.* iv. 38, in the affair of Voleatius Moschus.

[5] *Roma quae Achaeis, Rhodiis et plerisque urbibus claris jus integrum libertatemque cum
immunitate reddiderat* (Seneca, *De Ben.* v. 16). Cf. Pliny, *Hist. nat.* v. 29. It is known that
there were eighteen free cities in the province of Asia, and these were not all.

prevent what the people of Amisus wish to do, since they use a right which is given them by the treaty of alliance."[1]

Municipal life was equally active and free in the cities possessing the *jus Latii*, for a writer of the time of Augustus and Tiberius declares cities of this kind removed from the jurisdiction of the provincial governor.[2] With greater reason was it the case in the municipalities possessing the *jus civile*, which preserved down to the second century their peculiar legislation and their tribunals;[3] and even in the colonies, where all was Roman, and whose condition, though more dependent, was considered as more honorable.[4]

These cities, in fact, must have participated in the condition of the Italian cities. In the ancient French law, Parisian usage has considerably modified many provincial usages. The municipal law established by Caesar for Italy exercised a still greater influence, for when the Romans organized in the provinces colonies and municipia, they certainly borrowed largely from that law which, in their eyes, summed up ancient wisdom and the experience of centuries in municipal questions.[5] The *lex Julia* became even for the jurisconsults of the third century the municipal law *par excellence*. If, therefore, we knew the powers which these laws gave to the Italian duumvirs, we should be near knowing those possessed by the magistrates of the Roman colonies and of the provincial municipalities, — two sorts of cities whose condition was so similar that in Hadrian's time the difference between them was no longer distinguishable. Now the *lex Julia* gave to the duumvirs in civil matters the decision of suits and the means of forced execution.[6] They exercised these rights without limit over

---

[1] Pliny, *Epist.* x. 93.

[2] Nîmes was a Latin city, and because of that (διὰ τοῦτο) was not subject τοῖς προστάγμασι τῶν ἐκ τῆς Ῥώμης στρατηγῶν (Strabo, iv. 1, 12). Cicero says also: *Gaditani, id est foederati* (*Pro Balbo*, 24). Still the governor, like the praetor in Italy, exercised in the Latin cities the superior rights of the *imperium* for reserved cases, of which we shall speak later.

[3] According to the classic passage in Aulus Gellius, xvi. 13: *Municipes sunt cives Romani ex municipiis, legibus suis et suo jure utentes, muneris tantum cum populo Romano honorari participes . . . nullis aliis necessitatibus, neque ulla populi Romani lege astricti.*

[4] *Magis obnoxia, minus libera* (Aul. Gell., *ibid.*).

[5] Aulus Gellius says of the colonies: . . . *jura, institutaque omnia populi Romani non sui arbitrii, habent* (xvi. 13).

[6] *Lex Julia*, lin. 117, 118, ap. *C. I. L.* i. 120. Ulpian said even in the third century: *Jus dicentis officium latissimum est. Nam et bonorum possessionem dare potest, et in possessionem mittere, pupillis non habentibus tutores constituere, judices litigantibus dare* (*Digest*, ii. 1, 1. Cf. *ibid.* ii. 1, 3).

the whole extent of their territory by themselves or their delegates, unless the parties preferred taking their suits to Rome for
settlement.[1]

The *lex Rubria* recognized equally in the municipal judge in
Gallia Cisalpina the right to adjudicate in civil causes, whatever
might be their importance (*de omni pecunia*); but in certain cases —
as, *e. g.*, in money loans — it limited his competence to disputes
which had reference to less than fifteen thousand sesterces.[2] When
this amount was exceeded, the litigants had to take their suit
before the praetor at Rome.

This arrangement, which limited municipal jurisdiction in
Cisalpine Gaul, had perhaps been introduced in the interests of the
citizens[3] and of public order. Did it form a part of the *lex Julia?*
Some maintain that it did.[4] It at least became part of the common law, for it is found in the third century applied to the whole
Empire. "The municipal magistrates," says Paulus, "could judge
only up to a determinate sum."[5] But at that time all the pro-

---

[1] *Die Gerichtsbarkeit der Duumvirn erstreckt sich auf alle Civilsachen ohne Einschränkung*
(Bethmann-Hollweg, *Civilprozess*, ii. 23). It is also the opinion of Puchta (*Cursus der Institutionem*, sect. 90, p. 395; *Unbeschränkte Rechtspflege*, by Keller, edit. Capmas, pp. 6, 7, etc.).

[2] *Lex Rubr.* cap. xxii., *quae res non pluris IIS XV millia erit.* Savigny (*Hist. du droit
rom. au moyen age*, i. 51 of the Fr. transl.) says: "In certain matters the jurisdiction of
the duumvir was unlimited, and the execution on property could be carried out." This is
also Mommsen's opinion (*C. I. L.* vol. i. *Ad leg. Rubr*, p. 118). French civil tribunals give final
judgment only to the amount of fifteen hundred francs in matters personal and relating to
movables, and to sixty francs of leasehold value in real estate. When the object of the suit
is of a higher value, they judge only in the first instance. Art. 69 of the *lex Mal.* seems to
have also fixed a limit for the *judicium pecuniae communis.* Unfortunately the text fails at
the most important point.

[3] Some political idea which escapes us is doubtless hidden under this provision. Might
it not be, that debts having been one of the great causes of anxiety of republican Rome, the
Senate sought to prevent, in the cities united to its fortune, the agitations which had distracted
the capital, through a regulation allowing the magistrates of the cities comprised in the *agro
Romano* only the decision, in matters of debt, of suits of small importance? When Italy
became Roman territory, this arrangement was applied to it with the religious respect of the
Romans for ancient prescriptions; so was it for the same reason to the Roman colonies beyond
the sea; then to the whole Empire at the period when this latter had the Roman citizenship.
This limitation, in place of being an attack on the authority of the municipal officers, would
then be a privilege of Roman citizens, — that of not being judged in respect of considerable
debts except by the praetor of Rome or by his representative in the provinces, as in cases of
criminal accusation they were only amenable to the governor, with the right of appeal to the
Emperor. This interpretation seems authorized by the *lex Sempronia*, which, in order to
lessen the evils of usury, prescribed *ut cum sociis ac nomine Latino pecuniae creditae jus idem
quod cum civibus* (Livy, xxxv. 7, to the year 561 U. C.).

[4] So Marquardt, *Handbuch*, iv. 67.

[5] *Sent.* v. 5a, 1. According to a fragment of municipal law (67 B.C. ?) found in the

vincials had become citizens. Paulus does not speak of the clause *de omni pecunia*, which possibly at that period had disappeared. Whether this view be correct or not, different texts of the first century authorize the statement that the privileged cities of the provinces were, in respect of civil jurisdiction, in the condition assigned to the cities of Italy by what we know of the *lex Julia*. On the *Bronzes of Osuna* the powers of the duumvir are summed up by the juridical words which express the power of the Roman magistrate, — *potestas* and *imperium*. The law of Malaga[1] declares: "Let the magistrate state the law and assign the judges." To the power which was recognized in him of preparing the sentence, a jurisconsult adds that of causing its execution;[2] finally, we know that at Genetiva the local judge could punish with a fine of a hundred thousand sesterces the infraction of a municipal regulation.[3]

What legally remained to the governor in civil matters as regards privileged cities? The causes that parties brought by appeal to him, the suits relative to municipal debts and credits going beyond a certain total,[4] and, lastly, the disputes which arose between two cities. Thus Trajan sent a legate extraordinary to Greece to fix the limits of the sacred territory of Delphi;[5] another

---

environs of Este in 1880, the duumvir was able, in *actiones famosae*, to deliver a formulary and appoint a judge or umpire when the interest at stake did not exceed ten thousand sesterces and the defendant agreed to the procedure. Esmein, in the *Journal des Savants*, 1881, p. 123.

[1] Art. 65: . . . *Jus dicito, judiciaque dato.* See p. 37, note 6, the commentary of Ulpian on the powers of the *jus dicentis*. On the division of the suit into two parts, — the procedure *in jure* before the magistrate invested with jurisdiction, who determined the subject of the pleading and indicated the line to be followed, and the procedure *in judicio* before judges whom he appointed to hear the cause and pronounce the decision, see Keller, *De la procédure civile chez les Romains*, sect. 1, trans. Capmas.

[2] *Regiones dicimus intra quarum fines singularum coloniarum aut municipiorum magistratibus jus dicendi coercendique libera potestas* (Siculus Flaccus, *Gromat. Vet.*, edit. Lachmann, i. 135). Cf. the curious passage in Strabo on the election of the Lycian body of magistrates and judges (xiv. 3, 3).

[3] In the third century Paulus still said in general terms: *Apud magistratus munic., si habeant legis actionem, emancipari et manumitti potest* (*Sent.* ii. 25, 4).

[4] *Lex Mal.* 69.

[5] See Vol. V. p. 291. Vespasian charges his procurator in Corsica to fix the boundaries of the two communes, and sends him for that purpose a surveyor, *mensorem* (Orelli, No. 4,031); Trajan does the same thing in Macedonia (*C. I. L.* iii. 591); Hadrian in Thessaly (*ibid.* 586), in Thrace (*ibid.* 749); Claudius in the Tyrol (cf. the curious *Table de Clès*, found in 1869, edit. Dubois). The Republic had done the same (cf. Or. Henzen, Nos. 5,114 and 5,115)

time he wrote to the proconsul of Achaia to examine into the
dispute between Lamia and Hypata, and himself give a decision.
For like cases the intervention of the sovereign power is still
needful at the present day.

These are, then, the various classes of cities, which were very
nearly autonomous in their internal administration;[1] and history,
in exhibiting the solicitude of the Emperors in behalf of the
provinces, furnishes proof that in the time of the Early Empire
these local rights were generally respected.

As regards criminal cases also, the texts of the third century show the municipal jurisdiction to be singularly limited.
The duumvir or the aedile had the right of pronouncing only a
fine against the freeman, against the slave only a moderate chas-
tisement.[2] These last words carry their date with them: they
could only have been written after the Antonines; in fact it is
Ulpian who uses them. Quite different was the right in the Early
Empire; and to measure the difference in municipal liberties at the
beginning and at the end of the period we are studying, we need
only contrast the slave of whom Cicero speaks, who was crucified,
after having had his tongue cut out, by order of the magistrates
of an Apulian town,[3] and him of the third century, on whom
these same magistrates could inflict but a *modica castigatio*. The
people of Minturnae believed they had captured a robber: they
judge him, condemn him to be tortured, and afterwards put him
to death.[4] This was the ancient jurisdiction: the new pronounces
a fine.

In Italy the right of urban courts was suspended in the matter
of crimes which the *quaestiones perpetuae* punished. So in virtue
of the Cornelian law *de sicariis*, Cluentius of Larinum, in Apulia,

---

[1] Bethmann-Hollweg (vol. i. sect. 18, p. 41) says of the Latin and federated cities: . . .
genossen sie übrigens vollkommene Autonomie, also eigne Gesetzgebung und Gerichte. Cf. *Id.*,
ii. 21 *et seq.* It is also the opinion of Kuhn. The tributary cities, which were least numerous,
remained, it is needless to say, while they had their own laws and a certain jurisdiction,
subject to the oversight and orders (προστάγμασι) of the governors. The edict of Cicero to
his province of Cilicia (*Ad Attic.* vi. 11, 15) shows how widely the proconsular authority
extended in these cities.

[2] *Modica castigatio* (*Digest*, ii. 1, 12). On the subject of penalties, see later.

[3] *Pro Cluentio*, 64-66. Another example at Catana. Cf. Cicero, *Verr.* iv. 45.

[4] Appian, *Bell. civ.* iv. 28. Cf. Livy, vii. 17, where two colonies desired to put to death
those of their citizens who had taken part in a war against Rome. I do not mention the case
of Marius, who, being proscribed, could be killed anywhere.

could not be judged in the city where the crime had been perpetrated; the matter was brought to Rome, before the " permanent commission." [1]

In the provinces the governor had criminal jurisdiction; [2] but he did not exercise it everywhere, nor always to the same extent. In the first place, preservation of public order in the cities was

PERISTYLIUM OF THE QUAESTOR'S HOUSE AT POMPEII.

necessarily cared for by the urban magistrates: for all the military forces of the Empire being at the frontiers, the security of the interior still depended, as under the Republic, upon the vigilance of the local authorities. [3] Each city had its prison, guarded by public slaves, [4] and in case of outbreak, misdemeanor, or crime, the duumvirs shut up the accused in it; in that of Pompeii have

[1] Cic., *Pro Cluentio*, 6. Polybins (vi. 13) shows the Senate of his time already capable of trying these crimes in whatever part of Italy they may have been committed.

[2] *Mixtum et merum imperium* . . . *Merum est imperium habere gladii potestatem in facinorosos homines.* Cf. Ulpian, in the *Digest*, ii. 1, 3.

[3] Appian shows (*Bell. cir.* iv. 28) the inhabitants of Minturnae going in pursuit of the bandits on their territory: ἐπὶ ζητήσει λῃστηρίου . . . περιθεόντων.

[4] Pliny, *Epist.* x. 40. These public slaves were in a peculiar condition: they could hold property, and even make a will: *Servus publicus populi Romani partis dimidiae testamenti faciendi jus habet* (Ulpian. *Reg.* xx. 16).

been found the remains of four men who were in fetters there at
the time of the catastrophe. At Philippi, a Greek city and Roman
colony, a tumult arising as a result of the preaching of Paul and
Silas, the magistrate ordered them to be seized, beaten, and thrown
into prison.[1] Things happened in much the same way at Lyons
in the case of the Christians of that city. But how far could the
duumvirs conduct the matter? At Lyons, the residence of the

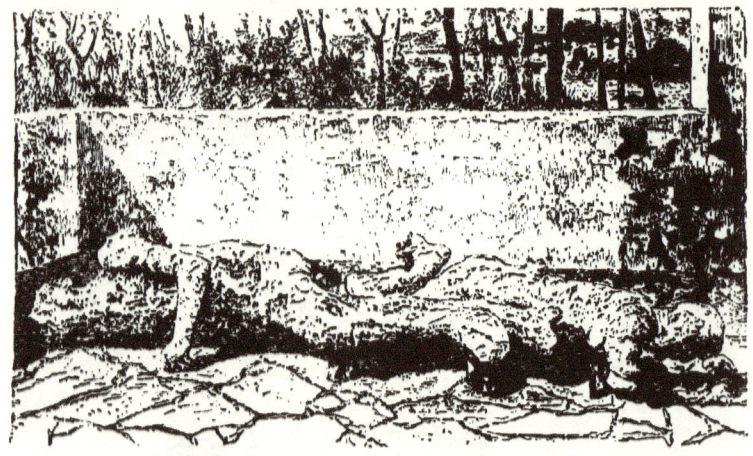

CORPSES BURIED UNDER THE ASHES AT POMPEII.[2]

governor, they make the preliminary inquiry, put the accused under
temporary detention, and await the supreme authority of the province; for it was a question of high treason. At Jerusalem, in the
trial of Christ, the proceedings go farther, because the matter did
not at first concern the Romans. He is arrested, examined, and
judged by the Sanhedrim, who then seek from Pilate the sentence
to the Roman punishment of crucifixion.

The *Acts of the Apostles* give another instance. On two occasions the priests ordered Peter and John to be imprisoned, and
then assembled to pronounce judgment. The first time fear of
the people stopped them; the second, they were about to con-

[1] *Acts*, xvi. 22–23.
[2] These corpses were restored by means of liquid plaster poured into the hollow left by
the destruction of the bodies.

demn them to death when, by the advice of Gamaliel, they were persuaded to let the matter drop. However, they did not release the prisoners until after having ordered them to be beaten with rods. Some months later Stephen was stoned, and no mention is made in the *Acts* of the intervention of the procurator. Paul himself reminds the Jews of the part he took in the trial and execution. Before his conversion he caused to be beaten in the synagogues those who believed in Jesus; he dragged them to prison and gave his vote against them when it was a question of punishing them with death. He adds: "I received authority from the chief priests." The latter even commissioned him to go to Damascus to seize the Jewish converts.[1] This mandate to bring to trial, delivered by the chiefs of the nation at Jerusalem, and to be executed outside of Jewish territory, proves, if it be authentic, that the Emperors recognized in the Sanhedrim, over those of their own nation, rights of justice and repression that were remarkably extensive.

After the outbreak which took place in Jerusalem when the report had been spread that Paul had introduced Gentiles into the temple, we see again appearing the right of the great national council to institute a criminal process. The priests wish to arrest the apostle and judge him; the Roman garrison interferes in the interests of public order, and Paul, snatched from the hands of the crowd, is sent to Caesarea. The high priest Ananias and some elders follow him thither; they complain to the procurator: "We have found this man a pestilent fellow, and a mover of insurrections among all the Jews throughout the world : . . . who moreover assayed to profane the temple : on whom also we laid hold."[2] Now the Jewish law punished with death profaners of the holy place; and that no one should be ignorant of it, the prohibition to strangers, under penalty of death, against entering the sacred precincts was engraved in Greek and Hebrew on the wall which separated the court of the Jews from that of the Gentiles.

But Paul possessed Roman citizenship, which made the affair more delicate; it dragged along for two years, the Jews continu-

---

[1] Saul is here, said a Christian of Damascus, with authority from the chief priests to bind all that call on the name of Jesus (*Acts*, ix. 1, 2 and 14).

[2] *Acts*, xxiv. 5-8.

ally demanding that the prisoner should be sent back to Jerusalem, as amenable to the tribunal of his nation and not to that of Rome. The procurator, whom this complicated case embarrassed, at last yielded to their wishes;[1] upon which Paul gained security by an appeal to Caesar.

Thus, according to the *Gospels* and the *Acts*, the chiefs of the people at Jerusalem, when the person concerned was not a Roman

citizen, order arrests, cast into prison, beat with rods, and condemn to death, but deliver the condemned to the Roman officer, who verifies the reasons of the sentence, and if he finds it just, proceeds to execution. This is the definitive judgment, having a sanction which the other had not.

COIN OF THERMAE,
THE ANCIENT
HIMERA.[2]

— the punishment. The former was nevertheless a real judgment, since without the sentence of the national judges Pilate would not have ordered the execution of Jesus.

The Areopagus of Athens had more liberty than the Jewish Sanhedrim. A man being accused of forgery, it condemned him; a proconsul passing through the city, one of the proudest patricians of Rome, asked pardon for the condemned, but it was refused him.[3] At Marseilles the judge sentenced to exile, which is a capital sentence.[4] In Sicily the praetor himself wished to decide in the trial of a citizen of Thermae for forgery of a public document; the accused person refused. "The Roman Senate and people,"

---

[1] Cicero says, in *De Legibus*, iii. 3 : *Quum magistratus judicassit, inrogassitve, per populum mulctae, poenae certatio esto.* Is it according to this principle that the procurator of Judaea, the Emperor's representative, *i. e.*, of the Roman people, fixes the penalty and orders the execution ?

[2] Woman standing and sacrificing: on the right a satyr receiving the water which flows from a fountain: in the field a grain of barley. Tetradrachm of Himera or Thermae Himerenses.

[3] Tac., *Ann.* ii. 55. The *crimen de falso* was one of the indictments which in Italy belonged to the jurisdiction of one of the *quaestiones perpetuae.* Cicero recalls a sentence of exile pronounced at Athens (*Tusc.* v. 37, 108); Demonax was there accused of impiety (Lucian, *Dem.* 11). Dion, in his seventh oration, mentions, in a town of Euboea, an assembly before which an inhabitant of the island was accused. According to the famous decree of Hadrian respecting the exportation of Attic oils, small infractions were adjudged by the Senate, great ones by the people (*C. I. G.* No. 375). The suit of the Athenians against Atticus Herodes was taken before the Emperor (Philostratus, *Herodes*), because Atticus was a Roman senator.

[4] Asconius, *In Milon.* p. 55.

said he, "have restored their city to the Thermitans, and their territory and their laws;" and he claimed to be judged by the magistrates according to his country's law.[1] Chaeroncia does not seem to have been even reckoned among the privileged cities, yet its senate pronounced a capital sentence against one of its noblest citizens;[2] and when an Italian duumvir is seen, in order to increase the attraction of a festival which he gave the people, to cause four men to be thrown to the wild beasts,[3] it appears that the one who orders the punishment had also pronounced the sentence. Appian shows us the magistrates of Minturnae condemning to torture and death. At Alexandria a revolt breaks out against the prefect of Egypt, the most powerful and feared of the governors. It is not he who takes action in the case: the municipal officers cause the offenders to be arrested, question them in the midst of the instruments of torture, discover the instigator of the disorder, and hand him over to the public assembly. Some demand against him a decree of infamy; others, exile; the majority, death: and he escapes it only by a precipitate flight.[4]

Only one fact more. In the *Tripolitana Regio* a quarrel arises between Leptis and Oea (70). Both sides arm and fight furiously, like two independent states. The people of Oea, beaten in a pitched battle,[5] appeal for help, not to the Romans, who are far away, but to the Garamantes, who prowl around the frontiers. These nomads throw themselves into the territory of the conquerors, ravage it, and the cohorts arrive from the province of Africa only to drive away these enemies of the Empire. Is it credible that the magistrates of these warlike towns sent across the desert to the proconsul at Carthage the slave, the *humilior*, or the captive, whom they desired to have executed? After these facts and this testimony we shall not be astonished to read in Apuleius that a slave was crucified, a gardener executed, a matron banished for life, by the decisions of muncipial officers, and that the author himself on one occasion had reason to fear being put to the torture

---

[1] Cic , *In Verr.* ii. 37. 　　　　　[2] Plutarch, *Cimon,* 1 and 2.

[3] . . . *Ob honorem quinq. spectaculum glad. triduo dedit et noxeos quattuor* (Mommsen, *Inscr. Neapol.* No. 6,036).

[4] Philo, *In Flacc.*

[5] *Discordiae quae . . . jam per arma atque acies exercebantur* (Tac., *Hist.* iv. 50).

and sent to execution.[1] It may be that this book by Apuleius is
only a romance; yet we can hardly imagine that this advocate.
the son of a duumvir. should have invented imaginary laws.

That these laws existed only among peoples specially privileged
under one title or another, we cannot doubt. But seeing that
certain cities of France in the sixteenth century and certain English
counties in the seventeenth held the right of life and death,[2]
we are the less surprised to meet with the same right in the
agglomeration of cities under diverse conditions which composed
the Roman Empire.

The historians of this period took no notice either of punishments or of those who underwent them. when only unimportant
persons were concerned. Tacitus. however. gives us an appalling
total : for the famous sham-fight on Lake Fucinus. Claudius called
together from the provinces nineteen thousand convicts condemned
to death. These were strong young men, since they were to serve
as marines or oarsmen in a naval battle ; it is therefore probable
that they had left behind them in the prisons many like themselves who had not been regarded as fit for the journey or the
show. Had the governors conducted this great number of trials ?
Must they not have been aided by the municipal magistrates. to
be equal to the task of causing order, security. and law to prevail.
without a single soldier. in the midst of a hundred millions of men ?
Many peoples from whom Rome had required only the surrender
of their external sovereignty. all those cities which we regard as
placed outside the Empire, must have for a long time preserved
the activity of their tribunals. In the reign of Marcus Aurelius, a
jurisconsult said : " For certain crimes the punishment differs in
the different provinces." [3] These differences arose from local customs which the conqueror had respected. What wonder that he

---

[1] *Met.* lib. ix. *sub fine*, and x. *initio.* Plutarch (*Praec. pol.* 19) speaks of a certain Petreus
who was burned alive by the Thessalians. but without saying whether it was the result of a
judicial sentence or a riot.

[2] The ordinance of Moulins, written out by L'Hôpital, recognized it as still theirs, and
Loyseau expresses surprise at it (*Traité des seigneuries*, cap. xvi. sect. 80). In the reign of
Charles II., in order to put an end to the raids of the Scotch marauders, the magistrates of
Northumberland and Cumberland were authorized to raise companies of armed men, and the
expenses were met by means of local rates (Macaulay, *Hist. of Eng.* cap. iii.). A similar evil
necessitated, in the first century of the Empire. the same remedy.

[3] Saturninus. in the *Digest,* xlviii. 19, 16. sect. 9.

also respected some of the ancient powers which were derived from them! The principal function of the duumvirs, indicated by the very name of their office (*de jure dicundo*), was to administer justice and see their sentence carried out. When we find that an obscure town like Genetiva possessed the right of arming its inhabitants and investing the duumvir who commanded them with the powers possessed by the military tribune in the Roman army, —that is to say, in certain circumstances with the right of life and death over his soldiers and captives,[1] — we cannot help believing that these magistrates had exercised all authority except in case of crimes, the cognizance of which, reserved in Italy for the Roman praetor, in the provinces must have belonged to the governors.[2]

Did the magistrates of the privileged cities act by virtue of a power of their own? Assuredly so in the free cities, for Athens, Alexandria, Haliartus, and Thermae passed condemnation and had the sentence carried out in cases of crimes provided for by the Cornelian laws. Similarly in the colonies, since by one of those changes so frequent at Rome, the judicial powers of the public assembly had been transferred by Augustus to the municipal senate.[3] We have seen that at Genetiva the duumvirs had the *imperium* and the *potestas*,[4] — doubtless with the obligation, as at Jerusalem,

---

[1] Art. 103. I am quite aware that Polybius (vi. 37, 8) confines himself to saying of the tribune, κύριός ἐστι καὶ ζημιῶν ὁ χιλίαρχος καὶ ἐνεχυράζων καὶ μαστιγῶν; but these are the rights of a time of peace. In war, in face of the enemy, a tribune at the head of an isolated detachment might be forced by circumstances to use the *jus gladii*, as in a similar case a colonel, or even a captain, would do among us. Tacitus (*Ann.* i. 38) relates that M. Ennius, only a prefect of the camp, caused two vexillarii to be killed to prevent a sedition, and declared that he should treat as deserters those who would not follow him, *bono magis exemplo quam concesso jure*, he says. The prefect of the camp was often only a *primipilus* (Orelli, Nos. 3,449. 3,509, etc.).

[2] Bethmann-Hollweg (*op. cit.* ii. 24) ascribes to the Italian duumvirs, according to the *lex Julia*, the entire criminal jurisdiction, except for crimes punished by the Cornelian laws and of which before these the Senate took cognizance (see p. 50, note 5, the quotation from Polybius). The *quaestiones perpetuae* (Vol. II. pp. 368-369) first of all succeeded to this jurisdiction, which passed under the Empire to the urban and praetorian prefects and to the consuls of the different regions. We read in the *Digest*, i. 18, 10-11 : *Omnia provincilia desideria quae Romae varios judices habent ad officium praesidium pertinent*. According to Gaius (*Comm.* i. 6) the governor in his province has the same jurisdiction as have the two praetors in the city.

[3] The celebrated inscription on the altar of Augustus at Narbonne (Orelli, No. 2,489) records that this Emperor *judicia plebis decurionibus conjunxit;* the fact could not be an isolated one. According to another interpretation, Augustus simply added to the decurions, for trials, a certain number of plebeians, as he did at Rome by creating the *decuria* of the *ducenarii*.

[4] *Bronzes of Osuna*, cap. cxxv. The *imperium*, which was conferred at Rome by a *lex curiata*, had been given to the magistrates of the colony *jussu C. Caesaris dict*. As regards the persons designated in cap. cxxvii., I believe it refers to Roman magistrates temporarily at

of referring to the governor for execution, and with the right of appeal.[1] Lastly, the Roman magistrate often delegated his right to judge;[2] an article of the *Bronzes of Osuna*[3] declares that this delegation can be made to those only who have in the colony the right to administer justice. *i. e.*, to the duumvir or aedile.

In the matter of jurisdiction it is therefore necessary to conceive the Roman province as divided into two different domains, whose frontiers, though often confounded by the republican proconsuls, were habitually respected by the imperial lieutenants: on the one hand, the provincial soil, the actual property of the Roman people, in which the full powers of the governor were exercised;[4] on the other, the territory of the privileged cities, where the Roman authority was limited by treaties and by the immunities recognized as belonging to these peoples. Within the former of these domains the governor decided all affairs of importance;[5] within the latter, in criminal matters, it would seem that he had, in the colonies, the municipia, and the Latin cities, only the cases reserved by the Cornelian laws, the examination of capital sentences passed by the duumvirs, the appeal from all other sentences, and recourse to his court by the cities or private persons.

Genetiva or who had come to that colony to try reserved cases; the hypothesis offered on this point by Mommsen seems, therefore, needless.

[1] Plutarch, blaming a tendency which already showed itself in his time, of having recourse to governors even for small matters, adds that this is to remove all authority from the senate, the people, the tribunals (δικαστήρια), and the magistracies (*Praec. polit.* 19). Nevertheless, he recommends his statesman to have recourse to the Roman magistrate in case of scandalous suits (δίκας ἀπρεπεῖς), which might disturb the city, in order, by putting them to unusual trouble, to take away from those bringing such suits the desire to go on with them (*Ibid.*, 25).

[2] *Mandata jurisdictione*. It is discussed at length in the *Digest*, i. 21, 1, and ii. 1, 16–17. The jurisdiction originating from a law, a senatus-consultum, or an imperial constitution, could not be delegated unless from absence, *si abesse coeperit; quae vero jure magistratus competant, mandari possunt.* " I have often heard it remarked by our Emperor," says Julianus, "that the governor himself is not compelled to judge. It is for him to decide whether he will conduct the trial or appoint a judge " (*Digest*, i. 18, 8–9). See in Vol. IV. p. 102, the judicial organization at Rome. Outside Italy the judges selected by the governor were taken from the members of the *conventus* and the notables of the province, *i. e.* the decurions and the duumvirs, *in albo decurionum*, says Keller (edit. Capmas, p. 41). This form of procedure, *judicium privatum*, lasted a long time; but judgment *extra ordinem* finally became the rule, and in Diocletian's time the revolution was accomplished.

[3] Chap. xciv.

[4] *Amplissimum jus* (Gaius, *Comm.* i. 6).

[5] Both for civil and criminal. See the enumeration made by Cicero (*Ad Attic.* vi. 1, 15). Claudius even gave to the governors the special jurisdiction of trusts. Cf. Suet., *Claud.* 23; Gaius, ii. 278. The title *de officio praesidis* in the *Digest* (i. 18) is applicable for the first two centuries only to the stipendiary cities.

The writings of the jurisconsults of the Early Empire. which might have enabled us to know its administrative system. being lost. a good deal of difficulty remains on this question. and we must be satisfied with but a glimpse of certain matters. Yet if we read two political treatises of Plutarch.[1] a contemporary of Marcus Aurelius, we shall find in them. in the midst of melancholy regrets for a lost independence, the proofs of a very active municipal life. The discourses of Dion Chrysostom show the interior life of cities under the same aspect.

The municipium had its own religion as well as its own system of justice. its administration. and its finances. Its priests. pontiffs, flamens, augurs. were as freely chosen as its magistrates.[2] but were not annual, as they were: and while it is true that the local divinities had consented to share their altars with the gods of Rome, the former still kept the affections of the inhabitants. who were resolutely attached to the national worship, the ancient festivals, — in fact. to all things earthly and heavenly which recalled the remembrance of their ancestors and of their old independence. The city was then a complete whole. having all the organs necessary for its multifold functions. liberty being its vital principle.

These cities were not. like ours. kept carefully isolated. The provincial assembly brought together their deputies [3] every year : some had besides close relations with their neighbors. They mutually contracted bonds of public hospitality, which established reciprocal rights, or they were associated for some common work.[4] or for games or festivals. Eleven Lusitanian cities built the bridge of Alcantara. which is still standing.[5] and a number of inscriptions

---

[1] The *Praecepta politica* and the *An seni gerenda sit*, etc.

[2] In the colony of Apulum (Carlsburg) the sacerdotal body was composed of a pontiff, an augur, a flamen. an aruspex. and some augustals (*C. I. L.* iii. 183). At Genetiva (cap. xci.) the pontiffs and augustals were chosen like the decurions. At Vienna the flamen was nominated by the curiae (Henzen. No. 5,996. and Herzog. Nos. 501. 518). The priestly office in the municipalities and colonies was perpetual. and it seems, according to certain inscriptions, that the office of pontiff exceeded in dignity that of flamen and augur. In the inscription of Orelli, No. 2,298, the office of aruspex is held by a freedman already *serir Aug.* : it was therefore of an inferior order. That of flamen was also bestowed on women : *Flaminica Aug. Herae*, etc.

[3] See several examples of these associations in Herzog, *Gall. Narb. pr. Rom. Hist.* p. 232.

[4] Orelli, No. 156. One of these inscriptions of Trajan's time (*C. I. L.* v. 875) runs : . . . *Ut incolae muneribus nobiscum fungantur.*

[5] *C. I. L.* ii. 759. See representation of this bridge facing p. 274 of Vol. V.

show cities bearing the expense of making roads useful to all.
The three colonies of Cirta,[1] with their metropolis, formed an actual
state, in which the municipal aedile was invested with the powers
granted to the Roman quaestor in the proconsular provinces.[2] The
twenty-three towns of Lycia were a sort of federal republic; and
there were said to be, besides the confederation of the three great
cities of the region of the Syrtes, a *tripolis* in the Isle of Lesbos,[3]
a *tetrapolis* in Phrygia, a *pentapolis* in Thrace,[4] etc.

We have now collected facts enough — and this is all that concerns political history — to give us the right to regard the Early
Empire not as a state in the modern sense of the word, with
officials everywhere present, acting always and everywhere in the
same manner, but as an aggregation of republican communities
which, subjected to a central power as regards political sovereignty
and taxation, were not as yet subjected to a vexatious administration. These communities in the regular course of things managed
their internal affairs according to their own judgment: the boroughs and colonies with greater liberty, the tributary cities with
less, the free and federated cities with a real independence. Doubtless in this society, where public law was ill defined, the Emperor
preserved over the whole Empire that superior authority which
the Senate had formerly exercised over Italy, — an authority which
at certain moments must have singularly restrained the liberty
of the cities.[5] Without doubt, also, two things sometimes came
into conflict, as may be the case in all periods, — law and fact.

[1] L. Renier, *Inscr. d'Alg.* Nos. 2,296, and 2,529, 2,530.
[2] *Ibid.*, Nos. 2,172, 2,173, 2,325, etc. Cf. Mommsen, *Hermes*, i. 65 *et seq.*
[3] Perrot, *Mém. d'archéol.* p. 174.
[4] This *pentapolis* became a *hexapolis*, after the time of Hadrian, by the addition of a sixth
city (*Id.*, *ibid.* pp. 192 and 417).
[5] According to Polybius (vi. 13, 4) the jurisdiction of the Senate over Italy was exercised
in certain clearly determined cases, — treason, conspiracy, murder, poisoning; and in others
which, on the contrary, were very vague : . . . εἴ τις ἰδιώτης ἢ πόλις τῶν κατὰ τὴν Ἰταλίαν, διαλύ-
σεως, ἢ ἐπιτιμήσεως, ἢ βοηθείας, ἢ φυλακῆς προσδεῖται, τούτων πάντων ἐπιμελές ἐστι τῇ συγκλήτῳ.
The imperial administration had certainly preserved these habitudes of republican administration. These were the " royal cases " of the old French monarchy. So, by virtue of a dominal
right, the Senate in its provinces, the Emperor in his, conceded to individuals the privilege of
opening public markets which were held twice a month (Frontinus, in the *Gromatici* of Lachmann, p. 53; Pliny, *Epist.* v. 4; Suet., *Claud.* 12; *Digest*, l. ii. fr. 1, and *Code*, iv. 60. Cf.
L. Renier, *Inscr. d'Alg.* No. 4,111, and Wilmanns, *Ephem. epigr.* ii. 274). By virtue of the
same right, the Senate had fixed the interest of money at 4 per cent per month in Cilicia,
and Cicero, ignorant of this senatus-consultum, had made it 1 per cent (*Ad Attic.* v. 21).

At wide intervals a bad governor encroached upon the liberties of the citizens, and a good Emperor would appear to disregard them, by appointing a commissioner extraordinary to correct the abuses of a province.[1] It has been usual especially to dwell upon these violations of rights or this momentary forgetfulness of them: it is the rights themselves which we have sought to establish; and this examination shows that the Roman people had known how to solve, at least in the first organization of its Empire, the difficult problem of harmonizing a monarchical government with local liberties, and a very strong central power with the existence of a number of cities habitually very free.

Later we shall see what were the consequences of this fact as regards the general history of the Empire; but let us now enter one of these cities, — Salpensa, Malaga, or Genetiva Julia, since a stroke of fortune has given us back a part of what one might call the charter of these three cities. Except some differences of detail arising from local usages, these laws would reproduce, if we possessed them in their completeness, the general principles of municipal legislation at the end of the first century of the Empire.

II. — Interior of a Roman City : The Public Assembly,. The Curia, The Magistrates.

The organs of municipal life which Graeco-Latin antiquity had everywhere established, — namely, the general assembly of the people. or the sovereign; the senate, or the deliberative body; and the magistracy, or executive power, — existed in our three cities. There were found also in them the two fundamental principles of the political organization of ancient Rome; namely, the duality of powers and the right of *intercessio*, — i. e.. of appeal to an equal or superior magistrate.

---

[1] As Pliny was sent into Bithynia, and Maximus to Achaia, *ad ordinandum statum liberarum civitatum* (*Epist.* viii. 24; cf. L. Renier, *Inscr. d'Alg.* No. 1,812). Wescher (*Delphes*, pp. 22–23) and Orelli-Henzen cite other examples (Nos. 2,273, 6,450, 6,483. 6,181. 6,506). These *missi dominici* were, however, sent to correct abuses, not to suppress ancient liberties. Trajan says this expressly to Pliny : . . . *Sciant hoc. quod inspecturus es, ex mea voluntate, salvis quae habent privilegiis, esse facturum* (Pliny, *Epist.* x. 57), and Pliny repeats this to Maximus (viii. 24).

The assembly was divided into tribes and curiae,[1] one of which, drawn by lot, included the *incolae* who had Roman citizenship or the *jus Latii*.[2] This assembly made the elections, voted on the propositions presented by the magistrates, and ratified the decrees prepared by the decurions. When it was a question of renewing the administration of the city, the eldest of the duumvirs presided. He received the declaration of the candidates, and to each of them addressed the following questions, which seem taken from the Julian law:[3] "Are you of free condition (*ingenuus*)?[4] Have you incurred any judicial sentence, or followed any trade which renders you legally incapable of holding office? Are you twenty-five years of age[5] and five years a resident of the city? What public office have you held? How many years have passed since the expiration of your term of office?"

The president also made certain that the candidate had the amount of property required for entrance to the senate and a sufficient fortune for the liabilities which he would incur in the exercise of his functions. At Malaga the duumvirs and quaestors must furnish bondsmen (*praedes*) and pledge a sufficient piece of real estate. The *Bronzes of Osuna* require this property to be in the city or its environs, not further distant than a mile, so that it could easily be seized in case of forfeiture.[6] If the candidates are fewer in number than the places to be provided for, the president

---

[1] At Berytus (Beirut) the curia was subdivided into thirties (L. Renier, *Bibl. de l'École des hautes études*, xxxv. 302). Certain cities even had the Roman division into *seniores* and *juniores*; at Lambese, for instance (L. Renier, *Inscr. d'Alg.* Nos. 1,525, 3,096, etc.). It is probable that there were also classes determined by a property qualification (cf. Cicero, *In Verr.* ii. 55); and one of the questions put to the candidate proves that precautions had been taken as in republican Rome, to deprive the poor man of his vote.

[2] This arrangement no longer leaves any doubt on the authenticity of the passage so much disputed in Livy xxv. 3: . . . *Ubi Latini suffragium ferrent.*

[3] In cap. viii, in which are mentioned the cases of disqualification for the decurionate, with a penalty of fifty thousand sesterces to the people's profit, pronounced against those who offered themselves for election when they belonged to those disqualified.

[4] *Lex Malac.* 54.

[5] *Bronzes of Osuna*, chap. xci. The Julian Law (chap. vi), the Pompeian Law for Bithynia, and that given by Claudius Pulcher to Alaesa (Cic., *In Verr.* ii. 2, 49) required thirty years of age: Callistrates says that in this matter the custom of the country was usually followed, *Lex cujusque loci* (*Dig.* vi. 5, sect. 1).

[6] *Lex Malac.* 57 and 60, and *Bronzes of Osuna*, cap. xci. The *praedes* were subjected to all the rigor of execution without trial, which constituted a very easy and sure form of obligation for the municipium, but very rigorous towards the debtor (P. Dareste, *Des Contrats de l'État en droit rom.* p. 56).

of his own accord proposes them; but citizens liable to bear this costly honor [1] have the right of naming others fulfilling the required conditions: after which all these names are posted up in a place where the people can read them.[2] The Julian law required in addition three years' service in the legionary cavalry, or six in the infantry. The requirement must have disappeared after the establishment of the standing army; but all the others were retained, and no new regulations were introduced restricting the choice. This method of election to the municipal senate lasted a hundred and thirty years after the Julian law, and was even in existence later under Trajan and Marcus Aurelius. At the beginning of the second century that organization was yet remote which was to close the curia against plebeians and was to change into an hereditary administrative body this deliberative assembly whose members had attained the decurionate by the way of having been elected to a magistracy.

The candidature once made public, the candidate had need to watch over his conduct. It was forbidden him, under a penalty of five thousand sesterces, to give or cause to be given any public festivities during the year preceding the election,[3] or even to invite to his house more than nine persons at one time; and such invitation must have been given only the evening before.[4] The municipium

---

[1] We see that at Malaga, as in Bithynia, there were persons who *inviti fiunt decuriones* (p. 280). Ulpian indirectly repeats the same thing in the *Digest*, l. 2, 2, sect. 8, and Papirius Justus cites on this matter a rescript of Marcus Aurelius (*ibid.* l. 1, 38, 6). This does not mean that in the first and second centuries persons were already avoiding municipal functions. Some did so, as is the case often among us, from a desire for quiet and contempt for popularity; others, not to risk their fortune. Thus, under Tiberius, an Alexandrian complains, on account of the insufficiency of his property, that the superintendence of the gymnasium was imposed on him (Philo, *In Flacc.* trad. Delaunay, p. 217). But the participation of the rich in civic administration was a necessity by reason of the onerous obligations which the magistracies imposed, and the law must have foreseen the abstention of those who did not wish to perform civic duties (*munus capere*). Yet the great severities belong to a time when Christianity made a void in the curia, because it was not possible to be a Christian and also a magistrate assisting at pagan rites. We have remarked that in the Early Empire the conditions of fitness for the decurionate were numerous, the causes of excuse rare, the exemptions but little desired (Houdoy, *De la Condition des villes chez les Romains*, p. 247).

[2] . . . *ut de plano recte legi possint* (*Lex Malac.* 51). This right of the president to nominate candidates for municipal offices was indeed an old Roman custom, and it paved the way for the later method of the curiae themselves making the nominations, the people having nothing else to do than confirm the election by acclamation.

[3] *Bronzes of Osuna*, cap. cxxxii.

[4] According to the Tullian law, presented at Rome by Cicero, these prohibitions lasted two years, as long as the *petitio*.

would not suffer it to be suspected that the people sold their votes,
or that the candidates sought to buy them. Rome in her most
austere days was not more scrupulous in preserving spotless the
purity of her comitia — or in seeming to do so — by her laws
against bribery.

At length the day of election arrives, and the president calls
the citizens to vote. Each curia assembles separately, and the voters
deposit their ballot (*tabella*) in a basket held by three citizens of
a different curia who have sworn to receive the votes and count
them faithfully. The duumvirs are first elected, then the aediles,
lastly the quaestors; and the president announces the names of
those who have the majority of votes. Five days later, the persons
elected take an oath in the presence of the assembly to obey the
laws and watch over all the interests of the city: "I swear by
Jupiter and the divine Augustus, Claudius, Vespasian, and Titus,
by the Genius of Domitian Augustus and by the Penates, to carry
out exactly whatever this law and the interests of the city require,
nor knowingly to do anything by deceit or fraud which may be
contrary to it; to prevent as much as in me lies others from doing
so; and to give no counsel or sentence otherwise than in conformity
to this law and the interests of the city." Any one refusing to
take this oath was condemned in a penalty of ten thousand sesterces,
to the profit of the citizens.[1]

If any disturbance prevented the regular holding of the comitia,
a Petronian law, otherwise unknown, authorized the decurions to
appoint prefects in the place of duumvirs.[2]

These honors were by no means gratuitous:[3] the newly elected
had to pay into the treasury the *honorarium*, often doubled by
those who wished to do the thing grandly.[4] This sum, which the

---

[1] *Lex Malac.* 59.

[2] Orelli, No. 3,679, and *lex Salp.* cap. xxiv.

[3] Unless the curia had decided that it should be so, — *duumviratus gratuitus datus
a decurionibus* (Mommsen, *Inscr. Neap.* No. 2,096, and many others); but this exemption was
the recompense for great services or previous acts of liberality which gave promise of others
in the future. On the *honorarium*, see L. Renier, *Archives des Missions*, iii. 319.

[4] A large number of inscriptions mention this usage. M. L. Renier has collected a large
number of them in Numidia and the two Mauretanias. Cf. Pliny, *Epist.* x. 113, 114, and
Fronto, *Ad Amic.* ii. 6, who, while speaking of the sums spent by Volumnius to obtain the
decurionate, show that this office was still, in the time of Marcus Aurelius, much sought after,
since it was bought with a large sum of money, and when lost was greatly regretted. See, in
the *Digest*, the title *De Sollicitationibus*, where the free gifts of the magistrates are treated of.

flamens, pontiffs, and augurs also paid, was always considerable; it was in some cases as much as thirty, forty, or even fifty-five thousand sesterces, without speaking of games and works of utility or embellishment for the city, on which the new dignitaries spent a good deal. A lady of Calama, in Numidia, elected priestess for life, gave four hundred thousand sesterces for the construction of a theatre,[1] and Dion Chrysostom reminds his fellow-citizens that his grandfather, his father, and himself had each in turn compromised his fortune in the offices which he had held. But then what honor and respect surrounded them, and how proudly these duumvirs and aediles walked the streets of their city, clad in the praetexta, as if they had been Roman magistrates of the early times! Preceded by two lictors, who bore the fasces before them, and followed by a crowd of public officers, — apparitors, scribes, tabellions, heralds, — they came into their courts, to sit in curule chairs and to give decisions in the name of the law. They were like two Roman consuls, and the pride of the cities was gratified by seeing in these local magistracies a reduced image of the supreme offices of the Empire.

The public assembly was not only an electoral power, but it was moreover the living representation of municipal sovereignty; and as such it was consulted regarding all the measures outside of the customary order. A number of Greek and Latin inscriptions mention the consent of the people ($\delta\hat{\eta}\mu o\varsigma$), even of the plebs,[2] to propositions made by the curia, the choice of a patron for the city, honors to be given to a citizen, a statue to be erected to some public benefactor,[3] etc. In certain cities, as Athens, Alexandria, the public assembly preserved even the judicial power.[4] At

[1] Henzen, No. 6,001; cf. Pliny, *Epist.* x. 48. At Diana the dignity of flamen cost ten thousand sesterces; at Lambese, four thousand; at Verecunda, two thousand (L. Renier. *Inscr. d'Alg., sub voc.*); at Pompeii, ten thousand sesterces were paid for the office of duumvir (Mommsen, *Inscr. Neap.* No. 2,378); and at Cirta a like sum for each of the three magistracies, — aedile, triumvir, and quinquennal (L. Renier, 1832, 1835, 1836).

[2] *Consensus plebis,* at Tuficum (Or.-Henzen, No. 7,170), at Narbonne (No. 2,189). The *cenotaphia Pisana* show the people of Pisa passing a decree in favor of the grandsons of Augustus.

[3] Cf. Orelli, at Histonium (No. 2,603), at Arretium (No. 2,182), at Sassina (No. 2,220), at Beneventum (No. 3,763), etc. The *Bronzes of Osuna* (cap. cxxxiv.) interdict magistrates in office from asking these marks of honor from the curia.

[4] See above, pp. 44 and 45. Similarly at Bantia, *Tab. Bantina*, sect. 3; but this law is ancient, being probably of the time of the Gracchi.

Rome the words *Senatus populusque Romanus* were nothing more than a formula of politeness towards defunct powers; in the municipalities the legend *Ordo et populus* was still a reality.

But what was a municipal senate, — the curia, or, as it was already styled, the *splendidissimus ordo?* [1]

In the colonies founded by the Roman people or in its name, the persons to whom the law, and later the Emperor, gave the duty of dividing the lands among the colonists, themselves appointed the decurions, augurs, and pontiffs of the new city.[2] This senate was afterwards filled up from the magistrates retired from office,[3] from those whose names the quinquennals inscribed in the list drawn up every five years. For the last a simple condition had to be fulfilled, — they must have the senatorial property qualification, which at Como was a hundred thousand sesterces.[4] Besides, custom required of them liberality towards their colleagues (*sportula*). How the curia was originally formed in the municipia and in the other cities we do not know; but it was everywhere renewed according to the rules above mentioned. It was therefore the people who at that time indirectly appointed the members of the city council, since they appointed the magistrates who renewed it. The contrary became the fact when, in the third century, it was requisite to have been a decurion in order to be a magistrate; but at that time the people had lost their importance, and the Empire was about to perish.

The council, generally consisting of a hundred members,[5] — the number being greater in the large cities, especially in the East, and fewer in the small,[6] — was called the "curia," whence the name

---

[1] Orelli, No. 139 and *passim*.

[2] So at Capua, according to the agrarian law of Rullus (Cic., *De Lege agr.* ii. 35). According to an opinion given by Pomponius, the decurions were, at the beginning, the tenth part of the colonists who had founded the colony (*Digest*, l. 16, 239, sect. 5).

[3] Decree of the decurions of Tergeste, about the year 150 according to J. C. Wilmanns. No. 693 : . . . *Prout qui meruissent rita atque censu per aedilitatis gradum in curiam nostram admitterent.*

[4] Pliny, *Epist.* i. 19, and, perhaps, Catullus, xxiii.

[5] Cic., *De Lege agr.* ii. 35; Orelli, Nos. 108, 3,448, etc.; De Boissieu, *Inscr. de Lyon.* The number of decurions must have increased when the popular assembly disappeared. The *lex Julia mun.* kept the number of senators always the same, by authorizing new nominations only to replace those deceased or those who had been expelled after condemnation.

[6] Kuhn, *Die Städt. Verfass.* i. 217, and Or.-Henzen, Nos. 4,031, 6,999. The *Tabula Heracleens.* (cap. v.) prohibits exceeding the prescribed number.

of its members, the decurions. who assumed also, like the senators of Rome, the title of Conscript Fathers,[1] and retained this title, also like them, for life, unless the *quinquennalis* or censor excluded them from the council by omitting their name from the senatorial list.

The Roman Senate was open to the sons of senators and of knights of the highest rank; the sons of the decurions and some young men of wealth (*praetextati*) were also allowed to be present in the municipal curia.[2] It was considered wise to give these persons opportunity for hearing the debates before taking part in them, and for studying state business before transacting it; they had no deliberative voice till twenty-five years of age. But in the case of rich young men of whom liberal gifts were expected, honors were often granted in advance of their years. At Ascoli a *praetextatus* of nineteen was augur and patron of the colony, — a crafty act of flattery. which levied a tax on vanity and was otherwise harmless, since for its discussions with men the city had other patrons,[4] and its affairs with the gods it felt quite willing to leave in the hands of a minor.

DECURIONS' COIN.[3]

The decurions wore insignia which pointed them out to public consideration,[5] and at the theatre, the festivals. the games, they sat apart from the common people.[6] Accordingly, some of those who could not fulfil the conditions required for the decurionship — rich freedmen, for example — sought to obtain by services done to the city these *ornamenta*, a kind of civic decoration. Emulation among the citizens was thus aroused, and municipal life had more vigor. It is easy to see that this organization, modelled upon that of the conquerors of the world, would give pride to those who

---

[1] *Lex Malac.*, *passim*. The inscription in Orelli, No. 3,796, runs thus: *Vir patribus et plebi gratus;* and Orelli adds: *Decuriones . . . patres videntur se interdum rocasse.* Cf. Cic., *In Verr.* ii. 49, the *Tabula Heracl.* (lin. 85, 86), and the *Index* of Or.-Henzen.

[2] See the *Album* of Canusium (*Inscr. Neap.* No. 635).

[3] EX CONSENSV D. (*ex consensu decurionum*) C. C. I. B. (*Colonia Campestris Julia Babba*). Babba, according to Pliny, was a Roman colony founded by Augustus in Mauretania, forty miles from Lixus. with the surname Julia Campestris. Bronze with the figure of Aesculapius.

[4] Orelli, Nos. 3,768 and 3,765.

[5] *Ornamenta decurionalia* (L. Renier, *Inscr. d'Alg.* 1,529; Henzen, Nos. 7,006, 6,328, 6,111, 5,231, etc.).

[6] *Bronzes of Osuna*, capp. cxxi. and cxxvii.

enjoyed its advantages, especially when we consider that to honors which gratified men's vanity was added the power which satisfied present ambition and opened the most brilliant prospects in the future, since municipal magistracies might and often did lead to the Roman Senate and to the great offices of state.

HOUSE OF A DECURION OF POMPEII (LUCRETIUS, FLAMEN OF MARS AND DECURION).

Like modern municipal councils, the curia deliberated on all questions in which the city or its territory was concerned. It passed decrees, and Hadrian had ordered obedience to them.[1] It determined the city's expenses, after appointing a commission to examine

---

[1] *Quod semel ordo decrevit non oportere id rescindi;* but he added, *Nisi ex causa, id est, si ad publicam utilitatem respiciat rescissio prioris decreti* (*Digest,* l. 9, 5). Thus we see, in this single expression, the old law of municipal liberties, and the new law, which was just coming in force, of the absolute dependence of the municipalities.

accounts,[1] it caused to be sold, when needful, the securities and pledges lodged in the municipal coffers, disposed of the common lands,[2] and appointed the priests.[3] Its liberty of action was great, for its decisions needed not the sanction of the governor of the province, who, however, had power to annul any which were contrary to the prerogatives of the superior authority.[4] The curia was thus in each city the deliberative power. It possessed, moreover, certain powers which we leave either to the executive power

THE THEATRE AT POMPEII.

or to the judicial authority. Thus, as heads of the great municipal family, the decurions could in some cases name the guardian whom the magistrate appointed for wards,[5] and see to the forms of enfranchisement being carried out when the master of the slave was under twenty years of age.[6] Later, they received documents and guaranteed their validity. They took possession of land for public uses, regulated compulsory labor for works in the city and the repairing of roads,[7] and decreed honors to those citizens who had

[1] *Lex Malac.* 63, 67, 68.   [2] *Ibid.* 62–64.   [3] Herzog, 561, 518.
[4] *Ambitiosa decreta decurionum rescindi debent* (Ulpian, in the *Digest*, l. 9, 4, and *Code,* x. 46, 2). This is the idea of Hadrian's rescript.
[5] *Lex Salp.* 29.   [6] *Ibid.* 28.
[7] M. Giraud (*Bronzes d'Osuna*, p. 12) considers "that the law of 1836 has done no more for our parish roads" than did the regulation at Osuna (cap. lxlviii). The payment in labor ought not to exceed, yearly, five working days for an adult male (from fourteen to sixty years of age), and three days for each wagon team. Chapter lxlix. contains a law of expropriation for the sake of public utility. This text seems to me to solve the question so often

deserved well of their country, or the erection of monuments for the adornment of the city. A number of inscriptions bear these words: " Erected by a decree of the decurions." After each election they examined acts of unworthy conduct or pleas of excuse of the elected, — a right which later passed to the central power, but in the first two centuries of our era permitted the decurions to annul the decisions of the people. There was an appeal to them against penalties fixed by the aediles and duumvirs,[1] which raised the curia above the magistrates; and to oblige the latter to call an extra-ordinary session of the senate, the demand on the part of one member was sufficient.[2] Lastly, at Osuna, where the curia seems, as it were, the old Roman Senate transferred to a little town, the decurions could call the citizens and residents to arms for the defence of the territory, send them into the field (*armatos educere*) under a duumvir or a prefect, furnish instructions to this officer, and invest him in the matter of discipline with the rights pos-sessed by a military tribune of a Roman legion. We have no other example of a similar provision in our fragments of municipal laws, which are indeed so scanty; but there is no reason for sup-posing that it was special to this small Spanish city. This right, so necessary for the security of the inhabitants, must doubt-less have been recognized, in the earliest times, as belonging to the municipal senates of all the important cities, they being held responsible to the supreme authority as to the purpose and the results of taking up arms, as was the case at Vienna and Pompeii. The legions ranged along the frontier would, without this precau-tion, have left the interior of the Empire to bandits and the coast to pirates, while the Germans and Sarmatians, the Arabs and

debated respecting expropriation as existent among the Romans. Absolute respect for Quiri-tarian ownership was the ancient principle (Cic., *In Rull.* i. 5 ; *De Off.* ii. 21 ; and the edict of Venafrum, Or.-Henzen, No. 6,428); moreover, Lic. Crassus was able to prevent a public aqueduct passing across his property (Livy, xl. 51). But the idea of the state and of the rights that its requirements created became so comprehensive that the rule had to yield, even at Rome. (Cf. *Revue de lég.* 1860, p. 97, and P. Dareste, *op. cit.* p. 40.) Outside Italy, the Roman people being the head landlord over provincial soil, the Emperor could expropriate without indemnity (*Digest*, xxi. 2, 11, pr., and vi. 1, 15, sect. 2). As regards cities whose public works were considerable, they could not have executed them unless the regulation of Osuna had been general. Ulpian shows (in *Digest*, viii. 4, 13, sect. 1) that by the side of the principle there was *custom* ; and we must conclude from Frontinus that he was paid an indemnity.

[1] *Lex Malac.* cap. lxvi.   [2] *Bronzes of Osuna*, cap. lxlvi.

Moors, breaking through the intervals between the camps, would have desolated the provinces within.[1]

When, in the third century, the popular assembly had been suppressed, the decurions inherited its electoral powers; they appointed to the magistracies and kept their own number full by cooptation; their importance seemed to have increased; even the levying of the taxes was confided to them. But they were held responsible for the tribute and for the heavy city obligations (*munera et curationes*), without having any hold upon the people whence their fathers had sprung, and hence were powerless; so that from the free magistrates that they originally were, they became the slaves of the administration.

The presidency of the curia belonged of right to the magistrate highest in dignity, and this president had the prerogatives that the Julian law assigned to him.[2] He made known the business of the meeting; then each senator, in order of rank, gave his opinion, either by speech or in writing, and the decisions were arrived at by the majority of votes. Also in many places, or in certain cases, to make the action taken valid, the presence of at least two thirds of the decurions was required,[3] — a regulation which appears in the *Digest* as the general rule.

The highest magistrates of the city formed in the colonies two colleges, those of the duumvirs and of the aediles; in the municipia, one only, that of the quatuorvirs.[4] The quaestors came next. All

---

[1] See the *Mém. de l'Acad. des inscr.* vol. xxix. 2d part, for my paper on the *Tribuni militum a populo*.

[2] *Senatum habere, sententiam rogare, ire jubere, sinere*, etc. The inhabitants of Aritium take oath to pursue by land and sea (*armis bello internecivo*), by a war of extermination. Caligula's enemies, — an interested oath, proving, however, that this people had arms, and would have gone forth to war like the men of Osuna.

[3] Thus at Venafrum : . . . *Cum non minus quam duae partes decurionum adfuerint* (*Edict of Augustus*, in Henzen, No. 5,428) at Malaga, under Domitian (capp. lxi. lxiv. etc. Cf. *Digest*, iii. 4, 3, and 4: l. 9, 4; and *Cod. Theod.* xii. 4,84). [A very large *quorum*, which proves good attendance. — ED.]

[4] In Lower Moesia and Numidia the free towns had duumvirs (L. Renier, *Inscr. de Troesmis*, p. 7), — a new proof of the want of uniformity which is found in so many cases. The inscriptions of Narbonensis contain the following magisterial titles, — *duumviri, quatuorviri, praetores IIviri, praetores IIIIviri, IIviri aerarii, IIIIviri ab aerario, aediles, quaestores, praefecti vigilum et armorum, triumviri locorum publicorum persequendorum* (Herzog. *op. cit.* pp. 213, 214). An inscription of Vienna (Isère) proves that the municipal magistrates had *scribae, praecones, lictores, viatores*, and *statores* (L. Renier, *Mém. de l'Acad. des inscr.* vol. xxvii. parts 1, 8). The superior magistracies were called *honores*, and the expression *magistratus* was kept for the duumvirs.

were elected for a year, and were eligible for re-election after an
interval which, at Malaga, was five years. The duumvirs convoked
the assembly of the people and the curia, over which they presided.
Being executive officers of the municipal senate, they administered

TEMPLE CALLED THE MAISON CARRÉE, AT NÎMES.

under its control the city and its territory, which was almost
always of considerable extent, for the adjacent hamlets, the *vici* and
castella, were, for the census, imposts, and jurisdiction, dependent
on the city. Thus on Nîmes were dependent twenty-four *oppida*,
or large villages,[1] on Genoa five *castella* ; the whole of Helvetia,

[1] Pliny, *Hist. nat.* iii. v. The *vici*, or κῶμαι, had special administrators, *magistri praefecti*
(cf. the *Index* of Henzen, p. 163). They could be raised to the condition of a *civitas* (Waddington, *Voyage de Lebas*, iii. 257), and a city was sometimes reduced to the state of *vicus*.
Thus Septimius Severus made Byzantium, which had sided with Niger, a town of the territory
of Perinthus (Dion. lxxiv. 14). The *lex Rubria* and the *lex Julia municipalis* mention in
Italy three sorts of cities or communities having their own administration and jurisdiction,
municipia, *coloniae*, and *praefecturae* ; and the *vici, castella, fora*, and *conciliabula*, territories
which were dependent upon them for administration and justice. Certain *vici* were the prop-

which before the war against Caesar reckoned four hundred *vici* and twelve *oppida*, formed under Augustus but one *civitas*, or " city," and the three Gallic provinces had only sixty; so that the division of France into dioceses has long corresponded to the division of Roman Gaul into cities: the bishopric of Tours and Touraine, for example, having the same limits as the *civitas Turonensis.*[1]

The duumvirs could contract in the name of the city and, in case of need, appear in court for it by a *syndicus* or *actor*, whom the curia regularly nominated.[2] Certain acts, as emancipation, adoption, and manumission,[3] were to be transacted before them, and they farmed out the public works at auction or by contract.[4] Like the Roman consuls, they gave guardians to wards and their name to the year; they presided at the electoral comitia and directed the deliberations of the Senate; their toga, like that of Roman magistrates and priests, was edged with a broad band of purple.[5] Those who were in office at the time of the census, which occurred every five years, took in addition the title of quinquennals, or censors, and drew up the list of the senators, *album decurionum.* Therefore the duumvirs of the fifth year were very carefully selected, and the most conspicuous citizens sought to obtain this office, which was the highest honor in the city.[6]

Besides being administrators of the city, the duumvirs were also its judges. We have seen above the extent of their jurisdiction. Their system of prevention, moreover, was expeditious and

erty of a single person (Cic., *Ad Fam.* xiv. 1). More frequently it was a union of private estates, *fundi* (Desjardins, *Table alimentaire de Veleia*, pp. xliii. *et seq.*). Ordinarily the landed proprietors lived in the city, while their *coloni* established on the land, cultivated it. The *vicani* had, however, their gods, altars, sacrifices (*sacra*), their *comitia*, their own revenues, since they could buy and sell (*C. I. L.* vol. i. No. 603, and Mommsen, *Inscr. Helv.* No. 86), and this gave them the character of a civil person. But all this administration seems to have been usually confined to matters of religious worship.

[1] The communes of France which have the widest extent of territory are in ancient Narbonnaise, the most Roman of the Gallic provinces. In the Bouches-du-Rhône they have an area more than three times greater than that which the communes have in an average department: Arles is the largest commune in France, — about 42 square miles.

[2] . . . *per actorem sive syndicum* (*Digest*, iii. 4, 1, sect. 1, and 6, sect. 1).

[3] *Lex Salp.* 28.

[4] Plutarch, *An vitiositas*, etc., 3. The Romans did not undertake the direct management of the public works.

[5] *Lex Salp.* 29, and Livy xxxiv. 7. Cf. Zumpt, *Comm. epigr.* pp. 166 *et seq.*; Kuhn, *Die Städt. Verfass.,* p. 241.

[6] See, in Apuleius (*Met.* x.), what concerns Thiasus.

simple : for young offenders, the rod and the cell ; for others, most frequently fines. These were numerous, because, for a penalty, the municipia preferred to imprisonment, which profited no one, a pun-ishment which was of public advantage, the proceeds of the fines being added to the funds for public games and festivities. The Kabyles, so Roman in their municipal customs, still do the same. Among them misdemeanors and crimes are compounded for, either in money, of which each takes a share, or in oxen and sheep, which the community consume, without excluding the man fined from the repast made at his expense. Every infraction of the municipal regulations was punished by a fine. The law of Osuna is full of these rules, which existed already in the Julian law and are met with in that of Malaga[2] : it was one of the characteristics of the municipal law.   All the citizens were interested in directing attention to breaches of it. — first, from respect for the law ; and then by the profits of the *delatio*, which probably formed a third of the fine.[3]

MEDAL OF A
DUUMVIR.[1]

The Roman principle of appeal to an authority either equal or superior, or the right of interference permitted to magistrates in respect to the acts of their colleagues, was practised in the municipia.[4]   We have seen that the curia received certain appeals ;[5] others were carried before the governor of the province, who in the end secured them all,[6] as he had had from the first, in the tributary cities, the decision of civil matters referring to the *imperium* rather than to jurisdiction.[7]   Representative of

---

[1] C. VIBIO MARSO PRCOS. C. CASSIVS FELIX A IIVIR (*.l. C. Vibius Marsus proconsul, C. Cassius Felix, duumvir*).   Bronze of Utica representing Livia veiled.   Coin of Utica.

[2] *Lex Julia municipalis*, capp. i. vi. vii. viii. x ; *Lex Malac.* capp. lviii. lxi. lxvii.   This custom was extremely Roman.   As the cities filled their coffers with the fines, the State filled hers with the confiscations pronounced after criminal prosecutions.   In a society like this, organized on the principle of the *census*, to lessen or annihilate a fortune was not only a financial punishment, but a political and social one also.

[3] *Senatus-cons. de Aquaed.* and *lex Mamilia Roscia*, ap. Giraud. *Jur. ecloq.* pp. 167 and 170.

[4] *Lex Salp.* art. 27, and *Table de Bantia*, sect. 1.   A public assembly dissolved by the *intercessio* of a magistrate could not be called together again the same day by the one who had convoked it the first time.   Cf. Bréal, *Épigr. italique*, p. 388 ; Giraud, *Tables de Salpensa* and *Lex Malac.* pp. 68 *et seq.*

[5] For example, at Malaga, respecting fines, art. 66.

[6] Cf. *Digest*, xlix. 1, 21, pr., and *ibid.* 4, 1, sects. 3 and 4.

[7] Paulus, in the *Digest*, l. 1, 26.   So the restoration to a property, the giving possession of an estate, or a dowry or legacy.   Yet the Italian duumvirs had the *missio in bona* (see above,

the Roman people, who had over the provincial soil the right of eminent domain, the governor could of his own will transfer possession, either in his own person at the assizes, which he held annually in different cities of his province (*conventus juridici*), or by judges whom he appointed to decide in his stead. The duumvirs therefore in certain cases formed, in the non-privileged cities, a jurisdiction of the first degree.

Yet, from the multiplicity of their duties, we can understand the prohibition made them of both being at the same time absent from the city. "When one of the duumvirs is absent," says the law of Salpensa, art. 25, "and his colleague wishes to leave the city, be it only for one day, the latter will choose, *ex decurionibus conscriptisve*, a deputy, *praefectus*, to whom he must administer the oath." If the Emperor or any member of the imperial family accepted civic office, he must also be represented by a prefect, whose term of office in this case is one year.[1]

To make room for merit or favor, the Emperors were accustomed to give to a person the title of *consularis, praetorius*, and the like, although he had never been either consul or praetor; and the free towns followed this example. We find at Canusium four *quinquennalicii* who had never held the office of which they had the name.[2]

After the duumvirs came the aediles for the supervision of the streets and public buildings, of the markets, weights, and measures, of baths and games, in fact, for the maintenance of good order and health in the city. They had also the supervision of the *annona*, *i. e.*, of provisions sold or distributed;[3] they drew up edicts on matters belonging to their department, such as cases of flaw or fraud in sales, defects in contracts of sale, the repairs or position of edifices, etc., and in their capacity of administrators they had these edicts carried out; or, as judges, they punished delinquents

pp. 334 *seqq.*); and this leads to the inquiry whether the magistrates of the Roman colonies and Latin cities did not enjoy the same right.

[1] L. Renier, *Inscr. d'Algérie*, No. 4,070, and the *Index* of Henzen. On the *praefecti legi Petronia*, cf. Marquardt, *Röm. Staatsv.* i. 494.

[2] Orelli, Nos. 798, 800, 922, 1,170, 1,178, 1,181; Mommsen, *Inscr. Neap.* No. 625. So at Lyons a citizen received the insignia of the duumvirate, although he had been only quaestor (Orelli, No. 4,020).

[3] Petronius, *Satyr.* 44.

by fine after having reported to the duumvirs.   So, at least, it
stands in the law of Malaga.   Apuleius cites the case of an aedile

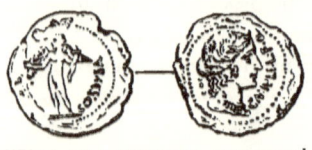

of Hypata causing the money to be
returned for a commodity sold at too
high a price which he had destroyed,
and the tradesman considering himself
fortunate to get off in this way without being beaten by the rods which the

MEDAL OF A MUNICIPAL QUAESTOR.[1]

apparitor carried after the aedile.[2]

The quaestor had no jurisdiction, but important functions, which
varied with the customs of each city.   He farmed out by auction
the public lands,[3] without being allowed himself to take them on
lease either directly or by a middle man, he reclaimed territory
illegally occupied, looked after the maintenance or repairs of public
buildings, invested the funds of the city, recovered its debts, made
all the contracts which the good management of its affairs required,
and kept the registers of the census up to date, entering therein
all changes of property.   He was the guardian of the public
wealth.

The cities, " uncertain persons," had only bona publica, such as
temples, walls, etc., or that which was regarded as being the
common property of all the citizens, like the common lands of
our time.   The Emperors granted them successively the right of
acquiring and possessing with all the rights of a civil person,
of receiving trusts and inheritances, of freeing their slaves, and
exercising over their freedmen all the rights of a patron.   Then
they had abundant sources of revenue, — the returns from urban
and rural properties, interests of invested capital, legacies, donations,
honoraria presented by the newly elected, inheritances from the city's
freedmen (since the Antonines), the labor of the city slaves, revenue from mines and quarries when they possessed such, rights
to tolls on the highways and in the ports, duties at the gates of

<hr />

[1] Coin of Corduba. CN. IVLI L. F. Q. (*Cnaeus Julius, son of Lucius, Quaestor*).   Head
of Venus   The reverse CORDVBA.   Cupid standing, holding a torch and a cornucopia.
Bronze coin.

[2] *Met.* i. and *Digest.* l. 2, 12.

[3] Sometimes the duumvirs kept this duty, as at Salpensa.   In certain cities the quaestorship was only a *munus*, in others a *honos* (*Digest*, l. 4, 18, sect. 2).   The inferior officers, *scribae,
librarii*, etc., received a stipend, which at Osuna varied from 1,200 to 1,300 sesterces.

the cities which had kept this privilege, levies for the maintenance
of highways. sewers. aqueducts from the owners of adjacent property, etc. To these sources of income were added sums voluntarily
expended by citizens who had accepted the oversight of a municipal
service. In modern times a man is at liberty to decline public
office. and salaries are paid to those accepting them; in the Roman
Empire, public service was obligatory, and imposed expenditure: it
was a civic obligation, *munus*.[1] Thus the administration cost little
or nothing. The large expenditures were for public works. An
imperial rescript appropriated a third of the revenue for these;

GENII OF GAMES.[2]

but this rescript is of the year 395, — that is to say, at a time when
the Emperor interfered in all civic matters.[3] Indemnities to physicians, professors, citizens sent on deputations to the Emperor, games,
and, in many cities, relief to the needy and to poor children, took
the remainder. When the municipal income was insufficient for
the expense of obligatory duties and public works, a rate was
imposed on the citizens and foreign residents (*incolae*), after the
consent of the governor of the province had been procured in the

---

[1] In the *Digest* (l. 16, 239, sect. 3), the *munus* is defined *publicum officium privati hominis*.
The *munera* were divided into *mun. personarum*, or obligations imposed on the person which
required labor or intelligence, and *mun. patrimonii*, or obligations which entailed expenditure
(*Ibid.* title iv. 1, sect. 3, and 18, sect. 1). If the citizen were absent, his estate was levied upon
for the fulfilment of the *munera personalia* (*Bull. de l'Acad. des inscr.* 1877, p. 128). The
enumeration of the *intributiones*, which the landed proprietors supported, will be found in
Kuhn, i. 40–69. These *munera*, voluntarily held, notably reduced the expenses of the city; but
they were already in the middle of the second century an onerous charge . . . *munera decuri-
onatus* . . . *onerosa* (decree of Tergeste); they became an intolerable burden when the progressive impoverishment of the Empire and the abandonment by Christians of municipal
functions forced a ruinous compulsion to take the place of an interested devotion. At sixty
the obligation of holding *munera* ceased: *leges quae majorem annis LX otio reddunt* (Pliny,
Epist. iv. 23). The *Digest* and *Code* give different ages. A rescript of Diocletian (*Cod. Just.*
x. 49, 3) put an end at fifty-five to the obligation of *munera personalia*.

[2] Bas-relief in the Museum of the Louvre.   [3] *Cod.* VIII. ii. and XI. 69, 3.

case of tributary cities.[1] In the others the rate was arranged in conformity with the registers of the census fixed by the quinquennals. Thus a considerable portion of the Empire had the free control of its finances,[2] as it had its free elections and its own jurisdiction, its own divinities, and its special forms of worship.

At the Antonine epoch there is observable in the financial administration of the municipia a change of which the results were very important. The irresistible tendency of municipal administrations which a superior power does not check is to burden the future for the profit of the present. The correspondence between Pliny and Trajan proves that many cities were at that time involved in debt as the result of ill-considered works or scandalous waste. The government was therefore led, in the interest of its subjects themselves, to exercise some control over their affairs.[3] Trajan gave a curator to Bergamum,[4] Hadrian to Como, Marcus Aurelius to a number of cities, — doubtless at their request and with the sole desire of restoring order to their finances; thus Apameia had begged Pliny to examine its estimates. The curator, an important personage of senatorial or equestrian rank, received from the Emperor, for a time not specified, the duty of verifying the accounts and of arranging the expenditure of a city. Far from being then an encroachment upon municipal liberty, this intervention of the superior authority was a service rendered to embarrassed communities,[5] as the Emperor rendered them another when he sent to the province a commissioner extraordinary to terminate

[1] The Emperors did not like to have the cities increase the municipal rates. See next page, note 4.
[2] Apameia was a Roman colony; when Pliny wished to examine its accounts, the inhabitants declared that no proconsul had ever done so. ... *Habuisse privilegium et vetustissimum morem, arbitria suo rem publicam administrari* (Pliny, *Epist.* x. 56).
[3] Pliny, *Epist.* x. 29: ... *Rationes ... esse vexatus ... satis constat.* (Cf. *ibid.* 46 and 48.)
[4] The institution of these curators has been traced to its origin in Nerva's reign, according to a decree of that Emperor inserted in the *Digest* (xliii. 24, 3, sect. 4); but the officer to whom this rescript refers is the *cur. loc. public. persequendorum*, who existed at all times at Rome and such as several free cities already had. Cf. Or.-Henzen, in vol. iii. p. 109, of the *Index*, a very long enumeration of *curatores rei publicae*; L. Renier, *Mél. d'épigr.* p. 43; and the dissertation of Henzen in the *Annali* of 1851, pp. 5–35.
[5] See, in Plutarch (*Praec. Pol.* 19), how the continual recourse of the cities to the sovereign authority compelled the Emperor to become more a master than he wished ... ἀναγκάζουσι μᾶλλον ἢ βούλονται δεσπότας εἶναι τοῖς ἡγεμόνας. It is still in France a national whim; and this whim had grave consequences for the Roman Empire, as it has had for us.

disputes respecting boundaries, to appease quarrels, to introduce order among men and affairs even in free cities.[1] The *consulares* of Hadrian, the *juridici* of Marcus Aurelius, as judges will be more just than certain municipal magistrates; the *irenarcha* appointed by the governor[2] will greatly assist in the preservation of public order; imperial coins of better standard will replace the civic coinage, to the great advantage of trade: lastly, the governors will interpose to prevent the cities from drying up the source of their prosperity by the imposition of excessive imposts[3] and useless works,[4] or ruining their wealthy citizens by repeated elections to onerous offices.[5]

Yet there are services dangerous in the acceptance. **The** temporary curator of Trajan will become the permanent director, in the Emperor's name and for his profit, of the municipal finances; the provincial governors, who, following the example of the *juridici*, will watch closely over the good order of the cities, will check their vitality; recourse[6] and appeal to the Roman magistrate will multiply; and by the development of extraordinary procedure we shall reach the suppression of the *judex*, so that in Diocletian's time, the jurisdiction of the duumvirs being reduced by all these causes to the most insignificant proportions, the city will become nothing more than a taxable district. At last the provincial coinage will, with good reason, fall into disuse; but with it will disappear the last sign of ancient liberty.[7] Then it will be found that these imperial legates who so successfully put an end to municipal rival-

---

[1] This was an old practice of the Roman Senate. Cf. Or.-Henzen, No. 6,450.

[2] He selected him from ten candidates proposed by the decurions (Aristides, i. 523, edit. Dindorf).

[3] Rescript of Septimius Severus: . . . *Non temere permittenda est nov. vectig. exactio* (*Cod.* iv. 62, 1).

[4] The Emperors at last kept in their own hands the right of authorizing public works (Ulpian, in the *Digest*, i. 16, 7, sect. 1; Modestinus and Macer, in the *Digest*, l. 10, 3, sect. 1, and fr. 6. Cf. *Cod. Theod.* xv. 1. 37. *anno* 398: and doubtless they assumed it very early in the case of the tributary cities. This tendency was already showing itself under Trajan (Pliny, *Epist.* x. *passim*).

[5] *Digest*, l. 4, 3, sect. 15. This intervention, called forth by abuses, will end by putting the nomination of magistrates in the governor's hands.

[6] At the end of the third century the distinction between *jus* and *judicium* will be suppressed. The governor, instead of establishing a *judicium* and appointing a *judex*, will himself bear the case to the end and pronounce the sentence. Cf. Bethmann-Hollweg, iii. 104.

[7] Under Antoninus or Marcus Aurelius a governor caused the silver coin of a city to be demonetized because it contained too much copper, *quasi aerosa* (*Digest*, xlvi. 3, 102, *proœm.*).

ries have also put an end to the rights which produced them. Augustus had, at Rome, " pacified eloquence ; " soon the Emperors will have " pacified," to the remotest provinces, the most unpretending liberties, — a fatal usurpation, which public necessities far more than greed for power at first imposed, and to which the whole Empire was accessory: the cities, by allowing abuses to increase in their midst ; the Emperors, by yielding to the temptation to think and act for all, in the interests of the general weal. It was often at the request of those interested that the government interfered, and it was by means of the best Emperors, the Antonines, that the movement towards centralization began. It would have been quite different if the provincial assembly, placed between the city and the Emperor, had been able, by an active control, to prevent the difficulties of the former and as a consequence the encroachments of the latter.

The municipal public service was completed by the religious service under the supervision of three pontiffs and three augurs. At least that is the number at Genetiva, and was most likely the same in many cities, for the body of Augustals had likewise six chiefs, the *seviri*. The importance of these sacerdotal functions is proved by the rank which the album of Thamugas gives the *sacerdotales*, and the laws of the Theodosian Code, which place them after the duumvirs in office, but before the other magistrates. The office of flamen was elective, and gave the individual an indelible character, or at least gave him a title which he kept for life, *flamen perpetuus*. Lastly, in order to be represented in court, the city appointed a *procurator*, or *syndicus*, to whom it confided the defence of its interests.

If the Roman city, which has handed down to us so many regulations and institutions, had in the first two centuries of our era much more liberty than the French commune of to-day, it differs from it, however, by its far less democratic spirit and by the rigorous responsibility which it imposed on its magistrates.

When the Romans founded a colony they reserved a part of the lands assigned to the colonists to form an *ager publicus* for

Hadrian suppressed the tetradrachms of Antioch, which were of too base a standard. In the middle of the third century the provincial mints had all been closed, except in Egypt (Mommsen, *Hist. de la Monn. rom.*)

the new city: for it was a settled principle that a city should possess a landed estate. All the municipia had therefore common lands (*praedia*), which were directly utilized by the citizens as public pasturage, or of which the revenue was added to the income from various sources which constituted the civic funds and were protected by the severest provisions of the law.

Before entrance on office the magistrates had to give security and furnish bondsmen to guarantee the city against the results of negligence or fraud.[1] They were responsible for rents during the whole period of the leases which they had made, and for a period of fifteen years in case of faults of construction in public works which they had directed;[2] their accounts, though verified and audited, might be invalidated until the twentieth year.[3] It was at their own risk and peril that they placed the public funds or that they neglected to claim a legacy or exact the payment of a debt. There was still another obligation, — the magistrate held responsible for the consequences of his own acts was likewise responsible for those of his predecessor if he had approved them, and of his successor if he had recommended the latter for election. Finally, in any prosecutions against him were involved not only his actual bondsmen, but those who might be considered as tacitly responsible for him: that is to say, his colleagues, the predecessor who had recommended his election, and even his father if the son had not been emancipated before taking office. All profit made by him in the exercise of his functions entailed a penalty of two hundred thousand sesterces; one of ten thousand was exacted for each infraction of a decree of the decurions, and at Osuna one of one hundred thousand for the violation of the municipal statutes.[4] Observe that the accounts are to be presented to the city, and not to the governor; it was to the city, and not to the Emperor, that the responsibilities are made good. The Romans had not, as the

---

[1] *Lex Malac.* 60, and *Digest*, l. 1, 38, sect. 6; *ibid.* 8, 9, sect. 4, and sect. 7.

[2] Such, at least, is the command in a rescript of the year 385; they shared this responsibility with the contractor, who, instead of furnishing security, as with us, also was required to present bondsmen. (See in the *Comptes rendus de l'Acad. des inscr.* July, 1875, a curious inscription of Cyzicus.) The heirs of a magistrate also inherited his obligations (*Cod.* viii. 12, 8). The extreme burden of responsibility laid upon these officials seems to be comparatively of late date. The code of Malaga is much less severe.

[3] *Digest.* xliv. 3, 13, sect. 1.

[4] Capp. lxlxvii. cxxix. cxxx.; see also *Table of Bantia*, sect. 2.

French have. constituted a special court for the public functionary. This is a further proof of the power of municipal life at the time.[1]

To the responsibilities of the administrator were added those of judge. Had the judge given force to a rule contrary to the established law, this rule was henceforth applied to him in all the suits which he himself had to sustain; did he neglect what the *formula* had prescribed. he owed reparation for the damage caused by his decision.[2]

How numerous the precautions to protect the property of the city. the municipal law, and the rights of the citizens, even though the most respected officials of the town should be ruined by penalties! But also how careful in their action must have been magistrates held so strictly responsible, how slow in their deliberations. how prudent in their projects. how vigilant in the execution of them, what admirable managers of the public funds concerning which they must give so severe account! On the one hand, great freedom of action : on the other, a responsibility equal to the power intrusted. This is how men are made; with principles like these the municipal system must flourish so long as they are respected. To this system, much more than to the Emperors, the Roman world owed those countless buildings whose grandeur and stability astonish us. It is these municipal administrations which, frequently uniting their efforts and resources, built amphitheatres and temples, threw bridges over rivers. aqueducts across valleys, and roads from one end to the other of their province.[3]

[1] The Antonines still further increased the number and extent of these responsibilities. Thus Trajan gave to a ward the right of bringing an action for indemnity against the magistrate who, in the absence of a legal or testamentary guardian, had made a bad selection of the man to whom he had assigned the guardianship (*Code*, v. 75, 5); and Hadrian fined a duumvir forty *aurei* who allowed a corpse to be interred in the city (*Digest*. xlvii. 12, 3, sect. 5 ; cf. Capitolinus, *Marc. Aut.* 13). M. Pierre Dareste (*Des Contrats passés par l'État en droit romain*, p. 102) well says : " The principal or subsidiary responsibility of the functionary, . . . which took the form of a responsibility stipulated by contract of civil law, is an idea quite peculiar to the Roman Empire. We are at the present time accustomed to see in the functionary an almost irresponsible mandatory. . . . In the Roman Empire he was the first to feel the consequences of his own acts. . . . One cannot deny that there was a very just idea at the basis of this system. Despotism exaggerated in the interest of its own finances a system which offered great advantages for the collection of revenues . . . ; but the abuse should not prevent us from comprehending and appreciating the ingenious and just practice of previous centuries."

[2] Keller, edit. Capmas, sect. 86. This rule had existed elsewhere at all times, even for the Roman praetor.

[3] In Pliny's correspondence (lib. x.) we observe in a single province and in less than two

Citizens cannot be found in our time exposing themselves to like dangers merely for a simple civic distinction. By reducing the communes to infinitesimal proportions in comparison with cities containing the population of a kingdom, and by keeping them all under strict state guardianship, our great modern communities have destroyed local patriotism. In the municipium of the Flavians and

BISELLIUM IN BRONZE, FOUND IN THE THEATRE OF HERCULANEUM.[1]

the Antonines it preserved all its ancient energy. Each man loved his city and desired it to be prosperous and beautiful, and many thought, like Caesar, that it was worth more to be first at one's own home than second elsewhere. Thus the offices which a century later will be avoided with alarm were at the period we are now considering sought for eagerly. It is regret at leaving them which most afflicts the exile of whom Plutarch speaks. "Alas!"

years the following works projected or in course of completion, — at Prusa, magnificent baths; at Nicomedeia, a forum and an aqueduct, for which the city had already expended 30,529,000 sesterces; at Nicaea, a theatre which before completion had cost 10,000,000 sesterces, and a gymnasium so vast that the walls were 23 feet thick; at Claudiopolis, baths of colossal size; at Sinope, an aqueduct over fourteen miles long; at Amastris, the covering in of a streamlet which ran through the city, etc. As regards roads, there were three kinds. — *publicae, privatae, vicinales* (*Digest,* xliii. 8, 2, sect. 22); these are the French national, departmental, and communal routes. The first only were made at the public expense, *publice muniuntur* (Siculus Flaccus, *De Agr. cond.* p. 27, edit. Giraud). Yet they had to be maintained by the owners of adjacent property (*Digest,* viii. 6, 14, sect. 1).

[1] This seat of honor (from the Museum of Naples), enriched with carving, is very high on its legs. A marble stool was used to mount up to it (Monaco, *Le Musée nat. de Naples,* pl. 119).

he exclaims, "I no longer command as magistrate, I no longer
give counsel as senator, I no longer bestow prizes at contests," etc. :
and he might have added : "I no longer traverse the city clad in
the *praetexta*, which from a distance attracts men's eyes, and preceded by lictors who cause the crowd to give way before me."
These men were vain, doubtless; but how many services vanity has
done the world!

This seeking after municipal honors was such that the cities
enriched themselves with their titles of decurion and with all the
decorations which they could bestow (among them being the *bisellia-
tus honos*),[1] and even with the citizenship, as our kings do with their
titles of nobility or offices; and they found persons ready to buy
for one or two thousand denarii the honor of a seat in the curia,[2]
for five hundred drachmae the right of voting in the public
assembly.[3] Others, aspiring higher, thought that the duumvirate,
in bringing them to the Emperor's notice, would help them to
attain the honors of Rome and offices under the imperial government. In this respect municipal offices were the necessary step
for ambitious men in the provinces, since experience in city affairs
prepared them for state offices; and since many provincials had the
right of Roman citizenship, no obstacle arising from their condition
barred the way of those whom favorable circumstances placed on
the road to the highest offices of the Empire, so long as these
offices were open to the most able men.

---

[1] The *bisellarii* had obtained or purchased the right of having conveyed by their slaves to
the games, theatre, or festivals, a double seat (*bisellium*), which they occupied alone, so as to
give them more room (Orelli, Nos. 4,013, 4,011. Cf. Millin, *Descr. des tombeaux de Pompéi*,
p. 78).

[2] Pliny, *Epist.* x. 113 and 48, and many inscriptions. Cf. Léon Renier, *Arch. des Missions*,
ii. 319.

[3] For example, at Tarsus (Dion Chrysostom, *Orat.* ii. 44, edit. Reiske), and elsewhere.
Women were accustomed to buy this right . . . *civis recepta* (*C. I. L.* ii. 813 ; Orelli, Nos. 1,663,
3,710). A tribune says to Paul (*Acts*, xxii. 28) : "With a great sum obtained I this freedom."
Augustus had interdicted the Athenians from selling the right of citizenship (Dion, liv. 7).

III. — ARISTOCRATIC CHARACTER OF THE ROMAN CITY; MUTUAL RELATIONS OF THE CITIZENS.

JUSTINIAN well understood these ancient institutions when he wrote in one of his *Novellae:* "Those who in the past constituted our republic judged it needful to unite in every city the notables (*viri nobiles*) into a body which should transact public affairs and do all in an orderly manner." This aristocratic organization, which dates from Rome's earliest days, was in the provincial cities strengthened by various customs,— the gratuitous character of the public service, the onerous burdens imposed by it, and the terrible responsibilities which were incurred in the exercise of the magisterial office. Municipal interests, which in France are guaranteed by administrative control, were in the Roman Empire guaranteed by the financial responsibility of the magistrates, which would have been illusory if poor men could have attained the duumvirate. The municipal senate was therefore open only to *viri nobiles,* — a nobility of birth and wealth which sat by hereditary right in the senate so long as it kept its fortune, or at least the fortune required for the duumvirate. At Prusa, Dion, his father and grandfather, exercised in succession the highest functions ;[1] with four hundred thousand sesterces they would have had the right to claim to be enrolled in Rome itself among the judges of the five *decuriae.*[2] Lastly, as this society had for its principal civil institutions slavery and clientship, it did not profess equality, but preferred distinction of ranks. Thus, for inscription on the senatorial list, a real hierarchy was established ; at its head the *honorati* who had held office in the city and the province,[3] or had enjoyed Roman honors, and the patrons of the city ;[4] then those who had

---

[1] De Bréquigny, *Vie de Dion.*

[2] Or.-Henzen, No. 6,167.

[3] The persons who had held the provincial priesthood in the temples of Rome and Augustus (*sacerdotales*) formed a separate order, often mentioned in Africa (L. Renier, *Inscr. d'Alg.* Nos. 1,146, 1,528, 1,718, 1,851). Similarly, the Asiarchs in Asia.

[4] In 321 the practice was still continued for the cities to obtain a powerful patron : *Quod Faustianenses patronum cooptarent, cum liberis posterisque ejus sibi liberis posterisque suis tesseram hospitalem cum eo fecerunt, uti se in fidem atque clientelam vel suam vel posterorum suorum reciperet . . .* (Orelli, No. 1,079).

held municipal offices.[1] Age, marriage, number of children, the number of votes obtained, were causes of promotion; the lot decided all else. An inscription has preserved the names written on the *Album* of Canusium, drawn up in 223; with this document we enter the senate-house and can observe the session of a municipal senate, as the laws of Salpensa and Malaga have enabled us to be present in the public place at the elective comitia. More than a hundred and twenty decurions are there assembled.[2] First notice in the place of honor the seats of the patrons, — personages of too great importance to condescend to be often present. Next the ex-magistrates, bearing a title derived from the name of the highest office which they have filled,— seven *quinquennalicii* and their four coadjutors having held the censorship,[3] twenty-nine *duumviralicii*, nineteen *aedilicii*, nine *quaestoricii*, then thirty-two *pedarii*, or decurions who have not yet held office. Behind them, twenty-five *praetextati* listen to the orators; they are becoming acquainted with the concerns of the city, the rules of law, and the method of conducting public affairs.[4] The deliberations are not noisy, for age and condition are respected; each speaks and votes according to his rank and according to the order of inscription on the table. Thus experience has the precedence of ignorance, and wisdom of rashness.

This order was changed in one case only. If one decurion accused another of unworthy conduct and obtained judgment against him, he took the latter's place.[5] This was a means of compelling every member of the curia to keep watch over himself.

[1] *Scribantur eo ordine quo quisque eorum maximo honore in municipio functus est: prča qui duumviratum gesserunt, si hic honor praecella!* (Ulpian, in the *Digest*, l. 3, fr. 1 and 2).

[2] On the list are found a hundred and sixty-four names; but the thirty-nine patrons, persons of consideration (thirty-one senators, eight Roman knights), were almost always absent, and twenty-five *praetextati* did not vote: so that the number of effective decurions was one hundred. But all bore this title. See Mommsen, *Inscr. Neapol.* 625. M. Masqueray has discovered (December, 1875) another *Album,* — that of Thamugas.

[3] *Allati inter quinque nnalicios.*

[4] According to the *Theodosian Code* (xii. 1, 4) those who had exercised magistracies were seated, the rest standing. This classification still existed in the second half of the fifth century. Cf. Sid. Apollin., *Epist.* i. 6. M. Heuzey has found in Macedonia some inscriptions which mention children of five and six years already members of the curia (*Mission en Macédoine,* p. 140); the same at Lyons (*Inscr. de Lyon*), and elsewhere. These nominations had been marks of gratitude towards the father, or an interested choice in the hope of obtaining a liberal gift from the family.

[5] At least this was the law at Genetiva Julia, cap. cxxiv.

These distinctions were valued so highly that they are recorded upon tombs, where we read the offices held and the grades of rank obtained. When the practice of paying a salary became general, its amount was also mentioned in the inscriptions, to do honor to the deceased. A future Empress, Julia Soemias, in this way recalls the fact that her husband had been successively centenary, ducenary, and trecenary procurator; *i. e.*, that he had received yearly 100,000, 200,000, and 300,000 sesterces.[1] When a man could not claim distinction from the crowd by birth or wealth, he valued himself according to the sum of money which he had cost the state. This order was observed at the public festivals and even in the gratuitous distributions; each received a share of provisions and a number of ases[2] proportional to his rank. Some magistrates boast of being men of a share and a half, or even a double share.[3] It was like the "fat and lean people" of Florence.

A society where wealth was so highly esteemed must find room for any man who knew how to acquire it, even for those whose condition destined them to remain at the lowest level. The expression *libertinae opes*[5] had passed into a proverb, and Narcissus, Pallas, Crispinus, and a thousand others had justified it. It is easy to understand how these fortunes were made. Having formerly been slaves, the freedmen had the habit of work among a people who labored but little, and they were not shackled by any prejudices in the midst of a people who had many. On obtaining freedom, sometimes by their vices, but frequently by their intelligence, they knew how to make their way through the crowd, as they had done through servitude. By the stain on their birth they were below the poorest of free-

DENARIUS OF DISTRIBUTION.[4]

---

[1] Orelli, No. 946.

[2] At Radiae a money distribution gave twenty sesterces to each decurion, twelve to each Augustal, etc. (Orelli, No. 3,858); at Lyons, a *summus curator civ. rom. prov. Lugd.* gives, *ob honorem perpetui pontiff.*, to the decurions, fifteen denarii; the members of equestrian rank, to the *seviri Augustales*, and to the wine-merchants, thirteen denarii; to all the authorized corporations, *licite coëuntibus*, twelve denarii. Orelli, No. 4,020, and *passim*, for many similar instances.

[3] Or.-Henzen, Nos. 6,086, 7,181, 7,199 . . . *Ob duplam sportulam collatam sibi . . . et magistri sesquiplares.* This usage existed in the army under the name of recompense of honor . . . *ob virtutem* (Varro, *De Ling. Lat.* v. 90).

[4] EX A. P. (*ex argento publico*). Victory in a quadriga. Reverse of a denarius of the *gens Julia*.

[5] Martial, *Epigr.* v. 1, 3.

born men; by the means of gold they rose above the noble who had nothing to live on but the glory of his ancestors. Tacitus shows them to us filling even at Rome the tribes and decuriae. In the Latin provinces they had invaded the popular sacerdotal office of the Augustals, whose annual heads, the *seviri*,[1] chosen by the decurions, became, on the expiration of their office, life-members of a college forming a sort of intermediate order between the senate and the mere *possessores*;[2] at Lyons the *seviri* were as much honored as the knights of the city.[3] Into this college entered many freedmen who, unable, in spite of their wealth, to obtain municipal honors, took refuge in the priestly office:[4] Trimalchio was a *sevir Augustalis*. This too was a rank which was purchasable.[5] Some men boast in their inscriptions of having obtained it without cost (*gratis factus*);[6] and they were right, this exemption was in their case a brilliant distinction.

The first Augustals sacrificed in honor of the *gens Julia*; then Claudiales, Flaviales, etc., formed colleges, sometimes distinct, sometimes united to that of the Augustals; and all, priests of the national deities, but also of the Augusti and of the imperial majesty, consecrated by religious rites the apotheosis which the Senate had decreed. For this institution, as well as for many others, we must give up the hope of finding a uniform rule, which was habitual neither in the general administration nor the affairs

[1] A *sevir* states in his inscription that he has held the office twice (Orelli, No. 3,921). The *seviri Augustales* of the provinces must not be confounded with the *sodales Augustales* of Rome, — a college instituted by Tiberius and composed of the greatest personages of the state, — nor with the associations which were formed, *in modum collegiorum* (Tac., *Ann.* i. 73), in the capital to honor the new deity.

[2] By reason of their religious functions the Augustals were ranked so near the decurions that politeness might sometimes confuse them. Thus in 140 a freedman of Domitia offers ten thousand sesterces *ordini decurionum et sevirum Augustalium*, and obtains *ut ex reditu ejus pecuniae, III idus febr. natale D., praesentibus decurionibus et seviris discumbentibus in publico arquis portionibus fieret divisio* . . . (Orelli, Nos. 775, 3,939, and *passim*).

[3] Orelli, No. 4,020. At Narbo the priesthood of Augustus, established A. D. 11, was composed of three knights and three freedmen. A shipowner of Puteoli was *sevir Augustalis* in this city and at Lyons (*Inscr. de Lyon*, No. 358; cf. *ibid.* No. 406).

[4] Orelli, No. 3,914: . . . *Omnibus honoribus quos libertini gerere potuerunt honoratus.* This and other inscriptions show that the *sevir Augustalis*, the *primus* and *perpetuus*, owed this title to a decree of the decurions, and that they themselves could not obtain the decurionate.

[5] *C. I. L.* ii. 100. It at last, like the others also, became hereditary. Cf. Marquardt, *Handb.* i. 516.

[6] Orelli, No. 3,920. The corporation had a chest (*area*) to receive the gifts of the new associates or of its members (*ibid.* Nos. 3,913, 7,116, and 7,335); but it seems that an authorization was needed.

of the cities. The fact itself is clear of doubt, and that alone is of importance to political history.

A more significant custom was the division of the citizens into two classes: I do not speak of the division into free men and slaves, but into *honestiores* and *humiliores :* or, as they were termed in the Middle Ages, nobles and villains. Thus the former could not be beaten with rods,[1] crucified, fastened to the stake, or thrown to the beasts, these atrocious punishments being in case of condemnation the ordinary lot of the poor man who had been unable to rise from his humble condition. In former times the *lex Porcia* protected the citizen, whatever his condition, from the rod and other

CARPENTER.[2]

punishments reserved for the foreigner. When citizenship had been given to the greater part of the inhabitants of the Empire, and the *peregrinus* was disappearing, the poor citizen took his place: a slow revolution, which was not effected till the third century. Then the higher classes and the lower, placed by political and penal law in different conditions, formed two distinct peoples, between whom it is difficult to draw the boundary line: for in this society, land and man had not been marked, as they were later, with indelible marks.

A MASON.[3]

This much is sure, — at one extreme we may place the decurions, the magistrates, and those who, having obtained civic honors, formed the senate: and at the other, along with those who had undergone judicial sentences, the *coloni*, ancestors of the serfs of the Middle Ages, — the artisans, day-laborers, small tradesmen, whom

---

[1] *Fustibus caedi solent tenuiores homines, honestiores vero . . . non subjiciuntur.* See on this point the author's paper in the appendix on the *honestiores* and the *humiliores.*

[2] From a Gallo-Roman tomb.   [3] From Trajan's Column.

Cicero had already styled the dregs of the cities,[1] and all those whose calling was regarded as ignominious; these were called the *plebeii* or *tenuiores*. In the upper class there were also placed the members of the corporation of the Augustals, the *possessores*, or landed proprietors, — who will in later times be summoned in certain matters to deliberate with the decurions, — veterans who had obtained the *honesta missio*, professors and physicians.[2]

These *tenuiores* were very numerous. The state employed many of them, along with freedmen and slaves, for the service of the temples, of the magistrates, and in public works. Poverty tending to equalize both conditions and feelings, some free-born persons competed with slaves in the lowest occupations for a living. They multiplied the number of shops in the streets and public places, and they exercised in wretched cellars a thousand industrial occupations which the rich in former days imposed on their slaves, — in the house, for domestic needs, and out of doors hiring out their strength, their intelligence, or selling the products of their toil. There had always been artisans at Rome: there were many more when the showy tunic of the slave put to shame the citizen's thread-bare toga. To the latter no calling now seemed degrading, neither to go upon the boards as an actor, to enter the arena as a gladiator or the brothel as a procurer, nor to live by the often insulting charity given to the parasite and client.

To recapitulate: when, putting aside political history, which often shows only the surface of things, we penetrate into the inner life of the Roman world, we find a society in which the grades were as numerous as ever they have been in any. At the bottom, the slaves and plebeians (*humiliores*): above, the free man possessing landed property (*possessor*); then a twofold aristocracy of rank and wealth. The first, beginning with the provincial who had obtained Roman citizenship, ended with the consuls and the patrician order, which the Emperors continually renewed, just as the kings of England take care to keep up the numbers of the nobility by filling up titles that lapse. The second was arranged according to the fortune. One hundred thousand sesterces, in important

---

[1] *Opifices et tabernarios, atque illam omnem faecem civitatum* (*Pro Flacco*, etc.).

[2] The professors were nominated by the curia, and physicians received from it a license to practise, which was always revocable (Modestinus, in the *Digest*, xxvii. 1, 6, sect. 6).

cities, qualified for the decurionate; two hundred thousand classed a man, at Rome. among the ducenaries; four hundred thousand throughout the Empire raised to the rank of knight; twelve hundred thousand gave access to the Senate. Thus a nobility of wealth existed at the side of the nobility of birth, and the two conservative forces which descent and wealth constitute concurred in maintaining at the same time order and movement in this great community, wherein, nevertheless, existed no impassable barrier for any one. Here is the secret of that "Roman Peace" which the writers of the first two centuries praise so enthusiastically.

This division of the citizens into two classes might have been the cause of troubles in the city if sundry customs had not drawn together those whom political and penal laws separated. These customs were due to two causes. The first of these was the organization of the Roman family. in which servants, slaves, and freed persons were considered as forming part of the household; so that the obligations of patronage imposed on the rich the position of protectors to a large number of poor. The second was the confused yet deeply rooted notion of a sort of fraternity existing from the first among all the inhabitants of the municipium. and of the protection which in former days the weak had sought for at the hands of the strong. This idea, which had its expression in clientship and in the old institution of public services or *munera*. prevented the aristocracy of the provincial cities from being as haughty and unpopular as aristocracies have been in other countries. The *munera* were the duty accepted by rich citizens of superintending a large number of public services and of contributing to the expenditure which they entailed : thus a *curator ludorum* made up the deficiency in the sum set apart by the city for the celebration of a religious festival or of public games; another took the charge of heating the baths or repairing the pavement of a street. At the present day municipal expenditure falls upon everybody; in the Roman city it was for the most part a charge on the rich. They it was who built the bridges still existing at Merida and Alcantara, the aqueducts of Segovia and the Pont du Gard, and those temples and amphitheatres the ruins of which meet us everywhere. In seeing the aristocracy pay for its privileges by sacrifice of time and money from which they themselves profited, the poor felt neither hate nor anger towards them. As clients, they experienced still more directly the effects of aristocratic liberality: and as this bond which attached the small to the great was voluntary, it wounded no one. We said just now that the wealthy provincials followed the example of the Emperors, who covered Rome with costly edifices. Good rulers advised the wealthy to act thus. A discourse of Nerva, which has not been preserved, exhorts them to show munificence;[1] and to prevent cities being deceived in their expectations, as the legacy-hunters often were, Trajan established the principle that every promise made to a city should be binding on the promiser or his heir. The Emperor would not permit municipal patriotism to be trifled with, or a miser's vanity to take advantage of a senate's credulity.[2]

At Herculaneum, Mammianus Rufus had constructed the theatre at his own cost; Nonius Balbus, the basilica. We know the prodigious liberality of Atticus Herodes at Athens. For his stadium he had ransacked the marble quarries of Pentelicus, and the list of his debtors included almost the whole city. His biography affords us another insight: it shows that some of the new nobility did not disdain, in spite of the decree of Marcus Aurelius, to live in their provincial cities. Although Herodes was senator and of consular rank, he scarcely ever left Athens; Plutarch also, after a long stay at Rome, returned to his little city of Chaeroneia; Martial did the same, with less philosophy; and the provinces gained in thus winning back some of the celebrities of Rome.

When the municipal treasury was empty and the donations insufficient, the city opened a public subscription and gave to the praetors a mortgage on its walls, porticos, and temples, or on a branch of its revenues. Cnidus, wishing to erect a portico to Apollo, proceeds thus: she promises to carve on the monument the names of those who will not demand the interest of their

---

[1] Pliny, *Epist.* x. 24: . . . *Omnes cives ad munificentiam.*

[2] On the capability of the cities for receiving legacies and donations, see Vol. V. p. 280. In spite of Hadrian's rescript, difficulties arose sometimes between the donor's heirs and the city as legatee; Antoninus overcame them by prescribing that for the future the action of the decurions should be regarded as binding the legal personality which the city constituted (Gaius, *Comm.,* ii. 195). Before this new legislation the cities had already been able, with the authorization of the Senate or the Emperor, to accept a legacy. Cf. Suet., *Tib.* 31. Ulpian enumerates (in the *Digest,* xxxvii. 1, 3, 4) the bodies which could possess property, — *municipia, societates, decuriae corpora.*

money; to others she offers as guaranty of repayment the impost of the fiftieth and the profits of the office for oaths, where were registered the contracts of sale between private individuals.[1]

We are disposed to dwell on this aspect of civic manners which unhappily is now so strange to us. Ummidia Quadratilla builds at Casinum an amphitheatre and a temple;[2] Secundus, at Bordeaux, an aqueduct which costs him 2,000,000 sesterces.[3] One of Lucian's heroes, Peregrinus, gives up during his lifetime all his property, thirty talents, to his native city. Crinas, of Marseilles, expends 10,000,000 sesterces in rebuilding the walls of the Phocaean city; the two brothers Stertinius, a larger sum in decorating Naples, their native city, with public buildings;[4] one Hiero gave as much as 2,000 talents (over $2,000,000) to Laodicea, his native city.[5] The younger Pliny spent less at Como, — 11,100,000 sesterces. How greatly he was interested in embellishing it with monuments, honoring it with useful institutions, and making it a prosperous and famous city! "Towards it," said he, "I have the heart of a son or of a father."[6] "One ought to give to one's native place," he says again;[7] and he encourages his friends and neighbors to imitate his bounty. He founded at Como a library, a school, and a charitable institution for poor children.[8] Outside the walls he built a temple to Ceres, and spacious porticos to shelter the trades-folk who came to the fair which was held during the festival of the goddess. One of his friends made a present of 400,000 sesterces; his grandfather had erected a costly portico and furnished the money necessary for the decoration of the city gates.

---

[1] *Bulletin de corresp. hellén.*, 1880, p. 341. M. Dareste, author of the commentary on this inscription, makes the remark that by Greek and Roman law mortgage applied both to movables and immovables.

[2] Orelli, No. 781.

[3] *Revue épigr. du Midi de la France*, p. 179.

[4] Pliny, *Hist. nat.* xxix. 8. One of them was that physician Stertinius who, after having doubled the ordinary fees of the Emperor's physician, 250,000 sesterces, affirmed he was still a loser, his practice bringing him in 600,000; another demanded for a cure 200,000 sesterces; a third in a few years gained 10,000,000. The sesterce of those days may be valued at 17 or 18 centimes, — nearly 3½ cents; so that about twenty-eight were equivalent to a dollar.

[5] Strabo, xiii. 578.   [6] *Res publica nostra pro filia vel parente* (iv. 13).

[7] ix. 30.

[8] Henzen, p. 124. Pliny's correspondence contains six letters in which he mentions his gifts to individuals.

Observe, too, that these acts of liberality towards a single city, made known to us by the accident of a few letters which have escaped oblivion, were done in the space of a very few years and in a way by a single family, and all during the lives of the donors, — a fact which allows us to suppose there were many

PALMYRA: PORTICO OF THE COLONNADE.

others. They mark one of the characteristic features of municipal life in the Roman Empire; and inscriptions would furnish a multitude of similar examples, even in places which have become impassable deserts. At Palmyra, for example, the long porticos which border the principal streets were built by private individuals, who often received the honor of a statue decreed during

life by the senate and people.[1] Later, the Emperor's authorization
became necessary for works executed at the expense of the cities; but
this was not the case for monuments erected by individuals.[2] This
exemption from long and troublesome formalities was an encouragement to donors, who often followed one another through several generations. A consul of Trajan's time had given 3,300,000 sesterces
to Tarquinii : his son increased the amount to enlarge and complete
the baths which had been begun.[3]

The aristocracy also sought to interest the multitude in their joys
and their griefs, and there was no solemnity in the midst of a
rich family which was not celebrated by some entertainment for
the people, some public festival or games. " Those who assume the
toga," says Pliny, " those who marry, or enter on office, or dedicate
some public work, are in the habit of inviting to the feast all
the Senate of the city, and even many members of the lower classes,
and giving to each guest one or two denarii."[4] The Romans of
the Empire, even senators of Rome, did not feel ashamed to accept
money, even the most trivial sum. A rich private person having
imposed on his heir the obligation of giving a certain sum annually
to the Conscript Fathers.[5] Domitian annulled the will. The senators considered the Emperor too thoughtful of their dignity, and
he indemnified them for their loss. On one occasion at the theatre,
as the lottery tokens which he threw into the midst of the audi-
ence had all fallen on the third benches, — those of the people, — the
next day he had fifty prizes thrown to the seats of the Senate.[6]
These habits of liberality prevailed throughout the whole Roman
world. At Oea, in Africa, a widow distributes, on the day when

---

[1] Cf. De Vogüé, *Inscr. sémitiques*, Nos. 8-11, etc. Some of these inscriptions enumerate
the bronze ornaments and the glazing with which the columns and architraves were covered,
— the polychrome architecture of Athens transported to the desert !

[2] *Digest*, l. 10, 3, sect. 1. This fragment is from Macer, a jurisconsult of the third
century. If Pliny consulted Trajan from day to day respecting the works projected in Bithynia,
the reason was that he was fulfilling in that province an extraordinary mission. It is possible
besides that in the tributary cities the government had reserved betimes the authorization of
expenses which might interfere with the returns of the state impost.

[3] Henzen, No. 6,622. Cf. Orelli, No. 80: . . . *Quod liberalitates in patriam civesque, a
majoribus suis tributas, exemplis suis superaverit.* . . .

[4] Pliny, *Epist.* x. 117. This usage was very ancient; for Plautus, in the *Aulularia*
(v. 107), speaks of money distributions.

[5] *Ingredientibus curiam* (Suet., *Dom.* 9). It was a sort of fee given for attendance.

[6] Suet., *Dom.* 4.

her son assumes the toga, fifty thousand sesterces. The next day she contracts a second marriage; and to escape the repetition of a burdensome generosity, she goes to be married a long way from Oea,[1] — a clear proof that custom would have imposed on her a second largess, in spite of the previous evening's liberality, if the marriage had taken place in the city.

Maximus lost his wife, a native of Verona. He gave the city, in honor of the deceased, a combat of gladiators,[2] — an old religious

AMPHITHEATRE OF VERONA.

usage which had been turned into an amusement: first, blood to appease the manes; later, blood to amuse the multitude. A corpse was carried by chance through the streets of Polentia on the way to a burial-place at some distance. The inhabitants made a riot and would only allow the procession to pass after the heir had promised them what doubtless they were accustomed to receive at the funerals of their principal men, — a gift of gladiators. At Minturnae can be read on the base of a statue: " In four days he exhibited eleven pairs of gladiators, who did not cease fighting until half of them, all the most valiant of Campania, were stretched

---

[1] Apuleius, *Apolog.*   [2] Pliny, *Epist.* vi. 31.

on the arena; besides, he gave a hunt of ten terrible bears."
And the author of the inscription exclaims proudly : " Noble fellow-
citizens, you well remember this!" [1]

Everything was acceptable, — struggles between old athletes,
combats of low gladiators,[2] slaughter of wild boars, even of hares;
and after the pleasures of the show those of the table, were it but
some scanty pittance, which richer men changed into a feast. In
ancient times religion ennobled everything; these feasts were acts
of devotion, as were the early agapae of the Christians.[3] Religious
faith had vanished, but the custom remained. Pliny had founded
a temple at Tifernum; on the day of its consecration he gave
a repast to all the inhabitants: it was part of the sacred festival.
It was the same in the case of pious foundations made to honor
some deceased person by a festival annually given to the decurions, the Augustals, the fellows of a college, etc.

Ideas of another sort constantly called forth acts of liberality
of the same nature to clients, and even to all the people of a city.
In some houses large halls were arranged, in which on certain
days open table was kept (*triclinia popularia*).[4] Trimalchio wished
to be represented on his tomb scattering a sack of gold pieces
among the people. "For you know," he says to the architect,
"that I gave a public feast and two gold denarii to each guest.
Represent the *triclinia* and all the people heartily enjoying
themselves." [5]

These repasts were so usual that they had the name of *pub-

---

[1] Henzen, No. 6,148. An inscription of Ancyra says of a citizen that he surpassed every
one by his gifts, enriched his country by distributions, adorned it with fine works of art, etc.
(Perrot, *Galatie*, p. 235, No. 125.)

[2] Martial (iii. 16, 59) ridicules a shoemaker — whom he calls, it is true, *sutorum regule* —
and a fuller who had given combats of gladiators, the one at Bologna, the other at Modena. In
the *Satyricon* (45) there is in contemplation "gladiators at two sesterces apiece, decrepit,
ready to drop if blown upon, and dead in advance; real refuse stock." Cf. Juvenal, *Sat.* iii.,
and Persius, *Sat.* iv. Yet in the reign of Tiberius a senatus-consultum had been passed prohibiting the giving of games if the donor were not possessed of at least four million sesterces
(Tac., *Ann.* iv. 63).

[3] *Festis insunt sacrificia, epulae, ludi* ... (Macrob., *Sat.* i. 16).

[4] Cf. Pliny, *Epist.* i. 3.

[5] Petronius, *Satyr.* 71. These donations were of all kinds. The little city of Acraephion,
near Chaeroneia, has handed down to posterity, in a pompous inscription, evidence of its gratitude for the feasts, sweetmeats, and delicacies given by one of its citizens to the whole population, even the slaves (*C. I. G.* No. 1,625). Cf. Egger, *Mél. d'hist. anc.* pp. 76 and 87.
Others furnished oil for the games or the baths, etc. Another curious example may be found
in *C. I. G.* No. 2,236, and Lebas, *Inscr. de Morée*, No. 149.

licae cenae. But the Emperors were very distrustful of these assemblies, fearing that the nobles might find there assassins for hire, — *bravos,* in fact, such as the great Italian lords had for so long a time in their pay. Nero prohibited these banquets,[1] allowing only the *sportulae,* or baskets filled with provisions and given to indi-

COUCH FOR THE REPAST.[2]

viduals. The thing was still more simplified; the *sportula* was replaced by the gift of some sesterces, the more willingly accepted because they served to satisfy other wants than hunger. These distributions of money were in their turn suspected, and Domitian suppressed them and again substituted the *sportula,*[3] *cena recta,*

[1] *Publicae cenae ad sportulas redactae* (Suet., *Nero,* 16).
[2] Before the person a round three-legged table (*monstripus*); near the table a cup-bearer (*pocillator*). Bas-relief in the Museum of the Louvre, No. 44 of the catalogue.
[3] . . . *Sportulas publicas sustulit revocata rectarum cenarum consuetudine* (Suet., *Dom.* 7).

Trajan. who disliked anything of the nature of an association, did not. however. dare to destroy this last relic of republican manners; he seems to have left the choice to those interested between the two forms of the *sportula.* — in provisions or in money. Spain and Spanish America still preserve these Roman customs.

These liberalities took place under exceptional circumstances; others occurred daily for the benefit of the clients. When the client gave the patron his vote in the comitia, his blood on the battlefield. and his fidelity everywhere. clientship was that solid institution to be found under one form or another in all aristocratic societies. In the second century of the Empire it was nothing else than organized mendicity : *i. e.*. an institution of decay. If a man were poor, or only straitened in means, and lazy. admission was gained into a body of clients. It was an easy matter. for one of the vanities of the rich was to appear in public preceded or fol- lowed by citizens in togas, — *turba togata ;* as the *grand seigneur* of former days never showed himself at court but with a numerous retinue of gentlemen. Consideration being proportionate to the num- ber of clients. the patrons made it a point to have a good number of them. " What a thick smoke ! " exclaims Juvenal.[1] " It is the *sportula* they are distributing. A hundred are rushing thither, each armed with his kitchen apparatus." Nor did they feel any more shame than a hidalgo with a torn mantle going to obtain his soup at the convent of Toledo.

Doubtless in this multitude were sometimes heard muttered mur- murings. and there was much secret ill-will against " the king and lord " who on certain days showed haughtiness or niggardliness : " You invite me. Sextus. and while you enjoy a grand supper you give me a hundred quadrantes. Am I invited for supper. or to be envious of you ? "[2] But for a service which gave little trouble.[3] and in which the ancients did not see the servility which we find in it. the daily salary, 25 ases,[4] or 2.280 sesterces for the year. was a good deal of money taken from men who had too much, and

---

[1] *Sat.* iii. 249.   [2] Martial. *Epigr.* iv. 68.

[3] Yet Martial terms it *ingenuas cruces* (x. 82). But he was very idle, and in spite of his practice of extending without shame his hand with its gold ring, the little dignity left in the poet's soul rebelled in the presence of certain patrons (cf. x. 70, 74, and many other places).

[4] 100 quadrantes, or 25 ases. were worth 625 sesterces.

bestowed upon those who had not enough. To the daily quadrantes
must be added the occasional largess. — gifts now and then, an old
cloak, a half-worn toga, invitations to dinner, a corner in the
palace to lodge in,[1] sometimes even, in a lucky moment, a field
like that which Martial received,[2] and about which the begging
poet does not seem to care after he has got it, in order to obtain
more. "You have given me," said he, when reproaching his
patron for his meanness, "some land at the gates of Rome; I
have a larger extent on my window. . . . A caterpillar would starve
there, a swallow would carry off all the straw for her little
ones' nest, and a spoon would hold the harvest." Then, too, the
clever ones would secure several patrons, and with good legs they
were equal to a manifold service. Therefore it was, whatever the
disappointed may say of it, a trade on which one could live, — on
the condition, it is true, of not being too proud. These figures are
for Rome and the suburbs;[3] in the provincial cities the *sportula*
yielded less. But I am quite certain that it was always given where
scanty means and much vanity existed: two things which often go
together, and which in the Empire were never wanting.

The Emperor had his clients like other rich men; the palace was
crowded with them. They followed him in his travels, ate at his
table or in its neighborhood, and received his gifts, — which Quintilian calls *congiaria*, like the distributions to the people.[4] But the feeling of natural or social inequality was so deeply rooted in the heart
of this society that the Emperor and all who reckoned a sufficiently
large number of clients or "friends" divided them into classes,
under very different conditions, without thereby exciting any opposition; there were friends of the first, second, or third degree.

---

[1] *Digest*, ix. 3, 5, sect. 1.   [2] xi. 18.

[3] At Baiae, Martial received from Flaccus the one hundred quadrantes. Martial (*passim*),
Juvenal (*Sat.* i.), and Fronto (*Ad Marc. Aur.* 5; *Ad Ver.* 7) show that under this form the *clien-
tela* was still in full vigor in the time of the Antonines; it is found even later, but it no longer
carries the idea of fidelity on the one part and actual patronage on the other. See the complaints of Martial against Pontieus, who refused him every kind of assistance. Yet we must
distinguish between mere transient clients, runners after *sportula*, to whom applies what was
said before, and family or civic clients, by which I mean those who were hereditary clients by
virtue of a contract in proper legal form between the first patron and the first client, for them
and their posterity (cf. Orelli, Nos. 1,079, 3,056 *et seq.*), the freedmen over whom the ancient
master had the right of correction, and the inhabitants of a municipium who had been given a
patron in perpetuity (*Id., ibid.*).

[4] vi. 3, 52.

Even cities made themselves the clients of a rich and influential patron, sometimes of several. Canusium had thirty-nine patrons,

of whom thirty-one were Roman senators and eight Roman knights.[1] These men of the South, always lovers of games, spectacles, and noisy demonstrations, knew how to make the most of the lavish, the seekers for popularity, and the vain who liked to hear men say: "There goes the patron of this or that important city!" In

COIN OF A PATRON OF A CITY.[2]

this community, where the manners of the republican aristocracy had left so many traces, it was remembered that Scipio and Marcellus, Brutus and Cato, all the great citizens of Rome, had been patrons of cities or peoples.

At that time this patronage had been useful even to those who exercised it, now it was merely honorable; but it was so in a high degree, and the most considerable personages did not at all disdain to place this last relic of the distinctions conferred by the people at the side of titles which the Emperor[3] had conferred. To the cities, this patronage was a protection

GLADIATOR'S HELMET (MUSEUM OF NAPLES).

against the excesses of a governor, who from the depths of the most remote province was restrained by the fear of the formidable accusers whom an injured people might raise up against him in the Senate of Rome.[4] This selfish interest was by no means concealed; the document which officially constituted the bond between the people and their patron often contained these words: "We offer you this, the highest honor of our city, in order that we, by

---

[1] Mommsen, *Inscr. Neapol.* No. 625. See the advice that Fronto (*Ad Amic.* ii. 10) gives to his compatriots for the choice of several patrons.

[2] MVNICIPII PATRONVS, and an *aplustre* : i. e. an ornament which decorated the stern of ships. Bronze medal of Cadiz.   [3] Orelli, No. 784.

[4] See the discourse of Thrasea in the Senate, and the examples furnished by the younger Pliny.

means of you, may always be secure and well protected." Should also this bond be relaxed or broken, it was renewed, *renovavit hospitium*.[1]

To choose a patron, the senate was called together. A decree had been prepared by the decurions, presented to the public assembly, and voted as a legislative act;[2] it was a contract which bound the posterity of the protector and of the protected.[3] Thus Bologna was under the patronage of the Antonii.[4] Lacedaemon of the Claudii, Sicily of the Marcelli, etc.; even women and children were patrons of a city.[5] The act was engraved on a tablet of bronze or marble (*tabula hospitalis*), which was preserved in a temple. and of which a copy was solemnly deposited in the patron's house;[6] from that time he became the official defender of the city before the central government, and of its citizens before the tribunals. For his clients he exhausted his credit and his purse; he rebuilt their decayed monuments or erected new ones; he gave them games of athletes or gladiators. festivals, public repasts; he made to them distributions of money, or, like Pliny, founded some provident or charitable institution. But then he walked, when in the city. at the head of the magistrates; he had the first place in the temple, at the theatre, and at the feasts : he was offered presents, which he returned a hundred-fold ; during his lifetime inscriptions. busts, and statues were voted to him; and at death a tomb. on which were the words : " This monument has been erected at the expense of the community by a decree of the decurions, in gratitude for the services rendered by N. to the city."[7] The patron's protection was more effectual than that of Jupiter; like the god, he was paid with incense, pomp, and acclamations, and everybody

[1] Orelli, Nos. 4,036, 4,037.

[2] *Consentiente populo* (Henzen, No. 7,171). At Malaga (cap. lxi.), at Genetiva Julia (cap. cxxx.), the choice of the patron was made by a decree of the senate passed with a majority of two thirds.

[3] . . . *Eamque cum liberis posterisque suis patronum cooptaverunt* (Henzen, No. 6,413). We know of many acts of this sort.

[4] Suet., *Octav.* 17.

[5] *Puer egregius ab origine patronus ordinis et populi* (Orelli, No. 3,767). A daughter of Marcus Aurelius had this title at Guelma (L. Renier, *Inscr. d'Alg.* Nos. 2,718–2,719); a priestess of Venus at Peltuinum (Orelli, No. 4,036), etc.

[6] Orelli, No. 784.

[7] . . . *Eique ob merita ejus erga rem publicam scholam et statuas decrevit* (Orelli, No. 344). Cf. No. 3,853 ; two statues, a silver shield, etc.

was satisfied, — most of all the man who had half ruined himself in order to appear of importance.[1]

To the liberality shown by the rich during their lifetime were added testamentary legacies, which were very common, the law giving the father the absolute disposition of three-fourths of his property, and custom demanding that he should make a will. Before the Apronian senatus-consultum, passed under Trajan or Hadrian, cities could not receive a gift or inheritance. except by special authorization, as in the case of Marseilles under Tiberius, or by an evasion of the law, as when Pliny secured to Como a revenue of fifty thousand sesterces. But friends and companions of the deceased, even strangers who did honor to the city or the state, received unexpected gifts in wills. Pliny writes to Trajan: "Julius Largus, of the province of Pontus, whose face I never saw and whose name I never heard, has in his

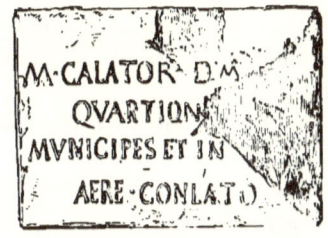

INSCRIPTION PLACED UNDER THE STATUE OF MARCUS CALATORIUS.[2]

will begged me to accept fifty thousand sesterces out of his estate, and to divide the remainder between the cities of Heracleia and Tyana, to be employed in public works or in quinquennial games." [3] The Roman family was strengthened rather than weakened by this testamentary freedom, which obliged the son to show more respect to his father, as well as more prudence in his own affairs; and the city was the gainer also, by not having within its walls men considering themselves as strangers in the midst of their fellow-citizens.

These relations, established by custom between the different classes of society, gave a peculiar character to municipal manners, in spite of the offensive distinction established by the law between the

[1] In this case the city sometimes afforded help to the patron's family. Women or children whose husbands or fathers had perhaps been ruined in the public service obtained from the decurions what was at that time one of the great anxieties of life, — a tomb (*Inscr. de Lyon*, No. 191).

[2] It must be completed thus: Marco CALATORIO Marci filio QVARTIONI MVNICIPES ET INcolae AERE CONLATO : " To Marcus Calatorius Quartio, son of Marcus, the citizens of the city and the inhabitants, with the money which they have collected " (Naples Museum; cf. Roux, *op. cit.* vol. vi. pl. 86, and p. 167).

[3] *Epist.* x. 79. Augustus in twenty years had received fourteen hundred million sesterces by legacies in wills, although he refused many which were made him (Suet., *Octav.* 101, 66).

honestior and the *humilior*, — a difference which, after all, the evil-doer alone felt. The rich seemed to be responsible for securing the pleasures, and to some extent the subsistence, of the poor.[1] It was quite as much for them as for the senators that they erected buildings, since the whole community occupied seats in the same theatre, bathed in the same baths, walked under the same porticos. With us it is rare for the rich and poor to know one another; in the Roman city they were in continual communication, by means of the clientship, the patronage, the lavish gifts which associated the one class in the amusements of the other. Games, spectacles, and exercises were common to all. From all this came a spirit of mutual good-will and order which secured the tranquillity of the Empire.

Why is not this the case in modern society? For several reasons. We do not possess the great Roman municipium, with its habits of close relationship between the citizens; we have the law of a compulsory division of property, which prevents testamentary acts of liberality, by making the father's fortune the inalienable property of the son. In the family, by depriving its head of the right of disinheriting the child who throws disgrace on his name, domestic discipline has been destroyed; and throughout the population our continual revolutions have caused a fierce sentiment of false equality which has expelled patronage from our manners and respect from our public life. Each is his own master, — which is a good thing; but many in this way remain isolated in the immensity of the state, and are ready to charge society with the ills of which this isolation is the cause.

IV. — COLLEGES AND BENEVOLENT INSTITUTIONS.

HITHERTO we have considered a Roman city in its totality; but the municipium contained, like so many little communities, corporations (*collegia, universitates*) formed by all those who found interest or pleasure in being associated. For a long time

---

[1] There are many examples in Greek inscriptions of generous citizens importing corn in time of scarcity and selling it at a low price. At other times this is done by the magistrates in the name of the city (*Bull. de corresp. hellén.* February, 1881, p. 89).

the right of association was practised without restriction, and there existed guilds of handicraftsmen from the earliest times of Rome's history.[1] When, in the last century of the Republic, they became a cause of disturbances, they were suppressed, except a few colleges which their antiquity or their religious character specially protected. Clodius, in order to provide himself with a revolutionary army, re-established them in 58 B. C. and created new ones from the dregs of the people. Caesar compelled them to dissolve, and

WEIGHING OF LOAVES AT A BAKER'S.[2]

Augustus tolerated only those which were founded by virtue of a senatus-consultum.[3] His successors continued faithful to this policy and subjected the members of illegal associations to the most terrible punishments. Ulpian says: "Whoever forms a society without permission, is liable to the same penalties as those who by armed force hold the public places or the temples."[4] And these

---

[1] Gaius, in his *Commentary* on the Twelve Tables, says: *Sodales sunt qui ejusdem collegii sunt, quam Graeci ἑταιρίαν vocant. His autem potestatem facit lex pactionem quam velint sibi ferre, dum ne quid ex publica lege corrumpant.* He regards this right of association as derived from a law of Solon, which he quotes, in which the extent and variety of this right are shown: ἐὰν δὲ δῆμος, ἢ φράτορες, ἢ ἱερῶν ὀργίων, ἢ ναῦται, ἢ σύσσιτοι, ἢ ὁμόταφοι, ἢ θιασῶται, ἢ ἐπὶ λείαν οἰχόμενοι, ἢ εἰς ἐμπορίαν . . . (*Digest*, xlvii. 22, 4). The Twelve Tables only forbade night assemblies, and the Gabinian law only clandestine meetings (Porc. Latro, *Declam. contra Catil.* sect. 10). On the *collegia, corpora, sodalicia, scholae artificum et opificum*, see capp. xvii. and xviii. of Orelli, the *Index* of Henzen, the dissertation of Mommsen, *De Collegiis et sodaliciis*, Boissier, *La Religion romaine*, ii. 274, and Levasseur, *Les Classes ouvrières*, vol. i. liv. i. cap. vi.

[2] Bas-relief on the tomb of Eurysaces. See this tomb, Vol. IV. p. 116.

[3] Dion, xxxviii. 13; Suet., *Caesar*, 42; *Octav.* 32; Josephus, *Ant. Jud.* xiv. 10, 8. Cf. the senatus-consultum *De Bacch.* (*C. I. L.* i. 195); Ulpian, *Ad leg. Juliam majestatis* (*Digest*, xlviii. 4, 1). All disorders were readily attributed to these associations; the first measure ordered by the Senate towards stopping the dispute between Nuceria and Pompeii was to suppress the colleges, *quae contra leges instituerant* (Tac., *Ann.* xiv. 17). The passage well shows the two contrary tendencies, — in the people, the desire of multiplying the colleges; in the government, the wish to restrain them. Chapter cvi. of the law of *Genetiva col.* interdicts *coetum conventum conjurationem.*

[4] *Digest*, xlvii. 22, 2: *collegium illicitum.*

penalties were those attached to high treason; namely, banishment or death. We have seen Trajan's jealous repugnance towards
all associations, although he himself constituted at Rome, in
the public interest, the guild of bakers; and Gaius said, moreover, about the year 150:[1] "They are authorized only for a few
reasons. Thus the farmers of taxes, the workers of gold, silver,
and salt mines, are permitted to form themselves into societies.
Rome has besides many corporate bodies legally established, such
as that of the bakers, the boatmen of the Tiber, and others.[2]
Some exist also in the provinces. These associations can possess
property,[3] as can the city, a common chest, a syndicate for managing
their affairs and defending them in the law-courts."

Yet we have noticed, beginning with Hadrian, an expansion in
this policy, at least in respect to the Christians: and this certainly
agrees with another regarding the trade and festive societies, for
a decree of the "Divine Brothers" — Marcus Aurelius and Verus —
proves the existence of the usage by the very prohibition which
they make against being members of two colleges at the same
time, while granting to these associations the right to receive legacies and to emancipate their slaves, — hence to inherit from their
freedmen.[4] Half a century later Alexander Severus himself formed
all the trades into guilds.[5] Manners led to it. Feeling themselves
lost in the immensity of the Empire, men attached themselves the
more strongly to their city: and in the city itself the movement
towards concentration, arising from the increasingly aristocratic character which municipal administrations were taking, had long im-
pelled the *humiliores* to associate according to their wants and
their ideas. Political considerations had combated without destroy-
ing this inveterate custom of the Graeco-Latin world; and as is
always the case when manners are in opposition to the law, it is
the former which conquer: the old usages had triumphed over
the reluctance of the government. This custom had moreover, been

[1] *Digest*, iii. 4, 1.

[2] The scribes of whom Martial speaks (viii. 38) formed one of the colleges at Rome.

[3] The widow of a rich freedman left to a college a site for a chapel, a marble statue of
the god, a terrace sheltered by a roof with a gallery, where the fellows could hold their collegi-
ate repasts (Orelli, No. 2,417).

[4] *Digest*, xlvii. 22, 1, sect. 2; xxxiv. 5, 20, and xl. 3, 1 and 2.

[5] Lamprid., *Alex. Sev.* 32. Hadrian had established something similar for the artisans
whom he took with him in his travels.

strengthened by the example of the companies authorized by government for the service of the state or the public needs. Then men of the same trade, of the same district, of the same street, the freedmen of the same master, the worshippers of the same

PRACTICE OF SINGING, OR MUSIC.[1]

Lares at the nearest cross-roads, those adoring the same divinity at a neighboring temple, the merchants from the same country,[2] or the Romans (collegium urbanorum) and the veterans settled in a foreign city, many others also,[3] associated together for the purpose of rendering mutual help, for religion, or for pleasure.

[1] Mosaic in the Museum of Naples.

[2] Collegium peregrinorum. Thus at Tomi existed ὁ οἶκος, or the chamber of the Alexandrine armorers, etc. Cf. Perrot, p. 67. An inscription (Orelli, No. 1,246) reads: "The people of Berytus, worshippers of Jupiter of Heliopolis, established at Puteoli;" and there are many similar to this.

[3] For example, corporations of artists, musicians, and actors. Cf. Egger, Mém. d'hist. anc. p. 31. Slaves could not enter a college without the consent of their masters, dominis volentibus (Digest, xlvii. 16, 3, sect. 2).

Men formed associations for feastings,[1] or, like the French clerks of
the Basoche, to celebrate some holiday by scenic representations, or
for the practice of singing, music, and gymnastics, etc.[2] Especially
there were funeral associations.[3] To be certain of a tomb was at
that time every man's chief care. The rich made theirs ready on
their own domain; the poor, who had not a spot of ground to hold
the sepulchral urn, bought in common a corner, where they would
be protected by the "members" better than a knight was, in his
sumptuous tomb, against the indignities of placards and announcements, sometimes against the intrusion of another corpse, which
from economy the heirs might try to place in some old sepulchre.[4]
Nerva had encouraged this institution, by establishing a fund to
aid the poor in meeting their funeral expenses; and as these societies
were by far the most numerous, since they had been authorized
by a senatus-consultum, others took the form of a burial society
to give a legal character to meetings of a different sort.

We have the rules of one of these colleges, that of Lanuvium.[5]
To become a member, there was a payment of a hundred sesterces
and an amphora of good wine (about six gallons); to continue in
it, six ases a month must be paid to the common fund. In consideration of this, each member was assured of having a funeral pile and
a tomb, costing the fraternity three hundred sesterces, fifty of which
were paid to the members who should follow at the funeral to do
honor to the deceased. If the subscriber had died within twenty
miles of Lanuvium, three members, selected for this purpose, set

---

[1] Tertullian (*Apol.* c. 39) makes allusion to societies for feasting: *Epulae potucula cora-
trinae.* . . . In an inscription of Orelli, No. 4,073, the associates call themselves "boon companions." — *convictores qui una epula vesci solent.*

[2] The *ludi juvenales* celebrated by *collegia juvenum,* which are found in great number in
Italy in the first and second centuries. Cf. L. Renier, *Comptes rendus de l'Acad. des inscr.*
1866, p. 164, and Orelli, Nos. 1,383, 3,909, 4,091, 4,101, etc.

[3] Ὀπόταφοι. See the curious passage in Gaius quoted at p. 95. These colleges, or
something analogous, still exist in Germany, — *Sterbekassen,* or *Grabkassen.* For a very moderate premium the family receives, at the death of the assured, a certain sum for his burial, —
Begräbnissgeld: the same thing exists in England and Ireland.

[4] See, in the *Comptes rendus de l'Acad. des inscr.* for 1866, an inscription of Thasos, in which
the proprietor of a tomb threatens with a fine of four thousand denarii, to be paid to the
city, those who might try to put another corpse in it. There are many such inscriptions. The
infliction of the fine was certain, because it went either to the municipal or to the imperial
treasury (*arcae pontificum*), and public authority was aroused against violators of sepulchres
(*Digest,* xlvii. 12, 3, sect. 3).

[5] Henzen, No. 6,086.

out at once for the funeral, and they were paid twenty sesterces as travelling expenses. If he died at a greater distance, they paid the customary *funeraticium* to the undertaker. Lastly, if a master, "from spitefulness," refused to give up to the association the corpse of his deceased slave, none the less on that account did the dead associate receive the semblance of funeral rites.[1] Suicides had no right to anything. The black and white penitents of Southern Europe keep alive to this day the memory of these funeral associations.

The slave-member of a college who obtained his freedom was expected to give, on this joyous occasion, an amphora of wine, which was reserved for future use. Six times a year the members dined together. The fare was plain, — for each guest a loaf of bread, four sardines, and a bottle of the wine which, with curious forethought on the part of a burial society, they had in store.[2] But the company were not at those times occupied with gloomy thoughts; they loved to laugh, and to drink also, and would not be drawn aside from their pleasures until they had emptied the twenty-four gallons (four amphorae) put on the table. "If any one desires to make any complaint," says the rule, "or to make any proposition, let him await the stated meeting of the college; we wish on holidays to dine quietly and pleasantly, *ut quieti et hilares . . . epulemur.*" As in the city, breaches of the rules were punished by fines, — four sesterces for having taken at the feast a seat which was not a man's own, twelve for having made a disturbance, twenty for rudeness towards the president; these fines doubtless served to increase the bill of fare. The managers of the feast[3] must furnish the cushions for the couches, the plate, and the hot water[4] which it was common to mix with the thick or honeyed wines of the time.[5]

[1] *Ei funus imaginarium fiet* (Henzen, *ibid.*).
[2] Many other inscriptions mention this distribution of wine : cf. Orelli, No. 2,417. A special legacy secured twice a year to the ordinary members of this college, two denarii and three sextarii of wine (over two quarts), to the servants double, to the officials three times as much, and to all four loaves each.
[3] *Magistri cenarum ex ordine albi facti.*
[4] The taste for hot drinks was so general that there were many thermopolia at Rome . . . *In thermopolio . . . calidum bibunt* (Plaut., *Curcul.* II. iii. 13, 14).
[5] This picture of the interior economy of a Roman brotherhood is taken from a long inscription found at Lanuvium (Henzen, No. 6,086), which is of the year 136, and which bears at the top the senatus-consultum authorizing burial societies. We infer from this text that the quotation of Marcianus in the *Digest*, xlvii. 22, 1, which has not the words *in funus*, which are in the inscription, was incomplete. This jurisconsult speaks of the principle established by the

These corporate bodies, in which the slave sat down at the same table with the free man, and by means of which were secured to him a funeral and a tomb, show how Roman society, in its ideas

BAKERS KNEADING DOUGH.[1]

and in some of its institutions, had already taken a step towards Christianity.

The guild had its patron also. He was very humbly begged to accept this onerous title, and to allow the decree of appointment

whole of the imperial rescripts, *mandatis principalibus praecipitur*, and not of the senatus-consultum mentioned at Lanuvium. He sums up the principle in these words, — that *sodalicia* are prohibited, and yet that the poorer classes are allowed to have a common purse, supported by monthly payments, on the condition that meetings do not take place more than once a month. Marcianus goes even farther in saying : . . . *Religionis causa coire non prohibentur* (*ibid.* sect. 1), and with their masters' permission slaves can be affiliated, *collegia tenuiorum* (*ibid.* sect. 2). Opposed to this passage from Marcianus are the following words of Ulpian : *Sub praetextu religionis vel sub specie solvendi voti coetus illicitos nec a veteranis tentare oportet* (*Digest*, XLVI. ii. 2). I see here a precaution against military disorders, and I can comprehend that after so many barrack revolutions the government, regarding every meeting of soldiers as dangerous, had placed under a general prohibition, aimed at illegal assemblies, those of veterans, who might allege the pretext of a sacrifice or a vow in order to meet and plan a rising. It was impossible to interdict religious assemblages, for this would have been to suppress public worship. Marcianus does not speak differently. But there was need to strike at societies which concealed their true purposes under the guise of religion : this is the purport of Ulpian's words. The Romans, like the English, had certain very rigorous laws which were generally left dormant, but which they used in case of need. Thus a well-decided principle of the imperial policy was to interdict associations, and the constant usage was to tolerate, even in the camps (cf. Renier, *Inscr. d'Alg.* 57, 60, 63, 70), all those which seemed to be inoffensive. Against others there was always in reserve the law, which could be applied ; this was what was done against the Christians. Nevertheless, Mommsen admits that those colleges in which he saw only burial associations would have meetings *ad epulas et res sacras quoties res ferebat* (p. 88), and he adds that every association which required a monthly subscription took, without constituting itself a special college, the legal form of a burial society. I do not ask more ; with that alone all the rest can pass. The prohibition cited previously against being a member of two colleges at once proves, contrary to the opinion held by Mommsen, that there were different kinds : for I do not think that any one desired to be affiliated to two funeral colleges for the sake of having two tombs. Walter (*Gesch. des Röm. Rechts*, No. 339) thinks also that the funeral colleges were only one of the classes of those authorized, and he says respecting Mommsen's statement : *Seine Gründe sind nicht überzeugend.*

[1] Bas-relief on the tomb of Eurysaces.

to be carved above his door, with many compliments for his meritorious action and his generosity; and there could always be found some well-to-do merchant who was delighted to accept this dignity in the absence of another.

DIANA WITH DOG.[1]

The trade societies, like our ancient guilds, sometimes sought patrons in heaven. On the 19th of March the weavers, fullers, and dyers betook themselves, headed by their standard,[2] to the temple of Minerva; the 19th of June was, for the millers and bakers, the feast of Vesta and of their guild. Others were worshippers of

---

[1] Statue in the Vatican, Hall of the Biga, No. 622.
[2] *Vexilla collegiorum* (Vopiscus, *Aurel.* 34, and *Gall.* 3).

Diana and Antinous, of the chaste goddess and the imperial favorite whom a strange syncretism had united in one temple at Lanuvium. In fact all the divinities of the Roman Pantheon, the new as well as the old, were invoked, even those ill-defined and yet popular divinities that were styled genii (*collegii genio*). For them a chapel was built at the place where the guild held its meetings; on the holiday they were offered incense and wine, a grain of the former and some drops of the latter, and a victim, of which the complaisant god left a good share for the faithful, being himself satisfied with the sweet smell which arose from the fat burned on his altar.

Thus by the side of the trade societies which old usages and the competition of the slaves had compelled the free workmen to form, there existed others which recall the brotherhood or guild of the Middle Ages.

The college with a certain pride called itself "the republic," and its members were "the people;"[1] it was in fact organized after the pattern of the city. Like the latter it possessed that character of a civil person which Marcus Aurelius had recognized when he gave it the right of receiving legacies.[2] It had statutes, discussed in the general meeting (*conventu pleno*), which were its law; monthly subscriptions, which represented the state tax; its *album*, or list of associates, revised every five years; its annual heads elected to office, and its distributions of food or money given by some generous patron.[3] Moreover, like the decurions in similar circumstances, the dignitaries of the college received a better portion[4] or a larger sum; but like them also they were condemned to burdensome liberalities. This mode of recognizing the dignity of the chief by serving him better at table had a famous precedent. At Sparta the law gave a double portion to kings; in this manner Rome always honored the courage of her bravest soldiers,[5] and the Church [imitating the Mosaic law] will do the same towards her priests.

---

[1] . . . *Populus collegii* (Orelli, No. 2,417, and elsewhere).   [2] *Digest*, xxxiv. 5, 20.

[3] Under Antoninus four senators of Rome were patrons of the boatmen's guild of Ostia (Guasco, *Mus. Cap.* ii. 185).

[4] . . . *partes duplas* . . . *sesquiplas* (Or.-Henzen, No. 6,086). See at No. 2,417 the very curious regulation of the college of Aesculapius and Hygeia.

[5] Pliny, *Hist. nat.* xviii. 3.

This strange practice covers an idea which was true at the time when combats were often hand-to-hand fights. To recompense a brave man he was given the means of increasing his strength, in the gift of a larger supply of food; conversely, the coward was punished by weakening him : bleeding was a disciplinary punishment in the Roman army. This people, very tenacious of their usages, honored the peaceful decurions of the Empire in the same way that their ancestors had honored the heroes of ancient days.

These associations, which were a legacy from the Empire to the Middle Ages, raised the poor man in his own eyes and in the eyes of others. By their union, the members of the college took a position in the city and made themselves of account there. Isolated, they would have been despised ; united, they became one of the organs of municipal life. Some of these colleges even secured to their members, by virtue of a concession of the Emperors, the freedom of the urban offices ;[1] and this privilege of certain corporations increased the consideration of the others. Thus it often happened that a decree of the decurions assigned at the theatre special places to the members of an important corporation,[2] that on public distribution days they received their share before the plebeians, and that they had a better one. Even in the elections, the support or opposition of an inferior college was a matter of importance, which gave to these people of humble rank the ability of speaking out, at least for the moment. An inscription at Pompeii states : "The fishermen nominate as aedile Popidius Rufus." — an announcement somewhat bold, and very likely to influence the undecided and to intimidate opponents.[3]

We also see that at this period election was practised everywhere, in the corporation as well as in the city, and that it constituted the strength of the system. But we also find in it another thing. These little cities contained in the great one were often animated by a real spirit of fraternity. These poor people[4] loved one another. A freedman wrote on the tomb of his wife, a former slave : "To the best of women, who never did me anything unto-

---

[1] *Munera* (*Digest*, l. 6, 5, sect. 12).   [2] Boissieu, *Inscr. de Lyon*, p. 396.

[3] *C. I. L.* iv. 826. Boissier, *Relig. rom.* ii. 332.

[4] See *C. I. L.* iii. 633, the sixty-nine names inscribed on the album of one of these colleges; they are only people of the lower class, almost all of them freedmen, four slaves of the colony, three of private persons.

ward except that she departed from me;" and he erected this tomb
for her, for himself, and for all his freed men or women.[1] Many
funeral monuments are raised "by a friend:" *C. Julius Flavius
amico suo.* They treated one another as "brothers;" one of them
we see giving "to his brothers composing the college of Velabrum"[2]
a monument which he had restored. Others announce that they
have consecrated an altar to Jupiter "with the assistance of the

FUNERAL MONUMENT DEDICATED BY A HUSBAND TO HIS WIFE.[3]

brothers and sisters." In another case it is a friend who, on the
anniversary of the birth of the friend whom he has lost, makes a
distribution "to the grateful and pious multitude" of his old
brothers.[4] These usages were general, and it was not the poor
only who helped one another. The senators of Rome, who many
times under the bad Emperors had acted as informers against each
other, under a better rule offered voluntary subscriptions to aid
a colleague in giving games or in rebuilding his palace when

[1] Orelli, No. 575.   [2] Orelli, No. 1,485.   [3] Museum of the Louvre.
[4] Martial, *Epigr.* viii. 8. The monument reproduced on the following page was erected
by Q. Marcius to his brother: *D. M. Mamertino Q. Marcius Chamo* (?) *Fratri piissimo et
Parthenope conjugi bene merenti* (Piranesi, *Vasi*, vol. ii. pl. 170).

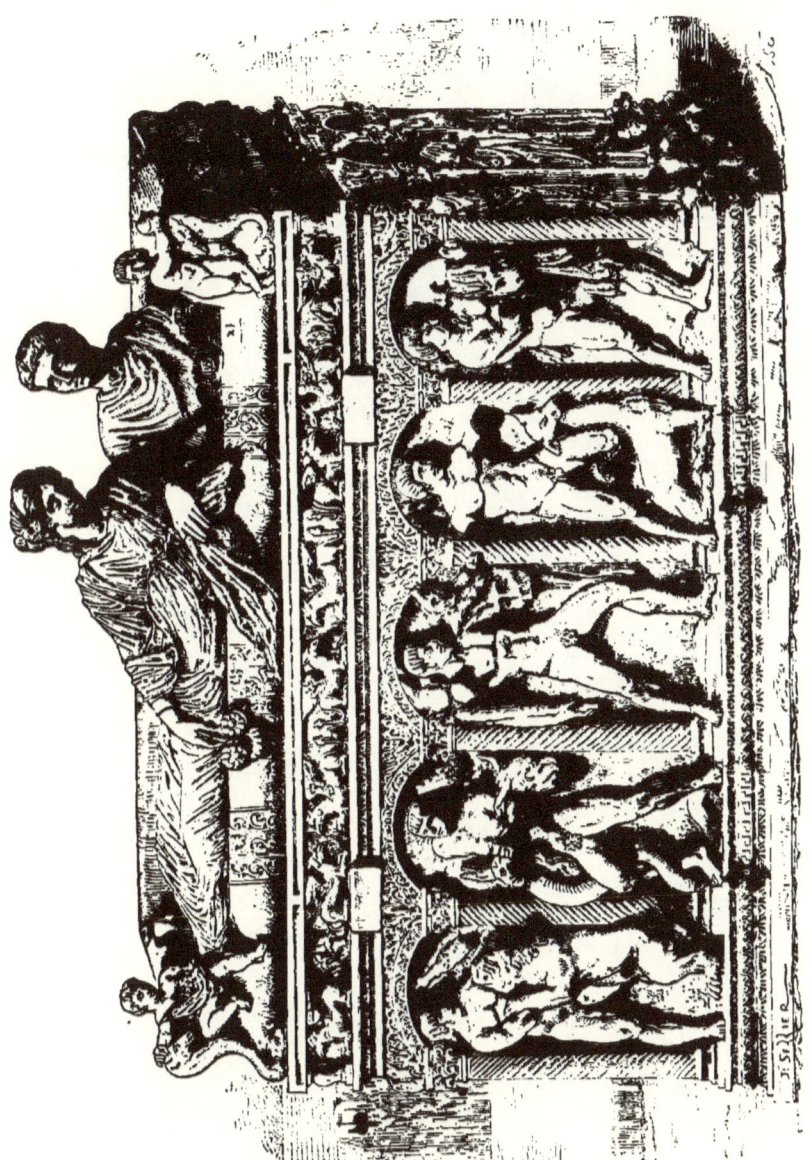

CINERARY URN ENCLOSING THE ASHES OF A MARRIED COUPLE.

burned down;[1] and amidst the eulogies pronounced on the deceased it would have been fitting to carve on more than one patrician sepulchre these words, which are often seen on the tombs of the common people: "He was devoted to his family, to his college" (*pius in suos, pius in collegium*). As early as the time of Augustus a rich freedman inserted in his epitaph that he had always been a "friend of the poor."[2]

The inscriptions of Lambese have disclosed a practice which, since there is no reason why it should be peculiar to the legion cantoned there, must have been general in the Roman army, — the existence of military colleges and the favor which, in spite of the express prohibition by law, the legates themselves extended to them. These colleges had formed, from the subscriptions of their members, what was really a relief fund;[3] and it is not rash to conclude from this fact that some civil corporations had devised similar institutions.

There was also in the corporation the spirit of discipline and order. Classes existed in the college as in the curia; ranks were assigned and were kept. At the head of the *album* were inscribed the patrons of the corporation, its elected chiefs, its dignitaries; then the freemen, the freedmen, and the slaves. Order was pleasing to them, and they accepted quite naturally the subordination of ranks, which the teaching of a barbaric equality had not as yet confused. Accordingly, no more docile subjects were to be found. In those immense provinces which had not a single soldier, there is no mention made of insurrection.[4] The armies revolted, but not the peoples. Religious feeling caused riots against the Jew or the Christian; but there were none against the magistrate or the law, or against society. At the very most, in times of famine there were

---

[1] Seneca, *De Benef.* ii. 21, 5; Juvenal, *Sat.* iii. 216.

[2] *Misericordis, amantis pauperes.* The inscription reads *pauperis.* But this pearl-merchant of the Via Sacra, who built on the Appian Way a tomb in which other freedmen were buried, could not be called a poor man. Besides, *is* for *es* was often used, not to speak of the solecisms common in inscriptions. See Egger, *Mém. d'hist. anc.* p. 356.

[3] Cf. Léon Renier, *Inscr. rom. de l'Algérie*, Nos. 69 and 70. The associate when travelling received his travelling expenses, the veteran before setting out on his leave five hundred denarii, etc. The Greek countries had long been filled with similar associations. The θίασοι formed religious societies, as well as for mutual help, credit, assurance against fire, etc.; and their dignitaries, the *clerotes*, have perhaps given their name to the Christian clergy.

[4] The two wars of the Jews and the war of Civilis, which had their special causes, must be excepted.

riots against so-called "monopolists," such as have been seen even in our days.[1] During its whole duration the Empire had neither the Servile wars nor the social commotions which had so often deluged the Republic with blood. Cicero, in one of his orations against Catiline,[2] refers to the conservative spirit existing in the Roman lower middle class; three centuries later Herodian notices the same thing.

Many causes concurred in producing this peaceful spirit. The principal one was this character of a society, aristocratic, and yet open to all, which preserved slavery, but progressively ameliorated the lot of the slave and was already giving attention to the wretchedness of the poor; in which the magistrate was not necessarily an enemy, as he is often considered among other peoples; where, too, respect was preserved for the honors and authority conferred in the name of the majesty of the Senate or of "the divinity of the Emperor," and even for the great families, which were said, or which men wished to believe, to be sprung from the gods. The plebeian was as proud of his historic families as are the common people in England of theirs; he thought that these pontiffs of the city, the province, and the Empire, could offer to Jupiter prayers heard with a more favorable ear.[3]

It is curious to find still in existence after eight centuries this religious reverence (*pietas*) for the country and family, for the laws and discipline established by a man's ancestors, which we have seen was from the very first the foundation of Roman character. Political revolutions had not been able to destroy this solid social education of ancient Italy.

England is still nearly in this condition: the French nation has ceased to be so; nor have we known how to replace, by a moral discipline in our hearts, that social discipline which has disappeared from the state. The Empire of the Antonines had both: men honored the law; the order established by it was loved: and every man occupied, generally without envy or hate, the condition in

[1] Thus at Prusa, where Dion Chrysostom's house just escaped being burned by the mob.
[2] iv. 7-8; Herodian, vii. 2, 5.
[3] Tacitus praises Tiberius for having taken the nobility into consideration in the distribution of office (*Ann.* iv. 6), and he mentions the case of all the people of Rome taking the part of a great Roman lady against her husband, who was rich but of low birth (*ibid.* iii. 22). These feelings still existed in the third century, and even later. Cf. Marquardt, v. 249.

which he was born, seeking indeed to raise himself, sometimes by crooked ways or shameful means, but never by outbreak.

The city was completed by certain institutions for teaching and public aid. It had professors for its schools, medical men for its sick ; and these professors and medical men were the only functionaries of the city who received fees[1] and had exemption for themselves. their wives and children, from all municipal services,[2] guardianships, deputations, lodging of soldiers and public functionaries, duties as judges and priests. and even from military service.[3] To all these advantages were added the *Minerval*, which scholars paid their masters and which rich patients gave their physicians. This practice was old ; Strabo had already stated of the Gallic cities : " They give salaries to physicians and rhetoricians." The Republic had shown no concern for the men whose business it was to care for the mind and the body. On this point, as on so many others, the Empire introduced a new policy. By his decree in favor of physicians and the professors of the liberal arts, Caesar had elevated their social condition and paved their way to wealth.[4]

---

[1] *Multis in locis: praeceptores publice conducuntur* (Pliny. *Epist.* iv. 13 ; *Cod. Theod.* xiii. 3, 2 and 3. Σοφιστὰς . . . κοινῇ μισθούμενοι, καθάπερ καὶ ἰατρούς (iv. 1, 5). Fronto (*Ad Amic.* 7) seeks to obtain one of these positions for a client. Even women practised medicine. An inscription says : *Juliae Saturninae . . . incomparabili medicae* (De Laborde, *Voy. en Espagne*, vol. i. 2d part, inscr. No. 15. and Wilmanns, 241 and 2,493).

[2] The masters of small schools, *qui pueros primas litteras docent*, having some other occupation, had no right to these immunities unless they had been appointed by a great society like that of the mines of Aljustrel, which had exempted theirs from all civic offices in order to secure their best services as teachers. Ulpian does not recognize them under the title of professors : *Licet non sint professores* (*Digest*, l. 13, 1, sect. 6). But he recommended the president to be careful that they should not be burdened beyond their ability (*ibid.* 2, sect. 8). Furthermore, Rome recognized every class of master, — the preceptor. who had often only board, lodging, and two hundred drachmae (Lucian, *De Merc. cond.* 35 and 38), going. like the father of Statius (*Silv.* v. 5, 176) to give lessons in the city, and the one who received his pupils into his house at the rate of five aurei for the school year of eight months (*Schol. ad Juv.* vii. 243). Remmius Palaemon gained by his school a profit of four hundred thousand sesterces (Suet., *Ill. Gram.* 23). The Emperor Pertinax began his career as a professor, but without success (Capit., *Pert.* 1).

[3] The deputations, from which physicians and professors were exempt (*Digest*, xxvii. 1, 6, sect. 1), were very frequent and burdensome. At any remarkable event in the life of the Emperors they were sent to Rome ; others came to ask the settlement of some difference with a neighboring city when even the matter in question was something quite paltry. We have just recovered a letter from Antoninus to the Coronaeans to thank them for having brought a message of condolence on the occasion of Hadrian's death, and their felicitations respecting the adoption of Marcus Aurelius. Another letter of the same Emperor shows that the deputies of Coronaea had asked him to decide whether certain plethra of pasturage belonged to them or to Thisbe (*Bulletin de corresp. hellén.* for 1881. p. 456).

[4] See Vol. III. p. 533.

To Vespasian the honor is due of having created, at the expense of the state, higher literary teaching, by bestowing on certain Greek and Latin rhetoricians a salary of a hundred thousand sesterces, payable by the imperial treasury. Quintilian was the first to receive this salary; and it may be concluded from an expression used by him,[1] that at the end of twenty years these public professors obtained a retiring pension, as the legionary had a right to the veteran standing after a service of equal length. Hadrian and his two successors multiplied the number of chairs supported by the state, and the cities imitated their example. Como, not having any public teachers, sent her sons to study at Milan. Pliny

A SURGEON DRESSING A WOUND.[3]

regretted this; he called a meeting of the heads of families, represented the need of having a school in the town, engaged to pay a third of the expense, and the school was founded.[2] Thus by the united action of the Emperor, the magistrates, and individuals, was organized in the cities a new and important service, — that of public instruction, which the Barbarians were never able completely to destroy. At first free, this instruction was by degrees subordinated to public authority, either that of the Emperor or of the

municipal council. In a rescript dated 362, Julian says: "As I cannot be present in every city, I forbid those who wish to give instruction, suddenly and rashly to undertake this function. Let the candidate be examined by the *ordo*, and, with the consent of the *meliores*, let him deserve that the *curiales* should pass a decree

---

[1] *In prooem.* i. Had public professors from the earliest times public rations (*annonae*)? It is probable, since all the administration had them. In 376, at Trèves, the *rhetor* received thirty shares, the *grammaticus Latinus* twenty, the *grammaticus Graecus* twelve (*Cod. Theod.* xiii. 3, 11).

[2] *Epist.* iv. 13.   [3] From a Pompeian painting.

in his favor." A century earlier Gordian had already prescribed this examination.[1] The same plan was followed for medical men.

These liberalities on the part of the Emperors towards rhetoricians, grammarians,[2] and philosophers did not produce any great literary works, for genius can alone do that; but the advantages granted, or rather officially recognized as due, to physicians show an aspect of the social life of antiquity which has been too much left in the shade. The practice of medicine, at first exercised by magicians or religious impostors, was soon secularized. Hippocrates made it a science; and as it proved lucrative, many followed it. Medical practitioners were found everywhere; medical assistance even became a municipal service. Each Greek city had one or more public medical men who visited the sick in the city and suburbs. Each had also a large dispensary, *iatrium*, where the

A SURGEON ATTENDING TO A WOUNDED MAN (FROM AN ENGRAVED STONE).

practitioner, aided by his pupils and slaves, held consultations, performed operations, and distributed the needful medicines. Some beds were also reserved there, — probably for patients who could not be removed, or for persons attacked by very serious complaints.[3] The rich being able to be cared for at home, those who needed the aid of the public dispensary were the poor; and we know that in that state of society the isolated poor — I mean without patron and "without brothers"[4] — were not very numerous. The cities had not, therefore, in order to possess an *iatrium*, to go to the enormous expense which the hospitals of the present day cost; and we may assume that it existed almost everywhere. A precept of

[1] *Code*, x. 52, 2 and 7. The word *meliores* signifies in this passage those most fitted to act as examiners, — *probatissimi*, as is said elsewhere. The *ordo* could revoke them, *si non se utiles studentibus praebent*.

[2] The *grammarians* explained the poets and commented on them; they criticised the texts and explained the rules and methods of the language. The *rhetoricians* taught, by the study of the great writers, not eloquence, which cannot be learned, because it is a natural gift, but all the resources open to an orator's use to produce conviction by disposing his arguments in the best order and giving to his discourse the strength of ideas and the ornaments and graces of style.

[3] This is inferred from different passages in the Hippocratic treatise περὶ ἰατρείου (Dr. Dechambre, *Revue archéol.* of 1881, p. 53).

[4] That is, those who were not members of a college having a mutual benefit fund. See our cap. lxxxiii.

Hippocrates recommends the care of the poor.[1] Inscriptions show that this was followed. One of them is a decree granting a crown of gold to Metrodorus, who, " for twenty years a public physician, has saved many citizens, and now lives in poverty, having refused from them any fees."[2] The whole city paid a special rate, the *iatricon*, for supplying the expenses of this municipal service. One of the most delicate and generous obligations of the modern practitioner was also imposed on the ancient; summoned into the interior of families, it was his duty, having ears, to hear not, and having eyes, to see not. This professional loyalty is prescribed by Hippocrates.

We see then one half of the Empire well provided with medical help; whence we may conclude that, thanks to the effect of

XENOPHON, THE IMPERIAL PHYSICIAN.[3]

example, the other was not without it. The army had its medical staff for the wounded and sick, the *lanista* for his gladiators, the rich man for himself and his slaves, the Emperor for his own person and the numerous servants of the palace. Even the artisans sought to attach to their colleges poor practitioners who would be satisfied with very moderate fees, and we know from Plautus that Rome had many apothecaries, with shops where they sold their advice and medicines, and where they even lodged some patients.[4] Augustus increased the privileges which Caesar had conferred on them; and later, the physicians of Rome made part of the administration in an official capacity. There was for each of the fourteen regions of the city a doctor for the poor, whose title, *archiatrus*, indicates that he had

[1] " . . . Sometimes even you will give your attendance for nothing, προῖκα " (*Œuvres d'Hippocrate*, edit. Littré, vol. ix. *Præcepta*, sect. 6). The obligation of attending the poor, of which Valentinian reminds the medical men (*Cod. Theod.* xiii. 3, 8), is not a new duty which he imposes on them, it was one to which they had been always subjected.

[2] An inscription recently found at Cos is an honorary decree regarding a physician who during an epidemic had particularly distinguished himself by his devotion. Another, discovered at Athens, speaks of several public physicians practising in that city (*Bull. de corresp. hellén.* 1881, pp. 203 and 205).

[3] Bronze coin of Cos. Xenophon, the physician of Claudius, was under Nero chief physician to the imperial family, ἀρχιατρὸς τῶν Οἴκων Σεβαστῶν, before Andromachos, who is stated up to the present time as having first borne this title (*Bull. de corresp. hellén.* 1881, p. 468).

[4] *Menæchm.* V. v. In the *Amphitryon* and the *Epidicus* Plautus again speaks of these dispensaries. Cf. Dr. Briau, *De l'Assistance médicale chez les Romains*. [Aristophanes alludes to them at Athens in the fourth century B. C., when δημοσιεύειν was the technical word for such practice. So Herodotus speaks of Democedes. Cf. my *Social Life in Greece*, chap. v. — ED.]

subordinates under his orders.[1] Lastly, we learn that there existed
at Rome, at Beneventum, and at Avenches (Aventicum), which
was then an important city, *scholae medicorum*, or places of meeting for the profession, — perhaps also schools for instruction in
medicine.[2]

1. LANCEOLATED CAUTERY, WITH TURNED TRUNCATED HANDLE (POMPEII).

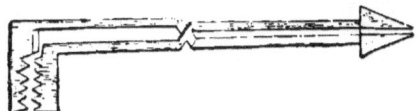

2. PINCERS FOR EXTRACTING FOREIGN BODIES FROM THE GULLET
(MUSEUM OF ALBUCASIS).

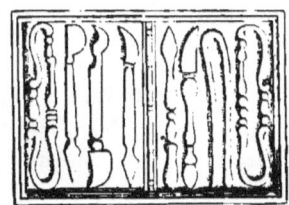

3. BOX OF INSTRUMENTS (BAS-RELIEF OF THE
CAPITOLINE MUSEUM).

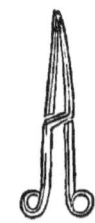

4. FORCEPS (MUSEUM OF
ALBUCASIS).

5. BISTOURY (MUSEUM OF ALBUCASIS).

6. CASE OF INSTRUMENTS (POMPEII).

7. SERRATED FORCEPS WITH RUNNING KNOT
(POMPEII).

8. A PHYSICIAN'S OR OCCULIST'S
STAMP.[3]

It has however been believed that medical assistance could not
be obtained in the cities of the Western provinces. If this obser-

---

[1] *Cod. Theod.* xiii. 3, 8.

[2] A passage in the *Protagoras* of Plato, where there is a question of a sum of money paid
by a young man to Hippocrates of Cos, in order " to become a physician," shows that medical
instruction was not gratuitous.

[3] Saglio, fig. 1,412.

vation were well founded, we should reply with the remark which
will shortly be made, — that the time for the great institutions of
benevolence had not come for Roman society, because these institutions were not as yet absolutely necessary. But although the
inscriptions which represent physicians as salaried by the Latin
cities are not very numerous,[1] there are enough to authorize us in
the supposition that medical men were found everywhere.

The juris-consults often make reference to them; they tell us
what property was left by them, — collyria and salves, surgical
instruments, and apparatus for the preparation of medicines; and
also what a terrible responsibility lay upon them. Let one of
their remedies kill the patient, and it became to them a matter of
banishment or death. This responsibility entailed the obligation,
then as now, of the physician signing his prescriptions; and there
have already been found more than a hundred and fifty of their
seals.

We are confirmed in the opinion that the medical service of
the cities was a general usage, from the rescript of Antoninus
which has been given under the reign of that Emperor. This
rescript is a decree which reorganizes and not one which founds.
The institution was sufficiently ancient to have already produced
abuses, which Antoninus proposed to repress. When he fixed the
number of public doctors which the large, lesser, and small cities
were not to exceed, he protected the municipal finances; and by
limiting the number of citizens exempted from the *munera* he
diminished the weight of the common burdens for the inhabitants.
This rescript, addressed to the Greek province of Asia, "applies,"
says the jurisconsult Modestinus, "to the whole Empire."[2]   A
statement of Galen adds also the fact, that in nearly all the cities
was found the *officina medicalis*, the ἰατρεῖον, without which the
public doctor would have found it difficult to fulfil his duty
towards the poor.[3] After many centuries we have revived this
institution, due to the benevolence of Greece.

[1] Orelli, Nos. 3,507 and 3,994; *C. I. L.* v. 37 and 5,377, etc.; Paulus, *Sent.* iii. 6, 62;
v. 23, 19.
[2] *Digest.* xxvii. 1, 6, sect. 2.   The same idea will lead Constantine to limit the number of
the clergy (*Cod. Theod.* xvi. 2, 3, 5, and 6).
[3] . . . νῦν κατὰ πολλὰς τῶν πόλεων (*Galeni opera*, vol. xviii., *Comm. de med. off.* 1, 8,
edit. Kühn).

ANTONINUS PIUS.

From the Villa Hadriani at Tivoli (Museo Chiaramonti. No. 682).

We now see what the often-repeated statement is worth, that charity was unknown to the ancients. To what has here been said, add the mutual assistance given by cities, the subscriptions throughout a province to repair any local disaster,[1] the numberless subventions of the Emperors made to cities desolated by conflagrations or earthquakes, and lastly, the great alimentary institution founded by Trajan, which was imitated by rich citizens in all the provinces, in the depths of Dacia, Spain, and Africa quite as much as in the heart of Italy.[2] Our legislation taxes the property left by the poor as it does that of the ˉrich : the imperial treasury, less hard and avaricious, released from this formidable tax of the twentieth all property under a hundred thousand sesterces ; that is to say, all the small inheritances of those countless Roman citizens established in the provincial cities. Augustus had established this privilege, and Trajan confirmed it.[3]

It may be said that policy rather than benevolence had inspired these measures. The two ideas were combined in them, as in the case of the distributions of corn made to the people of Rome. Did not Pliny write these beautiful words : " It is a duty to seek out those who are in want, to bring them aid, to support and make them in a sense one's own family " ? " There is in life but one beautiful thing." runs the inscription of a tomb, " and this is beneficence." [4] Christianity says nothing finer.

The idea of charity is clearly shown in the foundations of Antoninus and of Marcus Aurelius. By the distinction given to these measures, the Emperors invited the provincial cities to follow their example ; and the cities did not fail to do so. Trajan had already recommended them to economize in the use of their revenues, so that they should be able to succor their poor,[5] — a recommendation which was soon changed into a command. In order to secure resources for the alimentary institution, the jurisconsults

---

[1] Aristides, *Palin. of Smyrna.*

[2] See Vol. IV. pp. 265 *et seq.* There are many other examples; thus at Seville, *C. I. L.* vol. ii. No. 1,171, and the inscriptions relative to the *curatores* and *procuratores alimentorum.*

[3] Pliny, *Paneg.* 40.

[4] . . . *Quos praecipue scias indigere, sustentantem foventemque orbe quodam societatis ambire* (Pliny, *Epist.* ix. 30). . . . *ἐν βίῳ δὲ καλὸν ἔργον ἐν μόνον εὐποιία* (*C. I. G.* 3,515). The elder Pliny says, with his usual emphasis: *Deus est mortali juvare mortalem* (*Hist. nat.* ii. 15). See in cap. lxxxvii. sect. 2. the opinions of the philosophers on charity.

[5] . . . *Ad sustinendam tenuiorum inopiam.*

laid down the principle that the surplus of the municipal revenues should be employed, among other uses, for furnishing food to the poor and instruction to the children.[1] "Donations," says Paulus. "may be made to the city, either for its adornment (*ad ornatum*), or for its honor (*ad honorem*); and among the things which honor a city the most is the practice of giving support to infirm old men and to young children of both sexes."[2] The decurions who had been ruined in the public service had a right to these allowances.[3]

While all the curiae did not, like the Emperor in the capital, give corn to the plebs gratuitously or below the market price,[4] yet many gave the poor man a great advantage by selling to him at the wholesale price, and even lower.[5] As at Rome a special administration existed for the distributions,[6] so some of the provincial cities set aside annually a sum to provide for the expense of the *annona*;[7] and these cities were so numerous that the Emperor Maximin, when at the end of his resources, seized everywhere the funds destined for these distributions. The *Digest* reckons among the ordinary public duties (*munera*) the care of watching over the use of this money and its division among the citizens:[8] this is one of the duties which Plutarch reserves for the old men whose

---

[1] *Sive in alimenta vel eruditionem puerorum* (Marcianus, *Ad L.* xxx. 117). The legacies left *ad alimenta puerorum* became so numerous that a rescript of Severus reduced them by the Falcidian fourth (*Digest*, xxv. 2, 80).

[2] *Hoc amplius . . . alimenta infirmae aetatis, puta senioribus, vel pueris puellisque* (*Digest*, xxx. 172).

[3] *Digest*, l. 2, 8.

[4] See *Digest*, l. 1, 8, and title, 8, 5. The distributions of corn to the poor in the municipia were made under the oversight of the aediles (*Digest*, xvi. 2, 17), who are sometimes styled *cereales* (Orelli, Nos. 3,992–4). The inscriptions frequently extol the liberality of this or that person, *qui . . . annonae populi saepe subvenit* (Orelli, No. 80). On the distributions of corn or oil in free cities at the expense of individuals, see Or.-Henzen, Nos. 708, 2,172, 2,818, 5,323, 6,759, 7,173, and Mommsen, *Inscr. Neapol.* 190; Guerin, *Voy. en Tunisie*, 233. Other examples: *C. I. G.*, Nos. 378, 2,930, 3,831a. Rhodes had a complete organization for the relief of the poor. They were given bread and work. Strabo (xiv. 2, 5) gives some curious details on this subject. See also an important passage in Saint Augustine (*Civit. Dei*, v. 17), which will be quoted under Caracalla's reign.

[5] Ulpian, in the *Digest*, vii. 1, 27, sect. 3: *Solent possessores certam partem fructuum municipio viliori pretio addicere.* Cf. *ibid.* l. 8, 5.

[6] *Fiscus frumentarius.*

[7] *Area frumentaria, pecunia ad annonam destinata* (cf. Hirschfeld, *Annona*, pp. 83–85, and Kuhn, *op. cit.* i. 46 et seq.).

Annonae divisio (*Digest*, l. 4, 1, sects. 2 and 18, 5).

age compelled him to give up military service. We have just seen
that many cities supported medical men for their poor; an inscription shows that charity already was assuming all sorts of forms.
An herbalist bequeaths to his successor three hundred pots of
drugs, with sixty thousand sesterces, on the condition that the sick
poor should receive gratuitously at the surgery mead and remedies.[1]
Finally, the new policy, which had imposed on the provincial
governors[2] as a sacred duty the protection of the young, led on
to the further idea of being also under obligation to succor the
poor, or at least to encourage foundations for their aid. Hence
doubtless the readiness of these magistrates to permit, contrary to
the law, the establishment of so many colleges whence the unfortunate might obtain from time to time a morsel of bread, and at
the last an honorable burial.

The gods set the example. They had their poor, who lived
near the temple, at the expense of the sacred treasury, and who
were styled in the Island of Cyprus the *gerim*, and in the Greek
cities "the parasites of the gods." The Christians imitated this
custom; the *matricularii* of the primitive churches were also "God's
guests."[3]

Doubtless, all this is not equal in value to our modern charitable institutions. But among the ancients, these institutions were
not so much needed, because agricultural communities, whose whole
work is done by slaves or serfs, knew not, except in the great
capitals, the formidable proletariat of our industrial communities.
In the latter, the workman who lives on his wages is exposed to
the disastrous results of being out of work, of illness, misconduct,
and idleness; in the former, the master maintains the slave in
his house, the *colonus* or the serf on the land that he tills, and
their subsistence is as secure as his own. We have seen[4] that the
patron was bound to furnish food to his freedman. Besides, as
not long ago in Spain each convent had its own poor, so in the
Empire every rich family had its clients, who every morning
received their *sportula* or a piece of money, every city had colleges

[1] Orelli, No. 114, in the very small town of Lorina, near Caere.
[2] *Ne potentiores viri humiliores adficiant. ad religionem praesidis prov. pertinet* (*Digest*, i. 18, 6).
[3] *Acad. des inscriptions et belles-lettres*, report for Nov. 28, 1880.　　[4] *Supra*, p. 307.

furnishing certain help to their members; and there still remained
something of the hospitable manners of ancient times, when the
guest and the beggar were looked upon as sent by Jupiter.[1] We
rightly prefer the poverty which labors to that which begs; but
this notion is neither Roman nor Greek, nor even Christian. The
institution of clientship, still in full vigor during the period of the
Antonines, was, so far as the great were concerned, the price paid
for their fortunes. Then also, in the delicious climate which the
countries bordering the Mediterranean enjoy, poverty is not, as in
the North, a state of actual suffering added to want. The sun
there is at half the expense of clothing and lodging; some water
and a loaf of bread suffice for nourishment. Now, the municipality
furnished the former plentifully, the latter cost but little, and the
poor man who did not find these resources sufficient sold himself
on certain conditions.[2] The time for the creation of great charitable institutions had not, therefore, arrived, since they did not
make part of the social necessities of the age. We are even disposed to believe that, the Roman family and city being organized
as they were, there were fewer persons exposed to death from
starvation at that time than now.

The whole municipal system is summed up in two words,
which often recur in the language of the jurisconsults, — the *honor*
of the city, which was the second religion of the Romans when it
was not the first;[3] the *dignity* of the citizen, which included all the
qualities by which a man commanded public respect and esteem.[4]
Under the influence of these two sentiments there were moulded
in the cities at this fortunate period men in whose eyes the aim of
moral life was dignity of character and conduct, and the aim of
social life, the fulfilment of their civic duties: precious virtues,

---

[1] πτωχοὶ γὰρ Διός εἰσιν ἅπαντες | ξεῖνοί τε πτωχοί τε (Homer, *Od.* vi, 207, 208; viii, 546).

[2] These voluntary sales were so frequent that the jurisconsults took notice of "the free man who sold himself" (*Digest*, i, 5, 21); and they are a proof that at that epoch slavery was not always the abominable institution which modern society condemns.

[3] Pliny writes to one of his friends: . . . *Quod patriam tuam omnesque qui nomen ejus aucerunt, ut patriam ipsam reverearis et diligis* (*Epist.* iv, 28). The inscriptions often state in reference to donations made by a citizen, . . . *secundum dignitatem coloniae* (Mommsen, *I. N.* No. 1,040).

[4] This expression applies to the state as well as to the individual; and to offend the dignity of the Roman people or its representatives was one of the crimes punished as high treason (see Vol. IV, p. 463).

though easily acquired, which all men might, and many did attain; as, for example, the younger Pliny, and the large number of honorable persons to whom he refers in his correspondence. It has been said that the Germans brought into the world the sense of honor. To that savage pride which is so ready to draw the sword and has been often the only virtue of fine gentlemen, I far prefer the old Roman notions, which moulded citizens whose great ambition was to honor or adorn their city, and men, some of whom, by their own self-respect, have made themselves respected in history.

Since we are seeking the ideas which underlie words, let us further remark that "antiquity" had, besides its usual meaning, the signification of a thing preferred: *Nihil mihi antiquius est*, says Cicero. — "Nothing is dearer to me."[1] From this union of affection and respect for old laws and old usages there arose a pious feeling which was a powerful conservative force, — a force which no longer exists on the shifting soil of modern societies. Says the younger Pliny: " Sages teach me that nothing is finer than to follow in the footprints of one's ancestors, — especially," he takes care to add, " when they have taken the right path."[2] When we shall have shown that corruption had not invaded these cities so much as is believed, it will perhaps appear that the provincial towns were then in a condition analogous to that of Rome in the best period of the Republic, with laborious habits and much municipal liberty, which indemnified them for the loss of political liberty, about which, moreover, they at this time cared very little. Doubtless in these cities by the side of excellent things were many bad ones, — a religion which had never possessed any moral influence, and a creed passing into superstitions sometimes unwholesome, or satisfied with outward observances; for public amusements, festivals too often licentious or sanguinary; in some houses lawless manners and shameless vice; in many servility, because in a community which was divided into clients and patrons, or, as Martial says, into servants and kings, there were too many ready to beg for the *sportula*, and too many ready to throw it. What grotesque or odious details in Juvenal, Petronius, Martial, and Lucian, in

---

[1] Aur. Victor repeats these words. Sallust says also, *tantum antiquitatis curaeque*, which must be translated by "so much reverence and solicitude" (Fronto, *Epist. ad M. Ant.* 3).

[2] *Epist.* v. 8.

respect to the client, the parasite, and the crafty plotter after
bequests; in respect to the baseness of the hungry and the insolence of the parvenu, the latter in their turn cringing before those
who had risen higher;[1] and finally, the universal adoration of
His Most Sacred Majesty Gold! (*sanctissima diritiarum majestas.*)[2]
But this is seen under other forms and other names at all
times, — even among the freest people, who are the humble subjects
of the " Almighty Dollar." — because these vices or infirmities
belong to human nature; and in this respect successive generations
differ only in having them to a greater or less degree. We do not
believe, moreover, that civic liberties would have been able of themselves to save the state. Well-ordered free cities are certainly a
good foundation on which to rest the social edifice; these and
the wisdom of civil laws contain a promise of prosperity. But if
the political laws are bad, they will in the end ruin the civil.

Thus when the municipium of the first centuries, which was
a civil person, and in respect to its interior affairs a sovereign
state, which had renounced only the right of wielding the sword
under the twofold form of war and of capital punishment, regu-
lating its life according to its own judgment, making contracts
and assuming obligations, which had its magistracies, its finances,
its schools, and its public religious ceremonies, with the most complete religious and philosophic independence; when this free city
shall become, by the deadening influence of Church and State,
an automatic wheelwork in the immense machine which was to
make the Empire a void; when, finally, all things shall be fixed
by heredity and administrative formalism, — then the movement
upwards will be arrested, the sap will no longer rise from the
roots to the branches, and the withered tree will fall.[3]

We must also add that Christianity, by unceasingly pointing
to the heavenly country as the only true one, will cause the

---

[1] We see by Amm. Marcellinus (xxviii. 4) and Claudian (*In Rufin.* i. 442; *In Eutr.* ii. 66;
and *Laud. Stil.* ii. 152) that these manners lasted to the end of the Empire.

[2] Juvenal, *Sat.* i. 112.

[3] Already, shortly after the Antonines, Papinian said: *Exigendi tributi munus inter sordida
munera non habetur et ideo decurionibus quoque mandatur* (*Digest*, l. 1, 17, sect. 7); that is to
say, that there was then no incompatibility between the municipal functions of decurion
and those of collector of the tribute for the state. But the decurion was interdicted from
farming the imposts of his own city: *Decurio sune civitatis vectigalia exercere prohibetur*
(*Dig.* l. 2, 6, sect. 2).

earthly one to be despised; that in changing beliefs it will change duties; that in replacing the legitimate pride of the citizen by the humility of the believer, it will draw away the latter from seeking municipal honors; that, finally, it will precipitate the ruin of the city by the disgust with which it will fill men's minds for institutions grown up around the altars which it seeks to overthrow.[1]

But before reaching this point, the municipal system had produced the age of the Antonines. Formerly between Italy and Rome there had been a current of young rich blood which tended unceasingly to renew the exhausted blood of the ruling class. The same exchange had taken place in the Early Empire between Rome and the provinces. Out of those flourishing free cities came forth artists and poets who had given birth to a new age in literature and art; philosophers who, softening the roughness of Stoicism, had exchanged the desire to speak well for that of doing well; lastly, those numerous *gentes* whom Vespasian had taken from them for reconstituting the Roman aristocracy. Then the Senate and equestrian order, whence the Empire recruited its administrators, were filled with men belonging to families who had long been in possession of municipal honors, who were well qualified to transact the affairs of the state after those of the city, and whom the Antonines, themselves provincials, gathered around them to second their own wisdom. This invasion of the high Roman society by the municipal nobility produced a revolution which was doubly salutary. Public affairs went on better for it, and the manners of private life resumed their strictness. Tacitus bears witness to this, and Pliny shows it.

---

[1] When Tertullian was converted to Christianity he declared that he gave up public affairs (cf. his *De Pallio*). In his *De Idololatria* he required his disciples to discontinue connection with civil society; he condemns every calling which in any degree touched on idolatry, — art, which lived on it, and literature, which spoke of it. He absolutely interdicts Christians from performing *public duties*, permitting only *private ones*; i. e., being present at birthday and marriage celebrations in a friendly family, etc. In his *De Corona militis* he prohibits military service. Yet a rescript of Severus, *eis qui judaïcam superstitionem sequuntur* (*Digest*, l. 2, 3, sect. 3), authorized Jews, and probably Christians, to accept military rank, with a dispensation from the obligations contrary to their creeds. But the Christians, — if they are here designated, — less tolerant than the Emperor, generally held aloof. The author of the *Letter to Diognetus* had already said (cap. v.) : " The Christians live in their native land like strangers." When the Church had become mistress of the Empire she sought to attach the faithful to civic duties; but it was then too late. See in the *Comptes rendus de l'Acad. des inscr.* 1872, a paper by M. Le Blant on *le détachement de la patrie*.

That no more fortunate period has ever been known to the world is due certainly to the eminent men who in that century reigned like philosophers; but it is also due to that municipal system in which institutions, ideas, and manners all tended to make capable magistrates, prosperous cities, and populations obedient to the law. A close tie at that time united the fortunes of the cities to the fortune of the Empire: the prosperity of the former made the strength of the latter, because the local liberties still subsisting formed men whom political liberty, now suppressed at Rome, no longer formed.

[1] Head of Pallas, with a laurel crown and the letters PV*blico argento.*

SILVER COIN OF THE GENS LUCILIA.[1]

CHAPTER LXXXIV.

THE PROVINCES.

I. — Prosperity of the Provinces; Progress in the West and on the Right Bank of the Danube.

THE storms which seem to upheave the ocean from its lowest depths in reality disturb only its surface; a few fathoms below, the waters remain tranquil, and the sands are unstirred. So was it in the Empire: the tumults at Rome, the wars on the Rhine, the Danube, or the Euphrates, did not affect the peacefulness of the interior provinces. While there was slaughter in the capital, among the Dacians, or beyond the Tigris, the nations at peace were developing industry and commerce, opening roads and schools, filling their cities with monuments and wealth. The conquered, says Aelius Aristeides, congratulated themselves on their defeat, and losing even the remembrance of former independence, amalgamated their own existence with that of the Empire. Men possessed security and well-being; they freely enjoyed the fruits of their labor, and the pathway to honors was open to all.

Plutarch, who had seen so many revolutions make the city of the Caesars run with blood, nevertheless calls Rome "a sacred and bountiful goddess;" and elsewhere "the steadfast anchor which stops and holds firmly human affairs in the midst of the whirlwind by which they are driven along." He spoke the truth: Rome had calmed the world and drawn on herself alone the storms which were yet to break forth. Aristeides was a pagan, a worshipper of Aesculapius, and Tertullian a rigid Christian; but both speak in the same way. The orator exclaims: "Men have laid off their iron armor to put on festal garments, and your provinces are covered with rich cities, jewels of your empire, which glitter like a costly necklace on a rich lady. The land is but one immense garden."[1] The sombre imagination of the Christian brightens at the smiling aspect of the Empire: "The world is every day better known, better cultivated, and more wealthy. The roads are open to commerce. The deserts are changed into fruitful domains; tillage goes on where once forests rose; sowing, where once were seen only barren rocks; marshes are drained, and the flocks fear no longer the wild beast. Now no longer is there any island which inspires horror, nor rocks causing fear; everywhere are houses, peoples, cities, everywhere is life!"[2] Appian's words are not rhetorical, like those of Aristeides; but the evidence of the cool, sagacious historian is the same. He says: "For two hundred years has the imperial system lasted; in that space of time the city has been adorned in a marvellous manner, the revenues of the Empire have increased, and by the blessing of a constant peace the peoples have attained the height of happiness."[3]

It is easy, in fact, to imagine what the cessation of war during two centuries must have produced for peoples who till then had passed a life of continual fighting, and what prosperity peace developed in the provinces and liberty in the cities. All this the tragedies enacted at Rome tend to conceal, and this we shall endeavor to bring to view.

It is not that the Romans deliberately undertook to become the benefactors of the provincials. It did not pertain to them, as to some modern nations, to connect with the idea of conquest that of the amelioration of the conquered. They had subdued the world from motives of pride and greed, to have no equals, and to gain wealth without giving themselves the trouble of creating it; accordingly, the province in their eyes was before all a *praedium*, — a farm with a fixed revenue; and in organizing it they cared only for securing the tribute from it. All else, municipal liberty and individual security, the independence of some or the subjection of others, mattered little to them. This had been the policy of the Republican Senate; the early Emperors pursued it also. Both were satisfied to have the subject-peoples administer their own affairs,

---

[1] Aristeides. *Paneg. Rom.* in the year 145: . . . ὥσπερ γυναικὸς πλουσίας ὅρμος (*Orat.* xiv. 224). See also his *Paneg. Cyzic.*

[2] *De Anima,* 30. In the book *Adv. gentes,* he says: . . . *Romanae diuturnitati, favemus.*

[3] *Praef.* 6. Add to this quotation the famous passage in Pliny, *Hist. nat.* iii. 6.

provided they paid the impost with exactness, and that the general good order which guaranteed its payment was not disturbed. Thence proceeded, at least in early days, their disdainful indifference as to local privileges or the semi-independence of cities, tribes, dynasties, or of kings, who sometimes called themselves the procurators of the Roman people and fulfilled the duties of that office. In a word, they intended to govern loftily and remotely, which was to wield a useful sway, and they were quite unwilling to govern in detail, not wishing to be embarrassed with a laborious guardianship. Tiberius, by his vigilance in restraining his proconsuls, exhibited clearly this heartless policy, yet not unwise, which he thus summed up : " A good shepherd shears his sheep, but does not flay them." In this respect Claudius and the Flavii were of his school. The Antonines impressed a new character on the government. They regarded themselves not only as the masters, but as the fathers of the Empire. They ameliorated its laws, they founded charitable institutions, and they were more preoccupied with the happiness of their subjects than with the interests of the treasury. Thus, from different motives, the rulers of the Early Empire acted with beneficence towards the provinces; and this, combined with the advantageous results of the municipal system which we have described, brought that prosperity the proof of which will be found in a rapid survey of the Empire.

Since Augustus the territory held by Rome had been increased by the addition of Britain under Claudius, of Dacia under Trajan, and under Marcus Aurelius of a part of Mesopotamia, — an uncertain and precarious possession, the theatre of continual fighting.[1] With the exception of Britain and the acquisitions of the two Antonines, which were rather outposts than provinces, the successors of Augustus had not passed the limits which Nature itself had fixed for the Empire ; viz., the Atlantic, the Rhine, the Danube, the middle Euphrates, the cataracts of the Nile, and the African deserts.

The ancient partition made between the Emperor and the Senate still existed, but new provinces had been formed either by

---

[1] In his preface Appian, who wrote under Antoninus, puts the frontier of the Empire at the Euphrates, and does not include in it Great Armenia, "which pays no tribute, but receives from the Empire its kings." In the reign of Hadrian I have shown what countries bordering on the Black Sea were placed under the administration or influence of the Romans.

conquests or from the older ones and from allied countries. There were twenty-six under Augustus; under Marcus Aurelius there were forty-five, six of which remained to the Senate.

Thus the number of provinces had been nearly doubled, without the territory having much increased. The fact is, the Emperors had already practised the system, ordinarily attributed only to Diocletian, of dividing the governments in order to diminish the power of the governors and promote the influence of the Empire over its subjects.

Britain, Gaul, and Spain. — Britain formed but one province, so well protected by the double line of defence established by Hadrian and Antoninus that the Picts and the Scots had but rarely disturbed the work of civilization going on there.[1] The toga had everywhere taken the place of the Barbaric *sagum*; temples, porticos, and beautiful villas arose in places where straw huts and Druidic altars had lately stood; and these Britons, the greater part of whom in the time of Augustus knew neither how to till the ground nor to utilize the milk of their herds, were now exporting corn to Gaul. The schools increased with the cities, and the Celtic tongue, like the old manners, fell back before the new language.[2] The British nobles spoke Latin; the descendants of Cassivellaunus and Caractacus came before the proconsul's tribunal to practise all the rules of Quintilian and rival in eloquent verbosity the barristers of Bordeaux and Autun. "Already," says Juvenal, "Thule proposes to employ a rhetorician;" and Martial was able to boast that his verses, written for the Roman nobles, were read even in that island which was the boundary of the habitable world.[3]

Some patriots indeed had sought liberty and scope for their resentment in the highlands of the Picts, whence they will descend

---

[1] Strabo, iv. 200. Britain, till Severus' time, formed but one province, governed by a consular (Tac., *Agr.* 13), who had under him a procurator, *proc. Aug. prov. Brit.* (Orelli, No. 222).

[2] [The numerous and splendid Roman remains found at York show how luxurious and refined was this great military post in the far north of England. The museum at York in this respect is truly astonishing. — Ed.]

[3]   *Gallia causidicos docuit facunda Britannos,*
   De conducendo loquitur jam rhetore Thule.
                    JUVENAL, *Sat.* xv. 111-112.
Cf. Martial, *Epigr.* xi. 111. Yet in the time of Constantine a Gallic orator said: . . . *Latine loqui Romanis ingeneratum est nobis elaboratum* (*Pan. Veteres,* ix. 1. Cf. Dieffenbach, *Celtica,* ii. 84).

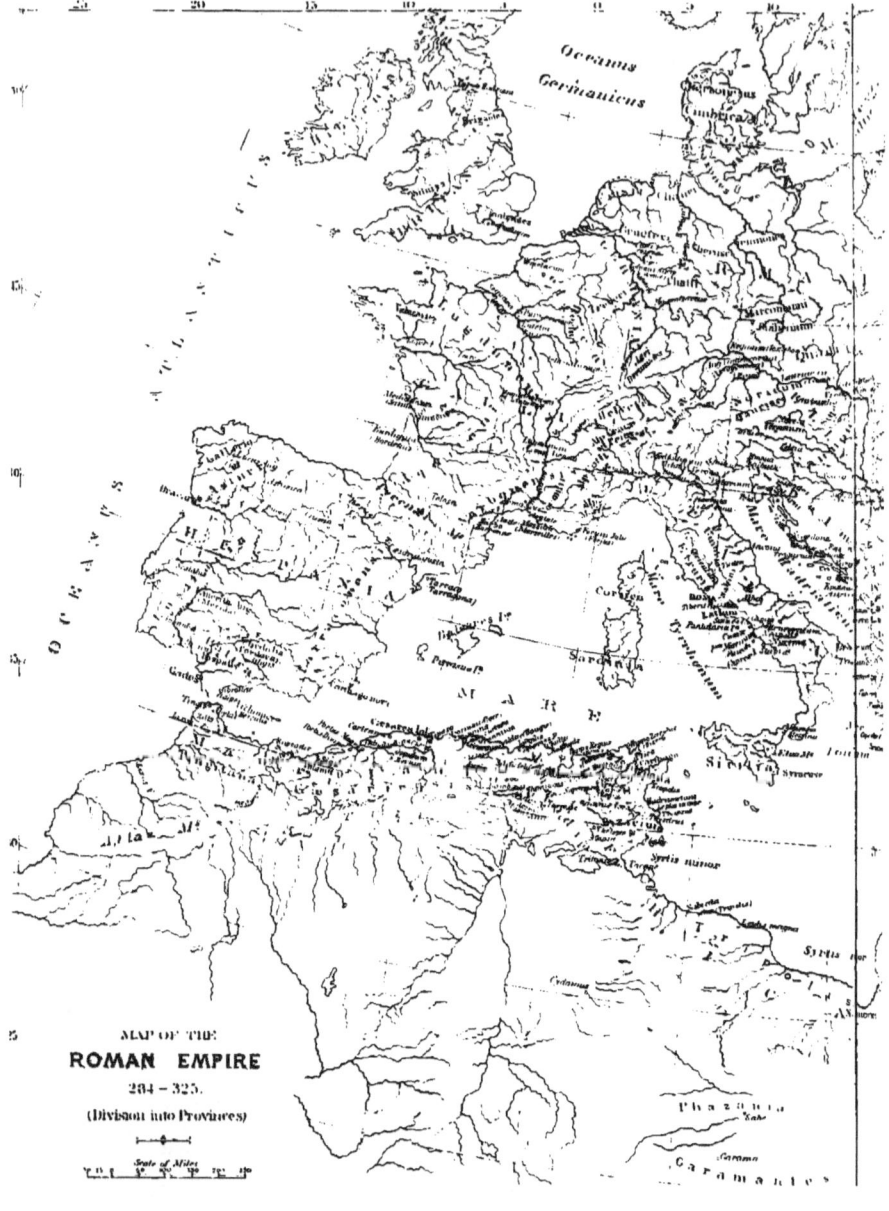

MAP OF THE
ROMAN EMPIRE
284 – 325.
(Division into Provinces)

Scale of Miles

to make this servile civilization retreat in its turn. But the mass of the nation, except the brave tribe of the Brigantes, joyfully entered upon this new life, and allowed the best of their sons to go and serve afar off in the Roman armies. Thus Britons were in garrison in Pannonia, while Germans came into Britain, in the same way that the Batavi were sent into Illyricum and the Spaniards to the Rhine.

Gaul had more quickly adopted Roman civilization and had made more advance in it. She had received its rays from closer range, especially in that zone of French territory whose shores are washed by the sea and warmed by the sun of Italy. The imperial government, of which Gaul, from its geographical position, formed the most important province, had studied to gain the heart of its inhabitants. In Narbonensis were seven colonies, twenty-nine Latin cities, two allied peoples; in Gallia Comata, ten free peoples, eight colonies, four federated cities, a number of Latin cities, and a multitude of men who had individually received the *jus civitatis.* Lyons had engraved on bronze, that it might always be before the eyes of Gaul, the speech in which Claudius expressed the liberal policy which had made Rome's fortune and the happiness of the provinces.[1] Galba and Otho from interested motives, Trajan and Hadrian from a comprehension of the wants of the Empire, had acted similarly, and Gaul, fortunate in the lot which war had brought to her, never desired to change it. We have seen the part she played in the revolutions of the Empire. From her breast arose the cry of disgust and revolt against Nero; there Galba and Vitellius had been proclaimed, and there also Civilis and Sabinus had erected, before the astonished eyes of the transalpine nations, the standard of the Gallic empire: a premature attempt! Gaul herself had deserted her own flag and her provincial Caesar. She had something else to do besides founding royal houses. Her noblest sons aspired to the senatorial laticlave. As regards the people, led on by the general movement towards works of peace, they expended in the search for prosperity that activity which had hitherto been spent on intestine wars. " From being fighters," says Strabo,[2] " they have become workers." The Druidic

---

[1] Tac., *Ann.* xi. 23. In relation to the discourse of Claudius, see Vol. IV. p. 535.
[2] iv. 1, 2, and 14.

forests fell under the woodsman's axe, or were pierced by roads
which carried light and life into their darkest depths. Everywhere
traffic was honored, and already Lyons assigned the same rank to
her wine merchants as to her knights and *seviri Augustales*.[1] The
powerful corporation of the boatmen of the Saone and Rhone (*utri-
cularii*) had agents everywhere for the navigation of the Gallic
rivers. In the amphitheatre of Nîmes forty places were reserved
for them.

Of old the most flourishing cities had sprung up at the points
where Gaul touched upon Italy, and this corner of French territory
has still more Roman remains than any other of the ancient provinces of the Empire. At Narbonne not a single Roman monument
is standing; but one cannot take down a wall or strike a pickaxe
into the soil without finding there fragments of friezes, of bas-
reliefs, and of tombs which attest its ancient grandeur. By the
classic beauty of its daughters, Arles was a Greek city, by the
splendor of its monuments, a Roman one. The culture and opu-
lence formerly concentrated in this " Italia Transalpina" had withdrawn from the frontier into the interior, and this change of social
activity indicated the general prosperity of the country. Toulouse
surpassed Narbo. Nîmes,[2] adorned by the Antonines or by itself
with monuments which still command admiration, eclipsed the old
Phocaean city; while the latter, losing its strict manners, gave rise
to the saying with which idle pleasure-lovers were in those days
taunted: "You are on your way to Massilia."[3] Then, as now,
commerce was heaping up gold in that city, and this wealth she
spent on fleeting pleasures, instead of devoting it, like Nîmes, to
lasting works of art. Thanks to her hot-springs, Aix was a resort
of the rich Massiliotes and one of the pleasure-cities of the province.
Lyons, the ancient metropolis, beheld two rivals growing up, — the
city of the Remi and that of the Treviri, whence the governors of
Belgica and Lower Germany kept watch upon the Barbarians, as

---

[1] Orelli, No. 4,026.

[2] From Strabo's time (iv. 190) Nîmes had more inhabitants than Narbonne. It was in
honor of the grandsons of Augustus, Lucius and Caius Caesar, the latter of whom was patron
of Nîmes, that the temple now called the *Maison carrée* was erected (see above, p. 62). The
edifice is 49 Roman feet high from the ground to the summit of the pediment, — a number
regarded as doubly fortunate, since it was the square of 7 (*Rev. épigr. du Midi de la France*,
No. 287). Tacitus calls this city *ornatissima colonia valentissimaque* (*Ann.* ii. 24).

[3] Athenaeus, xii. 5.

BRONZE TABLET CONTAINING THE SPEECH OF CLAUDIUS (MUSÉE DES ANTIQUES AT LYONS).

from Lyons they had long kept watch upon Gaul when that country was still a source of distrust. Vienna, the place of exile for dethroned kings or guilty governors; Autun, with its schools;

A MOSAIC OF LILLEBONNE.

Arras, with its manufactures of red cloth rivalling the Eastern purple; Langres and Saintes, with their manufacture of *caracallae*.[1]

---

[1] Cloaks of thick napped coarse cloth, introduced from Gaul into Rome by the Emperor Aurelius Antoninus, who thence acquired the surname by which he is commonly known. In the third century the greater part of the Gallic cities took again the name of their people. Thus *Andomatunum* became *Lingones*, *Augustoritum* was called *Lemovices*, etc.

which they exported to the whole of Italy; Bordeaux, the principal port for Spain and the British Islands; Juliobona (Lillebonne,
near the mouth of the Seine). where so many Roman remains
have been found; and many other cities, — exhibit life extending in

SILVER VASE FOUND AT BERNAY.[1]

every direction, in the centre as well as on the circumference, along
the Rhine, the Atlantic, and the British Channel, as well as on
the coasts of the Mediterranean. Although the Senate had estab-
blished in Gallia Comata only a very small number of colonies,
Roman life had changed the language, religion, and customs, and

[1] *Cabinet de France.*

had spread abroad luxury and wealth. In places but lately desolate, sumptuous villas arose, decorated with rare marbles and mosaics, of which we find traces, and with objects precious from their material and workmanship, like the fine collection of vases from Bernay which a fortunate discovery has restored to us.[1]

The Gallic divinities were at this time those of Rome, and the peoples erected to them magnificent temples, such as that whose imposing remains have lately been discovered on the summit of the Puy-de-Dôme. As for the Druidic worship, it had assumed the last form taken by religions before dying out: it was pagan (*paganus*); no longer to be met with except in those remote districts where the last priests of Teutates concealed themselves. Such will be the case with the Roman official religion after Constantine, when Jupiter, in his turn driven out from the gilded *cella*, will preserve only the rustic altar erected by peasants in the depths of the woods. To the honor of Rome, the Gallic conversion took place without violence. The skilful policy of Augustus and Tiberius had therefore succeeded; these Gallic divinities, associated in the same temples with the worship of Rome and the Caesars, had become zealous servants of the Empire.

This attraction of a superior civilization was equally exercised on the Celtic language, which defended itself no better than the Druidic religion had done. Like the latter, it also abandoned the cities and towns, where the affairs of government, justice, and commerce were transacted in Latin, and the descendants of the Gallic bards, now diligent readers of Catullus, Ovid, and Martial, strove to imitate the poets and orators of the sovereign people. Already Rome had inscribed among her great literary names those of the grammarian and poet Valerius Cato, "the Latin siren;" of Antonius Gnipho, who had taught in Caesar's house and counted Cicero among his hearers; of Varro Atacinus, a didactic poet; of Cornelius Gallus, the friend of Vergil; of Trogus Pompeius, the

[1] The Bernay Treasure, found by a laborer in the year 1830 at Bernay (a town in France, in the Department of Eure, on the River Charentonne, some twenty-five miles from Evreux) under his plough, consists of sixty-nine silver articles which belonged to a temple of Mercury, and seem to have been buried towards the end of the third century after Christ. The inscriptions on the articles are as late as that, and go back to the time of Augustus. M. Chabouillet has given in his *Catalogue* a description of all these objects.

first Latin author of a Universal History; of Domitius Afer, the instructor of Quintilian and the most eloquent orator whom the latter had heard, but a man who dishonored his genius by his baseness. Petronius also soiled the Latin muse by his *Satyricon*, an immoral picture of a society whose vices only he points out. But Marcus Afer has had the honor of being taken for the author of a dialogue which bears the name of Tacitus, and later still, under Hadrian, was conspicuous the sophist Favorinus. Favorinus was of Arles, Petronius of Marseilles, Gallus of Fréjus, Trogus Pompeius of the country of the Voconces, Varro from the banks of the Aude, — all from the province of Narbonensis.

Gallia Comata had also poets and orators; but the provincial muses, like the indigenous divinities, remained unknown outside the walls of the city, and the competitions at Lyons were more celebrated for the oddity of their rules than for the renown of the laurelled victors. Southern Gaul, which gave Rome so many men of letters, furnished also generals and consuls, — from Vienna, Valerius Asiaticus, who twice held the fasces; from Toulouse, Vindex; Agricola from Fréjus; and many others.

All this labor of hand and head to which Gaul had devoted herself with so much ardor was favored by peace, which since the time of Civilis prevailed on the banks of the Rhine. Barbarism, as if fatigued with having for two centuries expended useless efforts in that direction, had fallen back towards the Danube. Gaul enjoyed, therefore, between the league of the Cherusci and that of the Franks, between Arminius and the first Merovaei, nearly two centuries of respite; and we have seen how she profited by it.

Spain, still better sheltered from the Barbarians, had advanced more quickly along the ways in which Augustus had directed her. To rescue the country from Barbarism, the Romans had early multiplied cities. Pliny reckons up four hundred of importance, not to mention two hundred and ninety-three of subordinate rank; this was five or six times as many as in Gaul. Here, therefore, is one of the most lasting contrasts between the two countries. The municipal system, in fact, took such complete possession of the Iberian peninsula that fifteen centuries have not been able to uproot it. To this day, thanks to these old institutions so perfectly in accordance with the geographical character of the peninsula, there are indeed in Spain cities and provinces, but how hard it is to form a Spanish nation!

In general, the system of Augustus had the results that he expected from it. Each of the numerous cities was a focus of riches and of light; as early as the time of Strabo, Baetica and a part of Tarragona were quite Latin. We have seen that two Spanish governors successively attained the imperial power, and Vespasian considered it Roman enough to give it the *jus Latii*. We notice under this Emperor the establishment at Merida of a numerous body of Jews, the original stock of this race, which soon rapidly increased in the peninsula. Domitian continued towards Spain the favor of his house. He encouraged the extension of public works, and allowed the younger Pliny to pass condemnation on a governor of Baetica. — who was dreaded, however, at Rome as an offi-cial informer. Under Trajan there was a similar example of justice: the property of the faith-less governor served to indemnify the victims. Hadrian, who lovingly visited his native land, extended over it his active surveillance, and

COIN OF TARRAGONA.[1]

bore with patience the refusal of a general assembly to furnish levies which he asked to recruit the legions of the frontiers. That fact is important, for it proves the repugnance which the most warlike populations had at that time for military service.

The principal Spanish cities were always, — Italica, the birth-place of two Emperors; Cordova, the Iberian Athens; the coast cities, which trafficked with Italy and Africa: Tarragona, where the deputies of Hispania Citerior assembled, and where Licinius Sura, the best of Trajan's generals, was born; Gades, famous for its five hundred knights, but also for the lascivious dances of its *manolas*.[2] Her trading fleets went as far as Senegal, — perhaps farther still; and the city irreverently laid claim to preserve in her temple of Hercules that hero's bones, as Crete showed the tomb of Jupiter.

---

[1] C. V. T. T. (*colonia Victrix togata Tarraco*). An altar surmounted by a palm. Bronze. (See another coin. Vol. II. p. 210.) The engraving facing p. 132 represents an aqueduct conveying to Tarragona, on a double row of arcades above a valley, water obtained seven leagues away. (Delaborde. *Voyage en Espagne*, vol. i. pl. lv.)

[2] Mela, iii. 2; Juvenal, *Sat.* xi. 162; Martial, *Epigr.* v. 78. Martial praises Canius, the gay poet of Cadiz (i. 62); he is unknown to us.

We know that Trajan and Hadrian were from Italica; Spain had therefore the honor of furnishing the first two provincial Emperors. This fact implies that it was no longer a mere province, a foreign land. Before placing in the palace of the Caesars Emperors whose family were natives of the banks of the Baetis, Spain had sent to Rome quite a colony of poets and rhetoricians; she had conquered the Eternal City by literature before conquer-

ing it by the glorious services of her children. The two Senecas, Lucan, Pomponius Mela, Columella, Quintilian, Martial, Silius Italicus, Hyginus, perhaps Florus, were Spaniards. One recalls the contempt of Cicero for those poets of Cordova who dared to make the Latin muses speak: what would the great orator have said had he seen these provincials now opening

COIN OF ITALICA.[1]

schools and holding the sceptre of the new eloquence? The Senecas rule at Rome; the last of the great Roman poets is their nephew, and it is a Calagurritan who becomes the lawgiver of Latin literature! Elsewhere we shall show the value of this importation from the provinces; here we simply desire to draw this conclusion, — that in the time of the Antonines the education of Spain was completed, and Rome had nothing more to teach her, having given to her all that she herself knew and possessed: social life

COIN OF CALAGURRIS.[2]

and the taste for literature, with an immense development of industry and traffic; also, unhappily, her sanguinary amusements, the games of the circus, to which Spain added bull-fights.

The three countries which we have now passed in review were destined later to form one of the four prefectures of the Empire, — the one called by the name of Gaul; for that province from this time forth draws her two neighbors into her own sphere of political activity: and this preponderance will continue increasing as the frontier that she guards becomes more and more exposed to attack.

[1] MVN. ITALIC. IVLIA AVGVSTA. Livia seated, holding a sceptre and some heads of corn. Bronze. (See other coins of Italica, Vol. II. p. 215, and Vol. III. p. 83.)

[2] MVN. CAL. II VIR. Augustus bareheaded. Bronze.

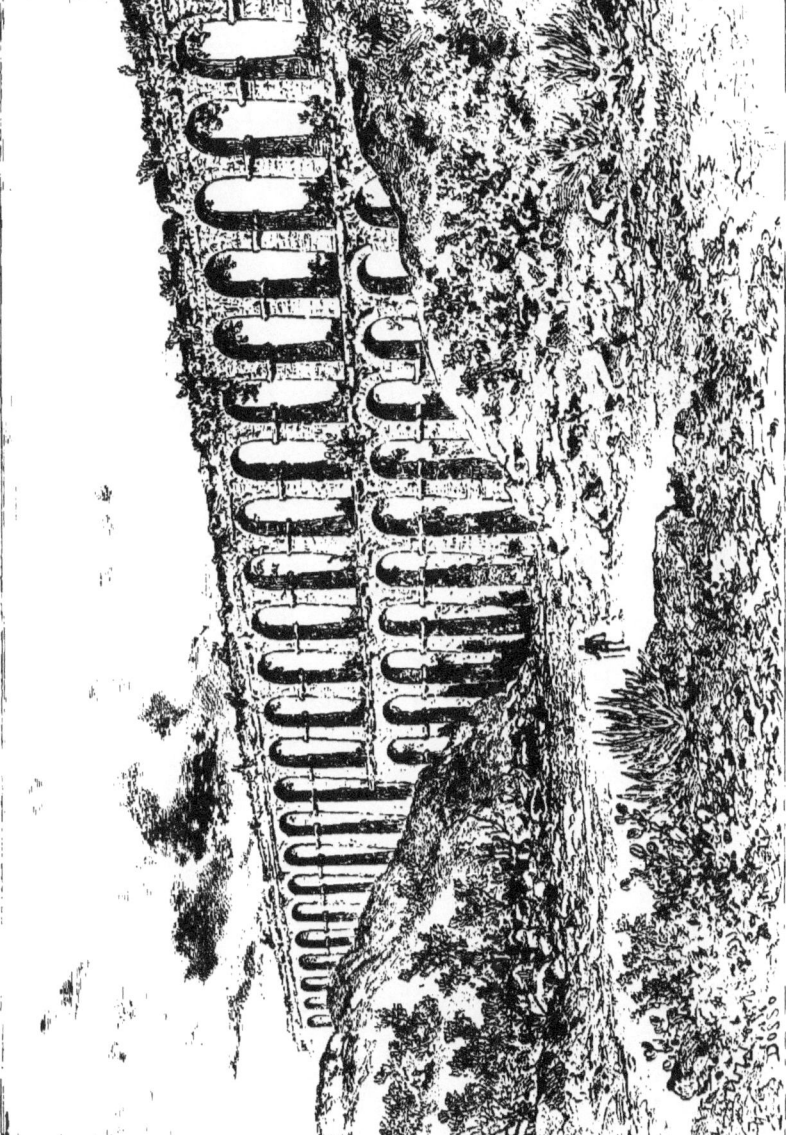

AQUEDUCT OF TARRAGONA. SEE NOTE L, P. 131.

Illyricum. — The mountainous countries which extend from the Alps to the Danube were divided into five provinces, — Rhaetia as far as the. Inn; Noricum as far as the Kahlenberg (*Cetius mons*)[1]; Pannonia as far as the Save; Illyria and Dalmatia from the Arsia to the Lissus; Moesia from the Drina to the Black Sea. We have chosen to leave to this vast region the general name of Illyricum, which Appian gives it;[2] for the nature of the soil, the character and civilization of the inhabitants, offer, in spite of numerous differences, general features of resemblance. While Roman life was richly and fruitfully developed in the group of western provinces, on this slope of the Alps and the Haemus, descending to the Danube, towards Germanic and Slavic barbarism, manners were still coarse and violent. There were few cities, colonies, or municipia; but, on the contrary, camps, fortresses, and, among the indigenous tribes, the daily use of arms, made necessary by the neighborhood of the enemy.[3]

Yet the conquest of Dacia and the transference into that province of a numerous Roman population had opened an era of prosperity for those regions. The noble river now flowing between two Roman banks was to be lined with flourishing cities, and Illyricum was destined to become one of the vital parts of the Empire, because its inhabitants will still preserve their martial habits in the midst of their peaceful industry. Thence, in fact, will arise the only great Emperors (Theodosius excepted) who for a while are to check the decadence of Rome, and the most illustrious of the Emperors of the Later Empire, Justinian.[4]

Rhaetia at that time included all the country of the Vindelici. In order to direct towards the Danube the attention and the

---

[1] Rhaetia, from the western end of Lake Constance to the confluence of the Inn with the Danube, and Noricum from Passau to Klosterneuburg, near Vienna, had been for a long time governed by procurators, and seem only in the time of Marcus Aurelius to have adopted the organization of provinces administered by imperial legates. Cf. *C. I. L.* iii. 588 and 707.

[2] Κοινῇ δὲ πάντας Ἰλλυρίδα ἡγοῦνται (*Illyr.* 6). Tacitus never gives this name to Rhaetia or to Noricum, but to Dalmatia, Pannonia, and Moesia. Cf. *Hist.* i. 76, and ii. 85, 86, and Suet. *Tib.* 16.

[3] *Raetorum juventus sueta armis et more Romanae militiae exercita* (Tac., *Hist.* i. 68).

[4] Decius was from Budalia, near Sirmium, Claudius II from Illyria, Aurelian from Pannonia, Probus from Sirmium, Maximian from Sardica, Diocletian from Salona, Constantine from Naissus, Justinian from Tauresium, near the Haemus. *Quis dubitat,* says Mamertinus (*Paneg. ad Maxim.* 2), *quin . . . Italia sit gentium domina gloriae vetustate, sed Pannonia virtute.*

strength of these valiant tribes, too much in the habit of looking
towards Upper Italy, which they had long ravaged, the first Emperor
had given them as their principal city Augusta Vindelicorum, on
the Lech (Augsburg).[1]

In Noricum and Pannonia the native race had been almost entirely exterminated by the Cimbri, Dacians, and Romans. However, the deserted lands of the Boii, which were a part of these two
provinces,[2] began to be re-peopled, and Claudius had sent thither
the colony of Savaria (Stein-am-Anger), where, as at Lyons, an
altar to Augustus was erected, surrounded by statues which represented the other cities of the province.[3] A city, Scarabantia (Oeden-
burg), which in remembrance of some imperial favor bore the
surname of Julia or Flavia, served as a halting-place between
Savaria (Stein-am-Anger) and Carnuntum, the great Roman post on
the Danube (Petronel). A little higher up the river, at Lauriacum
(Lorch), a strong garrison and a flotilla defended the entrance
to Noricum, and lower down the river Vindobona (Vienna) had
already been founded, perhaps by Vespasian. Noreia (Neumark),
the ancient capital of the Taurisci, had now ceased to exist; but in
its place there were four colonies which the Romans, with their
usual skill, had thrown out in front of the Julian Alps, the most
vulnerable part of the frontiers of Cisalpine Gaul. One of these,
Virunum (Mariasaal, to the north of Klagenfurt), was situated at
the point where the roads from Noricum and Pannonia met; the
three others[4] were established in the upper valleys of the Save and
the Drave, so as to protect that rich corner of Italy where every
year population and wealth accumulated more and more, where
before many years Pola attained thirty thousand inhabitants and
Aquileia a hundred thousand, and where already five hundred of
the citizens of Padua wore the knight's gold ring.[5]

These precautions had not appeared sufficient. In order the
better to guard the two grand highways which the Save and
Drave open through Pannonia from the country of the Dacians to
the Julian Alps, the Romans there doubled their military posts.

[1] Tacitus calls it *splendidissima Raetiae provinciae colonia.*
[2] *Deserta Boiorum* (Pliny, *Hist. nat.* iv. 12).   [3] *C. I. L.* iii. 525.
[4] Solvea, Celeia, and Emona (Seckau, Cilly, and Laybach).
[5] Strabo, iii. 169. No city of Italy and the Latin provinces, Rome and Gades excepted, had a like number of knights.

Aquincum (Alt-Ofen), on the Danube, and Mursa (Eszeg), on the Drave, were colonized, the latter by Hadrian. The fortifications of Taurunum (Semlin), at the confluence of the Save and the Danube, made this place the advanced post and protection of the great city Sirmium (Mitrovic), situated some leagues behind it. Sirmium, much nearer to the Barbarians than Siscia, now eclipsed Siscia, an old colony and stronghold founded by Tiberius. A military road which was bifurcated at Servitium (Gradiska), sending a branch to the Adriatic, closely followed the Save, connecting with one another the fortresses established on its banks. It is manifest that the Romans had not forgotten the lessons taught them by the revolts of the Pannonians under Augustus and the alarm caused by the Dacians under Domitian.

Pliny, so unequal in his descriptions, is less brief than customary respecting Illyria and Dalmatia. He says this region was divided into three judicial districts, whose chief towns were Scardona and Salona, which have kept their names, and Narona (Viddo). In the first were comprised the Iapydes, fourteen Liburnian cities, of which six enjoyed the *jus Italicum*, and a seventh which had moreover the title and advantages of the *immunitas*. In the second district were the Roman city Tragurium (Trau), celebrated for its marbles, the colonies of Sicum, of Salona, the latter being the principal post of the Romans in Illyria, and lastly, different Dalmatian peoples, divided into 924 decuriae. The third contained three colonies, seven Roman cities, and ten tribes divided into 463 decuriae.[1]

This is the first time Pliny mentions these subdivisions, resembling those which existed in Thrace and Cappadocia under the name of *strategiae*. As this mountainous region with its numberless valleys possessed few cities, the Romans had further divided these turbulent tribes into small territorial areas, over each of which a native chief was placed, who answered with his life for the preservation of order in his district. To watch them and keep them in bounds, also to deprive them of the sight of the sea, which recalled to these old pirates so many recollections and so many dangerous temptations, a multitude of colonies and Roman cities were placed along the coast between them and the Adriatic.

---

[1] Pliny, *Hist. Nat.* iii. 26.

Dacia, Moesia, and Thrace. — The administration of Trajan was marked by the same greatness and rapidity that characterized his military enterprises. When he had made the Carpathian Mountains the frontier of the Empire he clearly saw that a few garrisons scattered through that vast province would not be sufficient to hold the Dacians in check, and that Barbarism, though driven back, would return as the victors withdrew; accordingly, he introduced a whole population from the older provinces. In spite of fifteen centuries of misfortunes, the Roumanians at this day number twelve millions of men. Trajan in a few years had done the work of a century.

MOESIA SUPERIOR.[1]　　COIN OF TOMI.[2]

This vast focus of Roman life established beyond the Danube extended a beneficent influence over the neighboring provinces. Moesia had remained uncultivated and without cities, but civilization in crossing it had let drop some germs of that prosperity which was to be abundantly sown in Dacia.[3] Ratiara (Arzar-Palanca), Viminacium (Kostolacz), and Nicopolis, which still keeps its name, soon vied in prosperity with the old cities of Greek origin on the coast, Tomi (Kustendjé) and Odessus (Varna). Before a

COIN OF NICOPOLIS AD ISTRUM.

century had passed, the right bank of the Danube was dotted with cities more in number than it has to-day. Widdin, Sistova, and Nicopolis, its largest towns, are of Roman origin; and from these recently Barbaric regions were to go forth the last defenders of the Empire. Thrace had a bad name; it was called the parent of the nations most to be feared. Accordingly, Claudius had placed it under a double supervision; he had made it a province (46) administered by a procurator, and he had placed this procurator under the authority of the governor of Moesia, who was always at the head of considerable forces. Roman life did not readily take root

---

[1] P. M. S. COL. VIM. (*Provinciae Moesiae Superioris Colonia Viminacium*). Woman standing between a lion and a bull. (Bronze coin of Viminacium.)

[2] ΜΗΤΡΟ ΠΟΝ(του) ΤΟΜΕΩϹ (Tomi, metropolis of Pontus). Jupiter seated. (Bronze.)

[3] Moesia formed, from the time of Domitian, two provinces separated by the Cibrus (Cibritza).

there: in all Thrace only three or four colonies existed; but on the coasts and along the great military road which ran from Amphipolis to Byzantium there were very many Greek cities. Vespasian, Trajan, and Hadrian, obeying the impulse which from that period on drew the Empire eastward, had founded or enlarged there several cities. — Trajanopolis (Orikova ?), Plotinopolis (?), and Adrianople, whose site was so well selected that it has continued ever since one of the great cities of Europe.

COIN OF
TRAJANOPOLIS.[1]

As in Dalmatia, so in the interior of Thrace there were absolutely no cities. The Romans had, however, grouped its scattered population into *strategiae :* a rude copy of municipal life. Before the elder Pliny's time fifty of these were in existence; Ptolemy found but fourteen. — a proof of the progress of urban life in that region.[2] We have seen a similar growth take place in Spain, and it was the case everywhere: Pergamum had a hundred and twenty thousand inhabitants, Caesarea in Cappadocia, four hundred thousand.

COIN OF
PLOTINOPOLIS.[3]

II. — ITALY AND GREECE.

THE difficult work of assimilation which was the aim, the very life, of the Empire, and which remains its justification in history, went on less rapidly doubtless in the valley of the Danube than in that of the Rhine, because the populations were more diverse and ruder there; but it advanced rapidly enough to give ground for the hope that Illyricum would effectually protect Italy and Greece against Barbaric invasions from the North.

Great need of such a rampart had these two ancient queens of the world, whose strength and life were fast failing. Always venerated by the nations, they still see their capitals grow more

---

[1] ΗΓΕΤΟΥ Α ΜΑΞΙΜΟΥ ΑΥΓΟΥCΤΗC ΤΡΑΙΑΝΗC. City gate. (Bronze.)

[2] Pliny, *Hist. nat.* iv. 40; Ptolemy, *Geograph.* iii. 11, sects. 8–10.

[3] ΠΛΩΤΕΙΝ/ΠοΛΕΙΤΩΝ (the inhabitants of Plotinopolis). Minerva offering food to a serpent curled round a tree. (Bronze.)

beautiful year by year: Hadrian has just completed at Athens
the temple of Jupiter, and the Flavians and the Antonines have
made Rome a city of wonders. But where is to be found the
vigorous population who, by arms or by intellect, had subdued

ROMAN STATUE IN THE MUSEUM OF PRINCE TORLONIA.[1]

the world? If we except Rome, whither all the beggars of Italy
flocked, Southern Etruria,[2] which had revived under the influence
of order and peace, and a few cities along the Brundusian
road, which leads to Asia, and on that of Aquileia, the route

[1] *Atlas du Bull. archéol.* vol. xi. pl. xii. The two statues represented on this page and
the following were found, the one in the circus of Maxentius, near Rome, the other at the
villa of the Gordians, on the Praenestine Way. Some learned critics see in them, in spite of
the numerous restorations to which they have been subjected, the expressions of two different
phases of art, the one Greek, the other more Roman. Von Duhn says (*Ann. dell' Instituto di
Corresp. archéol.* li. 189): *Ciascuno . . . potrà a colpo d' occhio ravvisare la differenza tra la
forza e naturalezza greca e l' eleganza ed artificiosità del lavoro romano.*

[2] Canina, *Ann. dell' Instit.*, 1837, p. 62, and Dennis, *Etruria*, i. 204–210. As regards the
prosperity of Etruria under the Empire, see chapter lxv. *ad finem.* In the Roman Campagna
the cultivator was not everywhere driven away from these fruitful plains by the malaria, which
was still here and there kept down by the system of underground drainage which the early
inhabitants had organized. The mephitic atmosphere of this region is caused by the numer-

TRIUMPHAL ARCH AT ANCONA.

to the Danube, what was there apart from the Flaminian and
Appian Ways? Every day desolation was extending. For one
city prospering, how many were there on the decline? Capua,
Otriculum, Tuder, Rimini, Bologna, Verona, and Pola, did indeed

GREEK STATUE IN THE MUSEUM OF PRINCE TORLONIA.[1]

build amphitheatres, the ruins of which astonish and charm us;[2]
Ferentinum, a theatre; Beneventum, Ancona, Rimini, and Susa,
triumphal arches which are still standing.[3] The sulphur springs

ous deposits of stagnant water which remain just below the level of the ground in Rome and
its Campagna, from which under a burning sun disease-germs (*bacilli malariae*) are set free, so
numerous that the laborer collects them in the drops of sweat which cover his face. Man
escapes their influence on any ground a few yards higher than these subterranean pools,
whence the water never drains off because their basins are formed of an almost impermeable
tufa. For this reason the Romans reclaimed the soil by means of subterranean channels, one
of which, found in modern times and put in a state of repair, has cleared the neighboring
lands of their stagnant waters. See Tommasi-Crudelli, *Sur la distribution des eaux dans le sous-
sol de la Campagne de Rome* (Mém. de l'Acad. des Lincei, 1880), and for the *cuniculi* of the
Pontine Marshes, De la Blanchère, *La Malaria de Rome et le drainage antique* (in the *Mélanges
de l'École française de Rome*, fasc. i.).

[1] *Atlas du Bull. archéol.* vol. xii. pl. xi.

[2] That of Pola (facing p. 140), eighty-two feet high, measures two hundred and ninety-
five feet in its greatest diameter, and is of rare elegance.

[3] Except Ancona and Susa, all these cities are situated on the Appian and Flaminian
Ways or their extensions.

of Gabii had caused that city to recover more than its ancient prosperity; in its ruins has been found, among many other works of
art, one of the most beautiful statues of antiquity, the Diana which
bears its name. But what had become of Magna Graecia, the central region, and those twelve hundred cities of which the ancients
speak? A sepulchral stone has been found, on which is carved
the figure of a lion, and beneath it the name of an Italian soldier; this is all. Such was Italy destined soon to become, — an
empty tomb beneath a grand figure!

THE DIANA OF GABII.[2]

We have seen[1] the sad picture drawn by Columella of the plains of Italy less than a century after the *Georgics* of Vergil; notwithstanding his urgent appeal, very few had returned to the plough, and the large land-ownership had continued its struggle against the small. But why had not this new condition of landed property at least saved Italian agriculture and produced in the peninsula the same prosperity which it has caused in England? It is because in England the landlords long held in check by their tariff the competition of foreign corn, while policy obliged the Emperors to give up the Italian market to the importers of corn from Africa, Sardinia, and Egypt. England, moreover, has three sources of wealth, — manufactures, commerce, and agriculture, all of which are turned to the profit of its aristocracy, because after having

---

[1] Vol. IV. p 34. [2] Parian marble statue, discovered in 1792. Museum of the Louvre.

RUINS OF THE AMPHITHEATRE OF POLA.

made them available by its intelligence, it supports them by its capital. The Italian aristocracy had but one, — land ; and the reason has just been given why it would have been ruinous to make this land arable. The people fed as it could on some meagre harvests here and there. Now the population is always in proportion to the means of subsistence ; the latter being insufficient, the former diminished. Facts in political economy therefore explain the continuous decadence of Italy at the very time when the provinces were prospering around her.

Greece was even more unfortunate. To people Nicopolis, Augustus had brought together the inhabitants of all the neighboring towns. The foundation of a single city had ruined two provinces : Acarnania and Aetolia were deserted.[1] In many parts there was no other rural industry than the rearing of horses, — a sure sign that the population was neither rich nor numerous. This did not, however, arise from any harshness on the part of the imperial government towards Greece ; it had secured to that country a profound peace, and in return for the applause that Greece had given him, Nero had even freed her from imposts. Vespasian thought, it is true, that the recompense exceeded the service ; and taking occasion from some disorders to say that the Greeks had unlearned liberty,[2] he again placed them under praetorian authority, — a fact which Plutarch was still lamenting in the time of Hadrian. However, the Flavian Emperor allowed to exist in Macedonia, Epirus, Achaia, and the Isles, ten colonies, sixteen free states, two cities exempt from tribute, a Roman city, Stobi, near the confluence of the Axios and the Erigon ; and, as in the days of liberty, the Amphictyons continued to meet at the sanctuary of Delphi, while Olympia also kept its festivals.[4]

COIN OF STOBI.[3]

---

[1] Strabo, vii. 325. I do not speak of Sicily, which formed a province, nor of Corsica and Sardinia, which formed another. But while the whole of Sicily had the *jus Latii*, the entire Sardinian territory was *ager publicus*, and had consequently to pay the tithe of its harvests.

[2] Ἀπομεμαθηκέναι τὴν ἐλευθερίαν τὸ Ἑλληνικόν (Pausan., vii. 17, 14).

[3] MVNICIPI STOBENSIVM. Upright figure, with turreted head, holding a Victory and cornucopia ; on the earth, a helmet, cuirass, and buckler. (Bronze.)

[4] Beulé, *Le Péloponèse.* Three inscriptions which he quotes show that the priestly functions were still in exercise in the third century.

142 142 THE EMPIRE AND ROMAN SOCIETY.

It was not then a considerable share of liberty and of order that was lacking to Greece, it was in men that the country was deficient.

In a passage of the *Histories* of Polybius which we may well consider, this wise statesman seeks the causes of the ruin of Greece. He does not accuse, as a vulgar mind would do, fortune and the gods, but the people. He says: "We have had neither an epidemic nor war of long duration, and yet our cities are depopulated. We do not charge it to the gods, and we will not consult the oracles; the remedy, like the evil, is in ourselves. In our cities, from debauchery and sloth, marriage is avoided; and if children are born of transient unions, only one or two of them are kept, in order to leave them 'as rich as their parents. But let sickness strike down one of these children and war the other, and the house is left childless. Thus have our cities perished." [1] And unhappily we may say as he does: "Thus is our country depopulated." A singular similarity between two so different civilizations, in which the same anxiety for comfort has produced the same effects!

The evil pointed out three centuries before by Polybius had only gone on increasing. That which was then true of Greece becomes true now of Italy. We see the rewards promised by Augustus to the heads of numerous families, but in vain: all failed against the selfishness of these nobles who now lived only for pleasure. Shameful vices, the plague-spot of the East in all ages,[2] and the credit which, even with important personages, a fortune without heir secured, increased daily the number of men who avoided the duties of paternity. Among those even whom the law condemned, some avoided its stroke and usurped the privileges reserved for useful citizens. The unmarried were seen claiming a place of honor in the theatre in virtue of the *jus trium liberorum*: so that the law (*Julia Poppaea*) was found to have put at the Emperor's disposal one privilege the more for the reward of egotism and vanity. "Now," says Pliny, "we boast of having barren wives, and not even an only son is desired." "A man denies his own," says also Seneca.[3] "Children are abandoned," adds Tacitus.

[1] Polybius, xxxvii. 7.

[2] Cf. Zumpt, *Ueber den Stand der Bevölkerung und die Volksvermehrung im Alterthum*, pp. 14–16.

[3] Pliny, *Epist.* iv. 15; Seneca, *Consol. ad Marc.* 19.

This conduct of the higher classes turned against themselves: they perished by their own vices more surely than by the hand of the executioner; between the time of Caesar and that of Marcus Aurelius nearly all of the most illustrious houses had ceased to exist. In vain had Caesar and Augustus created new patricians; under Claudius these had already disappeared.[1]

One of the causes of the colonial power of England is certainly her fecundity. She is rich in men, and her population, growing up like the thick close grass of her meadows, overflows unceasingly by all the great highways of the world upon America, India, and Oceania. Thus Ancient Greece had spread itself over all the borders of the Mediterranean, and Italy over the countries of the West. But in those countries whence so many colonies had emigrated there was now a dearth of men, ὀλιγανδρία, according to the expression of Polybius; and as man is the best and surest productive agent, — and this was specially the case in ancient times, when machinery did not replace him, — when man failed, all failed. "The Greece of our days," says Plutarch, "would be unable to muster three thousand hoplites."[2] That is the number of soldiers which the city of Megara alone had furnished against the Persians.

Besides all this, the Hellenic genius, like a river reducing its own volume by spreading in a thousand little channels, had become enfeebled and inefficient by its own expansion, and Nature herself, growing unfriendly to her favorite race, no longer gave great men to Greece, because circumstances now made life too easy there. The race that formerly took delight in following the masters of thought upon those lofty heights bathed in the light of the ideal, were now occupied in selling or hiring out, at a good profit, what remained to them of the intellect or the art of their fathers. Daily from Hellas or from Asia some contractor set out for Rome ready to supply education or pictures, poetry or statues, philosophy or religion. Slaves born in Asiatic Greece were numerous in the capital of the Empire; but these men of pliant disposition and smooth speech did not remain in servitude. Soon enfranchised.

[1] . . . *Nec ideo conjugia et educationes liberum frequentabantur, praevalida orbitate* (Tac., *Ann.* iii. 25; xi. 25).

[2] Plutarch, *De defectu oracul.* 8. Some cities, however, had increased: "Tithorea, in Phocis, was not at that time so considerable a city as it is now" (*Id.*, *Sylla*, 21).

they governed their master,[1] and when the latter was an emperor they governed the Empire.[2] Thus in France for the last eighty years the clever speakers from our southern provinces have made our revolutions and our ministries. Artists or rhetoricians, physicians or astrologers, freedmen of a grand house or artisans in humble life, all these Greeks understood wonderfully how to utilize the Roman by ministering to his national vanity. As the Bedouin in his rags has only disdain for his French rulers, so the Greek in his heart scorned those minds, which to him seemed dull, and those heavy hands which had enslaved his country. From Dionysius of Halicarnassus to Libanius, not one Greek speaks of Horace or Vergil.[3]

On the contrary, with what ardor on the shores of the Tiber, where so many Greeks taught, and on the banks of the Ilissus and the Meles, did they repeat the great names and heroic deeds of their ancestors! Lost in the immensity of the Roman Empire, they made it their work to keep alive the memory of their native land. They celebrated, as in the time of Aristeides and Cimon, on the anniversary of the battle of Plataea, the festival of the Deliverance,[4] and the warriors of Marathon were as well remembered in their tombs as on the day when Demosthenes swore by their glorious death. At Delphi the *soteria* recalled the victorious repulse from the temple of the Gauls, pierced by Apollo's arrows. Eleusis preserved her mysteries, which Claudius desired to transfer to Rome. Sparta had no longer a Leonidas, but she had still her bloody sacrificial games. After a long indifference there was a return of pious fervor for the national religion and glory. Ancient

---

[1] Cf. Juvenal, *Sat.* iii. 57–114. This descendant of the Volsci did not like the Greeks. "The city has become Greek," says the poet, "and that I cannot tolerate. From Sicyon, from Andros, from Samos, from Tralles or Alabanda, imported to Rome by the same wind that brought the plums and figs, they swarm to the Esquiline, destined to be the very vitals and future lords of great houses. They have a quick wit, desperate impudence, a ready speech. The hungry Greek has brought with him whatever character you wish, — grammarian, rhetorician, geometer, painter, trainer, soothsayer, rope-dancer, physician, wizard; bid him climb up into heaven, he will do it. In truth, it was neither Moor, nor Sarmatian, nor Thracian that got him wings, but one born in Athens" (*Ibid.* iii. 69–80).

[2] The most famous of these freedmen of whom we have just spoken are, Callistus under Caligula; Narcissus and Pallas under Claudius; Polycletus, Doryphorus, and Helios under Nero; Icelus under Galba; Asiaticus under Vitellius.

[3] We must except Plutarch, who had lived at Rome and who once quotes Horace (*Lucullus*, 39).

[4] Plutarch, *Aristeid.* 21

1. Sacrifice.

2. Purification.

3. End of Initiation.

ELEUSINIAN MYSTERIES.[1]

Greece was discovered as fifty years ago we discovered the Middle Ages; and Hellenism, eclipsed for three centuries, began to exer-

[1] Copied from a vase discovered a few years ago in the tombs of the freedmen and slaves of the Statilian family (the early days of the Empire). The engraved representations around this vase are the same as those of the marble bas-reliefs and terra-cotta friezes which decorated ancient buildings, of which a number are preserved in the Campana collection. The circular bas-relief is composed of three groups, which represent three successive parts of the sacred ceremonies. — 1, the neophyte, assisted by a priest, offers the goddesses of Eleusis the preparatory sacrifice of a young pig : 2, the priestess places on his head the mystic vase (he is seated, veiled, with his feet placed on the skin of a ram). — the rite of *catharsis*, or purification ; 3, Demeter and her daughter admit him to caress the familiar serpent, — the rite of the *epopteia*, the crowning of the initiation. (Communication of the Comtesse Lovatelli, presented to the Institute by M. Heuzey, 13th June, 1879.)

cise a new influence on the world's ideas. Thanks to her renown and to her monuments, over which six centuries had passed already without tarnishing their youthful splendor, Athens, in spite of her poverty,[1] became once more, after a long silence, the city of Minerva. Again she had her clamorous schools, and artists in the suite of Emperors thronged within her walls. On entering into this ancient sanctuary of intellect, the philosophers cried out: "Let us here bend the knee!"[2] Hadrian has just completed the work of Pericles, — the temple of Olympian Zeus; and for what does Pausanias, who at this very time is exploring it, seek on this ancient soil? The traces of gods and heroes. He forgets the miseries of the present, to tell of that famous past by which live the heirs of Homer and of Leonidas.

Thus in the European possessions of the Empire we have three groups, — the countries of the North, which are awaking to social life; the western provinces, which enjoy it fully; the central regions, which are growing poor, decayed, and silent. This is the modern movement beginning, the life which leaves its place and moves northwards, as if to challenge Barbarism to fight that great battle which will cause the ancient civilization to be lost to view until the distant day when it shall emerge, stronger and better, from under the ruins which the Germans heaped upon it.

III. — AFRICA AND THE EAST.

On the other side of the Mediterranean lay the six African provinces, — Egypt, Cyrenaïca, Africa proper, Numidia, and the two Mauretanias. These provinces formed two distinct groups, separated by the deserts of the Syrtes, — on the east, Cyrenaïca and

---

[1] The Romans had left her several tributary islands and cities. — Oropus, Haliartus, Salamis, Lemnos, Imbros, Paros, Scyros, Ios, Sciathos, Ceos, Peparethus, Delos, and Cephellenia. Yet the city was so poor that in the second century A. D. she endeavored to sell Delos (Philostratus, *Vitae Soph.* i. 23), and had to give up incurring the smallest expenses (A. Dumont, *Popul. de l'Attique*, in the *Journal des Savants*, December, 1871); and in the third could not continue working the mines of Laurion. By the computation of M. Dumont (*Ephébie attique*), its population under the Antonines did not reach twelve thousand. Horace in the time of Augustus had already said of it . . . *vacuas* . . . *Athenas* (*Epist.* II. ii. 81).

[2] Philostratus, *Vitae Soph.* ii. 5, 3.

Egypt; on the west, the country of Carthage, the Numidians, and the Moors.

It was by way of Carthaginian territory that the Romans had first seized on Africa. They had so firmly established themselves there that Tunis is still covered with the ruins of their cities; and many of these ruins are among the most imposing that remain to us. The amphitheatre of Thysdrus recalls that of Vespasian, and equals in grandeur, with perhaps more elegance, that of Verona.[1] Formerly it was crowded by the population of a great and wealthy city; now all the *gourbis* of an Arab village live in its shade. What vigor had this municipal system, which could erect such colossal buildings on the very edge of the desert!

From Africa proper the new manners had spread through the neighboring countries. To hasten the transformation of these regions, Augustus and his successors had founded numerous cities in the two Mauretanias, even as far as the Atlantic coast, but facing Baetica, whence encouragement and help came to them.[2]

This attempt had been unsuccessful, or perhaps Augustus hoped to make more progress by giving the charge of this important affair to a native chief; he relinquished Mauretania to Juba. This learned king, to whom Athens erected a statue, employed a reign of fifty years in spreading among his people the taste for Roman manners. His capital, Iol, or Caesarea, now called Cherchel, was an Italian city. This prince, one of the *reges inservientes* of Tacitus, was more useful than a proconsul in preparing the way for the  imperial domination. Caligula took away the kingdom from Juba's son (40), and Claudius divided Mauretania into two provinces, — Tingitana and Caesariensis, separated by the Malva, which river is now the frontier between Morocco and the French province of Oran.[4]

COIN OF CAESAREA.[3]

[1] Its greatest diameter is 492 feet, its smallest 436, and its height 115; that of Verona is 505 long by 413 broad. See Guérin, *Voy. arch. dans la régence de Tunis.*

[2] Otho rendered this action more direct by placing Mauretania Tingitana under the jurisdiction of the governor of Baetica. Augustus had already made the same arrangement for Zilis: *Zilis jura Baeticam petere jussa* (Pliny, *Hist. nat.* v. 1).

[3] Head of Africa covered with an elephant's skin. On the reverse, CAESAREA under a dolphin. (Bronze.)

[4] The two Mauretanias, which extended from the Atlantic to the Ampsaga (Oued Roumel, or Oued-el-Kebir), were several times united under a single procurator, who commanded different corps of auxiliary troops. Marcius Turbo seems to have held this command under Hadrian.

From that time the whole of North Africa formed part of the Empire.

For a century and a half, therefore, the influence of Rome had preponderated in Africa, — for nearly two centuries if we go back to Scipio Aemilianus; for two centuries and a half if we date from the battle of Zama. Nothing great can be done without time. We do not sufficiently consider this in our unjust complaints concerning the slowness of the French progress in Algeria, — we, who take the place of Rome on that coast where Carthage, Masinissa, Bocchus, and Juba labored for her, and where for us there have been greater obstacles and no assistance.

Still, it was not without resistance that this race succumbed. History has not preserved an account of all the wars which had to be undertaken to stifle the protests against a foreign yoke. We know only the expeditions of Suetonius Paulinus, who crossed the Atlas, and of Geta, who pursued the Moors as far as the Sahara. The revolt of Tacfarinas is better known, thanks to Tacitus. Although this leader did not possess that religious aid which the Marabouts employ against the French, he held the troops of Tiberius in check for seven years, and deserved to have his name associated with those of the heroes of national independence in the first century of the Caesars, — Civilis, Sacrovir, Simon ben Giora, Caractacus, and the dauntless Boadicea.

This war had extended from Sitifis, which was its centre, to the country of the Garamantes, whose king made his submission after the death of Tacfarinas. This did not, however, relieve the province from all disquietude. The tribes of the Sahara, the Musulames and Getuli, for a long time tried the patience of the governors. To make the work of repression quicker, while at the same time weakening the too great power of the proconsul of Africa, Caligula deprived this governor of the army and gave it to an imperial legate. The same anxiety had led to the prohibition of the residence of state criminals in Africa; for the tranquillity of that province, which gave Rome abundance or dearth, — that is to say, the content or the displeasure of the Roman people, the security or the anxiety of the Emperor, — was too important not to be protected by all the prudential means possible.

Vespasian, whose wife was the daughter of a Roman knight

THE AMPHITHEATRE OF THYSDRUS (EL-DJEM); PRESENT CONDITION.

living at Sabrata, doubtless felt the same solicitude for Africa that he did for the other provinces; but all we know of his administration is the despatch of a colony to Icosium (Algiers). The pacification of Tripoli, which was begun by him, was completed under Domitian, who in order to put an end to the plunderings of the Nasamones, exterminated the greater part of them. Hadrian and Antoninus had to repress some commotions of the Moors; and under Marcus Aurelius we have seen the tribes of the Atlas start up and respond to the voice of the Barbaric world, which arose in confused clamors on the banks of the Danube.

Three causes rendered these revolts inevitable, — the natural features of the country, which offered so many secure retreats; the government by natives, from which Rome almost always derived considerable advantage, while at the same time it had its dangers, because the fidelity of the national chiefs was occasionally shaken; [1] lastly, the custom of carrying arms, which the Moors preserved. We have already seen that the provincials on the banks of the Danube had the same military habits; but the latter were kept in check by the nearness of the enemy. The Moors had to fight only with wild beasts; and these hardy hunters of the lion often forgot that master of the forests and hunted men instead.[2]

But Africa has never belonged to itself, because it has no geographical centre. These revolts would remain, therefore, without serious consequences

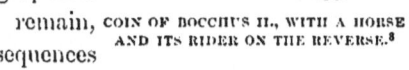

COIN OF BOCCHUS II., WITH A HORSE AND ITS RIDER ON THE REVERSE.[3]

until the time when they were supported by a foreign conqueror. Up to that time the organization given by the Romans to Africa sufficed to hold it. It is true that this organization was worthy of their usual skill.

Rome had a double interest in establishing herself on that coast. The first was to forge there the last ring of the chain which she had thrown around the ancient world, and to enclose the Mediterranean within her territory. Formerly a Carthaginian general forbade the

---

[1] Under Hadrian, a Moor who had been made consul had instigated or furthered the risings of this province. Cf. above, p. 8.

[2] Herodian and Zosimus say that the Moors were always armed with their arrows.

[3] On the obverse, the head of king Bocchus II.; on the reverse, a horse with a rider without bridle; in a cartouche, letters signifying: "To Bocchus, the kingdom." (Bronze.)

Roman sailors to dip their hands in the Sicilian Sea: now it is
the Mediterranean in its whole extent whose shores Rome will
not suffer to be trodden by a hostile foot.   Her second object
was to employ for her own advantage the riches of the African
continent.

These riches were very various.   Tingitana doubtless exported
then, as now, cattle to Baetica: but the Romans obtained thence
only tables hewn whole out of those gigantic primeval trees which

VINCASNONVI
NCASTEAMA
MVS POLIDOXV

RACEHORSE.[1]

grew in the magnificent forests at that time covering the foot of
Mount Atlas.[2]   Of Numidia. Pliny gives the inventory in two
words; he says: "Fine marbles and wild beasts."   He might have
added, horses incomparable for swiftness. if not for beauty of form.
Mauretania had on the reverse of her coins a horse without bridle,
and this inscription has been found: —

> "Daughter of the Getulan Harena,
> Daughter of the Getulan Equinus,
> Rapid as the winds in their course,
> Having always lived a virgin,
> Speudusa, thou dwellest on the banks of Lethe."[3]

In Byzacena, where the increasing dryness of the climate has
made the soil somewhat less fertile. corn returns a hundredfold;

[1] Fragment of the mosaic of Pompeianus, found near Constantine.   The inscription signifies: "Whether you win or not. Polidoxus, I shall always love you."
[2] Tingitana also furnished elephants for the circus (Pliny, *Hist. nat.* v. 1): none are found
there now, but the entire character of this coast has changed, and the mountains are no longer
covered with forests.   Traces of large rivers, of immense spaces which were covered with
water, are seen there, and the proofs of a formerly luxuriant vegetation.   Rabbi Mardochee
found in 1875, south of Mogador and very far beyond Cape Ghir, fertile regions, ancient
ruins, and tombs with carved figures, doubtless anterior to the Mohammedan era (*Bull. de la
Soc. de Géogr.* January, 1876).   [3] Orelli, No. 4,322.

thus Africa was represented as a girl with her two hands laden
with heavy corn-ears.[1] The fruitful soil of Byzacena and Zeugitana
extended into a part of Numidia; the Arabs still call the plains
lying between Setif and Constantine "the gold country." Hence
it was easy to interest the Numidians in agriculture; and Rome

COIN OF ZILIS.[2]   COIN OF HIPPO REGIUS.[3]

did not fail to do it. As regards Mauretania, the part which
formed the basin of the Malva was sterile; but at its western
extremity, where it had been attacked by Augustus, the country
was almost equal to the two neighboring provinces.

COIN OF HADRUMETUM.[4]   COIN OF THAPSUS.[5]   COIN OF LEPTIS MINOR.[6]

To possess this rich territory, Rome was not satisfied with
holding simply the African coast by the maritime cities; this
restricted occupation was regarded in the same light then as it is
at present. She penetrated into the interior, went as far as the
Atlas, crossed those mountains, and descended to the Sahara.

But first she established herself strongly upon the coast. From
the Lixus (Oued el-Kous,[7] which falls into the Atlantic, to Lake

[1] Pindar (*Isthm.* iv. 91) calls Africa τὰν πυροφόρον, fruitful in corn; *Faruch* in Syriac.
Ferik in Arabic, mean a certain state of the ear of corn.

[2] Head of Mercury; on the reverse, two ears of corn. (Bronze.)

[3] Beardless head, and the inscription HIPPO in Punic characters. On the reverse, a
panther; above it, TYPAT in Punic. (Bronze.)

[4] HADR. Head of Neptune; before it a trident. (Bronze.)

[5] THAPSVM IVN. AVG. Head of Livia, veiled and crowned with ears of corn.
(Bronze.)

[6] ΛΕΠΤΙ. Bust of Mercury. (Bronze.)

[7] Two and a half miles from El-Araïch, the Oued el-Kous surrounds a rocky peninsula
where have been found the ruins of an ancient city with Cyclopean ramparts. Opposite

Triton, which the sands and cliffs of the coast separate from the Syrtis Minor, she stretched a long chain of colonies, municipia, and Roman cities. Of these the most important were Zilis (Ar Zila), where have been found many coins of the kings of Mauretania; Lixus (El-Araïch), the Garden of Flowers; Tingis (Tangier), which shows its immense "shield of Antaeus" of elephant's hide; Siga, the rich and populous capital of Lyghax; Portus Magnus (Mers el-Khapir), the best natural seaport of Algeria; Hippo Regius (Bona), the old capital of the Numidian kings, a very strong position; and Tabraca (Taburka), which marks the boundary between Algiers and Tunis, as twenty centuries ago it marked that of Numidia and Tingitana. So little changes have taken place in that region!

Tabraca had the title of a Roman city; so also had Utica, the ruins of which, as a consequence of the alluvial deposits of the Bagradas, are situated in the midst of cultivated fields more than six miles from the coast.[1]   Hippo Zarytus (Byzerte), Carthage, Neapolis (Nabel), Hadrumetum (Sousa), Thenae, at the entrance to

the Syrtis Minor, Tacape (Gabes), were colonies; Thapsus, Leptis Minor, and twenty-seven other cities of the province had the rights of free cities.[2]

COIN OF CIRTA.[3]

In the interior, colonization was checked in Mauretania Tingitana (Morocco) by the deserts adjacent to the Malva and by what are called the mountains of the Rif.   But in the other provinces, which correspond to Algeria, Tunis, and Tripoli, it rapidly developed.   The innumerable valleys formed by the ramifications of the Atlas had each its city, connected with neighboring ones by the roads crossing the whole province from west to east and descending in one direction towards

El-Araïch the site of the Garden of the Hesperides has been thought recognizable (*Mém.* of M. Tissot on his travels in Morocco, 1874)!   A few leagues from Mequinez the ruins of the Roman city of Volubilis, with the remains of a temple, a triumphal arch, and the inclosure, cover an entire hill.   What discoveries might be made there—although these ruins have long served as a quarry for the construction of Mequinez—if Morocco were not so inhospitable!

[1] Hadrian gave it the title of colony (Aul. Gellius, *Noct. Attic.*, xvi. 13).

[2] Pliny, *Hist. nat.* v. 29.   To these twenty-nine free cities Pliny adds fifteen *oppida vicium Romanorum* and six colonies; but in the time of the Antonines there were many more.   Many military posts, *castella, turres*, had become cities.   Thus an inscription of *Tarris Tamalluni* praises Hadrian as the *conditor municipii* (Guérin, i. 244).   Marquardt (iv. 320–323) gives a long list of the colonies and free cities of Numidia.

[3] Struck in 43 B.C. with the figure of Sittius.   (Bronze.)   In regard to Sittius, see Vol. III. p. 490.

the maritime towns, and in the other towards the desert and the posts established at the foot of Mount Atlas.[1]

The Romans, like the French, had much difficulty in penetrating the mountainous central region of Kabylia; but by occupying all

MOSAIC OF IGILGILIS (DJIDJELLI).[2]

the entrances to the mountain chain, they forced the Kabyles to acknowledge, in order to exist, the supremacy of those who held the valleys, finally gaining a foothold even in the mountains themselves. The same policy was followed, but with different means, in respect to the Sahara. The Romans had closed by defences the gorges of the Aurasius to check the incursions of the nomads; they had even crossed the high plateau and descended into the desert, where they had seized some of the oases. We have been as far as Laghouat only

COIN OF THYS-DRUS, BEARING THE HEAD OF ASTARTE (BRONZE).

---

[1] Thus, Mount Aurasius, part of the Atlas range, which occupies the southern portion of the province of Constantine, between Batna and Biskra, forms a mountain mass, nearly four hundred miles in circumference, inhabited by the Kabyles, who have rarely been subjugated. Three valleys, of which only one is easily traversed, cross it. The ruins left in this district by the Romans prove that they had formed a quadrilateral, the sides of which abutted on Lambese, Ksar Baghaï, Bades, and Biskra (*Bulletin de la Soc. de Géogr.*, September, 1880: *Les Monts Aourès*).

[2] Delamare, *Expl. de l'Algerie.*

since 1854, and there are found at Géryville, in the same latitude. some vestiges of Roman occupation. At the foot of the southern slopes of Mount Aurasius they laid out a road, which was studded by military posts from Biskra for a long distance eastward. In the oasis of El-Outhaia to the south of El-Kantara, Marcus Aurelius had caused his soldiers to repair a ruinous triumphal arch,[1] and near Besseriani (ad Majores). not far from Chott Melghir, has been found a milestone bearing the name of Trajan.

For Numidia and Africa the centre of defence was at Lambese, where still exist the two camps of the Third Augustan legion and its auxiliaries, about ten thousand men, who furnished garrisons to all those posts, and even a cohort to the proconsul of Carthage.[2] Military roads, made by the soldiers. radiate hence in all directions.

The Romans. who had left autonomy to many cities, and to their magistrates[3] the Punic name of suffetes, had also recognized or established the authority of certain chiefs of tribes.

The desert of Sahara or the Atlas range could not be. like the Rhine and the Danube. bordered by a continuous intrenchment, nor was it necessary to maintain eight or ten legions on this frontier threatened by no danger. A few well-stationed posts kept the nomads at a distance. Modern travellers, who have at great risk lately penetrated into the southern portions of Tunis, have found in all the mountain gorges works. now fallen to ruins. which

defended the passage. Roman roads led to these, and aqueducts, one of which was not less than forty-three miles long,[4] brought water from the hills to the cities of the plain.

COIN OF ROMAN CARTHAGE, BEARING THE NAMES OF THE SUFFETES.[5]

As these precautions were not always sufficient to prevent raids and pillage. the government completed them by another means of defence : it gave a sort of investiture to certain native chiefs who

[1] L. Renier. Inscr. d'Alg. 1650.
[2] Cf. Henzen, Annali (1860), pp. 52–71 ; L. Renier, Inscr. d'Alg. 5 B.
[3] C. I. L. vol. v. Nos. 4,919–22.
[4] Guérin, Voyage en Tunisie, passim, and Archives des Missions pour 1877, pp. 362 et seq.
[5] ARISTO MVTVMBAL RICOCE SVF. Heads without beards and uncovered of J. Caesar and Augustus. On the reverse, KAR. VENERIS around a tetrastyle temple (Bronze).

RUINS OF A ROMAN AQUEDUCT NEAR CONSTANTINE.

undertook at their own risk to maintain order in the interests of
the Empire. These chiefs ordinarily built a fortress in the centre
of their territory ; and provided they paid the tribute and secured
the public peace, they could style themselves princes or kings and
govern as they liked. Rome showed no jealousy of them. Only
she kept near the more powerful of them a centurion or a prefect,
as a representative of her sovereign authority, who was always
ready to intervene to check plots or tumults that threatened to go
too far. They were like our heads of Arab departments (*bureaux
arabes*), overseeing the native aghas.[1]

We find a similar system on the other frontiers. To the
tetrarchs who held commands on the borders of the Syrian desert,
to the kings of the Cimmerian Bosporus, to the Barbarian chiefs
whom Rome pensioned on the north of the Danube, the Emperors
sent agents, who, residing at the courts of these princes, acted as
intermediaries between them and the Empire, and often controlled
their acts. This was therefore a general measure of government,
and, let us acknowledge, one of the most skilful.

This great province of Africa had been subject, since Caligula's
reign, to two different authorities, — the one civil, the proconsul,
who resided at Carthage ; the other military, the legate of the
Third Augustan legion, whose headquarters were at Lambese.
Hence arose conflicts and encroachments on the part of the legate,
who, having on his side the effective power and the longer duration of his duties,[2] finally secured the formation of Numidia into
a separate province, of which he was the head. There is also
another resemblance to Algeria ; namely, that as French colonization is hindered in the interior of our provinces by two conflicting
elements, the Arabs and the Kabyles, so also was Roman colonization by the Berbers and the Phoenicians. The latter in the
cities preserved their own worship, language, and manners, and
the Berbers kept the language which they speak at this day.
But Rome had this advantage over France, — her religious belief

---

[1] The history of Firmus (Amm. Marc. xxix. 5) shows that there were in this province
powerful chiefs, one of whom even bears the title of king. In an inscription of Trajan's time
found at Kamala in Numidia (L. Renier, *Inscr. d'Alg.* No. 2,715), there is mention of a Roman
praefectus gentis Musulamiorum : another inscription, found at Caesarea in Mauretania (*Ibid.*,
No. 4,033), mentions a *procurator Augusti ad curam gentium.*

[2] Tac., *Hist.* iv. 48.

did not excite the fanatical hatred of her subjects. Of the two
sentiments which constitute for a people their greatest power of
resistance against the foreigner, namely patriotism and religion,
the Emperors had nothing to fear from the latter, and historical
circumstances had singularly weakened the former.

Perhaps also the Romans found in this region, two thousand
years younger then than now, better conditions of culture, — mountains better wooded, springs of water more abundant, and especially more constant. Even in the Sahara — a territory burned by
an irresistible sun — there seem to have been in many places powerful watercourses, which now occur only in the form of subterranean pools. Withered palm-trees here and there bear witness to
the recent disappearance of the springs, and the Romans might
have seen a rich vegetation in the very place where we find only a
sea of sand. With good reason has been admired the system of
regular weekly, daily, and hourly irrigations which the Arabs have
established in the Huerta of Valentia. The same system was also
practised by the Romans. In Algeria stone tables have been found
with inscriptions indicating the hours during which each proprietor
had a right to the water.[1]

To conclude: from the sea to the Sahara were four zones, — the
maritime cities, that is to say, commerce ; the cities of the Tell,
or agriculture ; at the foot of the Atlas range, the military posts
and the native principalities ; beyond were the oases and the
desert nomads, who were dependent on the Tell for their supply
of corn.[2]

Such was the Africa of the Emperors, and such also is ours.
In this territory, whither we carry the civilization of Europe, the
name of Rome calls up that of France, and the two names become
unconsciously blended, as are the traces of the two peoples. But
we have not recovered all those which Rome has left.

In 1850 a French general, when crossing the Aurès on his
way to Biskra, thus wrote: "We were flattering ourselves that we

---

[1] Masqueray, *Ruines de Kenchela*, p. 3. The fauna of Algeria have changed, like the
water-system. In the south of Algeria are seen on the rocks representations of animals
such as the elephant, the rhinoceros, and the giraffe — which are no longer found there. The
elephant, still very common in North Africa in the time of Procopius, has entirely disappeared.

[2] Dr. Seriziat, who in March, 1865, was at Ouargla, the most southerly oasis belonging
to France, says that corn was worth 175 francs per 100 kilogrammes.

were the first to traverse the defile of Tighanimine. What a mistake! Half way through it, cut in the rock. . . . an inscription informed us that, under Antoninus, the Sixth Legion had taken the same route along which we were laboring seventeen hundred years later." [1] Others relate that during the expedition from Constantine the French soldiers were filled with admiration when, wearied by the dreariness of the route, they suddenly came upon the remains of a Roman city. No one expected such a discovery. These ruins in the solitude revived the enthusiasm of the army, reminding them thus solemnly that, centuries before, a great people had conquered and civilized this land. And since then, how often have our troops seen monuments, still imposing in decay. — the remains of baths, aqueducts, amphitheatres, temples, tombs, and triumphal arches, — from whose heights, one might say, the Genius of Rome seemed to be watching France beginning again the work of her legions. The Arabs, whom nothing astonishes, have yet been struck by the grandeur and number of these ruins; and they have said when pointing them out to those whom they call the *Roumi*: "Did your ancestors then believe they should never die?"

Africa, thus grasped by Roman civilization, yielded to this powerful embrace. She was destined to follow Spain and Gaul in furnishing emperors. There was already Libyan blood in the Flavian family; Septimius Severus, Albinus his rival, Macrinus the murderer and successor of Caracalla, were of pure African descent. From Hadrumetum came the great jurisconsult Salvius Julianus, and, as was proper, a provincial had compiled the law for the provinces.[2] This prosperity of Africa appears not only in the success of her sons, but also in the splendor of her cities, especially Carthage, which became once more the second city of the West. When the sap circulates actively and powerfully, fruit comes with the flower. Africa stood ready to seize that literary sceptre which Italy was again letting fall after having for a while recovered it from Spain and Gaul by the elder and younger Pliny, Juvenal, and Tacitus. The great names of Latin literature will henceforth be African, — Apuleius, Tertullian, Minutius Felix, Saint Cyprian, Arnobius, Lactantius and, noblest of all, Saint Augustine. For the time

---

[1] *Correspondance* of General St. Arnaud.   [2] Vol. V. pp. 391, 392.

Fronto reigns there, and Cirta is proud of having given to the world him whom she styles a new Cicero.[1]

I have not spoken at all of Tripoli, where the three cities Leptis, Oea, and Sabrata formed a sort of federal republic with an annual deliberative assembly which was still existing as late as the fourth century, — whose most illustrious time, however, comes later, since it was the work of Septimius Severus;[2] beyond the Syrtes we should enter into the Greek world, where the situation was nearly the same as it had been two centuries earlier.

COIN OF OEA (OBVERSE AND REVERSE).[3]   COIN OF SABRATA (WITH BEARDED HERCULES). (BRONZE.)

Cyrenaïca, while protected against the nomads by brilliant expeditions, yet saw its prosperity diminishing; Alexandria was causing its ruin, and the Emperors did nothing to arrest its decadence.

In Egypt the policy initiated by Augustus was still followed. The Emperors appointed as governors to this rich province only knights, sometimes even citizens of foreign extraction, — like that Jew who proclaimed Vespasian in Alexandria, and that Balbillus, grandson of a king Antiochus, whose daughter, the poetess Balbilla, engraved some pretentious verses and her genealogy on

---

[1] The first two governments in the Empire were those of the proconsular provinces of Asia and Africa, whose incumbents had a salary of two hundred and fifty thousand drachmas (Dion. lxxviii. 22). It appears also that the governors of Numidia enjoyed the privilege of being raised to the consulship on the expiration of their terms of office. At least M. L. Renier has found inscriptions of the reigns of Hadrian, Antoninus, Marcus Aurelius, and Septimius Severus, in which six legates, propraetors of Numidia, bear in the last year of their official life the title of consul-designate.

[2] Amm. Marcell. xxviii. 67. The territory of this republic — if we may so call it — was a dependency of the province of Africa, and Rome supported a garrison even in Fezzan. Barth (*Voy. dans l'Afrique centrale*, vol. i.) found in the mountains to the south of Tripoli a tomb, thirty-six feet high, which he believes to be of the time of the Antonines, and other sepulchral structures also on the route from Tripoli to Mourzouk.

[3] Woman's head turreted; behind, Oea. On the reverse, head of Apollo, laurel-crowned; in front, *quæstor* (?) *præfectus triumo*. (Bronze.)

the leg of Memnon.[1] The native civilization was nearly extinct ; but the country had always her rich harvests, her commerce with India, and her porphyry quarries, at that time worked for the whole Empire. Under the strong hand of her new masters she flashed out as in the days of the Pharaohs. Her numerous vessels ploughed the Red Sea ; her merchants again followed the route of the Rameses towards Nubia, and sought to solve the problem of the sources of the Nile.[2] The oases in the desert show to this day traces of Roman occupation, and inscriptions found on these remains bear the names of Galba, of Titus, and of Trajan.

We have traversed with Hadrian the whole Eastern frontier. In Syria, the cities of Baalbec. Palmyra. Gerasa. Rabbath-Ammon. and Bostra had begun the erection of those monuments whose ruins astonish the traveller who in fear and peril now penetrates the solitudes where in those days life was so crowded and busy.

In Asia Minor we should need to stop at every step to narrate the prosperity of those now desert provinces, where five hundred cities were then flourishing ; but in this work our chief aim is always the study of the manners and institutions of Rome. We have written at length respecting the western half of the Empire for the reason that all the activity of the Romans showed itself on that side. There they awakened civilized life ; there they made ready for the formation of the modern nations ; and they seem to have bequeathed to the latter that clear, exact mind which had aided themselves in doing their own great deeds.

COIN OF BOSTRA. STRUCK UNDER ANTONINUS (BRONZE).

In the East. coming after the Greeks as they did. the Romans were not able to dispossess them : and notwithstanding some Latin inscriptions and Roman names to be found here and there engraved

[1] Letronne, *Inscr. d'Égypte*, ii. 358.
[2] Dr. Schweinfurth found in 1874 the remains of seven Roman *castella* in the grand oasis of the Lybian desert, El-Khargué, eighty miles west of the Nile (*Bulletin de la Soc. de Géog.* June. 1874). Cailliaud (*Voyages à l'oasis de Thèbes*), the bold traveller of Nantes, had seen in 1818, fifty-six years before the German expedition, the ruins of El-Khargué, and notably more than two hundred Roman tombs. To the south of Syene a wall bars the Nile valley against Ethiopian marauders. Inscriptions speak of the guardians of the sacred gate, ἐπιτηρηταὶ ἱερᾶς πύλης Σοήνης (*C. I. G.* No. 4,878). This sacred gate was doubtless only an important post of the imperial customs.

on tombs, the Romans had not succeeded in causing their language and their usages to predominate. These countries, organized a very long time before the legions appeared in them, had preserved their own customs and peculiar genius in art, industry, commerce, temples, theatres, festivals; gladiators and amphitheatres there were none, or very few, except at Pergamus and Cyzicus,[1] but philosophers who are going to frame Christian theology, and a great number of sophists who will multiply heresies. It was quite another world; the difference was so profound that it still exists. From the Adriatic to the Atlantic, all had become Roman; from the Euphrates to the Adriatic, all was Greek.[2] In vain does Pliny talk in grandiloquent terms of the universality of the Latin tongue;[3] one half only of the Empire employed the language of Latium.

Latin was the official language, that of the army and of the administration. But in the second century every well-educated man spoke Greek, even at Rome; and under the external uniformity of the two languages, which divided the Roman world between them, local dialects, and consequently in a certain degree national peculiarities also, still existed. Since the language of the Druids has lasted in Brittany till our own days, and that of the Iberians in the Pyrenees, we should not be surprised that certain noble Arverni still made use of the Celtic dialect as late as the fifth century of our era,[4] that Saint Irenaeus was obliged to preach in Celtic in the Lyonnais district,[5] and that Saint Jerome found some genuine

---

[1] There was in the whole of Asia Minor no regular organization for gladiatorial games except at Pergamus and Cyzicus. These are the only cities in which the ruins of an amphitheatre are found (Texier, *Asie Mineure*, p. 217). Saint Polycarp's martyrdom proves, however, that games of wild beasts were given at Smyrna, Miletus, Ancyra, and Aphrodisias of Caria; and in Greece, Corinth, Megara, and even Athens, had them as well (Egger, *Mém. d'hist. anc.* p. 30).

[2] Apuleius says a Thessalian peasant could not understand a soldier who spoke Latin to him. [Only a dozen Latin words, concerning soldiers and taxes, are to be found in the Greek of the New Testament.—ED.]

[3] *Hist. Nat.* iii. 6. Saint Augustine says also of Rome: *Linguam suam domitis gentibus per pacem societatis imposuit* (*Civ. Dei*, xix. 7).

[4] Sidon. Apollinaris, iii. 3, v. 18, and Fauriel, *Hist. de la Gaule mérid.* i. 397. A Gallic inscription, found at Paris, dates from the fourth century (*Bull. de la Soc. de l'Hist. de Paris*, March and April, 1877, p. 36). Another is to be seen on a vase of the third or fourth century discovered at Bourges. Cf. *Revue critique*, 1882, p. 131.

[5] . . . *Nos qui apud Celtas commoramur et in barbarum sermonem plerumque vacamus* (*Adv. Haeres. procem.* 3).

Gauls in Galatia, although Greek prevailed throughout the whole East.[1] Some Italian contemporaries of Marcus Aurelius spoke Gallic and Tuscan[2] at the very gates of Rome, Umbrian at Iguvium,[3] Greek in Southern Italy, where, except at Brundusium, no Latin inscriptions are met with. The Emperor Septimius Severus was understood to be more fluent in the language of Hannibal

BAS-RELIEF FROM PERGAMUS; FRAGMENT OF THE GIGANTOMACHIA, REPRESENTING ZEUS.[4]

than in that of Scipio. The stepson of Apuleius, though born of a high family, knew but a very few Latin or Greek words; his maternal language was Carthaginian.[5] Two centuries later, in the diocese of Saint Augustine, the greater part of the country people knew no other speech; and it was still true in the time of Procopius of the Moors who lived near the Pillars of Hercules. Also in Algeria there have been discovered numerous Latin inscrip-

[1] *Comm. in Epist. ad Gal.* iii. The reasons which are given for doubting the evidence of Saint Jerome do not seem to me conclusive.

[2] Aulus Gellius, *Noct. Att.* xi. 7.   [3] Bréal, *Les Tables eugubines.*

[4] Berlin Museum. See in Vol. **V.** p. 36, another fragment called the Group of Athena.

[5] Apuleius in the *Apologia.*

tions containing Carthaginian names,[1] and there are constantly
found in Tunis Punic inscriptions of the Roman period.

Among the Emperor's secretaries we know that one was
required for the Arabic language; may we not infer from this
that there was one for each of the principal languages, since all
the subjects of the Empire had the right of appeal and of petition to the Emperor, and since agreements were valid written in
any language?

Another difference existed between the two great divisions of
the Empire: the right of coinage, withdrawn from the Latin countries, was for a long while preserved in the Oriental provinces, —
a measure which is explained by the greater activity of Asiatic
commerce and by the privileges of municipal autonomy granted
to a large number of transmarine cities. Rome, which had carried
her language and her institutions into Gaul, Spain, and Africa,
naturally carried thither also her monetary system, while the
East preserved its own, together with its language, its manners,
and its manufacturing industry.

Greece, which did nothing great in politics outside her own
territory, — nothing, at least, of a lasting nature, — has had in
matters of intellect an inexhaustible fecundity, and in philosophy
and eloquence a proselyting ardor which belongs ordinarily only
to religious beliefs. Without organization, and by the simple force
of its genius, this race was spread over Western Asia, where it
had occupied and penetrated everything. In its presence the
ancient civilizations had been effaced or transformed; the national
languages had disappeared, or existed only in the lower strata of
the population. Hellenic life had everywhere taken possession of
men and of cities.

The Greeks, above all things a rhetorical people, wished per-
petually to talk, to argue, and to teach. Wherever they came
they at once organized a place of discussion, a school, and they
allured the population to their disputes. Then men took sides
violently for rhetoric or grammar, for Zeno or Epicurus, and from
each city of Asia proceeded new masters. On the banks of the
Nile, old Egypt, affrighted, had escaped from Alexandria into the

---

[1] L. Renier, *Mél. d'Épigr.* 255–285; *Digest,* XLV. i. 1, sect. 6; and *Inst.* iii. 15
[sect. 1.

Thebaïs, whither a new enemy was soon to come to trouble her with a new creed; and even at the foot of Atlas, the palaces which took the place of Masinissa's royal tent had resounded with the names of Aristotle and Plato. All the Asiatic courts strove to speak Greek; the Parthian kings had some of the plays of Euripides acted in their presence, and India attempted to decipher those medals covered with Greek characters which she restores to us to-day, thus helping us to recover the lost history of a Greek state which flourished twenty centuries ago on the banks of her great river.

These active masters always found eager listeners. At Olbia the Scythians were in the vicinity, the war-standard planted on the towers; but Dion Chrysostom arrives, he speaks of Homer and Phocylides. All stop to listen; and then, to hear better, they lead the orator to the agora and listen to a long discourse on the city of the gods. Much flattered by the attention paid him amid circumstances so distracting, Dion adds: "So truly Greek were they in their tastes and manners."[1] Every rhetorician was then welcome, every discovery excited enthusiasm; and when these Greeks came into a country which had had its days of scientific culture, among a people whom without humiliation they could acknowledge as their elders (as Plato took pleasure in saying to the priests of Egypt), they immediately sought to make these unexplored treasures their own.

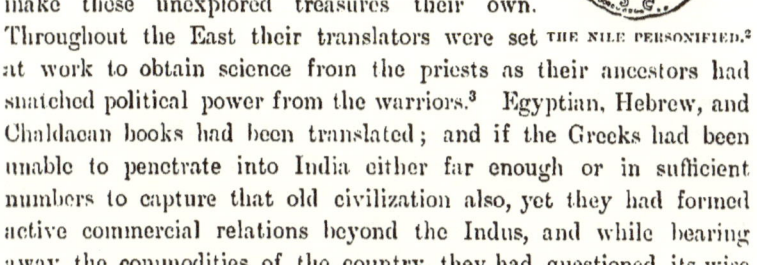

THE NILE PERSONIFIED.[2]

Throughout the East their translators were set at work to obtain science from the priests as their ancestors had snatched political power from the warriors.[3] Egyptian, Hebrew, and Chaldaean books had been translated; and if the Greeks had been unable to penetrate into India either far enough or in sufficient numbers to capture that old civilization also, yet they had formed active commercial relations beyond the Indus, and while bearing away the commodities of the country, they had questioned its wise men and carried off some of their teaching.

But the effort had already lasted long, and the Greek mind

---

[1] Dion Chrysostom, *Orat.* lxxx.   [2] Bronze of Hadrian.

[3] Strabo, xvii. 806: "They draw from the writings of the Egyptians as well as from those of the Chaldaeans."

was giving way under the mass of knowledge that it had acquired.
By being too much occupied in learning how others have thought,
a man forgets to think for himself; and as a strong political life
did not uphold the Greek mind, as its native land had become so
small and the land of its adoption so great that patriotism no
longer existed for these citizens of the world, the vigorous need of
knowing and believing, which animated men in the flourishing
days of the great schools of thought, had been replaced, in the
early days of the Empire, by the restlessness of a mind idle,
though still noisy. Strength was wanting to seek new solutions
outside the paths which the masters had opened, and there was only
a vain disquietude and a curiosity which satisfied with puerile
subtilties. Thus, after the grand movements of the ocean are
calmed, the agitation continues for a time longer in the shallows.
It is there that they end; but it is there also that they begin
afresh. These schools, now poorly occupied, will assume greatness
again when Greek philosophy, yielding to the influence of the revolution which had united so many peoples into one family, shall
lay aside metaphysics in order to undertake the moral education
of the world.

The more recent peoples of the West had neither fallen so low
nor risen so high. They had not obtained, when Rome made their
conquest, the luxuries of life; they lacked even its necessaries.[1]
They had everything to learn, and from Rome they asked everything, — laws, manners, language, both good and evil. Therefore
Rome put upon them her stamp, and twenty centuries have not
yet effaced it. Since the battle of Actium the Roman world had
leaned towards the West, the face of which had been renewed;
henceforth it was to turn towards the East. A time was to
come when this Empire will have but one language, that of
Athens, and when Rome will be at Byzantium; but then the
Empire will be nothing else than the Byzantine Empire.

---

[1] Cicero wrote to his brother, the governor of Pergamaean Asia, some years before Actium:
*Quod si te sors aut Afris, aut Hispanis, aut Gallis praefecisset immanibus ac barbaris na-
nibus (Ad Quint. i. 1, 6).* Juvenal still makes the same difference. After having raised the
laugh against the effeminate Rhodian, the perfumed Corinthian, and the hairless youth, — a race
engaged in polishing their legs, — he advises the insolent nobles who would have to govern
the western provinces to exercise prudence with such impatient subjects: *Horrida vitanda est
Hispania, Gallicus axis . . . Illyricum latus,* etc. (*Sat.* viii. 115.)

There is no need a third time to explain the provincial administration, which from Augustus to Diocletian remained the same in its general features.[1] With the exception of the creation of new governments and an interchange of provinces between the Emperor and the Senate, the principal change made was in the matter of the *procuratores*. At first mere financial agents charged with the levying of the tribute in the imperial provinces, they obtained from Claudius a jurisdiction over fiscal matters,[2] and finally possessed, under the higher authority of the military chief of the district, the administration of part of a province *cum jure gladii*.[3] Such were the procurators of Rhaetia, Thrace, and Judaea. As regards the *consulares* of Hadrian, the *juridici* of Marcus Aurelius, and the *curatores* of the Antonines, they belong to a new order of things which began then, resulting finally in Constantine's great reform. The time is not come for considering this; and we may say that since the reign of Augustus the government of the provinces had undergone no very important modifications.

We simply recall the fact that in certain circumstances extraordinary commissioners were sent to correct abuses,[4] and that great military commands were given from time to time to a prince of the imperial house or a famous general, as had been done in the case of Pompey and Caesar. The different provinces, reunited under one chief, were to furnish Diocletian with the idea of his division of the Empire into dioceses.

An unimportant change yet deserves mention here. After the Social War, the Italian soil, having become quiritarian, had ceased paying the land-tax. Some provincial cities obtained from the Emperors leave for their territory to be assimilated to the Italian land. This privilege was known as the *jus Italicum*.

---

[1] For the provincial organization under the Republic, see Vol. II. pp. 227 *et seq.;* under Augustus, Vol. IV. cap. lxvii. ; and in this volume the chapter on *The City.*
[2] See Vol. IV. p. 528.   [3] Orelli, Nos. 3,664, 3,888.
[4] Pliny, *Epist.* viii. 24; Philost., *Life of Herodes Atticus*, sect. 3.

The powers of the governor (*praeses*)[1] continue the same as in
the past. He has both civil and criminal jurisdiction, with the
exceptions which we have mentioned; the supreme authority in
the whole extent of his government, which he is required to maintain in peace and quietness.[2] His authority, as had been that of
the Senate over Italy, was not limited to the repression of crimes,
but had something of the moral jurisdiction of the censors. " The
governor," says Ulpian,[3] "ought to take care that no one make
an unjust gain or suffer an undeserved hurt." — a very vague
formula, which would permit any sort of interference. — " to prevent
the unjust seizures of property, sales compelled by fear, or pretended
sales which are not completed by an actual money payment." But
here is something new : " It is a sacred duty for him not to allow
the powerful to do wrong to the humble, nor, under pretence of
the arrival of functionaries or soldiers, to deprive the poor of their
only lantern or of their scanty furniture." This is like our
exemption of the indigent from billeting soldiers.

As to the fashion in which the governors acquitted themselves
in their functions, the writers of the imperial period show that
order being established had its necessary consequences. Doubtless not all the governors were Plinys or Agricolas, and there were
still abuses at rare intervals; but cases of extortion seldom occurred, because the peoples no longer had the resignation of older
times, now that they knew that the Emperor was interested in not
allowing any injustice to be committed, and that the Senate showed
no indulgence towards those whom the provincial delegates cited
and accused before it.

In noticing the short duration of proconsulates and legateships
we might be led to suppose that the public service would suffer
thereby; but the governors had at hand, besides their *assessores*
and counsellors, public slaves and freedmen, who, remaining per-

[1] *Praesidis nomen generale est* (*Digest*, i. 18, 1); . . . *majus imperium habet omnibus post principem* (16-1).
[2] *Digest*, i. 18, 13 pr., *Provincia pacata et quieta*. The state police was formed of soldiers taken from all the legions, and first of all kept at Rome (*frumentarii*), then sent into the provinces, where *omnia occulta explorabant* (Hist. Aug., *Hadr.* 10 ; *Macr.* 12); that of the cities was effected by municipal officers, the *irenarchs*, or justices of the peace, whom the governor selected yearly from a list of ten notables presented by the curia (Ael. Aristeides, *Sacr. Serm.*, IV. i. 523, edit. Dindorf).
[3] *De off. praes.* (*Digest*, 18, 6) : . . . *Ad religionem praesidis pertinet.*

manently in their positions, had charge of the papers and public
documents, prepared matters for settlement, and preserved the
routine. From numerous inscriptions found in a cemetery at Carthage it has become possible to draw up a long list of these
obscure and useful public servants in the proconsulate of Africa.
The head changed, but the departments remained, and affairs were
not interrupted. The inexperience of a new comer was set right
by the wisdom of his predecessors, which the subordinates of the
provincial government communicated to him, and in the carefully
preserved registers there were found for his use precedents bearing
on every question.

We shall see shortly that the departments of the central
administration had a similar organization; like those of the governors, they continued, even under an incapable chief, the accustomed
work. Thus imperial tragedies took place unnoticed by the provinces; they were revolutions of the palace, not of the Empire.

We have recently spoken of those provincial assemblies whither
the deputies of the cities came to declare their union with Rome.
An inscription of the year 238 shows the interested consideration
which the governors still manifested later than the Antonines
towards the influential members of these assemblies. "At the
time when I was imperial legate of the province of Lyons, I knew
many distinguished men in that city, among whom was Sennius
Sollemnis, one of the Viducasses, who had been appointed priest
of the altar of Rome and Augustus. . . . A particular reason
secured him my friendship. Some members of the assembly of the
Gauls, believing that they had cause to complain of Cl. Paulinus,
my predecessor, sought to enter an accusation against him in the
name of the province. Sollemnis resisted their proposal, and
declared that the people of his state, so far from directing him to
accuse the governor, had bidden him to eulogize the latter's administration. And upon this statement the assembly decided that it
would not prefer a complaint against Cl. Paulinus."

Thus, in the third century, the right of criticising the governor's conduct, and consequently of examining into his administration, was in full exercise. And documents give evidence, for the
fourth and fifth centuries, of the regular exercise of this practice.
It was accepted by the government as well as by the populations;

for in Dacia Trajan organized a *concilium prov. Daciarum trium*
which seems copied from that which Drusus had established at
Lyons under Augustus.[1] The province, with its own festivals, its
treasury (and. in the East. its royal right to coin money), its deputies
and its priests, its functionaries and its public slaves,[2] had therefore a life of its own derived from itself. and not from Rome.[3]
This might have been a source of strength for the Empire; but
the Emperors unfortunately did not know how to derive advantage
from it.

Not being made useful to the state. the provincials occupied
themselves with their own interests. By degrees they took possession of all the offices. even the highest. from the period of those
illustrious Antonines who were so great. only because they had
to second them a multitude of men sprung. like themselves, from
the free cities. By this the Empire gained energetic and able
Emperors. who appreciated the usefulness of the provincial assemblies. Trajan increased their number, and Hadrian took pleasure in
consulting them. But they seem to have been forgotten in the midst
of the troubles of the third century. and when in the following age
there was a wish to revive them. it was too late. This chapter
leads therefore to the same conclusion as the preceding. Much
municipal life and a little provincial life have made the grandeur
of the Empire; the ruin of these institutions was to cause its
decadence.

The prosperity of the provinces. manifested by the progressive
elevation of the aristocracy of the cities. is further proved by the
innumerable public buildings with which the cities covered the

---

[1] *C. I. L.* vol. iii. No. 1,454 *ad annum* 211 ; . . . *sacerdos arae Augusti* (Nos. 1,209,
1,509, 1,513) and *coronatus Daciarum trium* (No. 1,433).

[2] There were public slaves of the province, as of the city. Cf. *C. I. L.* ii. 28, 1, and
Henzen, No. 6,393.

[3] *Provincia Lugdunensis* had a *summus curator civium Romanorum* (Orelli, No. 4,020), —
another proof of the legal personality of the province. An inscription (Lebas, *Voy. archéol.*
No. 1,189) records a quarrel between two cities respecting their frontiers. The affair was
carried to the κοινὸν Θεσσαλῶν, composed of three hundred and thirty-four members, who met
periodically at Larissa. The voting took place upon oath and by ballot. To make the judgment binding, it needed the confirmation of the Roman governor. It has been concluded
hence that " the Roman administration shut up within very narrow limits the liberty of these
so-called autonomous communities and of their national assemblies." On the contrary, this
matter proves the extent of the powers of the assembly, which is judge in the first instance of
a question that in France the *Corps législatif* only could decide by a law. The right of fixing
the limits of municipal territory is of the very essence of sovereign power.

Empire, implying an amount of wealth never met with again until in our own days. This general condition of prosperity was the result of bringing into culture immense territories and of a commerce which carried everywhere the products of the soil, of industry, and of art. Let us also take note of three things. First, the nobility of those days had not the prejudices of our old military families. Dion Chrysostom shows us his grandfather, his father, and himself returning to business after having ruined themselves in the service of their city, and recovering their fortune previously lost in public life.[1] There were therefore in this social state fewer idlers than is believed. Next, very strict regulations respecting weights and measures and the permanence of the imperial coinage[2] gave a security to commerce which it had never known, and which it no longer knew in the third century, when, after the Antonines, the monetary system of the Empire became nothing else than "a permanent bankruptcy." Lastly, the military roads laid out by the Romans from one end to the other of their provinces, and the lesser roads connected with them, brought about the revolution which railways have effected in modern times. On the territory of ancient Gaul have been counted 22,000 kilomètres (13,200 English miles) of Gallo-Roman roads, and by no means all are identified.

The world was opened; the most secluded places had become accessible; all things circulated without let or hindrance. It was

---

[1] *Orat.* xlvi.

[2] Silver had been in all classical antiquity the dominant metal. The Empire retained it as such concurrently with gold, and thus had a bi-metallic standard. But in consequence of the alterations in weights and alloyage which silver money incurred, — to the extent that in the time of Severus these coins, containing from 50 to 60 per cent of alloy, became simply debased metal, — silver assumed more and more the nature of token money, and gold remained the sole standard. In the year 16 Augustus divided the Roman gold pound into 42 aurei (= 327.43 grs. = $214.30 of American money; whence we determine the intrinsic value of the aureus of Augustus, in pure gold = $5.10). Under Marcus Aurelius the pound equalled 45 aurei, which reduced the metallic value of the aureus to $4.76, *i. e.*, the small decrease of thirty-four cents in nearly two centuries; but these coins, always containing .96 of fine gold, and keeping their official value, continued to be received everywhere with confidence. Hidden treasures which have been discovered — one alone, that of Brescello, consisting of 80,000 aurei — attest the enormous circulation of gold coinage which took place at that period (Mommsen, *Hist. de la monn. rom.*, translated by the Duc de Blacas, vol. iii. *passim*). Gold is the coin of rich countries, and the Empire was rich. Requiring much gold for its innumerable exchanges, it drained all the neighboring countries of this metal, — as in our days America, whose monetary needs grow even more rapidly than its population, its commerce, and its agriculture, attracts the gold of the Old World.

free-trade, with its advantageous results in abundance and low prices.[1] All the produce of the world came into Rome by the Tiber, which Pliny calls *rerum in toto orbe nascentium mercator placidissimus.* The women of the Bernese Oberland bought their ornaments of a jeweller of Asia Minor,[2] as we now obtain from Smyrna or Caramania our best carpets. Merchants from Carthage and Arabia came to end their days at Lyons; Greeks, a Thracian

TOMBSTONE OF A CITIZEN OF PUTEOLI.[3]

woman, a citizen of Nicomedeia, found burial at Bordeaux;[4] Nabathaeans at Puteoli; a Puteolan at Rusicada, etc.: a certain Phrygian makes his boast of having rounded Cape Malea seventy-two times on his way to Brundusium or the Asiatic coast.[5] "Thanks to the festal peace which we are enjoying," exclaims Pliny, "an immense crowd of navigators traverse all the seas, even the Western Ocean, and find hospitality on all the coasts."[6] Merchants found it even on

---

[1] The colleges of the Early Empire (see p. 94 *et seq.*) differ from our trade-guilds in an essential point. they did not form privileged bodies, except certain societies established in the public interest.

[2] Mommsen, *Die Rom. Schweiz,* p. 24.

[3] This tombstone, found at Rusicada (Philippeville), and unfortunately broken, is only interesting from the inscription it bears: GEN(io) COL.(oniae) PVT(eolanorum) AVG(usto) SAC(rum). It is a proof of the commercial connection existing between the two maritime cities (*Musée du Louvre,* Frohner, *op. cit.* No. 173).

[4] Robert, in the *Comptes rendus de l'Acad. des inscr.,* 1872, p. 54, and Le Blant, *Inscr. chrét.* No. 225; Allmer, *Rev. épigr.* p. 180.

[5] *C. I. G.* No. 3920.

[6] . . . *pace tam festa* (ii. 15 and 67). Horace had already said: *Ter et quater anno recisus aequor Atlanticum.* We have seen that these navigators had lighthouses to guide their

the mountain heights; at the highest point of the Pass of the Great St. Bernard, between the lake and the spot where the present Hospice stands, have been discovered the ruins of a temple of Jupiter Penninus and more than thirty votal tablets in bronze. This temple had no doubt during the summer priests who gained a living from passing travellers.

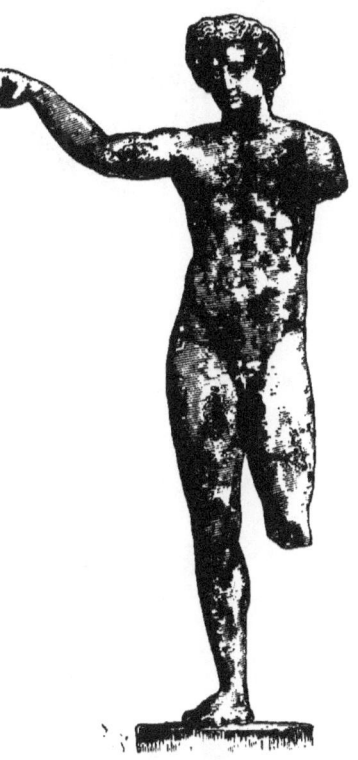

ROMAN FIGURE IN BRONZE FOUND IN POMERANIA.[4]

We have already noted the importance of this commerce in the early days of the Empire.[1] The general prosperity had increased it, but the objects of exchange were the same. It is therefore needless to retrace the sketch; we may only observe that Roman merchants had multiplied their relations beyond the frontiers. On all sides the old boundaries by land and sea were overstepped. Communications with India and Ceylon, though slower than in modern days, were as regular as they now are: the setting out and the return were fixed almost to the very day.[2] Some Italian merchants had trading-posts on the Malabar coast,[3] and used to sell their wines at Barygaza, at the head of the Gulf of Cambay; by way of the Indus they penetrated into Bactriana; by the Persian Gulf to the mouths

course, like those of Alexandria and Boulogne (above, Vol. IV. p. 509; Vol. V. p. 381), or sea-marks like the " towers of Hannibal " on the African and Spanish shores, and on the coast of Asia constructions from whose top the sea could be overlooked to a great distance and where on the approach of pirates could be lighted *praenuntiatiri ignes* (Pliny, *Hist. nat.* ii. 73). Strabo speaks also of lofty towers on all the coasts to observe the arrival of the tunny fish.

[1] Vol. IV. pp. 213-232.   [2] Pliny, *Hist. nat.* vi. 26.

[3] Many Roman coins have been found on the banks of a river in Malabar. Cf. Reinaud. memoir on the *Périple de la mer érythrée* and on the *Relations de l'empire commin avec l'Asie orientale.*   [4] *Archaeol. Zeitung,* 35th year, pl. 10.

of the Tigris; and from all these countries there came many times ambassadors to the Emperors of Rome. According to Seneca, ships even went from Spain to the Indies by rounding Africa.[1]

ROYAL DIADEM IN GOLD FOUND IN THE CIMMERIAN BOSPHORUS.[2]

On land caravans went as far as the centre of Ethiopia and the African oases,[3] which our merchants have so much difficulty in reaching; and in the north they penetrated to the farthest parts of Denmark. In the Island of Fünen, to the east of Jutland,

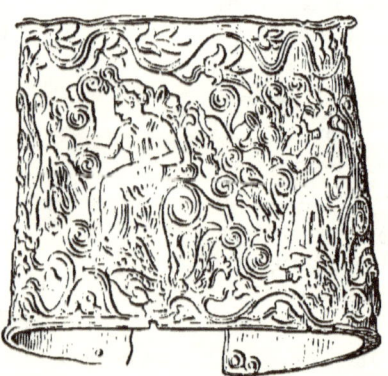

DIADEM OF A KING OF THE BOSPHORUS.[4]

and in the neighborhood of Königsberg have been found coins of the Antonine period with arms and utensils of Roman make. The kingdom of the Bosphorus was rich and flourishing;[5] at Dioscurias, at the eastern extremity of the Euxine, so many

[1] Quaest. nat. praef.   [2] Museum of St. Petersburg.
[3] Pliny, Hist. nat. vi. 34. Cf. D'Avezac, Afrique ancienne, pp. 33 and 58. The Roman Maternus seems to have reached the Soudan (Ptolemaeus, Geogr. i. 8).
[4] Museum of St. Petersburg.   [5] Vol. III. pp. 49, 120, 148.

Barbaric nations came to buy and sell that a hundred and thirty interpreters were required there.[1] We cannot say that Roman or Greek merchants had not at this period traffic with China ; and cities now inaccessible or entirely destroyed, as Petra,[2] Baalbec, Palmyra, "the ports of the desert," were crowded with a busy population exchanging the commodities of the Empire for those of

REPRESENTATION OF A SHIP SERVING AS A CUP.[3]

Babylonia and Parthia. "Every year," says Pliny, "we send to India fifty million sesterces in exchange for merchandise which is sold in the Empire at 100 per cent profit."[4] Prices rose to such a height because there were many purchasers seeking for the goods and an abundance of money to pay for them.

Yet the old harsh formula that the stranger is an enemy had not been forgotten. To sell iron, corn, or salt to the Barbarians

[1] Pliny, *Hist. nat.* vi. 5.

[2] Petra was not yet united to the Empire in Strabo's time, and still a large number of Roman merchants were found there (Strabo, xvi. 779). In the Arabian peninsula have been found traces of the working of gold mines, and Sprenger, in his *Géographie ancienne de l'Arabie*, believes that these operations were very considerable.

[3] Piranesi, *Vasi*, ii.

[4] Pliny, *Hist. nat.* vi. 26 : . . . *Quae apud nos centuplicato veneant.* In this passage Pliny speaks only of the commerce with India, the principal objects of which the *Digest* (xxxix. 4, 16, sect. 7), in a curious enumeration, makes known to us. The Romans also left much money with the Arabs, styled by the Romans "the richest people in the world," because the treasures of the Parthians and Romans came into their hands. "They sell the produce of their seas (pearls) and of their forests (odoriferous woods and incense), and buy nothing " (*Ibid.* 32).

was a capital crime, and the law sanctioned piracy towards peoples
who had no bond of amity or alliance or contract of hospitality
with Rome. On the seas and rivers of the Empire the government
kept armed fleets[1] to make traffic secure; the merchants were
also protected against barratry by laws borrowed from the experience of the Rhodians,[2] which decided questions of responsibility
in accidents by sea. Those who brought about a shipwreck, pil-

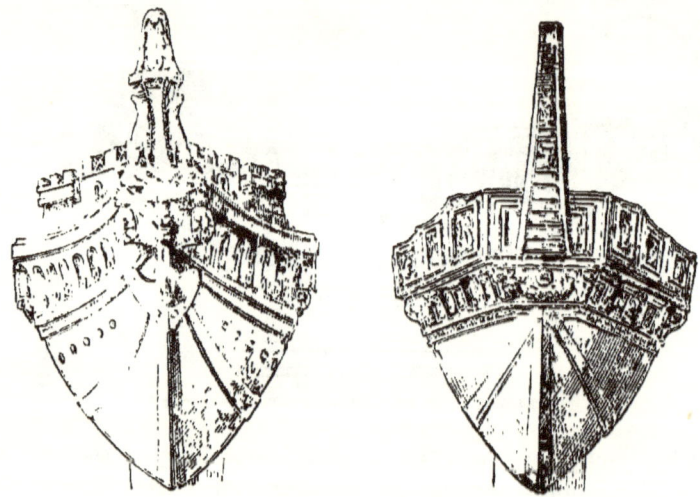

PARTS OF A VESSEL.[3]

laged a stranded vessel, or plundered the shipwrecked, were subjected to the penalties declared by the Cornelian law against
assassins.

Before landing, the merchandise must pass the custom-house,
which was very strict. If the shipowner had put on board any
contraband article, the vessel itself was confiscated; if the lading
had taken place in his absence by the act of the captain or a sailor,
the offender incurred the penalty of death and the merchandise
was detained, but the vessel was restored to the owner.[4]

The cargo being cleared, the merchant sold his goods at auction.

[1] *Digest*, xxxix. 4, 11, sect. 2; xlix. 15. 5. sect. 2. *Cæsar . . . lusoriis navibus discurrere
flumen ultro citroque milites ordinavit* (Amm. Marcell., xvii. 2, and xviii. 2).
[2] *Digest*, xiv. 2.   [3] *Piranesi, ibid.*
[4] *Digest.* xlvii. 9. 3. sect. 8 ; xxxix. 4. 11, sect. 2.

—an ancient practice which is attested by the first agreement be-tween Rome and Carthage and by the tablets of the banker Jucun-dus, found at Pompeii, existing throughout the whole Empire, where the words *vendere* and *venum dare* were synonymous.[1]

In order to insure honest dealing, standard weights and meas-ures were kept in the Capitol and in the cities; and frequently a decree of the municipal senate ordered the duumvirs or the aediles to make an unannounced inspection of the measures used by the merchants. Finally, banks of deposit, of payment, and of loan, kept by *argentarii*, facilitated business transactions,[2] and bills posted in the streets gave notice to passers-by of financial matters they were interested in knowing.

In this connection we may observe that, considered from an elevated point of view, commerce has at all times been one of the most powerful factors in the work of civilization. Not only does it interchange ideas as well as commodities, but it introduces into legislation, much more than do philosophies and religions, those notions of equity which modify the teaching of the jurists. In the past ages of humanity priests and philosophers have estab-lished tenets thought out *à priori* and almost always exclusive in their character, while commerce — taken in the widest sense of the word, as being the relations between men of different states and races — has furnished those facts of experience which have loosed the straitened bond of systems. Interested, for example, in causing good faith to prevail in contracts, it gave to social relations rules

---

[1] Cf. De Petra, *Le Tavolette cerate di Pompei*, and Caillemer, *Revue hist. de droit*, July, 1877. In vol. ii. of the *C. I. L.* No. 2,029, mention is made of an imperial procurator charged with collecting the *vectigal auctionum*, or duty on sales by auction. We have given in Vol. V. p. 174, a fac-simile of the tablets of Jucundus.

[2] Amm. Marcell., xxvii. 9, and Cod. Theod. xii. 6, 19, and 21; Orelli, Nos. 4,342–4,350; *Digest*, xvi. 3, 8. M. Perrot, in his paper on *Le commerce de l'argent à Athènes*, has shown to what an extent banking business was carried in the Greek cities. Three or four hundred years before the Christian era there were at Athens joint-stock companies and investors of funds receiving dividends. The bankers made advances on the deposit of title-deeds and articles of value; they had their account-books, wherein were entered receipts and withdrawals of funds, their agencies, and if not the bill of exchange, at least the cheque. Without possess-ing an official character, the bankers were the depositaries of documents and contracts which in modern times government officials receive. They made loans to the cities, and guaranteed in some form state loans. Roman legislation subjected the cession of incorporeal rights to numerous formalities; Athenian legislation, being much simpler, was probably in full force in the whole Greek world. [Cf. the chapter on the Business Habits of the Greeks in my *Social Life in Greece*. — ED.]

more and more rational and just, which from the practice of business men necessarily passed into the teaching of the jurisconsults. In
our days, what is it that has opened the gates of Japan and China,
and is to carry civilization into Africa? What on that continent
will destroy slave-hunting, the state of perpetual war, and all the
violent deeds and abominations which the slave-trade calls forth?
Commerce,[1] which has been successful many a time where preaching
had failed.

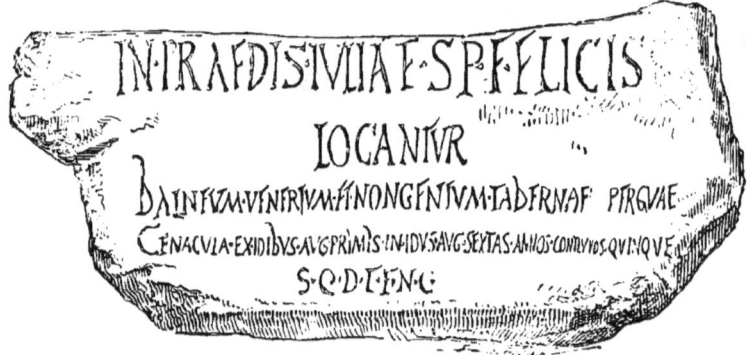

BILL POSTED IN POMPEII.[2]

The wealth of a people can be measured by the number of travellers it sends out. The travellers of that day were as numerous
as ours — perhaps even more numerous than ours — of fifty years
ago. Taste, as well as necessity, led men to undertake journeys.
" A quiet, tranquil life," says a poet of the first century, " in a
man's own home has no longer any charm. There is a love of
visiting new cities, of sailing on unknown seas, of becoming a

---

[1] At a congress of Orientalists (September, 1875) a successful Lyonese merchant, M. L.
Desgrand, said: " With us the man of business knows that his contract, properly understood,
enjoins on him honesty. In Asia the native acts towards the European as if he were convinced
that cleverness in cheating makes it legitimate. . . . Accordingly, the European banks have
been compelled to consider the signature of a native as absolutely worthless . . . it is requisite
that drafts should be indorsed by a European to make their negotiation possible. Let commerce develop, and it is certain that the Asiatic will change his way of looking at things, and
his civil life."

[2] Translation : " In the inheritance of Julia Felix, daughter of Spurius Felix, is offered to
let, from the first to the sixth of the Ides of August, for a term of five years, a bath called
Venus's [ET NONGENIUM?], some shops, stalls, and upper rooms. They will not be let
to any one exercising an infamous profession." For the explanation of certain difficult expressions in this inscription, see C. I. L. iv. 66, ad n. 1,136.

citizen of the world."[1] Accordingly, if Seneca is to be believed, one half the inhabitants of Rome, of the free cities, and of the colonies were only strangers led far away from the land of their birth by some voyage of business or pleasure.[2] How well does the Emperor Hadrian, the unwearied traveller, serve as the representative of his contemporaries!

The public post, instituted by Augustus and reorganized by Hadrian, always at the expense of the municipalities whose territory it traversed, could be employed only by government agents and those — a very limited number — who by special favor obtained from the Emperor the privilege of using it. But private enterprise came to the aid of ordinary travellers, and sought its profit from their tastes and wants by furnishing the means of satisfying them. Thus before his departure a man could seek on maps, in itineraries and guide-books,[3] all the necessary information. At the gates of the principal cities he found the carriages and horses of the *retturini;* on the route, relays, lodging-houses, *mansiones,* and inns, where the proprietor was held responsible for injuries suffered by travellers while in his house. An inn at Lyons bore this inscription: "Here Mercury promises profit, Apollo health, Septumanus good bed and board. He who will stop here will find himself well off. Traveller, take heed where you stay!"[4]

It was a time when all the world was in motion, — the trader hastening to his market, the centurion to his cohort, the administrator[5]

---

[1] Manilius, *Astr.* iv. 509–13. The *Acta* of the martyrs of Lyons show how many foreigners, even Asiatics, there were in that city, and the travels of Saint Paul, of the apostles, and of other Christian believers, establishing continued relations between the churches, prove with what facility the longest expeditions were undertaken.

[2] *Ad Helv.* 6. He goes so far as to say, with his usual exaggeration, that in Corsica, notwithstanding the savage condition of that island, there were more foreigners than natives.

[3] See in Vol. IV. p. 162, one of the vases or silver goblets found in the baths of Vicarello, on Lake Bracciano, in 1852. The Itinerary from Bordeaux to Jerusalem is a real guide-book, with geographical and historical information.

[4] *Colleg. jumentariorum.* Cf. Henzen's *Index; Inst.* iv. 5, 3: Orelli, No. 4,329.

[5] In a multitude of inscriptions the *cursus honorum* of the functionaries shows how frequently they changed their residence. There were centurions who in their military career had made the tour of the Empire two or three times; and similarly as regards the imperial legates. Thus a citizen of Laodicea in Syria serves as a soldier, then as centurion in the *Xa Gemina,* cantoned at Vindobona (Upper Pannonia); in the *IVa Flavia* (Upper Moesia), *XIIa Fulminata* (Cappadocia), *IIIa Cyrenaica* (Arabia), *Xa Fretensis* (Judaea), *IIa Adjutrix* (Upper Pannonia), and *Va Macedonica,* at Troesmis, where he died (L. Renier, *Inscr. de Troesmis,* p. 36).

to his duties, the invalid to the healing waters[1] and the altars
of the helpful divinities, the superstitious to renowned shrines[2]
and famous oracles, the idler to festivals and solemnities, and the
man of taste to places consecrated to history or art, to the archi
tectural splendors of Rome, Greece, and Egypt, where he wrote
his name on the Pyramids or the statue of Memnon. Every year
the sun or the malaria drove the rich from scorching cities and
the pestilential plain to the shady mountains with their murmuring
waters, or to villas built out into the waves of a peaceful bay.

Others travelled more economically, — the student on his way to
the great schools of Autun, Milan, Carthage, Tarsus, and Antioch,
or those of Rome and Athens, Berytus and Alexandria, which
eclipsed all the rest ; the professor and the physician in quest of
scholars or patients; the sage, the philosopher, and the scholar
seeking knowledge in the schools or in the revelations of the
mysteries;[3] the artist seeking wealth and renown; the charlatan
who explained dreams or exhibited curiosities; begging priests who
carried their guardian divinity about the villages and stretched
out the beggar's hand to the devout.

In their travels the ancients were brought face to face with
a nature as it were impregnated with divinity, and at every step
they came upon places full of mythological traditions which, without putting much faith in them, they yet loved to recall. The
grand phenomena of nature, which to us are the results of general
laws, were still for the majority of travellers acts of the divine
will. They excited admiration, combined with a sort of religious
terror; and those pantheistic beliefs which kept their ground in
spite of the increasing scepticism, those legends constantly revived
by their poets, sent numbers of tourists through the pacified prov-

---

[1] Inscriptions and authors tend to show that almost all the waters to which physicians
now send us were in those days known and utilized. A residence in Egypt was already in
vogue as a remedy for lung complaints (Pliny, *Epist.* v. 16), and milk-cures in the mountains,
and even a stay in pine-forests. (See Friedländer, ii. 1-15.) Galen sent cases of phthisis, as
we do, into warm, moist climates, with even temperature. — as, for instance, the Mediterranean
sea-coast.

[2] See the *Syrian Goddess* of Lucian.

[3] We have the accounts of many journeys made by Diodorus, Strabo, and Pausanias for
history and geography; by Dioscorides and Galen for botany and medicine; by Apuleius to
become initiated in the mysteries; by Apollonius of Tyana, the philosophers and rhetoricians
whose wandering life Lucian and Philostratus describe to us, etc. The *Digest* (xxvii. 1. 6, sect. 1)
speaks of grammarians, sophists, rhetoricians, and physicians as wanderers (*circulatores*).

inces.   They had not our modern enthusiasm for " pleasing horrors,"
but all their literature shows how much they loved sweet, smiling
Nature, the charming scenery of the sub-Apennine hills, the cool
valleys, the forest full of shadow and silence, and the wide horizons
of the sea.

Men still travelled for the gratification of the eye ; some went
even in search of the grand spectacles unfolded by Nature.   How
many, following the track of Hadrian, climbed Mount Aetna [1] and
Mount Casius, as we ascend the Righi to see a sunrise !   How
many others imitated Sabinus, that friend of Lucian [2] who went to
the very verge of the western provinces to hear the " hissing of the
sun when it plunges into the waves," [3] or, which was easier, to
contemplate the mighty waves of the Atlantic tides !   The bore of
the Seine and the *mascaret* of the Gironde must have greatly astonished these dwellers on the shore of a tideless sea.   The extensive
remains of a Roman villa have been recently discovered in the
Isle of Wight,[4] where the nobility of England at the present day
still seek out the charming situations which the contemporaries of
Hadrian or Severus loved.

Those who wished to travel fast made from fifteen to twenty
leagues a day ; much more when the Emperor permitted the use
of the public post.   Thus it was possible to go from Antioch to
Byzantium (nearly seven hundred miles) in less than six days,[5]
which gives a speed continued day and night of nearly five miles
an hour ; and more, if time for stoppages is allowed.[6]

By sea with a favorable wind the journey from Ostia to Fréjus
took three days ; to Cadiz seven ; to Carthage two.   It took six or
seven days from the Straits of Messina to reach Alexandria.[7]   But

[1] The tower on Etna called the Philosopher's Tower seems to be a Roman ruin.
[2] *Apologia*, 15.
[3] Juvenal, *Sat.* xiv. 278.
[4] At Morton Farm, near Brading (see plate).   Some coins of Victorinus (268) were found there.
[5] Friedländer, ii. 9.
[6] Tiberius travelled 74 leagues in 24 hours (Pliny, *Hist. nat.* vii. 20), and Caesar often 100 miles (37 leagues) a day (Suet., *Caes.* 57).
[7] Pliny, *Hist. nat.* xix. 1 ; Vegetius, v. 9.   There are many instances of a speed of from six to eight knots per hour; this is the average of our sailing vessels.   Suidas (s. v. *vaῦs*) assigns to the largest merchantmen 197 feet of length by 49 of breadth, which gives a measurement of about 1,500 tons.   [It should be remembered that in calm weather, when our sailing vessels lie idle, the ancients had slaves to row, and so exceeded our sailing speed.—ED.]

from November 11th to the 5th of March navigation was suspended, and all vessels were drawn up on shore, unless the Emperor was in haste to send an order to a province across the sea or a prisoner to his place of banishment.[1]

The customs officers were then detested, as they are now. "We are angry with them," says Plutarch, "for rummaging our baggage to make sure that we have no merchandise concealed in it; and yet the law prescribes this. If they did not do it, they would be held responsible."[2]

Notwithstanding the organization of municipal police and of the military precautions taken from time to time by the Emperors, and of the severity shown to bandits, there was reason to fear, especially in mountainous districts, highway robbers.[3] It was an endemic evil in the Taurus, in Corsica and Sardinia, even in Italy. The dangerous parts of the peninsula were the same then as now; the Pontine Marshes, the Gallinarian forest on the Campanian coast, and lower Italy. As is still the case, some of these bandits were famous for their exploits, their stratagems, and their generosity. A story which Dion relates resembles that of the legendary Frà Diavolo.

Severus was a strict disciplinarian; yet in his reign a bandit, Bullas by name, for two years ravaged Italy at the head of a band of six hundred men, notwithstanding the presence of the Emperor and of so many soldiers.[4] This brigand knew what important personages were on the road from Brundusium to Rome; he fell upon them unexpectedly, and released them for a ransom. If he found in their company any skilful workman, he detained him, made the most of his knowledge, then sent him back after having paid him more liberally than a Roman senator would have done.

[1] Thus Cicero and Ovid when exiled were obliged to set out in the winter. On the suspension of navigation in winter, see Vol. III. p. 470, note 2.

[2] Plutarch, De Curiositate, 71.

[3] In dangerous regions there were permanent posts. In 1865 was found on the bank of the Oued-el-Kantarah, where two roads intersect, the following inscription: Burgum commodianum speculatorium inter duas vias ad salutem commeantium (Annuaire de la Soc. arch. de Constantine, 1866, p. 22). Another post kept guard over the valley of the Adige at the point where a great part of the commerce between Germany and Italy passed. A number of small forts erected along the Danube stopped the smugglers, as those of the Atlas checked the nomads, and similar forts were established on all the frontiers.

[4] Dion, lxxvi. 10.

To save the lives of his comrades he risked his own. Two of his band had been taken and condemned to the wild beasts ; representing himself to be the governor of the country, he appeared at the prison-gate and effected the release of the condemned. On another occasion he went to the centurion in command of an expedition sent against the band and offered to deliver Bullas up to him. The officer went with him ; and being caught in the snare, found himself before a tribunal at which the bandit presided. The latter merely condemned him to have his head shaved, and then sent him back to Caesar with these words : " Go and tell your master : Feed your slaves, that they may no longer rob you." This bravado of Bullas cost him his life ; for Severus, enraged, after so many victories, at being mocked by a bandit, directed more forces against him, and especially a cleverer man, who in his turn entrapped the robber. The inevitable woman of the dramatic narrative was not wanting here. Bullas, betrayed and given up by a Delilah of low degree, was taken while asleep. Papinianus asked him : " Why are you a robber?" He replied : " Why are you a prefect?" This insolent retort did not save him from the arena, where, although Dion does not state it, we may believe that he bravely encountered the Alpine bear and the African lion.

"Robbery," says the same writer in another place, " is in human nature, and robbers there will always be." In perverse human nature, we may say ; but unfortunately such natures always exist. The Empire had therefore its share of them, and every year some merchant was held for ransom, some traveller carried off and sold as a slave.[1] But the general progress was not stayed. These were isolated incidents, to which the state and the cities gave no more attention than is given in free America to that which affects only the individual.

There are nations of which we rightly take no account, and periods which might have been omitted from history and humanity would have lost nothing thereby. But suppose for a moment that the Roman Empire had not existed : what a void in the world! Outside its frontiers the Barbaric world is torn by sterile convulsions, or the peoples vegetate in a miserable existence. In the

[1] Among the causes of legitimate hindrance from being at a certain place at a fixed time, Septimius Severus admitted the *incursus latronum* (*Digest*, xxvii. 1, 13, sect. 7).

Roman provinces, on the contrary, there are just laws and order, and what a contemporary of Marcus Aurelius was near calling "all necessary liberties;" there are labor and property, and a security which, although still insufficient, was such as the world had never yet known; and, lastly, there was no envy or hate between the different classes,—all things which singularly increased the happiness of existence.

RUINS OF THE GREAT AQUEDUCT OF MERIDA (EMERITA AUGUSTA).[1]

If with the picture which we have just sketched be contrasted that which represented the state of the provinces after the battle of Actium, we shall recognize the extent of the progress actually made. Better still, let us consider the ruins left by these peoples; let us go, for example, to the banks of the Guadiana, and in imagination reconstruct the ancient Emerita Augusta, colonized with veterans by Augustus. Observe its wall, fifteen miles in length, its theatre, its naumachia, its temples to Mars and Diana, its main

[1] Delaborde, *Voyage en Espagne.*

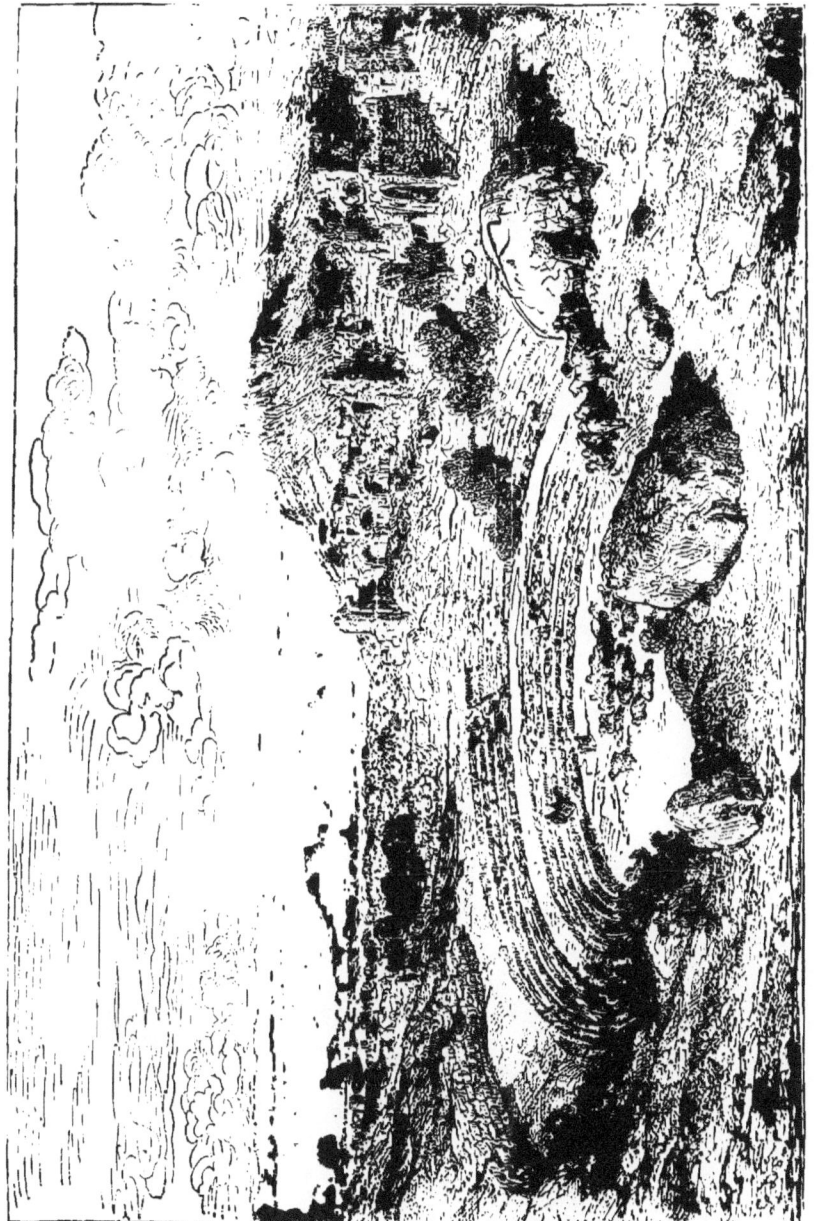

RUINS OF THE THEATRE OF EMERITA AUGUSTA (MERIDA).

street, having at each end a triumphal arch covered with white marble and having richly sculptured friezes. Two aqueducts, whose gigantic ruins by their imposing grandeur bring out in bolder relief the wretchedness of the modern city, brought pure water from the mountains. A great population went back and forth over its two bridges, one of which, wholly of granite and supported by sixty arches, is twenty-eight hundred feet long, and the other is still covered with the stout flagstones which the Romans laid down. An inscription found in the ruins of the theatre seems to say that the great Agrippa had a share in these gigantic works. In the neighborhood of Emerita were some hot-springs magnificently fitted up by a mother out of gratitude for the health of her daughter, which had been restored by them. The spring flows yet, as abundant and health-restoring as ever; but the Romans are no longer there, and it is almost lost in a swamp.

Elsewhere in the province imposing ruins such as the triumphal arch of Caparra, which now stands in a wilderness, the remains of a temple at Talavera la Vieja, or the bridge of Alcantara, show that flourishing cities, whose very names are lost, stood where now are only poor villages or miserable *posadas*.

Let us pass to the other extremity of the Empire. We will not speak of Palmyra, or of Baalbec, or of the dead cities, once so active, which dot the route from Damascus to Petra, in the province of Arabia. Let us stand on the arid plateau of Asia Minor, near the source of the Rhyndacus, and observe the immense ruins,—a theatre, a race-course, tombs, two marble bridges, three temples, one of which has colossal foundations, and another, of the Ionic order, is the most beautiful which has been found in the Asiatic peninsula. Upon these ruins may be read fragments of imperial letters and this sentence of a governor of the province : "The

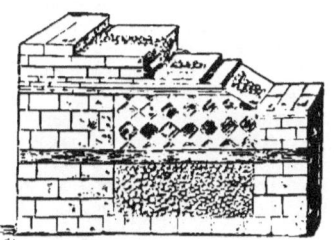

SPECIMEN OF OPUS RETICULATUM.

Emperor Hadrian has in his decision taken into account justice and humanity." We seek in history the name of this city, but we do not find it. Accustomed to see so many prosperous cities, Aezani did not seem to the early historians to deserve special

RUINS OF THE THEATRE OF ALZANI.[2]

admire the activity which she knew how to stimulate in those places where for many centuries nothing but silence has reigned.

Macaulay observes that the English not having seen, since

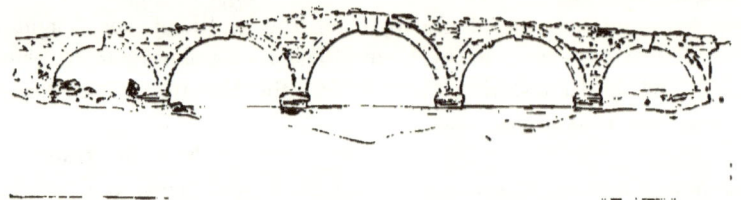

ANCIENT BRIDGE AT AEZANI. PRESENT STATE.[3]

the Revolution of 1688, a hostile flag floating on British soil or a mob break through the gates of Whitehall or Westminster, the

[1] We find in Strabo only the name of the district. Ἀζανῖτης (xii. 8, 11), and in Stephanus of Byzantium the name of the people, s. v. Ἄζανοι. The ruins are near the Turkish village of Tchafder-Hissar. Not all the ruins left by Rome are so fine or composed of such valuable materials, as here and there are to be found remains of buildings which are not worthy of this royal people. The cities used to build according to their means, often in great haste, in order to please the Emperor's taste and cheaply, to husband the municipal resources. Plenty of mortar was used, which was not always of the best quality; the stones found at hand were buried in it, and coarse masonry was faced with the *opus reticulatum*, which presented a good appearance, but had little solidity. See De la Blanchère, *Le Port de Terracine*, in the *Mélanges d'archéol.* of the *École française de Rome*, i, 347. There existed, at least in the following centuries, corporations of lime-burners (*calcis coctores*), who were obliged to burn the lime required for public buildings (*Code Theod.* xiv. 6, 1–5).

[2] Lebas and Waddington, *Voy. archéol.*

[3] Lebas and Waddington, *ibid.*

public prosperity had in less than two centuries increased at an incalculable rate. During a longer space of time the same thing had been true of the Early Empire. Its peaceable provinces had increased a hundredfold in wealth. On the evidence of Strabo, the prosperity of Egypt, so great under the Ptolemies, was nothing compared to that which the country enjoyed under the Romans;

ANCIENT BRIDGE AT ALZANI. RESTORED.[1]

and the Gauls, whose contribution was raised, in the middle of the fourth century, to an enormous sum, were grateful to the Emperor Julian for requiring of them only twelve times as much as they had paid to Caesar.

V. — THE JEWISH AND CHRISTIAN OPPOSITION.

UNHAPPILY all the inhabitants of this immense Empire had but one common bond, — the "Roman Peace." This was an interest, it was not an idea; and a nation is created only by community of ideas. There were even provincials who uttered protests against this well-being, and threats against this prosperity. While the greatest nations were submissive under the loss of their independence, monotheism, in the two forms which it had received at Jerusalem, refused to subject the external life of its adherents to the gods of the Capitol ; and in spite of their small number, its believers armed themselves against Rome with the sword to fight and with words to curse. On two occasions the Jews had held in

[1] Lebas and Waddington, *ibid.*

check the forces of the Empire, and the Christians had brought upon
themselves merciless judges. Their chiefs, the bishops, did indeed
preach obedience to the established authorities; but in the heart
of the new society was fermenting the implacable hatred of Isaiah
against idolatry, and fierce sectaries forgot the mild Galilaean
Master for the terrible Jehovah of the Exodus, the God of love for
the God of vengeance. An apostle had given the example. In
the days of Nero, Saint John had hurled at Rome his cry of mal-
ediction. Twenty-nine years later a Jew repeated, in the interests
of Israel, the Christian Apocalypse of the year 68.

He said: "Thy rule hath been by terror, and not by truth.
Thou hast destroyed the meek, thou hast hated the just and loved
the men of lies. Thy oppressions have come before the throne of
the Almighty; he hath consulted the times and hath seen that thy
measure is full. Thus thou shalt disappear, that the world may
breathe." It was after the fall of the Flavii, when Nerva trembled
in the presence of the revolted praetorians, that a seer, concealed
under the name of Esdras, testified that the hour of the great destruction was at hand. But Rome did not disappear; Trajan, on
the contrary, adorned her with fresh glory, — an insolent good fortune turning the promises of Jehovah into derision. Accordingly,
the Jews are ready to fall into despair. "Laborers, cease sowing
the land," exclaimed a new prophet, "and thou, O earth! to bear
harvests; what avails, O vine! the abundance of thy wine, since
Sion is no longer? Ye betrothed, renounce your rights; ye virgins,
adorn not yourselves with crowns; ye women, pray not to obtain
children. Henceforth it is for the barren to rejoice and for mothers
to weep: for why bring forth children in sorrow to bury them in
tears? Priests, take the keys of the sanctuary, cast them towards
heaven, restore them to the Lord, and tell him: Guard now Thy
house. And you, virgins, who spin the linen and silk with the
gold of Ophir, take it and throw it into the fire, that your enemies
may not enjoy it. O earth! have ears, and dust, take a heart to
make known in Sheol, and say to the dead: How happy are ye
in comparison with us!"

When those defeats occurred which darkened Trajan's last
days, the pseudo-Baruch believed that Jehovah had at last heard
Israel's cry. To the view of this writer the Roman Empire was

a forest which covered the earth with its deadly shade; towards
it flows a peaceful spring, — an image of the Messianic kingdom.
On approaching the forest the stream is changed into a furious
torrent which uproots the trees and mountains. A cedar alone
remains standing; it is the Emperor in the midst of his exterminated legions. But in its turn it is overthrown, and the vine says
to it: "Is it not thou, O cedar! who art the remnant of the forest
of evil? Thou seizest what doth not belong to thee, and holdest
in thy snares whatever draws near thee! Lo, thy hour is come!
Follow the fate of the forest, and let the dust of both lie together!"
The Emperor in chains is led to Mount Sion, where the Messiah
slays him. The vine then spreads in all directions, the earth is
clothed with flowers which do not fade, and the Messiah reigns
till the end of the perishing world.[1] The vision of the seer of
the year 117 was not fulfilled; but his threats and hopes doubtless
helped to bring about the great revolt which fifteen years later
Hadrian crushed.

The Sibylline oracles, more dangerous because they were popular,
fomented in the bosom of the Judaeo-Christian communities hatred
against the Empire, and doctors of the Church were accustomed to
prohibit public functions, and sometimes even military service, to
Christian believers. These oracles did not limit themselves to smit-
ing pagan society with loud reprobation, but they aimed at de-
stroying it altogether. Put together according to the circumstances
of the moment, they answered to the ideas which ruled in the extreme parties. These short, spirited compositions written in verse
in order to be more easily remembered, and circulating privately,[2]
filled the part which has in our days been played by certain jour-
nals and pamphlets inspired by the spirit of destruction. They

---

[1] This fragment and the preceding form part of the same apocalypse, which can be
assigned to the year 117, and which was found about 1866 in the Ambrosian library of Milan.
Cf. Renan, in the *Journal des Savants* for April, 1877.

[2] These oracles were so widely spread and seemed so odious to the pagans that the possession and reading of these books was prohibited under pain of death : *Sancita mors est in eos
qui legunt Histaspis aut Sibyllae aut Prophetarum libros . . . quod quidem in perpetuum efficere
non potuerunt, impavide enim non solum illos legimus, etc.* (Saint Justin, *Apol.* i. 44.) It
was, say the Benedictines (Preface to the works of Saint Justin, cap. vi. p. 84), the law *quae
futurorum curiosam inquisitionem prohibebat.* Saint Justin does not the less on that account
declare to the Emperor Antoninus that the Christians constantly read them.

formed the radical opposition of those days. Their invectives against the rich, their threats against the society which they devoted to eternal flames, show an intensity of hate which foretells how terrible will be the war of creeds and the shock of these hostile peoples.

[1] ΙΕΡΑ ΒΟΥΛΗ. Figure representing the Senate. On the reverse, ΑΙΖΑΝΕΙΤΩΝ. Cybele seated, at her feet a lion. (Bronze.)

COIN OF AEZANI.[1]

CHAPTER LXXXV.

GOVERNMENT AND ADMINISTRATION.

I. — THE EMPEROR AND THE NEW NOBILITY.

IN relating the history of the Empire from Augustus, we have exhibited this government in actual operation, and have shown the very simple parts of which the immense machine was composed. A few words will therefore suffice to sum up the details scattered throughout our narrative.[1]

The Romans were by no means theorists, and they would not have been at all able to understand our discussion on the social contract. The city, the state, or, as the ancients termed it, the republic, had been originally organized for the purpose of mutual defence against external enemies, and not with the desire of securing the greatest independence to each man. This was the case also in the family and tribe, in which the father and chief respectively disposed of everything. The first necessity is to exist; and in ancient times men could not exist without a strong family and state government. More than any other people, the Romans were forced, by the historic surroundings of their national existence, to establish and to preserve this vigorous discipline. The citizen had therefore given up to the state every right, in exchange for security ; or rather he had found himself naturally subjected under the Republic to the absolute power of the magistrates, even in the

---

[1] Dion Cassius, who was consul in 229 A. D., has left us a picture of the Roman government at the beginning of the third century. It is the discourse in which Maecenas is made to recommend to Augustus all that was done after him, even to the alimentary institution of Trajan (lii. 14–40). Dion is unable to imagine a better condition than that which he had under his own eyes, and the little that he adds to it — for instance, his sub-censor, an idea perhaps of Alexander Severus — does not impair the representation of the imperial constitution in the latter's time.

matter of his private life, which the censor penetrated, as under
the Empire he was subject to the absolute power of the Emperor.
In the former case liberty seems to have existed because it was
able to move freely among those various annual magistrates who.
being always two at the least in the same office, with the right of
intercessio against one another, preserved equilibrium. This was
the case in the best days of the Roman Republic. But these
magistrates, equal in authority, could also come to a secret under-
standing instead of being a mutual check; thus it happened after
the Gracchi, when a close aristocracy seized upon all public functions, even the tribunitian veto. This deviation from the constitutional principle became the law of the Empire. The prerogatives,
formerly divided and given for a very short time, were, after
Caesar, united, and relinquished to the Emperor during his whole
life, in such sort that no man could veto an act of him who had
no colleague, and that his decisions as judge were final, since
the *provocatio ad populum* was impossible against the perpetual
tribune, who, as representative of the entire people, acted in their
stead. The suppression of the double right of *veto* and *intercessio*
established absolute power; and here lies the sole difference between
the republican and the imperial systems. At bottom, the idea of
the complete sovereignty of the city or state exists in both, — represented at the period of the Catos, by many; at the time of the
Caesars, by one alone. Thus the Empire seemed at first to be only a
form of the Republic, as our fathers for a moment may have thought
it to be when they read on their coins the double inscription: *Répu-
blique française, Napoléon empereur.*

This union of all powers in the same hand — that is to say,
the permanency of the temporary dictatorship of the Republican
period — once being accepted by some as the end of civil disorders
and imposed upon others by the forty-five legions of Octavius,
there was not, on the establishment of the imperial power, any
great shock to the Roman world, nor any great change in its laws.
Yet, however small the difference seemed to those then living, it
was profound. A writer of the second century, Appian, says of it
in his preface: " Caesar preserved the name and forms of the
Republic, but seized upon all the power; and his successors have
kept what he took. They are called 'imperators;' in fact they have

the authority of a king." The jurisconsults speak in the same way with their customary rigor. "As circumstances had given the authority to a few," says Pomponius, "it came to pass that on account of factions it was found necessary to intrust to one man alone the government of the Republic when the Senate proved incapable of justly administering the provinces." This power was that of the most absolute king, since in this government there were neither hereditary bodies with the same interests as those of the Emperor, and yet capable of restraining him, nor those strong beliefs which, while surrounding royalty with a religious respect, yet imposed upon it certain reserves. The jurisconsults had even taken pains to spare the Emperor all hesitation respecting his omnipotence by furnishing him with legal formulas derived quite logically from the principle of national sovereignty,[1] constituting the individual reason of one man the collective reason of the entire nation, and the Emperor's will the popular law. "The Emperor," said they, "is not bound to observe the law;"[2] the law is his good pleasure, and the administration of justice is the same, for he annuls decisions or revises them.[3]

Formerly when the people, gathered in their comitia, wished to act as legislator, there must be the Forum or the Campus Martius, the consecration by the pontiffs, the convocation announced thirty days in advance, the flag on the Janiculum, the proposal of a magistrate, leaving to the sovereign nation only the choice between yes and no; and the law when passed was still subject to the veto of the gods as uttered through the augurs. To make a decree irrevocable, to establish an ordinance requiring absolute obedience,

---

[1] *Nec unquam dubitatum est quin id (constitutio principis) legis vicem obtineat, cum ipse imperator per legem imperium accipiat* (Gaius, i. 5). In virtue of the *jus majoris imperii* (Cic., *Cat.* iii. 6; Plutarch, *Cic.* 19; Livy, iii. 29, v. 9; Dion Halic., x. 25), he had the right of deposing any or all of the magistrates, even in the senatorial provinces.

[2] *Digest*, i. 3, 31 : *Princeps legibus solutus est.* He even had by law the right of altering wills, at least those in favor of cities (*Digest*, l. 8, 4) ; and this was an old republican right, for it was anciently necessary, in order that a testament be valid, for it to have been accepted by the people in the *comitia calata.*

[3] As perpetual tribune and invested with proconsular power, the Emperor heard appeals from the whole Empire (Suet., *Oct.* 33 ; *Digest.* xlii. 1, 27, and 33 ; xlix. 1). The ancient appeal to the tribunes or to a colleague *paris majorisve potestatis* had only a negative effect. The judge of appeal could annul the decision, but he could not alter it. The Emperor, or the judge whom he appointed, both annulled and amended. This right considerably increased the number of cases in the Emperor's courts, and was a cause of the increase of centralization.

the Emperor is hampered by none of those formalities which gave
reflection the time to speak and wisdom the opportunity of second
thought. Even Heaven itself cannot disturb his designs, for he is
chief pontiff and he makes the gods speak according to his will.[1]
A decree, an edict, a letter, a word, suffice; and he is not only
absolute master over the law (*dominus legum*),[2] he is so over
the property and persons of his subjects.[3] Lastly, every year, on the
anniversary of the Emperor's accession, the governors require the
soldiers and people to renew the oath of obedience to this limitless
will and this unchecked power.[4] Caligula had already uttered the
equivalent of the famous expression: *L'état, c'est moi !*[5]

The Emperor's relatives had no special privilege, except the
Caesar, or heir-presumptive, of whom we shall now speak. The
Empress was simply the head of the matrons; and to connect in
her majesty of rank with purity of life, the Augusta was seated
at the theatre in the midst of the vestal virgins.[6]

The Emperor, who was styled Your Eternity,[7] or Your Holiness,

[1] All the religious difficulties which arose in the Empire were decided by the two colleges of the pontiffs and *quindecimviri sacris faciundis*, of which the Emperor was chief. When he was unable to preside his place was taken by a *pro magistro*. From the day of his accession the Emperor was a member of the sacerdotal colleges.

[2] *Digest*, i. 1, 2, sect. 11; *Instit.* i. 2, 6; and Gaius, *Comm.* l. 5: *Constitutio principis est quod imperator decreto vel edicto, vel epistola constituit.*

[3] See Theophilus on sect. 6, *de jur. nat.* in the *Institutes: Caesar omnia habet.* Cf. Seneca, *De Benef.* vii. 6, and Orelli, No. 1,114: *Legum domino, justitiae aequitatisque rectori.*

[4] *Digest*, l. 1, 1; Pliny, *Epist.* x. 60. On January 3d solemn prayers were offered in the temples for the preservation of the Emperor (Pliny, *Epist.* x. 101).

[5] Νόμον ἡγούμενος ἑαυτόν (Philo, *Legatio ad Caium*). Under the Republic the edicts of the praetors and consuls were in force only during the time of their office; the Emperor being perpetual consul, his rescripts were in force for the whole of his reign, and remained law after his death if, in proclaiming him *divus*, the Senate had consecrated his acts, which could be altered only by the contrary act of a successor.

[6] Tac., *Hist.* iv. 16. Faustina bore the title of *mater castrorum* (Dion, lxxi. 10). The expression, "the imperial throne," which is so often used, is quite erroneous, the Emperors of the first two centuries having used only the curule chair of the consuls. This is especially the case as regards the Antonines, who professed to be unwilling to wound republican equality. In speaking of his accession to the imperial dignity, Antoninus said: "On the day when it pleased the gods to intrust this post to me" (*Quo me sumere hanc stationem placuit*).— *Letter to Fronto*, 6.

[7] Trajan allowed Pliny to swear by his eternity; the modest Antoninus called himself *mundi dominus* (Rescript to Eudem. Nicom., *Digest*, xiv. 29); and Fronto, speaking of this Emperor, wrote: περὶ τοῦ μεγάλου βασιλέως ἄρχοντος γῆς καὶ θαλάσσης (*Ep. ad Marc.* ii. 7). Elsewhere (*Ep.* 8) he calls Antoninus *Sanctissime Imperator*. Wine and incense were offered to the imperial statues; as regards the word *dominus*, Pliny, under Trajan, still applies it only to the Emperor; but under Marcus Aurelius, Fronto bestows it on everybody. Whatever might be his descent, the new Emperor was at his accession admitted a member of the patrician order.

wishes to be obeyed even after his death. If he has a son. the latter succeeds him. If not. adoption gives him one. whom he calls Caesar and Prince of the Youth. — that is to say, chief of the knights, — whom he invests with the consular and tribunitian powers, and to whom pass without difficulty on the day when The Eternity dies, the remaining titles and powers. These are given him by a senatus-consultum, and this decree of the Conscript Fathers is called the "Royal Law." In fact. while there are any children, — that is, either natural heirs or those made so by adoption, — heredity exists, under the guaranty of the *donativum* to the soldiers and with the formality of the senatorial assent.[1] In law, election is the constitutional principle, and this principle is applied by the Senate, but more frequently by the legions. which, entirely composed of citizens, seemed to represent the true Roman people; once even, in the case of Gordian III.. it was so by the populace of Rome. But this election, the result of a surprise, of violence, or corruption, is always the work of ambitious men, and never that of the nation, which has no means of intervening in the choice of its master, either actually of itself, since it is scattered over the whole surface of the Empire. or by its representatives, since it did not appoint any, and moreover was partial to the imperial authority, without even caring to know who possessed it.

Tacitus remarks, when speaking of the delays of the corn-ships. that the life of Rome was at the mercy of the winds and waves. Of the entire Empire we may say that its repose and security depended on the twofold hazard of circumstances and men. This people, under the Republic so far-sighted, had been able to foresee nothing under the Empire, and a hundred million of men intrusted their lot to the "blind divinity." "We have built a thousand temples to Fortune," says Fronto to Marcus Aurelius. "but not one to Reason."[2]

What, indeed, would this reason have counselled? Doubtless many things which history discerns. but which the men of those

---

[1] The fact of Maximin having reigned *sine decreto senatus* seemed extraordinary.

[2] He calls Fortune *dearum praecipuam* (*Letter* 5). See the passage in the elder Pliny (ii. 5) on Fortune, "whom in every place, and at all times, is invoked or accused . . . who, according to men, alone regulates the active and the passive, and who has been made God, she who is the very negation of the Divinity" . . . *ut sors ipsa pro Deo sit qua Deus probatur incertus.*

days did not see.   While it is true that a few men under the first
Emperors regretted the Republic, — that is, the absolute power of
two hundred senatorial families, — their opposition had not been popular.   Even Tacitus did not desire a new organization of power, and
he almost blamed Thrasea for his useless sacrifice.[1] Philosophy reproduced Plato's thesis: namely, that the best government was that
of one man, representative of the gods on earth and ruling everything with wisdom.[2] In the Empire, that which delights Aristeides,
as it did all the provincial writers, is the part which the Emperor
fulfils of chief justice, δικαστὴς μέγας, protecting the fortune
and honor of each and all.[3] Philo had said as early as Caligula's
time: "It is not fitting for the power to belong to many." Bossuet in the time of Louis XIV. speaks similarly. It is because,
in certain respects, the two powers are alike. As the kings of
France took the place of the feudal lords, so the Emperors took
that of the republican proconsuls, — a revolution which, at both
periods, was thankfully received by the people. The provincials
knew well enough that absolute monarchy also has its dangers,
and in the third century they sought separation from the Empire,
which was no longer able to defend them: but up to the time of
which we now speak they continued to regard it as the best
guaranty of their interests.[1]

Thus, to secure obedience, this government had no need either
of soldiers in the cities or of numberless agents in the provinces.
Its armies were on the frontiers facing the enemy, and we shall
shortly see how few in number were its functionaries.

In reality, never did any government encounter fewer adversa-
ries, though it was the object of innumerable competitions. No
man since Chaerea had proposed to change the Empire. But to
change the Emperor had been frequent. Let any man, indeed,
make himself a god upon earth, without being protected in his
usurpation by the absolute confidence of the people in his personal

---

[1] *Sibi causam periculi fecit, ceteris libertatis initium non praebuit* (*Ann.* xiv. 12).

[2] *Optimus civitatis status sub rege justo est* (Seneca, *De Ben.* ii. 20). . . . *Electus qui in terris
deorum vice fungeretur* (*De Clem.* i. 1).

[3] He still calls him ἄρχοντι καὶ κοσμητῇ, he who commands and co-ordinates the collective
life of all parties (*De Roma*, p. 213).

[4] Ἡ πολιτεία πρὸς τὸ βέλτιον καὶ πρὸς τὸ σωτηριωδέστερον μετεκοσμήθη (Dion, liii. 19). Cf.
id. xliv. 2, and Tertullian, *De Pallio*, i. 2.

character, and he will present a temptation to the ambitious to overthrow him and seize so splendid a position. The Empire will therefore have the life it deserves; namely, a succession of revolutions, not of political doctrines, but of persons. The happy intercalation of the Antonines was a lull which will never again occur, because one cannot count a second time on such a miracle as a succession of able men who through wisdom will impose upon themselves that moderation which institutions did not enjoin. Accordingly, the convulsions which had preceded the reigns of Vespasian and Trajan will re-appear after Marcus Aurelius with a more disastrous force; on the accession of Diocletian, out of forty-nine Emperors, without speaking of "the thirty tyrants," only eleven or twelve can be reckoned who died a natural death.

Who could have averted these disorders? Was it the Senate? This assembly had been renewed by the Flavians and Antonines. The old Roman families, destroyed by many causes, were rapidly disappearing. The second triumvirate alone had cost the life of three hundred senators and two hundred knights: such are the results of civil war. Under Claudius, thirty-five senators and three hundred knights perished. But how can we count the victims of Caligula, Nero, Domitian, and the murderous anarchy of the years 68 and 69? As far back as the days of Augustus and Tiberius there was a failure of patricians for religious functions, and in almost every reign the Emperors were obliged to create new senators. To fill up the gaps in the depopulated curia, Claudius opened it to the Gauls, and Vespasian to the nobles of the whole Empire. It was not at all from caprice, but from necessity; for the equestrian and senatorial orders, whence proceeded all the servants of the public administration, did not at that time amount to more than two hundred *gentes.* In order to reconstitute the exhausted aristocracy, the first of the Flavii summoned to Rome from the provinces a thousand municipal families.

What Vespasian did for the administration it was necessary also to do for the judicial office. At Rome the five decuriae of judges, composed of knights and ducenarii, were reduced like the Senate; they were filled up by provincial knights. Pliny, an old Italian who understands neither this necessary policy nor that historic law that close aristocracies do not last, exclaims with grief

(xxix. 8): "At the present time a man is summoned from Cadiz or from the Pillars of Hercules to decide in the most trivial cases."

Consequently, a hundred and twenty-eight years after the battle of Actium the provincials had invaded all things, even the supreme power, and not a single Roman by descent will ever again enter as master into the palace of the Julii and the Claudii. Cicero had said before the entire Senate (*Philip.* iii. 6): "How many are there among us who are not sprung from Italian municipia?" Concerning all men of any consideration at Rome and in the Empire, it might now be asked: "How many are there who do not come from the provincial cities?" *Sic vos non vobis.* Vergil had not foreseen that the subjects of "the Romulidae" would so quickly become their heirs.

These Spaniards[1] and Gauls, sitting in the Palatine, continued the policy of the Emperor who had made their fortune. Trajan gave the consular toga to a Mauretanian chief, Lusius Quietus; Hadrian to the descendant of a Galatian tetrarch;[2] Marcus Aurelius to several Africans.[3] Two Numidians, Fronto and Proculus, received Asia,[4] the province which was regarded as the leading government of the Empire. The proconsulship of Africa was the second. About the year 140 this was given to a Paphlagonian, who took as assessor or member of his council a decurion of Amastris, his native city.[5] From this same province of Africa were to proceed one after another three Emperors and an eminent jurisconsult.

Great distrust was felt of the Egyptians and Greeks, who had a bad name at Rome, and entered the Senate much later,[6] — the former in Caracalla's time, the latter under the Antonines, half Greek princes, who purposely surrounded themselves by those whose language they spoke. Arrian, Atticus Herodes, the Quin-

---

[1] The second personage in the Empire under Trajan, namely, Licinius Sura, was a Spaniard like himself, a native of Tarragona or Barcelona (Martial, *Epigr.* i. 50, and *C. I. L.* Nos. 4,282 and 4,536–4,548).

[2] Waddington, *Fastes des prov. asiat.* p. 218.

[3] *Alii quoque plurimi sunt in senatu Cirtenses clarissimi viri* (Fronto, *Ad Amic.* ii. 10).

[4] Fronto's illness prevented him from taking possession of his government. Proculus was from Sicca.

[5] L. Renier, *Comptes rendus de l'Acad. des inscr.* 1871, p. 200.

[6] Appian, who was of Alexandria, was invested with an important office in Egypt, which the word ἐπιτροπεύειν does not clearly indicate; but he did not become a Roman senator.

tilii.[1] Quadratus of Pergamus, and many others, obtained the consulship about that time. The father of Dion Cassius, a Bithynian, governed Cilicia and Dalmatia; the father of Avidius Cassius, a Syrian, held the prefecture of Egypt, which a Jew, Tiberius Alexander, and a descendant of the kings of the Commagene, Balbillus, had also held;[2] and finally, Marcus Aurelius gave one of his daughters in marriage to a knight of Antioch. Thus was effected the mixture of nations.

Martial and Juvenal, forgetful of their obscure birth, complained bitterly of the invasion of "these knights hastening to Rome from the depths of Syria, Cappadocia, and Bithynia, — sons of slaves, who left neither room nor wealth to the genuine descendants of Numa."[3] What would they have said if they had seen the Illyrian region furnishing later its contingent of generals, senators, and emperors? Thus, as the result of an inexorable law which was caused by the spread of Roman civilization outside Italy, and also as the result of the general prosperity of the period, there came for each province a time when the men whom the control of municipal affairs had trained, or whom commerce had enriched, were naturally called upon by the state for her various services. In the second century this new nobility were the senators at Rome, the higher officers in the army, and in the administration everywhere held the chief places. Their morals were better, their ideas more just; they did not regard the Empire as a usurpation of their rights; and the most ardent wish of their great interpreter, Tacitus, went no farther than to implore the gods that they would continue to give the world such emperors as Trajan.

Rome in the time of the Antonines was no longer, as under the Caesars and the Flavians, the scene of those continual intrigues against the Emperor and those retaliatory murders of inexpert conspirators or of innocent victims. The new aristocracy did not form conspiracies, except at wide intervals and as the last traces of a

[1] The Quintilii were of Alexandria Troas, and were consuls under Antoninus (Waddington, *Fastes des proc. asiat.* p. 229). For Quadratus, see *ibid.* p. 219.
[2] Respecting this Jew, cf. L. Renier, *Conseil de guerre de Titus,* and about Balbillus, Letronne, *Inscr. d'Égypte,* ii. 350. The great architect Apollodorus was of Damascus, Galen of Pergamus, Ulpian of Tyre, and Papinian of Phoenicia.
[3] Martial, *Epigr.* x. 76; Juvenal, *Sat.* iii. 81, vii. 14.

habit acquired by tradition from its predecessors. At most it only circulated little scandals respecting Trajan's suppers, the intimacies of Hadrian, or the insolence of the two Faustinas. Seneca says that Egypt set its wits to work to commit rude acts against those who governed it.[1] Rome in this matter kept pace with Alexandria. This petty gossip which the fault-finding spirit of great capitals hawks about daily from house to house is the tribute paid by power, by beauty, and by virtue, or sometimes it is the punishment of vice; and this tribute is paid by intelligent rulers without annoyance. Sprung from the ranks of the new nobility, the Antonines understood well their class, and knowing they had nothing to fear from it, showed it a confidence and respect which preserved a cordial peace between the palace and the senate-house.

But in the heart of this nobility was a corrupting germ, — freedmen had crept into it in great numbers. Curtius Rufus, a consul under Tiberius, was son of a gladiator; Vitellius was reported the grandson of a slave; and from Nero's time it was said that many of the senators and the majority of the knights had no other descent.[2] When certain old Romans, from wounded pride, objected to one of these parvenus on account of his low extraction, the Emperor replied: "He is the son of his deeds."[3] That was the motto of the new policy. Unfortunately, while among these former slaves who by dint of intelligence — sometimes also by unworthy means — had attained liberty and wealth, there were some capable of being excellent senators, very few of them had the ability to found those families wherein traditions of virtue and of self-respect prepare good citizens for the state. They understood public affairs and conducted them well, but their sentiments were rarely elevated with their fortunes: to mental flexibility corresponded a pliability of conscience; and the moral sense, the care of personal dignity, were often wanting in men who, having as their paternal heritage the remembrance of the humiliations of servitude, were, like the Rufus of Tacitus, "base flatterers of the

---

[1] *Ingeniosa in contumelias praefectorum provincia* (*Ad Helviam*, 17).

[2] Tac., *Ann.* xiii. 27: . . . *Plurimis equitum, plerisque senatoribus non aliunde originem trahi.* In the time of Pliny, the praetor Largius Macedo was the son of a freedman, — a fact which did not prevent him from treating his slaves so harshly that they killed him (*Epist.* iii. 11). The Emperor Pertinax was of the same condition (Dion, lxxi. 22). Under Caracalla a man who had been a slave was made senator (*Id.*, lxxviii. 13).

[3] Tac., *Ann.* xi. 21.

powerful, haughty towards their inferiors, disobliging towards their equals." In this way it came about that the Senate of the Antonines, politically more upright than that of the last days of the Republic and of the first century of the Empire, but containing impure elements, had at the same time so much experience in affairs and so much severity towards the Emperor.

II. — THE SENATE AND THE KNIGHTS.

JUDGING by appearances only, the Senate occupied an important place on the political scene; and its members seemed so indispensable for the proper guidance of affairs — or rather their residence in the provinces appeared so dangerous — that they were not permitted to leave Italy without the Emperor's permission. The Senate appointed to offices and gave legal decisions;[1] it administered and legislated; it watched over religion and the public treasury (*aerarium*); it exercised the most minute police control and political duties of the gravest consequences, at one time receiving foreign ambassadors or declaring the Decebalus a public enemy and beginning a serious war, at another authorizing some individual to establish a market on his lands,[2] or forbidding advocates to take fees from their clients. The senators said to themselves that they were the heirs of the national sovereignty; that they possessed more prerogatives than the Republican Senate; that, in fine, they were the source of all authority, even for the Emperor (*lex regia*). They saw the latter seek from them the confirmation of his title, sit with them as a colleague, and call himself only "the first of the Senate" (*princeps*). They shared with him the royal right of coining money. The Emperor, it is true, had reserved to himself the privilege of issuing gold and silver coin; but the bronze pieces were struck by the Senate and bore its signature: S. C.[3]

[1] All was so little fixed in this constitution that the Senate believed itself able, even in the course of a suit, to change the law, the application of which was the point in question; thus in the suit of Bassus (Pliny. *Epist.* iv. 9): *Senatui licet et mitigare leges et intendere*.

[2] Pliny, *Epist.* v. 4. There is another example in the *Ephemeris epigr.* vol. ii. fasc. iv. p. 271, of a similar senatus-consultum of the year 138 found in 1875 in Tunis. Cf. Pliny, *Epist.* v. 14 and 21.

[3] Yet we have seen, at p. 162, that a number of cities in the eastern provinces had kept

Lastly, at the Emperor's death the Conscript Fathers decreed him either heaven or the Gemoniae; they proclaimed him either a god or a tyrant, and either annulled his acts or confirmed them. The curia was moreover the great school for the officials of the Empire. To be placed at the head of a legion or of a province a man must belong to the Senate. Certain commands even were reserved for the ex-consuls; and this was one of the reasons which now obliged the creation yearly of eight or even twelve consuls, designated by the Emperor and appointed by the Senate, who gave them the curule chair and the ivory wand.[1] The terms of ancient politeness became official titles, and " the Magnificent Order " was now composed of those illustrious personages, "the *Clarissimi*." Their children, even the daughters, were thus addressed.[2]

What pomp in the forms employed! What splendor in the externals! And what a powerful personage the Roman senator must have felt himself to be who took his position seriously enough not to laugh, like the augur, on meeting with a colleague! But the Senate is only a useful machine; and Pliny, who styles the most respected of the old magistracies a vain shadow (*inanem umbram et sine honore nomen*),[3] portrays in his liberal Emperor an absolute master even of the property of his subjects.[4]

But let us enter the curia for a moment and see these men at work who bear so grand a title: the Official Journal of that time allows us to be present at a sitting. We are in the year 222. Elagabalus has just been murdered, his corpse dragged through the streets of Rome and cast into the Tiber, and the soldiers have proclaimed Alexander.

"Extract from the proceedings of Rome, the eve of the nones of March." The assembly is numerous; it invites the Emperor to be present in the house, and on his entrance salutes him thus:

---

the right of coining silver money (*cistophori*) and copper. This right of the Senate and the cities was important, "for it prevented the Emperor from uttering coin of a fictitious value " (Mommsen, *Hist. de la monnaie rom.* iii. 12).

[1] L. Renier, *Comptes rendus de l'Acad. des inscr.* 1873, p. 105, and Hist., Aug. *Aurel.* 13.

[2] Orelli, No. 922, for the times of Severus; *ibid.* No. 3,717; *clarissimi pueri*, and No. 4,911; *clarissimus juvenis.*

[3] *Epist.* i. 23.

[4] See Vol. V. pp. 263-4. Had the senatus-consulta the force of law? One could hardly doubt it, says Ulpian (*Digest.* i. 3, 9). " It is a question," replies Gaius (*Inst.* i. 4), — " a purely theoretic question, for in fact the Emperor was the master."

"Virtuous Augustus, may the gods protect you!

"Emperor Alexander, may the gods protect you!

"The gods have given you to us; may the gods preserve you!

"The gods have snatched you from the hands of a lustful man; may the gods watch over your years!

"You have suffered like ourselves under a wicked tyrant; the gods have destroyed him: may the gods protect you!

"We shall be happy under your rule; the Republic will be happy: may the gods grant long life to Alexander!"

The Emperor having thanked the assembly, it cries out anew:

"Antoninus Alexander, may the gods protect you!

"Antoninus Aurelius, may the gods protect you!

"Antonius Pius, may the gods protect you! We beg of you to take the name of Antoninus.

"In you is our safety, in you our life, in you our happiness!

"Long life to Antoninus Alexander! For the sake of our welfare let him bear the name of Antoninus!

"Let an Antonine consecrate the temples of the Antonines!

"Let an Antonine triumph over Parthians and Persians!

"In you, Antoninus, we possess all; by you we obtain all!"

The Emperor resists; seven or eight times the senators, without ceasing, repeat in chorus the same acclamations; and not being able to triumph over the honest obstinacy of Alexander in refusing a name which seemed too grand to bear, they suddenly adopt another manœuvre, which is carried out with the same harmony, in order to compel this young man, who as yet has done nothing, but whose name happens to be Alexander, to take the title of "the Great," given to the Macedonian hero after the conquest of Asia. The clamor begins anew. I will not repeat it, for the modern reader could not tolerate these litanies of insipid flattery. The Emperor remaining firm, they now begin boasting of his moderation, and on this theme continue for a long time, "according to usage," says the historian (*ex more*).[1]

[1] Lampridius, *Alex. Sev.* 6-12. Yet the historian has a reason for saying *ex more*, for these acclamations were a very old usage, which was followed at festivals, assemblies, the theatre, and at public recitations. What seems ridiculous and vulgar to us was then a national custom and a serious affair. There was in it a certain cadence, with a kind of musical modulation. Suetonius says of Augustus: *Revertentem ex provincia modulatis carminibus prosequebantur.* Nero regulated these acclamations, the number of which was given in advance by a master of ceremonies, ἐπεβῶμεν τά τε ἄλλα ὅσα ἐκελευόμεθα (Dion, lxxii. 20); and they were so much in use that we meet with them in the Church (Saint Augustine's Letters, No. 213), in the councils, — at that of Ephesus in 431, for example, — and they still existed at Constantinople in the tenth century, and in France upon the consecration of the Capet kings where the people approved, crying three times: *Nous le voulons.*

It may be urged that the Senate of Alexander Severus had passed through such ordeals that it might well have lost all dignity of character; but let us look at the Senate which Marcus Aurelius had left his son, — the Senate of the Antonines. He who speaks is an eye-witness and a man of consular rank:[1] "The games lasted fourteen days; the Emperor [Commodus] took an active part in them. All of us senators did not fail to be present with the knights. The aged Claudius Pompeianus alone remained absent. He indeed sent his two sons, but he never came himself, preferring to incur a violent death by his absence rather than to see the chief of the Empire, the son of Marcus Aurelius, giving himself up to such sports. According to the orders we had received we made different acclamations and repeated these unceasingly : ·You are our master, the first rank belongs to you! You are the most fortunate of men! You are conqueror! You shall be so! From time out of mind you alone are conqueror, O Amazonius!'" And a little further on : "The Emperor did something else which seemed to presage certain death to the senators. Having killed an ostrich, he cut off its head and advanced towards the places where we were seated. He held the head in his left hand, in the right his sword, still covered with blood, and directed its point towards us. He did not utter a word; but shaking his head and opening his mouth wide, he made us understand that he would treat us as he had treated the ostrich." There was good reason to tremble. Yet some of the senators, less struck with the danger they were incurring than with the grotesque appearance of this vanquisher of a peaceful bird, whose head he was carrying in triumph, so far forgot themselves as to smile. "The Emperor would have killed them on the instant with his sword if I had not suggested to those who were near me to pluck some laurel-leaves from their wreaths and chew them, as I was doing, so that the continued movement of our lips would prevent him from being quite sure that we had laughed." There is no need of other evidence to attest the servility of the Senate.

On the other hand, it would be easy to cite, on the part of many of the Emperors, both respectful words and acts of external deference towards this exalted assembly; but it was merely a

¹ Dion Cassius, lxxii. 29. See another scene, lxxvi. 8.

matter of politeness. The most courteous Emperors renounced not one of their valuable rights. In reality, under the Empire the Senate played no political part; or at least it had that only which the Emperor was pleased to give it.

Some learned men, who unite in themselves much imagination and much knowledge, have endeavored to see in the history of

ACCLAMATIONS AT THE CIRCUS IN THE PRESENCE OF THE EMPEROR.[1]

the Empire a struggle of three centuries between Caesarism and the Senate, till the reform of Diocletian. This is giving more importance to formulas than they deserve. The senators conspired against the Emperor; but between them and him there was never a political struggle.

We are already familiar with the judicial and administrative powers of the annual magistrates who sat in this assembly;[2] the

---

[1] Bas-relief of the pedestal of the obelisk of Theodosius at Constantinople (*Dict. des Ant.* fig. 36, p. 19).

[2] See Vol. IV. p. 89 *et seq.*, with notes.

eight [1] consuls, the eighteen praetors,[2] the ten tribunes, the six
aediles,[3] and the twenty quaestors. Their prerogatives, though still
considerable, were without independence ; so that the incumbents of
magistracies which had been the executive power of the Republic,
while holding a very important place in the administration, held
but a very trivial one in the government. It would be useless to
spend time in attempting to delineate the vague outlines of shad-
ows like these. History indeed devotes itself to the dead, but to
the dead who have once been alive. While the political insignifi-
cance of the Senate and its dignities is but too easily shown, and
baseness of character was an inheritance which many of the Conscript Fathers of servile origin had legitimately obtained, yet we
must regard this assembly as the grandest school of administration which has ever existed. At eighteen years of age, when
active life claimed him, the young noble who proposed to himself a
public career in the state entered the army, where he passed the
stormy years of youth receiving military instruction as a cavalry
officer ;[4] he then entered the vigintivirate,[5] and completed in the
courts his legal education, which he had begun with some jurisconsult of renown. After this twofold training in the Forum

---

[1] Four under Nero; six under Vespasian, namely, two, those whose names are in the
Fasti, and are called *cons. ex Kal. januariis*, serving six months, and the other four, three
months; eight, and sometimes twelve, from Trajan to Constantine. Commodus appointed as
many as twenty-five in one year. Public acts were, from Augustus to Caracalla, dated from
the consuls in charge, whether they were *suffecti* or not (L. Renier, *Comptes rendus de
l'Acad. des inscr.* 1875, p. 105).

[2] These sixteen or eighteen praetorships were drawn by lot by candidates whom the
Emperor had designated (Tac., *Agr.* 7).

[3] The offices of tribune and aedile were co-ordinate, so that a man might hold one or the
other, but never both successively.

[4] They were called *tribuni militum honores petituri*, or *tribuni laticlarii*. (See Vol. IV.
p. 90.) Those who had no military ambition were satisfied with a *semestrial tribunate*. Thus
the younger Pliny had as service in the army of Syria to keep the accounts, which left him
plenty of time to attend the lessons of philosophers; while Trajan, led on by his military
tastes, had followed the soldier's calling very seriously (*Panegyr.* 15). M. L. Renier (*Mél.
d'épigr.* p. 239) is the first who has unfolded the true nature of the *equestria militia*, or grades
of prefect of the auxiliary cohort, legionary tribune, and prefect of an *ala* of cavalry through
which the young nobles passed. These grades and that of *primipilarius* conferred the gold
ring on those who obtained them without belonging to the equestrian order. From Hadrian's
time the young nobles had to enter public life by the vigintivirate; fifteen inscriptions collected
by Wilmanns prove this.

[5] The vigintiviri (see Vol. IV. p. 90, note 1) formed but one college. They were therefore all of the same rank, the first grade of the official scale; and this permitted them all to
aspire, when the military stage was passed, to the magistracy immediately above, — the quaestorship. Cf. Dion. liv. 26.

and in the camps, the young man was appointed to one of the twenty quaestorships and entered the Senate. He was at this time but twenty-five years of age, and yet he already knew a good deal of practical life; he had been well instructed in the civil law and in military regulations; he had obeyed and had commanded. As Emperor's quaestor he carried the imperial messages to the senate-house and listened to the discussions which arose on them; as quaestor to one of the consuls, he became like a son to the latter, receiving his counsels and listening to his stories of war or of administration; as quaestor to a proconsul we see him a financial agent, in case of need a judge, and he had a large share in the government of the province. Later he became an aedile, with the oversight of the streets, markets, and public baths of Rome, or a tribune of the people, with the right of making propositions in the Senate or opposing his veto to the decrees of the curia.[1] What precocious maturity must have been developed by this continuous application of a man's faculties to services so very diverse! When thirty he reached the praetorship, and at thirty-three could obtain the consular office; that is to say, the great magistracies, the highest honors. But the state did not yet release him from public duties. Between these two offices a legion might be given him to command,[2] or a province to administer; and after his consulship, some other government, or an army, not to mention sacerdotal functions and great prefectures or curatorships to which he could be called.[3] His life thus passed half in councils where affairs are discussed, and half in functions by which they are carried out. Jurisconsult and judge, administrator and general, engineer making roads or building bridges, — he is all these, sometimes successively, sometimes simultaneously, and on a changing stage whose scenery grows broader every time he gains a higher grade.[4] To conclude, he knows one of

[1] Tacitus (Ann. xiii. 28) points out that in the time of Nero the tribunes still possessed some important judicial prerogatives.

[2] The command of the legions was given only to praetorii. Cf. Borghesi, Œuvres, iii. 152.

[3] Besides the highest offices there were many curatorships, — curatores riarum, aquarum, alvei Tiberis riparum et cloacarum urbis, operum locorumque publicorum, etc., praefecti frumenti dandi, alimentorum, aerarii Saturni, etc. These offices, formed out of the dissolution of the censorship, were intrusted to permanent officials. The provinces of Asia and Africa were assigned by lot among the ex-consuls; but in the time of Trajan the turn of each came only twelve years after quitting office (Waddington, Fastes des prov. asiat. p. 716).

[4] Subjoined is Hadrian's cursus honorum to the year 112, five years before he became

the secrets of a skilful administrator, — "Never be angry, speak little, listen much;"[1] and some are able to profit by the advice.

This is the career that almost all the senators passed through, followed in turn by their children. These dignities are in fact as if hereditary in the senatorial families, — first because the Conscript Fathers are hardly numerous enough to fill all the state offices, and secondly because the Emperor can only give the higher offices (the prefecture of Egypt and the praetorian prefecture alone excepted) to those who wear the laticlave. So he is often obliged to call to a place among the ex-quaestors and the ex-praetors citizens who have held neither the office of quaestor nor praetor,[2] and who in their turn will form a stock for public functionaries. But with this prerogative the Emperor had the means of keeping places for merit. This was the free promotion of modern times, which, when properly done, remedies the disadvantages of advancement by seniority.

We shall further notice that the arbitrary will of the Emperor was singularly restrained by this system, which advanced every senator in his turn to the great dignities of the state and the government of the senatorial provinces. The Emperor, at least, could not disturb the regular order of the *cursus honorum*, except only in those very serious crises of government which an intelligent ruler carefully avoids bringing about.

Emperor: decemvir *stilitibus judicandis*, prefect for the Latin *feriae*, *sevir* of the Roman knights, tribune successively in the legions *IIa Adjut. Va Maced.*, *XXIIa Primigenia*, secretary for the Senate's proceedings, quaestor of the Emperor and his *comes* in the Dacian expedition, tribune of the people, praetor *legatus* of the *Ia Minerv.* legion, legatus propraetor of the Emperor in Lower Pannonia, *sodalis Augustalis*, septemvir of the Epulones, and finally consul (*C. I. L.* vol. iii. No. 550). See also the case of Agricola. At nineteen Agricola served in Britain as military tribune; at twenty-five he was quaestor of the province of Asia; at twenty-seven tribune, and consequently a member of the Senate, to which the quaestorship gave him admittance; at twenty-nine he was praetor; at thirty-one he commanded the Twentieth legion in Britain, where he stayed three years; from thirty-five to thirty-eight he was governor of Aquitania; at thirty-eight he attained the consulship; at thirty-nine he returned to Britain as consular legate and remained there seven years; at forty-six he declined the government of the province of Asia. Mommsen sets forward the magistracies of Agricola by one year.

[1] A proconsul to whom the Emperor had just intrusted the command of several legions and the government of a great province asked of Demonax the best method of conducting affairs. The philosopher made him the reply above quoted (Lucian, *D monax*, 51).

[2] *Adlectus inter quaestorius, praetorios, etc.* An inscription (Or.-Henzen, Nos. 6,929 and 7,009) represents Antoninus recompensing a father who was not a senator by giving his son, a child four years old, the decorations of the Conscript Fathers, which insured him entrance into the Senate when he reached the proper age.

Modern society starts from another principle, — the division of labor and special training for the different offices. The plan is excellent for the orderly working of each office. The Roman system was more suited to form eminent administrators, and it did form such. But the political institutions of the Empire were adapted neither for forming citizens nor for improving their characters ; this is why this Senate, so rich in experience, was so poor in courage and true dignity.

IVORY TESSERAE USED AT THE THEATRE (MUSEUM OF NAPLES).[1]

In the equestrian order we see the knight by descent and the knight of fortune, the old hereditary estates and the recently acquired wealth of bankers, merchants, usurers, contractors for public works, or farmers of indirect taxes, — of all those, in short, who had known how to employ profitably their intellect and their capital. The former, especially since Hadrian's reign, filled the administration ; the others desired to follow them, and, after having gained wealth, to attain honors also. Vainly had Tiberius required

[1] Tesserae, or theatre-checks, found at Pompeii and Herculaneum. Some have a portrait on one side, and on the other the number of the place and a name, as we have indicated below each ticket. Others have only the name, and on the reverse of the ticket the number of the place. Those in the form of a pigeon should be noted, as they served to designate the highest row in the theatre, — pullarius, "the poulterer," now at Naples the piccionaia. These last have only numbers (Monaco, Le Musée nat. de Naples, pl. 126 and p. 23).

from citizens who aspired to the gold ring some proofs that their father and grandfather had both been free born and had possessed the necessary income; the elder Pliny was able to say: "In our days a man takes one leap from slavery to the equestrian order."[1]

To obtain the gold ring, the angusticlave, a place reserved at the theatre or the games, and to possess, if a man had a taste for it, the right to be insolent towards others, it sufficed to have gained, be it in the vilest employment, enough to buy the citizenship. There was no lack of indulgent protectors who would procure the concession and prevent any inquisitive questions as regards descent; and then, by virtue of his four hundred thousand sesterces, the new citizen was raised to the rank of knight.[2] Still, a dishonorable action, a legal sentence, a reverse of fortune, might deprive him of it. "From having given gold rings to girls," says Martial to a profligate, "you have lost your own." Claudius, during his censorship, deprived of the equestrian rank four hundred who had acquired it illegally, and he caused the freedmen who had thus obtained it to be sold as slaves.[3] Some veteran soldiers who had by merit reached the first centurionship of their legion or the military tribunate,[4] sometimes also, after the *honesta missio*, obtained the gold ring, with a money grant which gave them the income required of the knight.

But these parvenus of fortune or the army, so disdainful of the plebeians, were in their turn, objects of a like disdain on the part of the knights of high birth, who, having received the horse of honor (*equum publicum*)[5] from the Emperor, formed a class apart in the order, that of *illustres*. "It is neither gold nor military service which made me a knight," says Ovid.[6] In this class were

---

[1] *Vidimus Arellium Fuscum motum equestri ordine ob insignem calumniam* (*Hist. nat.* xxxiii. 8).

[2] *Quadringenarii* (Henzen, No. 6,469).

[3] *Epigr.* viii. 5. *Senatoriam dignitatem recusantibus, equestrem ademit* (Suet., *Claudius*, 24 and 25).

[4] This was the *militia* called *caligata* (*Digest*, xxxii. 1, 10, proœm., and Orelli, No. 3,465), in opposition to the *militia equestris*.

[5] See Vol. V. p. 101. They might be called "state knights," in opposition to those whom the inscription of Narbonne called "knights of the plebs."

[6] *Amor.* iii. 15, 6, and *Trist.* iv. 10, 7. It is hardly needful to add that the Emperor did not always take into account this distinction for nomination to lucrative employments (*procur., centenarii, ducenarii, etc.*). See in L. Renier, *Mél. d'épigr.* p. 88, the curious *cursus honorum* of L. Valerius Proculus.

to be found the candidates for the dignities of the curia, the offices of the palace, the provincial procuratorships, and the different prefectures, — the most important of which was that of the *annona*, with the civil jurisdiction over all frumentary affairs, — the vice-royalty of Egypt, and, above all, the prefecture of the praetorium, which was soon to become the highest post of the state. The senatorial order belonged exclusively to Rome and Italy, where the senators must fix their abode and have a third or a fourth of their landed property; the equestrian order, on the contrary, formed the provincial nobility. Each large city had its knights; and this character is well indicated by an inscription of Narbonne which, speaking of three wealthy colonists of that city, calls them *equites Romani a plebe*. These provincial knights could be summoned to Rome to sit in the decuria of judges.[1]

But by the invasion of freedmen and men of business, the order, even at Rome, daily lost ground in public esteem. This is already seen by a rescript of Hadrian which speaks of *libertini* having received the gold ring;[2] Septimius Severus will soon give it to all the soldiers; and under Constantine we shall find no mention of the equestrian order.

III. — THE PEOPLE. — DISTRIBUTIONS AND GAMES.

As, in speaking of the state, men still said "the Republic;" as there was a semblance of comitia,[3] an outward show of elections, and the shadow of the old Republican magistracies; and as men everywhere read the old formula: *Senatus Populusque Romanus*, — nothing prevented the Romans from still believing themselves to be the royal people, masters of the world and of themselves. But they did not, however, at all deceive themselves in this matter; they well knew where the power lay, and submitted without a murmur. Yet in numbers they had remarkably increased, for the Roman people now included all the inhabitants

---

[1] Pliny, *Hist. nat.* xxix. 8. On the equestrian order under the Empire, see the *Hist. des chevaliers romains*, by M. Belot.

[2] *Digest*, lx. 10, 6.   [3] See Vol. IV. p. 88, note 2.

of Rome and of the Empire possessing citizenship. Each citizen was enrolled in one of the thirty-five tribes,—a mere formality; for if those dwelling in Rome had no longer political rights, those who lived beyond the mountains and seas had not even the advantage of utilizing their title by being amused and fed by the Emperor and the rich. Yet they preserved an important privilege, —that of securing for their property the nature of an Italian domain ; that is, exemption from certain imposts.[1] Day by day the idea of Roman citizenship was becoming feebler, stifled by the rich development of municipal life. The Gaul, the Asiatic who had the *jus civitatis* belonged nominally to a Roman tribe ; in fact he was the citizen of a provincial municipality.

The urban tribes only continued organized and living, not in the matter of political rights, for we have seen what Augustus and Tiberius had done with these, but for the advantages secured to the poor of Rome. The Emperors had changed into a permanent institution the usage, often interrupted under the Republic, of selling to the citizens corn every month from the state magazines at a nominal price. There had even been given gratuitously to the very poor, tickets similar to the bread-tickets of our charitable boards, and this had ended by becoming a general distribution. In the year 58 B. C. Clodius had established the wholly gratuitous character of the distributions.[2] As there were in the city citizens belonging to the thirty-five tribes, the poor who had obtained the *tesserae* (which were doubtless numbered, for more regularity, according to the order of the tribes) formed thirty-five new corporations. These divisions preserved the ancient and glorious name which formerly designated the entire Roman people, now by a strange change of fortune to be applied only to the poorer classes. As used by Martial and Statius,[3] the words *tribulis* and *pauper* are already synonymous; and in that society which had so much respect for wealth, those who bore either name were the objects of the same contempt.

---

[1] Italian landed property had a partial immunity at least from taxes and the character of Quiritarian property, so that the holders of these estates had over them the *dominium*, and not simply, like the provincials, enjoyment (*possessio*).

[2] Cic., *Pro Sestio*, 25, 55 ; cf. Appian, *Bell. civ.* i. 21, and *Acad. des inscr.* new series, xiii. 23.

[3] Martial, *Epigr.* viii. 15, and Statius, *Silv.* iii. 10.

The plebs nevertheless had its millionnaires, as Martial shows us, — the contractors for works, for transport and funerals, the town criers, the farmers of certain imposts, and manufacturers of every sort, men who speculated on the vices or lived on the pleasures of the rich. The law declared certain of these occupations to be infamous, and on those fortunes there rested a stain, even in the eyes of some of the poor. But these parvenus cared little for men's esteem or contempt, being almost all of servile origin ;[1] for some centuries the population had been recruited from strangers, so that there were no more Romans in Rome than there are now Parisians in Paris.

We have recently observed a sitting of the Senate: let us become acquainted with the people. Sub-  joined is a letter which Aurelian addressed to them after having in Egypt overthrown the usurper Firmus : "Aurelian Augustus to the Roman people who adore him, health! After having paci-

TESSERA USED AT THE CIRCUS, IN LEAD, FOUND IN THE SAONE.[2]

fied the world, we have also conquered, taken, and put to death the Egyptian robber Firmus. You, the worthy children of Romulus, have therefore nothing more to fear. The corn of Egypt, which this robber detained, will reach you without the loss of a grain, if you live in peace and good friendship with the Senate, the knights, and the praetorians. I am able to preserve Rome from all disquietude. Go then to the shows ; go to the circus. The public needs are our business; pleasure is yours."[3] It is manifest that we have not gone too far in the expression of our contempt for this populace who dragged in the mud the greatest name the world had ever known, and had replaced noble sentiments by the lowest appetites. Influenced by those who look only at the

---

[1] . . . *Minore in dies plebe ingenua* (Tac., *Ann.* iv. 27 *et seq.*).

[2] *Gazette archéol.* 1876, p. 31. From the Museum of Lyons. The bas-relief is also published by the *Gazette archéol.*, *ibid.* pl. 10.

[3] *Vacate ludis, vacate circensibus. Nos publicae necessitates teneant, vos occupent voluptates* (Vopisc., *Vita Firm.* 5). Juvenal had already said (*Sat.* x. 78–81), —

. . . *qui dabat olim*
Imperium, fasces, legiones, omnia, nunc se
Continet atque duas tantum res anxius optat,
Panem et circenses ;

and Fronto (*Princ. hist.*) : "We lead the Roman people by two things, — *annona et spectaculis.*"

surface of things, the honor has been done this people of believing that it had some share in the founding and maintaining of the Empire. The people performed their last act of sovereignty when, in the Republic's vigor, but under the pressure of the first triumvirs, they gave Caesar the proconsulship of the Gauls; dating from that day, thirty years before the battle of Actium, the soldiers did everything, and they did what their victorious leader desired. What part did the people take in the accession of Tiberius and Claudius, in the death of Caius and Nero, even in the struggle between the Vitellians and Flavians? That of spectators, looking on at the duel between the Emperor and the aristocracy, or the

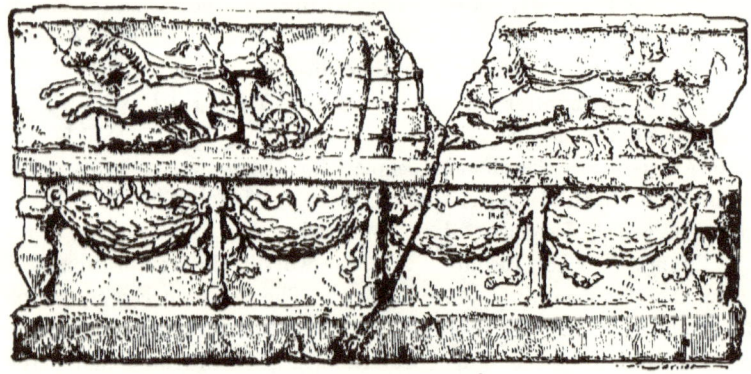

A RACE IN THE CIRCUS.[1]

murderous rivalries of ambitious men seeking the supreme power, with as much pleasure and coolness as at the gladiatorial combats in the arena.

As evidence that the popular sovereignty still existed, it has been said that the deserted Forum and the silent rostra were replaced by the circus and the theatre, where sometimes clamor arose. Certain Emperors, seeking popularity by unwise complaisance, did in fact sometimes yield to the random wishes of the crowd assembled in the theatre. But others received them with haughty disdain; and if the clamor continued, called in soldiers and pikes, whereupon immediately all became quiet.[2]

[1] Bas-relief found at Lyons in 1874.
[2] Cf. Suet., Dom. 10 and 13; Dion Cassius, lxix. 6; Josephus, Ant. Jud. xix. 14; Plutarch, Galba, 17. There were soldiers at the gates, and even inside (Suet., Nero, 21, and the Digest, i. 12, 1, sect. 12).

Let us be just even towards the populace of Rome. The distributions of corn received by it scandalize us, and political economists rightly regard them as detestable expedients. But the historian is compelled to see in these distributions. not a means of corruption skilfully employed by the Emperors. but one of the most ancient of Roman customs, and according to the ideas of those days a most natural institution. As early as King Ancus, *congiaria* were bestowed; and from the first century of the Republic the Senate, in time of scarcity. had been accustomed to buy corn and distribute it gratuitously or at a price far below its value. When the Roman people had acquired by arms the ownership of the provincial soil, a portion of it was assigned to some of their own number for the foundation of colonies; upon the rest were levied taxes in money to support the government, and in kind to feed the people, the armies. and the governors with their suites. Since the men of that time believed that all belonged to the conqueror, it is not strange that the distributions of corn at Rome should have been specially favored by the Gracchi, who were popular leaders, and by Cato. one of the chiefs of the Republican aristocracy.

Had the French in Algeria imposed on the Arabs a tax in kind, instead of a tribute in money. the corn they would have given would have served to support the African army, as the cattle taken in the *razzias* serve to improve the ordinary rations of the troops. Now at Rome. when the Republic permanently established distributions of corn, the army was still the people; therefore, even after Augustus, only the citizens *pleno jure* were permitted to take a share. The *vigiles*, for example. who had very important duties at Rome, but who were recruited from the freedmen. obtained only after three years the corn *tessera*. In these largesses, therefore. we must see only the benefits gained by victory secured by the heirs of the conquerors. Under one form or another, that has been done in all time, and will continue to be done so long as there are conquerors and conquered.

We have seen that Augustus had determined the quantity of corn required for the consumption of the palace. the soldiers. and two hundred thousand citizens,[1] and that the annual expense for

[1] Vol. IV. p. 116. Cf. *Digest*, XXXII. i. 36 pr., and Hirschfeld, *Die Getreideverwaltung in der Röm. Kaiserz.* p. 6. There were still 200,000 people receiving under Septimius

the gratuitous distributions and the sale under price perhaps equalled ten millions of francs [$2.000.000].[1]   From this total a fifth must be deducted for the corn supplied since Nero's reign to the soldiers in Rome and the suburbs whom the state had the duty of feeding, thus reducing the actual expenditure for the poor.   Whatever the amount may have been, we must admit that these gifts were dishonorable neither to him who gave, nor to them who received.[2]

In the Middle Ages, and even as late as 1830, the people on certain festivals had also their distributions of food : fountains of

Severus; but the *cives* had been reduced to 160,000, because 40,000 shares were reserved for the soldiers of all kinds who were in Rome or the environs, in garrison or provided for. In the Monument of Ancyra there is reference only to the *plebs urbana* (ὄχλος), and Fronto (*Princ. hist.*) distinguishes the corn-receiving plebs, who were kept by *congiaria*, from the entire people, who were amused by spectacles, at which all classes were present . . . *Congiariis frumentarium modo plebem singillatim placari ac nominatim, spectaculis universam.* Appian says (*Bell. civ.* ii. 120): τό τε σιτηρέσιον ταῖς πένησι χορηγούμενον ἐν μόνῃ Ῥώμῃ, and Dion Cassius, xliii. 21: σιτοδοτούμενος ὄχλος. Cf. Pliny, *Pan.* 25. These recipients of the *annona* were therefore the city poor, and at Rome, as at Paris, these poor were assisted without their moral conduct being taken into consideration (Seneca, *De Ben.* iv. 28. 2). But it must be noted that they received less than French soldiers, — whose daily ration is 950 grammes of bread, 300 grammes of meat, and a little vegetable, — and that consequently a family could not live in idleness on a corn ticket.

[1] At the death of Septimius Severus (Spartian, *Sev.* 7 and 23) the state magazines had enough corn for seven years at the rate of 75,000 modii a day.   The corn warehoused by Severus would therefore have sufficed for distribution to 456,000 citizens, and not to 200,000 What remained in store after the delivery to those having the right to the 60 modii according to regulation, was sold at a low price.   If we suppose that on these 256,000 other shares the state had lost half the price, the total expenditure would still have hardly reached the estimate which Hirschfeld gives (*op. cit.* p. 68). — 4 millions to 4½ millions of thalers; but it is probable that the allowance of 60 modii annually had been increased.   At Constantinople, Constantine raised the distribution to 80,000 modii *per diem* (Socrates, *Hist. eccles.* ii. 13).   Spartianus also speaks (*Sev.* 18) of a provision of oil for five years made by Septimius Severus and distributed gratuitously.   An inscription of Orelli makes us acquainted with a *procurator ad oleum.*   Respecting the sale of corn at a reduced rate, see Suet., *Oct.* 41; Monument of Ancyra, xv. ; Tac., *Ann.* xv. 39; Dion, lv. 26 : and on the gratuity of the ordinary *frumentationes,* Tac., *Ann.* xv. 72; Suet., *Nero,* 10; Hirschfeld, pp. 12-13.   There were also sometimes distributions of wine (Pliny, *Hist. nat.* xiv. 11), of salt (*ibid.* xxxi. 7), of meat (Lamprid., *Alex. Sev.* 22, 26), etc.

[2] It has been stated in Vol. IV. p. 118, what Paris expended on the poor in 1875.   For 1881, 125,000 persons are entered on the lists of the charitable boards; and if there are counted the sick received into hospitals, the infirm maintained in asylums, the 60,000 sick or lying-in women attended at their homes, and the necessitous temporarily assisted, it will be found that the protection afforded by public aid extends to nearly 400,000 persons   We must add to these charities that the city levies no tax on small quantities of articles of food brought within the walls, and that it gives 10,000,000 francs for free primary education. The boards of relief of the twenty arrondissements receive besides annually from private liberality amounts of money which in certain arrondissements exceed 200,000 francs : thus adding millions to the relief-fund of Paris.

wine were set flowing in the streets, loaves, sausages, hams were thrown among the crowd, who with loud cries jostled one another in their efforts to secure a piece. These coarse bounties proceeded from another principle, and were not repeated so frequently. Yet I cannot help saying that I prefer the strict and silent arrangement of the Roman *annona*.[1]

To the distributions of food were added from time to time those of money. Antoninus gave at the rate of a hundred and thirty-five sesterces per head yearly. Under the Caesars, from the Dictator to Claudius, this rate had been only forty-three. The latter seems to have been scarcely worth the trouble of stretching out the hand to take; but we know that in that society no man refused, however small the gift, or high the condition of the recipient.[2] .

Altogether, the distributions of corn and money to the Roman plebs amounted annually to perhaps fifteen or sixteen millions of francs [$3,000,000].

The public games were still less expensive to the state. According to a document of the year 51 A. D. there was scarcely paid out of the treasury yearly, for the most important, a sum total equal to 500,000 francs.[3] The city of Paris gives 800,000 francs to the Opera alone, which is never accessible to the poor, while in the Circus Maximus 385,000 spectators were admitted gratis. It is true there must be added to this expenditure the sums spent by the magistrates presiding over the spectacle, the praetors and consuls obliged by their official duty to celebrate certain solemnities,[4]

---

[1] Until recently a custom derived from the *frumentationes* existed in Rome. The cardinal governor of the city was obliged, on the evening of Shrove Tuesday, to offer a supper to all present at the Opera; it cost him from 20,000 to 30,000 crowns, according to his doing it economically or lavishly.

[2] See above, p. 85. By reckoning all the *congiaria* of which we know from Caesar to Claudius, we find that in a century there was distributed to the 200,000 *frumentarii*, 216,950,000 *denarii*; that is, 2,169,500 francs per annum, and about 11 *denarii* per head. Cf. Marquardt, II. i. 2d part. p. 110.

[3] Namely, for the Roman games, which lasted sixteen days, 760,000 sesterces; for the plebeian games (fourteen days), 600,000; for the Apollinarian games (eight days), 380,000; for the Augustal games, 10,000. (Cf. Mommsen, *C. I. L.*, according to the *Fasti Antiates*, p. 377b, and Friedländer, ii. 164.) To these public games, for which the state made a grant, must be added those of Ceres, of the Great Goddess, or the Megalesian (Martial, *Ep.* x. 41), of Flora, which cost 20,000 (*Id., ibid.*), and of Sylla's triumph. The number of games varied with the time: many under the Empire were successively created and abolished; the six ancient games lasted down to the fourth century. Cf. Tertullian, *De Spectaculis*, 6.

[4] The Megalesian games, which the praetor was required to give, cost him 100,000 sesterces when he was disposed to be frugal, and much more if he wished to make a display.

and the sums given by individuals who wished to make their
name or their fortune honored.[1] As vanity played its part and
there was emulation among these givers of public games, some of
them ruined themselves. A large fortune was divided and passed
into other hands; all that the state lost by the change was the
benefit that these millionnaires might have conferred by a better
employment of their money. But the ancients considered that in
spending it in this way it was extremely well expended. It
appeared to them that the rich possessed wealth for the benefit of
the public service, and those who held it shared in this idea. The
liturgies at Athens, the *munera* in the Roman cities, were onerous
obligations imposed by law and custom on those who solicited honors
or public consideration. With us all this is entirely different, and
we even find it hard to understand functions which cost money
instead of bringing it in. Yet facts to which all antiquity testifies
cannot be disputed, and we must accept that rule of historical
criticism and of strict equity which bids us in judging ancient
matters to take account of ancient ideas.

Besides, in their origin spectacles and scenic games, and even
the gladiatorial combats, were, like the old Mysteries, religious acts,
auto da fé, and in the pagan empire they officially preserved this
character; at some of them the statues of the gods were always
carried in procession. Under Domitian, even, the law *Genetiva
Julia* imposed on the duumvirs the charge of the games of the
circus and of the religious banquets, in the same category with
the inspection of the sacred buildings.[2] Accordingly, patriotism,
which in those days was a part of religion, hesitated at no sacrifice to make the celebration of these festivals worthy of the gods
and the city.

On the anniversary of his birthday Hadrian gave free games;[3]

Hence men avoided this office, and Constantine was obliged (Zosimus, II. 38) to take measures against the refractory. In case a praetor-elect died, his heirs were obliged to give the
games.

[1] When things were done liberally, there was expended for games which lasted three days
400,000 sesterces (Petron., *Satyr.* 45). The gladiatorial combats given every five years at
Pisaurum, by virtue of a legacy, cost only 150 or 180 sesterces, according as interest was reckoned at 5 or 6 per cent. Orelli (No. 81), who reckons it at 12 per cent, as being in the province, doubles the last figure. But there were gladiators at all prices. . . . *Dedit gladiatores
se sesterciarios, jam decrepitos, quos si sufflasses cecidissent* (Petron. *ibid.*).

[2] Cap. cxxviii.

[3] . . . προικα (Dion. lxix. 8).

there were some, therefore, which were not so. It was a widely spread form of industry which cost the state nothing. This we knew from Tacitus, Petronius, and Dion, and inscriptions confirm it.[1]

From these usages it resulted that, the citizens doing all, the state had scarcely anything to do. We see what was meant by *panem et circenses*, and how small the sacrifices really were demanded of the community by that crowd who desired, it is said, to be amused and fed at the expense of the Empire.

At the same time, while the sum entered in the official estimate for popular pleasures imposed on the treasury, the *aerarium*, was only a small charge, the Emperor's treasure, the *fiscus*, or what might be termed his civil list, bore a much heavier burden. Subjected by precedent to the same obligations with the magistrates and rich citizens, the Emperor gave festivals which the pontiff's calendar did not mention, and often aided his friends and kinsmen[2] to do things liberally when they had to offer a show to the people. The bad Emperors ruined themselves by these expenses; the good knew how to spend only their superfluous income. Augustus had given them the example of these liberalities, which custom made necessary, but which a wise firmness could keep within just limits.[3]

In the early days of the Empire the public games occupied sixty-six days in the year, sixteen of which were for races in the hippodrome, forty-eight for scenic representations, which were not very popular,[4] and two for the feasts which followed certain sacrifices. We have yearly fifty-two Sundays; by adding to these the public holidays, we shall reach nearly the same total of days of public rest, without counting all those which our workmen take of themselves. Official statistics give for the whole of France an average of only two hundred and twenty-six working days.[5] In

---

[1] A statue was erected to Caracalla from the proceeds of the seats let at the amphitheatre of Cirta.

[2] Thus Hadrian received two million sesterces from Trajan for the games it was his duty to give during his praetorship; Valerian gave five million to Aurelian for the festivals of his consulship (Spartian. *Hadr.* 3; Vopiscus. *Aurel.* 12).

[3] See in the Testament of Augustus an enumeration of the festivals given by that Emperor.

[4] The medals record buildings and the games of the circus and amphitheatre; they never refer to theatres or scenic representations.

[5] In pursuance of a rule of Marcus Aurelius (*Capit.* 10), the courts were to be open for 230 days yearly. Besides the annual games, Rome had some extraordinary holidays, due to

addition, our cities have amusements every evening: Paris alone possesses thirty-eight theatres or circuses, and a great number of other places of amusement. We are certainly more entertained, or think ourselves so, than the Roman people usually were, — at least we have the right to expect it, for in fact we do more work.

In course of time the Romans of Rome and the Greeks of Constantinople increased the number of games until they amounted to a hundred and seventy-five holidays in the year; that is the total given in a document dated 354 A. D.   But at that date we have reached the Byzantine empire; and in spite of the horror of the Church for shows, they were more popular even than in Trajan's time.   Even more was spent on them: for example, two thousand pounds[1] of gold for the consular games alone.

In imperial Rome the people's pleasures were full of a partisan-ship which was not dangerous, indeed, but was certainly scandalous. This feeling, having no longer great objects, attached itself to small ones.   In the circus, the Blues and the Greens divided the spectators, and the disputes raised by them agitated the whole city.   A man, the voluntary victim of a vulgar admiration, threw himself on the funeral pile which consumed the body of a famous charioteer,[2] and Juvenal dared to write: " If the Greens are beaten, Rome will be in the same terror as after the battle of Cannae."[3]   From Rome this passion reached Constantinople, where it became more keen, and survived the invasion of the Barbarians.[4]   The Christian Empire was still less wise respecting the *circenses* than the Pagan Empire had been; and the moderns in certain respects have outdone the ancients, — which ought at least to lead us to show indulgence to the latter.   Could not they also say, as do sober-minded men among the hundred thousand spectators at our races, that the vic-tors in the circus furnished good horses to the army and improved the breed of working animals?

imperial or individual munificence: in the year 80 there was a festival of a hundred days for the inauguration of the Colosseum; in 106, for the conquest of Dacia, 123 days of show, etc.

[1] This is the statement made by Procopius (*Hist. secr.* 26) in the reign of Justinian.

[2] Pliny. *Hist. nat.* vii. 54.

[3] *Sat.* xi. 197.   Lucian (*Nigrinus*, 29) does not like this mania for horses.   Yet he acknowledges that it is shared by a large number of very respectable people.

[4] The last king of the Goths of Italy, Totila, in 549, once more had chariot-races in the Roman circus (Gregorovius, *Hist. de Rome au moyen âge*, i. 436).

Many things have to be re-examined in this old history, which is only beginning to be studied in our days, — no longer with the forms of ancient rhetoric or of political passion, but with the severe scientific method which replaces facts amid their original surroundings, and seeks the truth, indifferent as to the results to which this truth may lead.

IV. — OFFICIALS AND DEPARTMENTS.

THE Republic had no disposition to multiply the offices of state, and it had possessed but a very small number of temporary administrators. As it farmed out the levying of the taxes and the execution of public works, there was nothing left for the Senate to determine but the sum it wished to receive from the provinces and what it intended to spend on works of general utility. The *publicani* brought the former into the treasury after their expense for collection had been deducted; the other was placed by the censors or the Conscript Fathers at the disposition of the contractors. In a word, Republican Rome governed, but did not administer, except in the case of her own affairs. Thus for the accounts of the *aerarium*, for the distributions to the people of the city (*annona*), for the coinage (*IIIviri monetales*), and the maintenance of its streets (*IVviri viarum curandarum*), she certainly had permanent offices.

The Empire at first pursued a similar plan. For a long time the state functionaries were few in number, — in the provinces, forty-five governors,[1] the legates of thirty legions, some procurators administering districts with the *jus gladii*,[2] others for the collection of the revenues of the imperial treasury; at Rome, the prefectures of

[1] The Emperor was invested with proconsular power in the imperial provinces, and his lieutenants had in them only the title of *legati pro praetore*, even when they had been consuls. In the senatorial provinces the governor was styled proconsul, and attained this post only after having held the consulship of the two consular provinces of Asia and Africa, and the praetorship for the others. The imperial legate had five fasces, the proconsul six. The provinces were drawn for by lot among the candidates designated by the Emperor. At the time of the Antonines admission to the allotment of the two consular provinces of Asia and Africa was granted only twelve years after having held the consulship. On the preparations which a consul had to make before setting forth, see Fronto's curious letter, *Ad Anton. Pium*, 8.

[2] See above, p. 165. Tacitus says (*Hist.* i. 11): *Duae Mauretaniae, Raetia, Noricum, Thracia et quae aliae procuratoribus cohibentur.*

the praetorium, of the city, of the *annona* and the watches, the offices of the vigintivirate and those whose holders had seats in the Senate.[1] All these functions were temporary or of short date,[2] except the urban prefectures. The prefect of the city often kept his office till death, and the command of the praetorians and of the watches was equally permanent if the officer retained the Emperor's confidence.[3] Thus, even in the first century of the Empire, Rome was indisposed to form a great body of permanent officials.

But by degrees the servants of the Emperor became public functionaries; the offices (*officia*) increased, and administrative centralization began. It was like a new empire when it received its true character from Diocletian; but its main principle from the first had been implied in the Empire.

The first public administration, in the modern sense of the word, dates from Augustus, who organized the postal service, with its numerous messengers, the *tabellarii*. This service, although performed by the cities, required a central office, and perhaps already, in the provinces, inspectors (*curiosi*) to insure its regularity. The second was the water-supply of Rome, instituted by Agrippa: he first employed for it his personal fortune, and constituted a whole *familia* of two hundred and forty *aquarii*,—slaves who at his death passed to the service of the state.[4] To collect the tax of a twentieth on legacies, heritages, and manumissions, and that of a fortieth on entries;[5] for the recruiting of the legions and the alimentary institution of Trajan, for the administration of the

---

[1] See above, p. 204.

[2] As a rule, the proconsulships were annual; the same was the case in respect to all the old Republican offices which had been preserved, except the consulship, now held for only three or two months. All the offices which were held directly from the Emperor had no other legal term than his will and pleasure. However, the imperial legations lasted on the average only three or five years (L. Renier, *Mél. d'épigr.* p. 124).

[3] The prefect of the city was at first charged only with keeping in check slaves and disorderly persons (Tac., *Ann.* vi. 11). His civil and criminal jurisdiction became later very extensive (*Digest*, i. 12). The prefect of the praetorium also had at first only the command of the guards (Tac., *Ann.* iv. 1 and 2), and ended by being the second person in the Empire (*Digest*, i. 11). The prefect of the watch, who had the duty of directing the nightly rounds, to prevent or check fires (Suet., *Oct.* 30), acquired, besides, criminal jurisdiction over incendiaries, thieves, and vagabonds (*Digest*, i. 15, 3). Thus the prerogatives of the Emperor's agents increased in proportion as those of the *magistratus populi Romani* diminished.

[4] Frontinus, *De Aquaed.*, and Dareste, *Des Contrats*, pp. 94, 110, etc.

[5] *Procurator XX hereditatum, quadragesimae, ad alimenta, ad bona damnatorum*, etc. Cf. Or.-Henzen, in the *Index*.

Emperor's domains, that of the property of those attainted, etc., there existed special permanent agents, whose jurisdiction often comprised several provinces.[1]

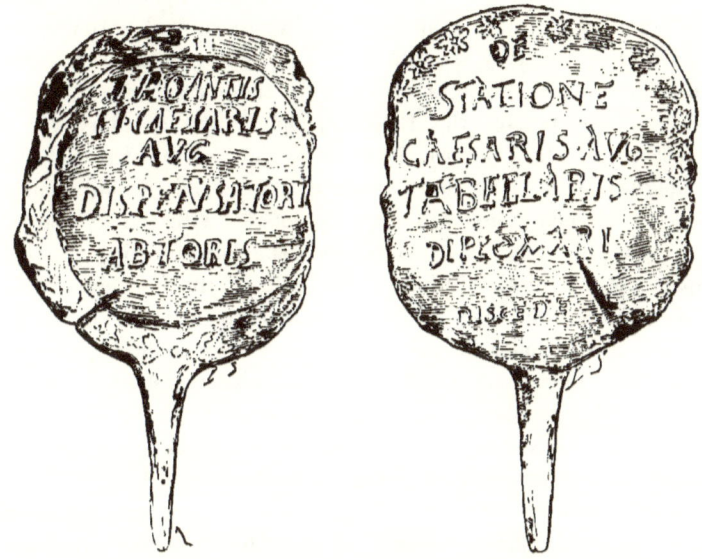

These officials received a salary of sixty, a hundred, two hundred, and three hundred thousand sesterces;[3] the proconsuls an indemnity of a million sesterces[4] and travelling expenses, with allowances of

---

[1] Thus Tib. Cl. Candidus was *procurator XX hereditatum per Gallias Lugdunensem et Belgiam et utramque Germaniam* (Orelli, No. 798, and many others).

[2] This bronze plate, the foot of which had to be fixed in a support, had a different notice on each of its faces. On face No. 1 is read: "(Office) of Thoas, (slave) of the Emperor Tiberius, put in charge of the table conches;" on the other is engraved, in the third century perhaps, the following words: "Withdraw from the office reserved for the messengers provided with the diploma of the Emperor's (postal service)." — E. Desjardins, *Bibliothèque de l'École des hautes Études*, xxxv. 72–73.

[3] *Procurator sexagenarius, centenarius, ducenarius, trecenarius.* Cf. the *Index* of Or.-Henzen. The inscription No. 946 gives to the *procurator rationis privatae* a salary of 300,000 sesterces.

[4] *Salarium proconsulari solitum* (Tac., *Agr.* 42). Dion (lxxviii. 22) gives the grand total as 250,000 drachmae or 1,000,000 sesterces ($50,000), without reckoning the corn of which the governor had need for his house (*frumentum in cellam*). His lieutenants — the quaestor, the praetorian cohort, and the assessors included — also received *cibaria* (Cic., *Verr.* i. 14, 36), or the *congiarium* and the *salarium*; i.e., at the beginning, wine and salt (Fronto, *Ad Ant.* 1, 2, and Pliny, *Hist. Nat.* xxxi. 41; *Digest*, i. 22, 4).

different sorts to meet the various burdens that were imposed upon
them. The republican principle had been gratuitous public services,
except an indemnity for expenses incurred by the magistrate in
the interest of the state. The principle of the imperial government
was, on the contrary, remuneration by an annual salary for the
services performed by the official. The two systems were concurrently followed. — gratuitous service by those who were still styled
" the magistrates of the Roman people," and a salary for the
Emperor's agents. But the latter were indefinitely increased, while
no addition was made to the number of the old republican magistracies, and soon there will exist no longer, with the exception of
the consulship, the praetorship, and the quaestorship, any other
unpaid officials in the Empire than those of the municipia.[1]

On this subject there is another remark to make. The example
of Cicero, — an honorable man, nevertheless, — who during his gover-
norship of Cilicia could put by over two million sesterces, shows the
effects of this republican unsalaried system. It was possible under
the Republic to make a fortune in public offices by exactions to
which the Senate shut its eyes; this could no longer be done
under the Empire, because of the Emperor, — a more inexorable
judge of extortioners, because it was for his own interest to
prevent his subjects from being oppressed.

The centre to which all affairs converged was the imperial
palace; accordingly, it had been from an early date crowded with
a multitude of slaves and freedmen, some charged with domestic
duties,[2] others forming administrative departments where the accounts
of receipts and expenditure were kept, despatches received and
examined, replies sent, and certain matters arranged for reporting
to the Senate, to the privy council which Augustus had constituted, and to the court where the Emperor heard appeals and
reserved cases.

At the head of all these departments were freedmen, who

---

[1] The inferior agents of the municipal and public administration were paid : those of the
state received *mercedem et cibaria ex aerario ; i.e.* a salary and allowance of food (Fronto,
De Aquaed. 100).

[2] Their titles, consequently, varied infinitely. A great number of them will be found in
chap. ix. of Orelli, which contains 254 inscriptions relating to the slaves and freedmen of the
palace. Under No. 2,974 Orelli has given a summary of the titles which accompany the proper
names in the *columbarium* of the slaves and freedmen of Augustus and Livia, in which were
more than three hundred names.

rapidly gained great influence; for where the monarch is everything and the whole Empire rests in his hands, there is one power
greater than himself, namely, the people about him, who control
or influence his will. Under Augustus and Tiberius these freedmen had been kept in the background; but from Caligula to
Vespasian they governed the palace and Empire. Helios, in Nero's
absence, condemned even senators to confiscation, banishment, and
death. Remitted to obscurity by the first two Flavii, these freedmen under the third regained their power, and the younger Pliny
could say: "The majority of our Emperors, those masters of the
citizens, were the slaves of their freedmen. They understood only
by means of them, they spoke by them, and by them were given
the praetorships, the offices of priests, the consulships." [1] Yet the
singular respect which he himself manifested towards Trajan's
freedmen, whom he declared publicly in the Senate to be worthy of
the senators' regards,[2] shows the credit which these men had under
the better Emperors. They formed a sort of permanent body, in
which were preserved the traditions of all that skill whereby a
master was made captive. The Emperor died; the freedmen did
not die, or at least their influence was perpetuated. They were
transferred with the furniture to the service of the successor.
Claudius Etruscus had served ten Caesars.[3]

The stain of their birth was concealed under the honors
bestowed upon them; many obtained the gold ring or military distinctions. Narcissus had the ornaments of the quaestorship, another
freedman those of the praetorship, and Claudius brought them with
him into the Senate. Some made distinguished marriages or
bought famous ancestry. Pallas became the man of highest rank
in Rome when it was thus proved that he descended from the
early kings of Arcadia, who in the person of Evander had founded
Rome itself. Accordingly, his arrogance equalled his wealth.
Not to soil his lips by speaking to slaves, this freedman communicated with them only by signs or by writing. It is a poet, Statius,

---

[1] Dion, lxiii. 12; Pliny, *Paneg.* 88.

[2] *Tanto magis digni quibus honor omnis praestetur a nobis (ibid.).*

[3] Statius, *Silv.* iii. 3. He died at the age of eighty, under Domitian. The Alexandrine
rhetorician Dionysios (Suidas, *s. v.*) was, from Nero to Trajan's time, set over the libraries,
the correspondence, the embassies, and rescripts. On royal secretaries among the ancients,
see M. Egger, *Mém. d'hist. anc.* pp. 220–259.

who, in his eulogy on Claudius Etruscus, gives us the most exact information respecting some of the offices filled by the freedmen of the palace. "To thee alone are intrusted the sacred treasures of the Emperor, the riches dispersed among the nations, and the tribute which the world pays to us. What Spain derives from her gold mines and that which glitters in the Dalmatian mountains, the harvests of Africa, the corn that the Egyptian crushes on his threshing-floor, the pearls which the diver seeks for in the depths of the Eastern seas, the fleeces brought from the pasturages watered by the Galaesus, and the transparent crystal, the citron from Mauretania, the ivory of India, — in fine, whatever the winds from south, east, and north waft to us, all is intrusted to thy watchful care. Thou dost estimate what is daily needed for the legions and the people; thou knowest the necessary expenditure for the temples, for the dikes which keep back the high flood, and for the military roads. Thou takest account of the gold which glitters on Caesar's ceilings, of that which forms the statues of the gods, or the coinage marked with the image of the Emperor." Etruscus, the treasurer (*a rationibus*), held what we should consider to be four ministerial departments; namely, of trade, public works, finance, and the Emperor's household.

The same poet makes us acquainted with another freedman, named Abascantus, who had charge of the despatches (*ab epistulis*). "To send to all parts of the earth the orders of the master of Rome; to know what laurels reach us from the North, what standards are on the banks of the Euphrates, the Danube, and the Rhine; how far the confines of the world have retreated before us towards Thule, at the limit of the roaring waves, — these are some of his duties. Is there need to call together trusty swords, he points out the one most capable to command a cohort or a hundred horsemen, him who deserves the glorious title of tribune, or who will best lead the swift squadrons. What does he not do besides? He needs to know whether the Nile has inundated the fields, or if the south wind with its fertilizing rains has watered sandy Libya. Less active is Juno's messenger, less prompt is Fame in her rapid chariot."[1] We may say that this secretary

---

[1] Statius, *Silv.* iii. 3, 86-105; v. 1, 85-105.

of despatches acted the part of a minister of war, of the interior,
and of foreign affairs.

His offices, in which intelligent slaves were at work, whom
liberty awaited as the reward of their services, were separated into
two classes, — one for the Greek-speaking countries, the other for
the Latin-speaking.[1] Here were employed intelligent and learned
men able to do honor, by their knowledge and style, to the
imperial government. We possess the works of one of them,
which by their precision of form and propriety of expression rank
among the best biographies in Latin literature; I refer to those
of Suetonius.[2] Not only was the style of the Latin or Greek
careful, but also the writing itself: the despatches were models of
calligraphy.[3]

The secretary of petitions (*a libellis*) and inquiries (*a cognitionibus*) had to listen to the crowd of petitioners and complainants,
to read the applications of those who from all parts of the Empire
asked for a place, a title, a favor, and who appealed to the imperial justice or clemency. He was supposed to render an account
of every matter to the Emperor, who decided it. The secretary
of inquiries, probably first appointed by Claudius, made a preliminary examination in affairs which the Emperor himself was to
decide or refer either to the Senate or to ordinary magistrates.[4]

These four secretaries — namely, of accounts, of correspondence,
of petitions, and of inquiries — remind us of the ministerial organization which France long had under the ancient monarchy, with
its four secretaries of state, whose duties were as complicated as
those of the Roman secretaries; and we are also reminded that it
was the principle at Versailles, as at Rome, to make a choice from

---

[1] An inscription (Orelli, No. 823) mentions even a *librarius Arabicus* (*Mém. de l'Acad.
des inscr.* I. 316), established doubtless in the *scrinium litterarum* at the time of the formation
of the province of Arabia; and this leads to the supposition that there were others for other
languages.

[2] Suetonius, the son of a legionary tribune and the friend of the younger Pliny, was
Hadrian's secretary, as was also the rhetorician Avidius, who was prefect of Egypt and father
of the ambitious Avidius Cassius. Titinius Capito, whom Pliny considered one of the best
writers of his time, had been Trajan's secretary. C. Vestinus, a preceptor and then
Hadrian's secretary, became keeper of the libraries of Rome, high-priest of Egypt, and
curator of the Museum of Alexandria (*C. I. G.* 5,900).

[3] Plutarch, *De Pyth. Or.* 7. Cf. Egger, *op. cit.* p. 224.

[4] Narcissus, under Claudius, had been *ab epistolis* (Suet., *Claud.* 28); Epaphroditus, under
Nero, *a libellis* (*Id.*, *Dom.* 14). The functions *a libellis* and *a cognitionibus* were often separated:
cf. Cuq, on the *magister sacrarum largitionum*.

men of low birth, — which did not prevent these humble individuals from becoming sometimes great men. The two governments had been led by similarity of circumstances to act alike, and they doubtless derived kindred advantages from this similar mode of action. In spite of the bad name of the imperial freedmen, I believe that with better information we should find that all were by no means harmful to their Emperor or useless to the Empire.

I remark that they had not given themselves up to a spirit of clique, which is so dangerous in public duties. The provincial administration was not carried on by their comrades in slavery or in enfranchisement; out of the eighty financial procurators which inscriptions make known to us, only eight freedmen are to be found, and these all belong to the early days of the Empire.[1] At the same time it would have been better to fill the high offices of state with men more respected by public opinion, and not belonging to the imperial household. We have seen Hadrian effecting this change by intrusting the duties of the secretaries to members of the equestrian order. Several Emperors had forestalled him in this direction without making, as he did, this reform a regulation of government. His successors followed it, and the administration became the better by this; but it was the beginning of that system which, followed out to the minutest detail, shackled society with so many bands that it became motionless and lifeless; so that we discover existing in the most brilliant period of the Empire the germ of those institutions which diminished its strength and prepared its fall.

The slaves and freedmen of whom we have just spoken lived in the palace, whither men of free birth daily came to dispute with them for influence. Under the Republic the great opened their houses to crowds of so-called friends, who in every case were their clients for the *sportula* and their partisans in any bold attack. The general with the army, the governor in his province, had also his band of young men attached to him and of friends who formed his council, carried his orders, or supervised their execution. Caius Gracchus and Livius Drusus had introduced the

---

[1] Starting from the Flavii, the *procuratores augusti* are true public officials taken from the knights (Tac., *Agr.* 4). The procurators of the early Emperors were stewards, like those belonging to private persons mentioned in many inscriptions. Cf. Henzen, *Index*, p. 187.

practice of giving a certain order to this retinue. They had friends of the first, second, and third degree, whom they treated accordingly: the last awaiting in the street a haughty salute, the second admitted to touch the patron's hand, the first to live on intimate terms with him, — a curious proof of the facility with which the Romans submitted to subordination and discipline. The Emperors maintained these usages, as they did so many others of the Republic; they also had their friends of different degrees, from intimate friends living with them, without title or duties,[1] to those who, simply agreeable, were scarcely distinguishable from domestics, unless they were learned men, artists, or eloquent and highly gifted persons, with whom Trajan, Hadrian, and Marcus Aurelius delighted to converse.

Under a personal government some of these friends of the Emperor, the companions of his travels or of his festivities,[2] and frequenters of the palace gained great influence.[3] Augustus had selected from them the members of his privy council,[4] — a genuine council of government, which examined matters referred to them at Caesar's order by the secretaries of state. For his judicial functions the Emperor called to his assistance any whom he judged fit. An example of these imperial sessions was given in the chapter on Trajan,[5] and this renders further comments unnecessary.

Friends of the Emperor, palace freedmen, and even slaves, these frequenters of the imperial antechamber were not always

---

[1] Seneca, De Ben. vi. 34; De Clem. i. 10.

[2] *Comites* and *convictores*. They had their special servants at the palace, the chief of whom had the title of *procurator a cura amicorum*. While travelling they formed the Emperor's retinue, and their expenses were paid by him. Augustus on one occasion gave to those of Tiberius, who had done no more for them than to furnish their food, six hundred thousand sesterces for the first-class friends, four hundred thousand for those of the second, two hundred thousand to the third (Suet., *Tib.* 46).

[3] *Nullum majus boni imperii instrumentum quam bonos amicos esse*, said Helvidius under Domitian (Tac., *Hist.* iv. 7). Homulus, under Trajan, thought the same. This title of " the Emperor's friend " came to be attached to certain duties: it became even a sort of title of honor which was inscribed on a man's tomb after mentioning the consulship. The prefects of the city and of the praetorium were of right " friends of the Emperor," as the marshals, peers, and cardinals were in France *cousins du roi*. Under the Merovingians, the king's *convive*, or companion, whose *wehrgeld* was double that of the other great vassals, was doubtless the successor to the Emperor's friend. This custom had existed besides in all the Oriental courts.

[4] See Vol. IV. p. 97, and Suet., *Tib.* 55. The consuls and high dignitaries of state formed part of it. These councillors had also a stipend of sixty thousand, one hundred thousand, and two hundred thousand sesterces (Orelli, No. 2,648).

[5] Vol. V. p. 261.

discreet persons. Some of them sold their real or pretended influence, and the news, true or false, which they had heard behind the door or feigned to have told in the master's ear. "The Emperor is sold," said Diocletian angrily; and Alexander Severus caused one of his servants to be suffocated who had made gain of the credulity of petitioners. During the execution a herald proclaimed: "Thus shall perish by the smoke he who has sold smoke!"

V. — THE ARMY.

THERE is no occasion to speak again of the activity put forth by the whole Empire for public works, — the municipal monuments, temples, circuses, amphitheatres, sometimes equalling those of Rome in beauty, and even in extent,[1] the bridges over rivers, the canals in the plains,[2] the aqueducts above the valleys,[3] the roads across mountains, the lighthouses on promontories, and, finally, the huge network of military roads, in all over fifty thousand miles in length.[4] The preceding chapters have exhibited this great work of civilization, which the moderns have surpassed only in our own days.

This brilliancy of civil life would have been soon extinguished had it not been for the army, which, permanently posted between the Empire and the Barbarians, protected the vast industry behind it. Under the Antonines the army was formidable, and we must speak of it with some detail; for of the two great originations of Rome, her law and her military organization, the latter remained a very long time incomparable.

Under the Republic, when war was over, the soldiers were disbanded; but after the rivalry between Marius and Sylla there was always some leader who found the means of keeping an army of

---

[1] The amphitheatre of Capua was almost as large as the Colosseum of Rome.

[2] The ancients did not understand dams, but they made weirs . . . *cataractis aquae cursum temperare* (Pliny, *Epist.* x. 69).

[3] Rome alone had as many as fourteen aqueducts, in all a length of 249 miles, of which fifty miles were on arches. The three which still remain in use are sufficient to make Rome the city in all Europe best supplied with water.

[4] It has been computed that the Itinerary of Antoninus names 372 great roads, which united would have made a road over fifty thousand miles in length.

his own. Octavius succeeded to all these forces; on the day after the battle of Actium he was at the head of seventy-six legions. Of these he kept twenty-five and dismissed the rest; Vespasian had thirty, — a total at which they remained for a long while.

Augustus declared these twenty-five legions permanent, and he stationed them in the provinces of the frontier, under the orders of legates appointed by himself and dismissible at will. To provide

ARCH OF THE AQUEDUCT CALLED ANIO NOVUS.

their pay he created new imposts, and established by the side of the public treasury a military chest, which received and expended all the money required by the army.

According to the list of the forces of the Empire presented to the Senate by Tiberius, the twenty-five legions were posted in the following manner. — eight along the Rhine, three in Spain, two in Africa, two in Egypt, four on the Euphrates, and six on the banks of the Danube or the Adriatic coasts.[1]

[1] In the time of Dion Cassius, the efforts of the Barbarians being directed upon the Danube, there were no more than four legions on the Rhine.

Thus all the military forces, except the garrison of Rome, were established permanently between the Empire and the Barbarians, far away from the cities, where discipline becomes relaxed. The camps, the fortified posts which connected immense lines of defence, served as a base of operations; and as there was no difference between a

LEGIONARY SOLDIER, XIVA GEMINA LEGION.[1]

LEGIONARY CAVALIER.[2]

peace footing and that of war, as the legions were within reach of their magazines or arsenals, and as behind them extended their principal recruiting[3] ground, they were always ready for action.

The conception was grand and novel, and a marvellous spectacle is presented by this Empire formidably armed on its frontiers, and governed in the interior without a soldier.

---

[1] From the Museum at Mayence.   [2] Museum of Saint-Germain.

[3] In general the legions were recruited in the neighborhood of the countries where they stayed; but when a cohort or auxiliary squadron was levied it was a rule habitually followed to send this cohort to a distance from the places where it had been raised. There was no general law respecting recruiting. When those who volunteered were not sufficient, the Emperor ordered a levy in such or such a province.

Yet many of the provincials were men vanquished but yesterday, who still preserved the remembrance of lost liberty. But the Romans had not the extreme solicitude which we have in respect to the maintenance of public order. They distinguished matters of general interest from those which were only of local or personal concern. It was quite possible that not all the roads were safe, nor all the cities at peace; it occurred even in the earlier periods that, through municipal rivalry, private wars sometimes broke out between two cities. The government cared little for this; it was a matter which concerned only the parties interested. But woe to the adventurer or the city compromising the general order or taking

INFANTRY ESCORTING BAGGAGE.

arms against the Empire! A sufficient number of cohorts were despatched from the nearest frontier, and the repression was as prompt as it was terrible.

We who have so long been accustomed to expect the state to watch and act in our stead, have multiplied indefinitely the small garrisons which destroy the military spirit, but are of great advantage to the cities which receive them. We station soldiers everywhere, at the risk of the army being crumbled to pieces and its discipline relaxed. The Romans placed them nowhere, except in face of the enemy. Their legionaries had but one duty, war. — one mode of life, that of camps; and this is why they became the best soldiers in the world.

Therefore it was only rarely that they were stationed in certain cities. When it was noticed that at Antioch, with its vain, insolent population, equally incapable of doing without a master and of keeping one, it was quite impossible to keep a soldier three months without his becoming effeminate or seditious, the garrison was removed from the city. although Antioch was an important point for the defence of Syria.

The legion consisted of 6,000 infantry and 730 horse, all Roman citizens; at different periods its number varied a little, without departing widely from what we may consider as the standard. It was divided into ten cohorts, the cohort into six centuries, excepting the first, which had ten, containing the flower of the legion. The 730 horse were divided into twenty-two companies (*turmae*) of thirty-three men. Each century had its standard, which in battle served as a rallying point. *Speculatores* and *exploratores* acted as scouts.[1]

The Italians were exempt from military service;[2] yet there were some of them who wished to follow the career of arms. For these persons and for the citizens who had not been able to gain admittance into the legionary service, special corps were created (*cohortes civium Romanorum*). The service in these was less severe than in the legions, the arms less heavy, the pay less tardy. Provincials, not being citizens. and the allied kings or peoples furnished the auxiliaries, the number of which, varying according to need, was nearly equal to that of the legionaries. These squadrons (*alae*) and auxiliary cohorts habitually bore the name of the province or people who had furnished them.

Each legion. amounting. with its auxiliaries, to twelve or thirteen thousand men, had its line infantry and its light infantry, which answers to our *tirailleurs*, its own cavalry and engines for hurling darts or demolishing ramparts; that is to say, a field and siege artillery. It was a complete army, and our divisions are still organized in the same manner, though with different means. But it is worthy of remark that the Roman army was always in divi-

---

[1] According to Vegetius (ii. 6), the first cohort, which carried the eagle and the images of the Emperors (*divina et praesentia signa*), had 1,105 foot soldiers and 132 horse: the nine others consisted of only 555 foot soldiers each and 66 horse; the total for the whole legion being 6,000 foot and 726 horse, which gives, for the time of Vegetius, a very much larger proportion of horse than in the ancient legions.

[2] Herodian, II. ii. and iii. 7. Levies took place there only under very grave circumstances.

sions, since the only formation known to it was the legion, which
represents a French division.

The golden eagle which served as a standard was the symbol
of country, duty, and honor, and to this symbol the soldiers paid
real worship. "The eagles," says Tacitus, "are the gods of the
legions." [1]

AN AUXILIARY HORSEMAN.[2]

In the organization of the legion we find no especial engineering
corps. The *fabri*, or smiths, who for certain work took the place
of our engineers, were not attached to the legions, but were divided

---

[1] . . . *Propria legionum numina* (*Ann.* ii. 17).

[2] Châlon-sur-Saône; cast at Saint-Germain, No. 20,325. The inscription, which contains
many orthographical errors due to the stone - carver, should read thus: ALBANUS
EXCINCI F(ilius) EQUES ALA(e) ASTURUM NATIONE UBIUS STIP(endiorum)
XII AN(norum) XXXV H(ic) S(itus) EST (instead of F, carved by mistake) RUFUS
FRATER ET AIRA (for *heres*): Albanus, son of Excincus, horseman of the wing of the
Astures, Ubian by descent, having served twelve years and lived thirty-five, lies here — Rufus,
his brother and heir.

among the military provinces under the supreme authority of the general, who himself appointed their chief (*praefectus fabrum*). All the soldiers were alike able to work in the construction of the fortified camp which was formed when in the enemy's country, though but for a single night's occupation. Hence the Roman soldier was ready for everything, because he had been taught to do everything, and his industry was even directed to works of civil utility when war was at a stand. Thus Marius, two thousand years ago, by the *fossa Mariana*, improved "the incorrigible mouths of the Rhone;" and we have but just now repeated his work in making the St. Louis canal, which up to the present time does less service. To pass around to the north of Germany, the soldiers of Drusus diverted a part of the Rhine into Lake Flevo, and the *fossa Drusiana* has become the Yssel; Corbulo's soldiers dug a canal between the Meuse and the Rhine, to render the inroads of the ocean less dangerous; Rufus opened up mines; one of Nero's lieutenants planned cutting the plateau of Langres to unite the Moselle and Saône by a canal, which was not completed till eighteen centuries after a Roman had conceived the idea of it. And I do not speak of the roads and bridges constructed throughout the whole Empire, nor of the harbors formed on every coast, nor of the marshes drained and hill sides planted with vines by their hands, nor of those immense fortifications with which they covered two thousand leagues of frontier.

These never-ending labors, to which history and inscriptions testify, were the great disciplinary means used by the Romans ; the generals dreaded the inactivity of the soldier to such a degree that they ordered him to do work which was actually needless. Thus Frontinus, the author of the *Stratagems*, praises the consul Nasica for having, during a winter, employed his legions in building a fleet for which he had no use.[1]

The Roman army was called *exercitus*, — *i. e.* the men who

---

[1] The Roman troops even built temples, porticos, basilicas ; and we read in the *Digest* that a proconsul was permitted to employ soldiers in the construction of public buildings in the provincial cities (*Digest*, i. 16, 7, sec. 1). In this case the cities provided the money. Thus a torrent swept away the road in the vicinity of Abila, near Damascus ; the legate of Syria ordered the 16th legion to open a new road in the mountain, *impendiis Abilenorum* (De Saulcy, *Voy. en Syrie*, ii. 506). The *legio IIIa Gallica* similarly cut through a mountain to make a road in Syria above the Lycus (*C. I. L.* vol. iii. No. 206); and there are many other examples)

worked; and it conquered the world as much with the pickaxe as with the sword.

To conclude, the most military people of antiquity were led by the experience of centuries to lay down the following principles :

1. No small garrisons.

2. The union of soldiers of all arms into twenty-five or thirty army corps, each of which was made up of a legion and its auxiliaries.

3. The stationing of the legions on the frontier, in face of and near the enemy, in intrenched camps, whose sites were so well selected that many of these camps have become important cities,[1] and that this army of three hundred and sixty thousand men was able for three centuries to make an immense frontier impassable, though bordered by rapacious Barbarians, and even by powerful kingdoms.

4. Incessant works of civil or military utility, imposed on the soldiers to keep them in good condition and to prevent inactivity and weariness, with the consequent loss of discipline.

5. Lastly, an ever-increasing importance of what we must call the siege and field artillery. "We may observe," says Gibbon, " that the use of machines in the field gradually became more prevalent in proportion as personal valor and military skill declined with the Roman Empire. When men were no longer found, their place was supplied by machines." In the time of Gibbon this observation seemed just; at the present day it has ceased to be so. Heroism in war changes its form without changing its nature, according as the struggle takes place hand to hand or at a distance, as happens where engines of war are employed. With the latter the soldier needs military virtues, — often more rare than boldness and impetuosity. The increasing use of artillery among the Romans does not, then, indicate the decline of military spirit, but rather the progress of science as applied to warlike matters ; and the *Poliorcetica* of Apollodorus is a proof of this.[2]

At Rome, in the grand period which formed the greatness of the state, military service was obligatory. It would not have

---

[1] Respecting the *castra* originating cities, see L. Renier, *Inscr. de Troesmis*, p. 22, and the Memoir of M. Robert on the *Emplacement des armées romaines.*

[2] See Vol. V. p. 323.

been understood that what belonged to all, *res publica*, should not be defended by all. The Roman citizen was required to arm and fight whenever his country called upon him, and this obligation began as soon as he had reached his seventeenth year.[1] A refusal to serve entailed the loss of property and liberty, and sometimes even the penalty of death. Under Augustus a Roman knight who had mutilated his two sons, to incapacitate them from serving, was sold as a slave, and refractory persons were executed.

The Republic also still further protected the military service, — a man could be a candidate for public office only after having passed at least ten years in the army. For two centuries and a half the Empire kept to this principle, but considerably reduced the duration of service.

In the eyes of the Romans the army was so much the native country itself that it was organized after the model of the latter. The slave was not considered as part of the civil society; accordingly, he remained outside the military organization, and any slave found in the ranks of the legion was punished with death. One class of citizens even were originally excluded from the service, — the proletariat, who, not paying taxes, had but a semblance of political rights. "This was very just." says Dionysius of Halicarnassus; "for arms should not be intrusted to citizens whose poverty offers no guaranty to the state." This condition ceased to exist at the beginning of the civil wars which destroyed the Republic, and Augustus did not again establish the exemption, or rather the exclusion, to which the proletariat had been subjected.

He preserved the distinction between the legionaries, who must be citizens, and the auxiliary corps, which were composed of *peregrini*. In law, all those who had the *jus civitatis*, except the Italians, were liable to military service; and the numerous cohorts[2] which they formed, prove that there were volunteers enough to fill readily, in ordinary times, the annual vacancies in the

---

[1] Aulus Gellius, *Noct. Att.* x. 28. In the second Macedonian war every man under forty-six was called out (Livy, xliii. 14). Under the Republic, therefore, military service was compulsory during a period of thirty years (17–46), unless a man had made ten campaigns in the cavalry and twenty in the infantry.

[2] We know the Thirty-second (Or.-Henzen, Nos. 90, 512, 6,756).

legions.[1] In the case of the provincials, the government determined, according to actual needs, how many soldiers each province must furnish;[2] and as a basis was required for the apportionment, that was taken which was the chief administrative engine of the Romans, namely, the census. Recruiting became a tax which landowners must pay: so many soldiers to so much property. A rich man was taxed in several recruits; several poor persons were united to furnish one; and even women paid this tax.

This system arose from ancient customs. Before the Roman sway had extended itself beyond Italy the Italians were bound to arm a definite number of auxiliaries, and Polybius tells us the number of the quotas which were ready in 225 B. C. to join the Roman army at the time of the Gallic invasion. In the evil days of the Second Punic War the citizens were made chargeable, each in proportion to his property, for one or more soldiers; and Augustus twice had recourse to the same means. He compelled the rich of both sexes to set at liberty certain of their slaves, so that he could immediately enroll these freedmen in the cohorts.[3] The Republic had therefore bequeathed to the Empire the practice of levying soldiers from its subjects, and the means of rendering these levies less onerous, by finding a general rule for them (*ex censu*). Augustus drew up a general rule doubtless to this effect. The state verified the age, the height, the bodily strength of the conscript; only the most vigorous were selected; and Dion adds. "and the poorest."[4]

Each legion was commanded by a legate of praetorian rank. After him came the tribunes in command of the ten cohorts; the prefect of the camp, acting as commandant in the castra and major in the field; sixty-four centurions or infantry officers; twenty-

---

[1] This is not contradictory to what has been said in the case of Tiberius. What that Emperor complained of was not a lack of volunteers, but of efficient ones.

[2] . . . *Inductis per provincias tirociniis* (Amm. Marcell. xxi. 6).

[3] *Viri feminaeque ex censu libertinum coactae dare militem* (Vell. Paterculus, ii. 111). . . . *Pecuniosioribus indictos et sine mora manumissos* (Suet., Oct. 25; Dion, liii. 31). Vitellius did the same (Tac., *Hist.* iii. 58).

[4] . . . . οἵ τε ἰσχυρότατοι καὶ οἱ πενέστατοι (Dion. lii. 11). Dion well formulates this system : . . . τοὺς μὲν ἄλλους πάντας ἄνευ τε ὅπλων καὶ ἄνευ τειχῶν ζῆν, τοὺς δὲ ἐρρωμενεστάτους καὶ βίου μάλιστα δεομένους καταλέγεσθαί τε καὶ ἀσκεῖν (lii. 27). Vegetius (i. 7. and ii. 1) says also: . . . *Possessoribus indicti tirones*, and the *Digest* (l. 1, 18, sect. 3) reckons among the *munera* the *tironum productio*. Cf. Code of Theodosian, vii. 13, 7, and the Code of Justinian, xii. 20, 2.

two decurions or cavalry officers; finally, eight or nine inferior grades of various names, collectively called *principales*,[1] our non-commissioned officers. The religious service was represented by the *victimarii* and the aruspices; the health service by surgeons and veterinary surgeons, and each camp had its hospital (*valetudinarium*).[2]

The pay was ten ases per day, or two hundred and twenty-five denarii per annum, — three hundred after Domitian, — out of which clothing, arms, and tent must be purchased and maintained. The state furnished only rations; but later it also gave clothing and arms.[3] Each cohort had a savings-bank, administered by *librarii*, or accountants under the oversight of the tribune. The soldier invested in it the savings from his pay, his share of booty, and the *donativum* accorded by the Emperor at his accession. The property of a deceased soldier without heir fell to the legion, as that of the decu-

---

[1] Levies were made by the *dilectator*, who acted in a more or less extended area, the *inquisitor*, who ascertained whether the recruit presented were fit for service, and the *legatus ad dilectus faciendos*, who centralized the work for a whole province and doubtless assembled the recruits there and sent them to their respective corps (L. Renier, *Mél. d'épigr.* p. 86; Cuq, Memoir on the *Examinator per Italiam*, pp. 11–23; and the *Acta sincera*, p. 299). Special commissions were given to legates (Caesar, *Bell. Gall.* vi. 1; *Bell. civ.* i. 30) and to senators (*ibid.* i. 12). Cf. *C. I. L.* vol. iii No. 1,157: *Missus ad juventutem per Italiam legendam*. Certain provinces supplied certain armies; *e. g.* in 64, levies were ordered in Narbonensis, and in proconsular Africa and Asia, to fill vacancies in the legions of Illyria, where many discharges had occurred (Tac., *Ann.* xvi. 13). As regards the total of the yearly recruiting, it can be determined in this manner: the thirty legions, with their auxiliaries, made up about 360,000 men. If discharge had always been granted after twenty years' service, a twentieth of the effective force, or 18,000 soldiers, would have been dismissed yearly; but for the reason I have given (Vol. IV. p. 388) it was usual to keep the number as low as possible. Supposing a third of this number to be retained, there would be 12,000 vacancies to be filled up. But the annual losses by death, by sick-leave, etc., were doubtless the same as in our army, nearly 4 per cent, and rather below than above this estimate, because the soldiers never left at all what we should call their garrison. Now 4 per cent on an effective force of 360,000 gives 14,400 dead, retired, etc. If we put it at 13,000, we shall have a total of 25,000 annual recruits, — a result reached by other calculations.

[2] Many inscriptions mention medical men as attached to the legions, the auxiliary troops, the corps doing garrison duty in the city, and lastly to the fleet. They had the rank, pay, and rations of the petty officers (*principales*), and probably there was one for every 250 men. They were commonly Greeks. Each camp contained a *valetudinarium*, which Trajan and Alexander Severus were accustomed to visit; there was even a *veterinarium* for the horses, and the field hospitals had their attendants, *optiones valetudinarii* (Briau, *Du service de santé militaire chez les Romains*). An inscription of Lyons, No. 320, speaks of a *sacerdos castrensis*.

[3] Lampridius, *Alex. Sev.* 52; Dion, lxix. 12. From the time of Polybius (vi. 39) the state gave four *modii* of corn per month, or forty-eight per year. This amount must have been increased and made the same as that of the distributions at Rome; namely, sixty *modii* per annum.

rion belonged to the curia. We have previously treated of the military colleges and their relief fund.

CENTURION OF THE ARMY OF VARUS
(18TH LEGION).[1]

In the time of Polybius the centurion received only twice as much, and the tribune four times as much, as the common soldier; in the second century the tribune's pay was twenty-five thousand sesterces, and we shall see Aurelian reach a much higher amount.

Under the Republic the military oath was taken in these terms: "In the army itself, or within a distance of ten miles, alone or with several, I will not take anything exceeding a sestertius in value. Should I find outside the camp an object worth more than a sestertius, I will within three days deliver it up to the officers. Never shall fear make me quit the standard, and I will never leave the ranks except to pick up a javelin, strike an enemy, or save a citizen."[2]

Under the Empire the soldiers swore to carry out, without hesitation or fear, the orders of the Imperator; never to desert; to die, if necessary, for the Roman people; and to do nothing contrary to the laws.[3] This oath was renewed every year on the 1st of January, and was faithfully kept; for if we except the two years of anarchy (68, 69), when the legions made three Emperors, we shall find, in the space of more than two centuries, only three military insurrections, not one of which succeeded.[4] This remark of course does not apply to the praetorians.

On reaching the camp the young soldier received a *signaculum*, or medal, usually of lead, which every soldier wore round his neck as a means of identification, and he was then given in charge to the instructors and drill-sergeants (*doctores armorum et lanistae*). His armor was heavy; during the drill he used arms heavier than those used in warfare, and he was taught, says Vegetius, to thrust, and not

[1] Museum at Bonn. Cast in the Museum of Saint-Germain.
[2] Polybius, vi. 21 and 33.
[3] Dion, lvi. 3; Vegetius, ii. 5.
[4] Those of Scribonianus in Dalmatia against Claudius; of Antoninus in Germany against Domitian; of Avidius Cassius in Syria against Marcus Aurelius.

to cut. He was furthermore trained in leaping, in swimming, and even in a sort of warrior dance, which was thought suitable, by its rapid movements, to astonish and intimidate the adversary. He was obliged to habituate himself to clearing ditches and hedges, to climbing steep slopes, and uttering the war-cry, — that terrible *barritus*, "itself enough," says Caesar, "to animate an army and terrify the enemy." The usual march was at the rate of four miles an hour, the quick march was twenty-three miles in five hours. Three times a month they went out to march.

They practised drill as our men do, the cohort being for them the tactic unit, as the battalion is for us; they had even what we call "sham fighting," the evolutions being regulated by the orders of the officers, the movement of the standards, and the sound of trumpets. Their exercises took place twice a day for the recruits, once daily for the old soldiers; and no man could be excused, except the veterans. This training, the most complete education of the physical man, gave the soldier his highest value as an individual, while the cohort gained by the precision of movements an admirable cohesion. Josephus says, "They never suspend their drills; it seemed as though they had been born with their arms." Even the name of the army, *exercitus*, told the soldiers as much.

But the great strength of the legions lay in their discipline, which Valerius Maximus calls "the most sacred discipline of the camps."[1] The soldier's obedience was absolute; and this respect for military law extended from the lowest of the legionaries up to the commander-in-chief. One day Trajan summoned to his tent a centurion, a man who later became the second personage in the Empire. Some tribunes were gathered outside the tent waiting to be introduced. Instead of taking advantage of this favor, the centurion said to the Emperor: "It is a shame, Caesar, for you to be in conversation with a centurion when tribunes are standing and waiting at your door." This is a trivial incident, but the spirit which it shows is extraordinary.

The disciplinary punishments were the reprimand, withholding pay, forced labor, degradation to an inferior service or a lower rank, expulsion from the army. Thus Caesar expelled a tribune who, in

---

[1] Some gold coins represent Hadrian followed by soldiers bearing standards with the inscription: *Disciplina aug.* (Cohen, *passim*).

the expedition to Africa, had loaded a vessel with his baggage, instead of putting soldiers into it.

Roman discipline admitted of corporal punishments, and very frequently the centurion's vine-rod fell on the shoulders of the legionary. The cases of capital punishment were numerous, the sentence being pronounced without hesitation and executed without delay. The Romans knew that victory depends on discipline, and discipline on strict obedience to rules, and that, not to have hesitating soldiers, which means the certainty of defeat, there must be placed behind those who fall back the law with all its severities. The troop which had fled was decimated; the coward was scourged or put to death; the deserter was either thrown to the wild beasts or sent away with his hands cut off; and disobedience received the same punishment as treason.

By a strange inconsistency the Romans did not make the general's want of skill a crime; they believed so much in Fortune, Destiny, and Chance — divinities very indulgent towards human weakness — that they were accustomed to charge to the gods that which often proceeded from the incapacity of men.

Thus the Roman citizen, so free and proud under the Republic, whose hearth was inviolable and life sacred, who could not be scourged or put to death, even by the sentence of the entire people, was, in the interests of his country, placed under the severest military system.

I pass to the system of rewards. They were of two kinds: the soldiers received either money (*donativum*) or arms, honorary collars, and medals, corresponding to our decorations, — a very ancient usage, since it took several men to bear those which had been given to Sicinius Dentatus, one of the victims of the decemvirs.[1]

---

[1] An acephalous inscription preserved in the Capitol says that the person to whom it is dedicated, probably Sura, served under Trajan as legate propraetor in the Dacian war, and there gained eight spears of honor (*hastae purae*, or pointless), eight standards (*vexilla*), two mural crowns, two siege crowns, two naval crowns, two crowns of gold, and that the Senate, at Trajan's request, decreed him the insignia of the triumph and a statue. Ordinarily a tribune could obtain only two spears and two standards; the legates, governors of provinces, and generals, four: from this double reward we infer that Sura had served in the two Dacian wars. To these decorations, which were worn on holidays, were added collars, gold or silver chains, and bracelets, medals (*phalerae*) of beautiful workmanship, the mural and civic crowns, etc. For the general commanding, the greatest military honor was the triumph. Orosius (vii. 9) reckons three hundred and twenty triumphs from Romulus to Vespasian;

Under the Republic the legionary could marry, because he was a citizen before all. and a soldier by circumstance; but entrance to the camp was forbidden to women. Under the Empire this prohibition continued: and as the soldier continued all his life, or but little short of it, under arms, it entailed the actual prohibition of marriage, or at least of what the Romans called *justae nuptae*, which alone had civil results and enabled a son to succeed to his father's property. As compensation. Claudius accorded to the soldiers the privileges established by Augustus in favor of fathers who had three children. But Nature asserted her rights, and many illegal unions were formed and tolerated. Still. it was only after having obtained his discharge that the veteran could exchange the *concubinatus* for the *justum matrimonium*, and that his wife became a matron, and his children citizens.

The discharge from the legions was obtained only after twenty, and later after twenty-five,[1] years of service. Then the veteran received the sum of 12.000 sesterces (about $570): this was our retiring pension, which is so much larger. He had the right to carry the centurion's vine-stock, he obtained exemption from certain taxes, and from all personal duties, which were very numerous in the cities. If accused of crime he was allowed in the prison a separate and better place. he could not be put to the torture, condemned to be beaten with rods, or thrown to the beasts in the amphitheatre.[2]

Instead of money, he was often, on the frontier, given land and a house, with the slaves and animals needful for farming. France has done the same thing in Algeria, and ought to do it more generally. Many writers have wrongly seen in these grants the origin of fiefs. Sometimes the cities honored these defenders of the Empire with a municipal benefaction. An inscription at Nîmes commemorates the fact that the decurions presented a veteran with

---

there were about thirty more up to the last which was celebrated at Rome, that of Diocletian (Eutropius, ix. 27).

[1] *Quina et vicena stipendia* is the usual formula; but inscriptions mention soldiers who had served forty-five years (*C. I. L.* iii. 266).

[2] These advantages were granted to those only who had obtained the *honesta missio.* We possess to this day seventy-three of these military discharges; the *honesta missio* assured the veterans of the auxiliary corps the *jus civitatis* and the *jus connubii.* — To complete what has just been said about the Roman army, see above. Hadrian's military reforms and his works of fortification on the frontiers.

a field near the walls, with fifty modii of corn to sow it, and with free entrance to the city baths.[1]

The legions with their auxiliaries represent the army of the line; the ten praetorian cohorts, or imperial guard, under the command of one or two prefects, and the urban[2] cohorts, commanded by the prefect of the city, formed, as it were, its reserve. The

QUADRIREME FROM THE REVERSE OF A BRONZE OF GORDIAN III.[3]

praetorian cohorts were at the beginning of the Empire formed of volunteers from Etruria, Umbria, Latium, and the older Roman colonies; later they were taken from the whole of Italy, the Spanish colonies, and those of the warlike provinces of Macedonia and Noricum.[4] From the time of Septimius Severus they were

---

[1] Herzog. pp. 109-110.

[2] Tac., *Ann.* iv. 5. Under Vitellius there were exceptionally sixteen praetorian cohorts and four urban, each with a thousand men (*Id., Hist.* ii. 93): afterwards a return takes place to the total of ten praetorian cohorts with ten troops of cavalry (Dion. lv. 24, and *Diplômes militaires* of M. L. Renier, Nos. 1, 2. 5, and 6, for the years 161, 208, 243, and 218). The four urban cohorts, of fifteen hundred men each, were next in rank to the praetorians, as is proved by three inscriptions of Lyons, which mention a *XIIIa coh. urb.*

[3] This coin bears the inscription: TRAIECTUS AVG. (The crossing of the Emperor.) Cohen. No. 323. (*Cabinet de France.*)

[4] Dion, lxxiv. 2.

composed of the flower of the legions, who, we have seen, came from all the provinces. Thus these soldiers, selected from the midst of populations which had been the first attached to the

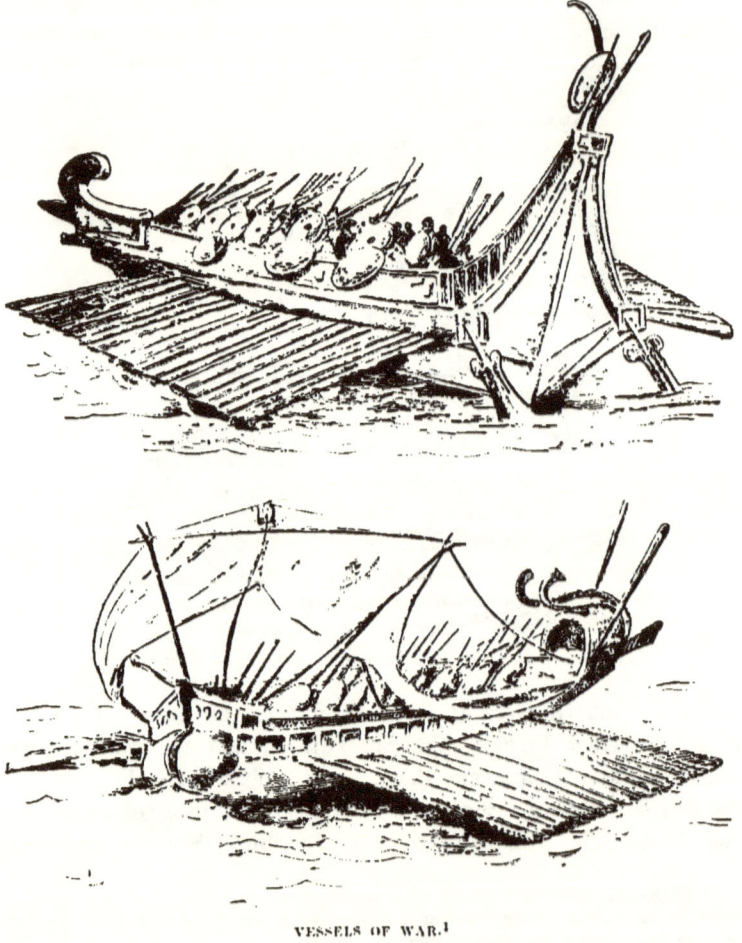

VESSELS OF WAR.[1]

fortune of Rome, or, as colonies, owed their origin to her, were in the imperial army, the most Roman element; and as in their ranks were found the choicest of the legionaries, the legions

<hr />

[1] Paintings of the temple of Isis at Pompeii, from Nicollini, vol. ii.

themselves accepted them as representatives of the army, although they did not share with it either the rough work or the dangers. After Nero's death the legions of Germany had sent secret messengers to the praetorians with this message : "Choose an emperor whom we can accept." This right of electing to the Empire exercised by the imperial guard as a power delegated to it by the army, was not at that time offensive, because as the legions admitted none but citizens, it seemed as if the best part of the people was that which was under the standards.

The praetorians had three times the pay of the legionaries, namely. two denarii a day, or thirty-two ases, in place of ten,[1] and a shorter length of service, — sixteen years, instead of twenty; but at first they did not have free rations. These Nero gave them, and Domitian increased the pay of all ranks by one third.[2] The pay of the urban guards was only half that of the praetorians. These troops protected the Emperor, Rome, and Italy. where several stations of praetorians have been identified. Accordingly, common opinion ranked them above the legions; but the seven cohorts of the

SHIP LADEN WITH TROOPS, ON A LARGE BRONZE OF HADRIAN.

watch,[3] each containing a thousand men. perhaps fifteen hundred, were ranked below the legions, because they were made up only of freedmen.[4] When we add to these troops a number of veterans (*evocati*) still remaining in the service; some German and Batavian horsemen, forming the Emperor's body-guard : some *singulares*. or the pick of the auxiliary cavalry : some marines ; some *frumentarii* drawn from all the legions and kept at Rome to fulfil various duties, — we see that the capital of the Empire had a considerable garrison. and a whole army ready to march to the Alps if any danger showed itself there.

The two praetorian fleets of Misenum and Ravenna guarded the Tuscan and Adriatic seas, and in case of need united their

[1] Tac., *Ann.* i. 17.
[2] Besides pay and rations, the soldiers seem to have obtained, in the third century, uniforms also. Cf. Lampridius, *In Alex.*, and Vopiscus. *In Aurel.*
[3] One for every two regions of the city.
[4] By three years' service they could get the corn *tessera*, and consequently the full freedom of the city.

forces with two divisions of the imperial fleet, of which Forum
Julii and Aquileia were the ports for equipment. The Euxine was

DIREME (BAS-RELIEF OF THE VILLA ALBANI).

guarded by forty vessels, carrying three thousand men ; the Archi-
pelago, the coasts of Syria and Egypt, and the British Channel, by the
fleets of Carpathos, Seleucia, Alexandria, and Britain.   The Rhine

LONG SHIP WITH FIFTY OARS, FROM A MOSAIC FOUND NEAR POZZUOLI.[1]

and Danube had powerful flotillas, and some vessels of light draft
were stationed on the Rhône, Saône, Seine, even on the lakes of
Como, Neufchâtel, etc.   The vessels of the fleet were called galleys

[1] Jal, Archéol. navale, i. 25.

of three, four, and five banks of oars, — *triremes, quadriremes,* and *quinqueremes,* according to the number of banks of oars or of the oarsmen in each row. The crews were composed of gangs of freedmen and *peregrini* recruited in the districts along the sea and rivers, who obtained their discharge and Roman citizenship only after twenty-six years of service. Instead of a rudder, these galleys were directed by two large oars acting at the two sides of the stern,[1] and at the

BIREME, CALLED THE IMPERIAL GALLEY (TRAJAN'S COLUMN).

bows there was a ram. For an engagement, legionaries came on board, and all the tactics of these vessels were those to which our modern fleets are returning: namely, ramming the enemy.[2]

Later we shall see this army, so long victorious, becoming unable to resist the Barbarians. Already we observe that the separation instituted by Augustus between civil and military society had had its inevitable consequences. First, it had been necessary to grant privileges to the soldiers as regards *peculium,* testaments, and mar-

[1] The rudder is an invention of the Middle Ages. It is found for the first time on a medal of Edward III. (Marquardt, vol. iii. part 2, p. 396.)

[2] On the organization of the naval forces, see Ermanno Ferrero, *L' Ordinamento delle armate Romane,* pp. 23–65, and Corazzini, *Storia della mar. ital. antica* (Leghorn, 1882). On the question so much discussed respecting the arrangement of the oars and of the rowers, the most recent work is that of L. Fincati, *Le Triremi,* Rome, 1881. I do not profess to solve the problem, but Admiral Fincati seems to me to take an excellent starting-point when he says of the *poliremi antiche, le quali lentamente et successivamente modificate per gradi figliarono le veneziane, le siciliane, le genovesi del medio evo, che non ne furono, perciò nè potrono esserne se non una continuazione non interrotta ed una riproduzione fidele delle loro parti più importanti.*

riage. without speaking of the gratuities procured them by changes
in the succession, by adoptions, and all the great events in the
Emperor's life. In the second century they were already, in the
eyes of the rhetorician Aristeides. a special class. which he compared
to the warrior caste under the Pharaohs. Juvenal mentions these
advantages of military life, nor does he exaggerate when he points
out "the man in a toga" vainly asking justice of the centurions
against the soldier who has broken his teeth or knocked out his
eye. In Thessaly a legionary meets a gardener riding on an ass
and addresses a question to him in Latin, which the Greek does not

TRIREME, FROM AN ANCIENT PAINTING OF THE FARNESE GARDENS.[1]

understand. The soldier is angry, strikes him. pulls him off his
ass. and then attempts to seize the animal. Upon this the peasant regains his courage. leaps at the soldier's throat. knocks him
down in turn, thrashes him soundly, and leaves him for dead.
The gardener takes refuge in a friend's house in the neighboring
town. But the soldier. reviving, stirs up his comrades: they accuse
the gardener of having stolen a silver vase: he is taken. condemned.
and executed.[2] This story, in which Apuleius wishes to picture
the insolence of the soldiery, must be as credible as Juvenal's
representation. The same thing has taken place wherever the
army has gained a preponderance in the state.

[1] Turnbull, *Treatise on Ancient Painting.* p. 1740.   [2] Apuleius, *Metam.* ix.

VI. — The Finances.

From what resources were the Romans enabled to build those vast constructions with which they covered the whole Empire? How were the expenses of the court, the administration, and the army provided for? We know whence the cities obtained their revenues, and their usual employment of the money; but we are not able to give the total of the receipts and expenditure. In this respect we have no more light upon the period of the Antonines than we had concerning the time of Augustus. We can only say that when the treasury[1] was not emptied by the senseless or shameful prodigalities of Nero and Vitellius, it was easily kept full, and enabled the Emperor, after providing for all the state services, to satisfy liberally the necessary expenditure for the splendor of the Empire.

We have already explained this financial organization; we shall need to return to it only at the period when the taxes, so light a burden for three centuries, will have become unbearable. For the early Empire it has no political interest, and from an administrative point of view a brief enumeration will suffice.

The services of religion cost little. The temples and priests were supported by foundations, the revenues from which covered the ordinary expenses of worship, — the purchase of animals for sacrifice, and the celebration of festivals. The state had occasion only to furnish assistance to enable the solemn feasts to be more worthily celebrated, especially the public games, which in their origin were religious acts; and we have seen how slight this aid was.

There was no body of judges nor diplomatic corps to pay, and the share of the state in the expenses of public education — an essentially municipal charge — was confined to the endowment of some professorial chairs and the support of the libraries of Rome and Alexandria. Private persons did the rest. The state expended more for the aid given by the *annona* and the *congiarii* to the

---

[1] I say the treasury, for the Emperor drew freely from three revenues, — the *aerarium publicum*, the *aerarium militare*, and the *fiscus* (see Vol. IV. p. 159), among which Dion declares (liii. 16) that there was no difference.

populace of the capital, and by the alimentary institution to poor children throughout Italy. If the state had not, as we have, a large sum of interest to pay on a national debt, it was compelled then, as now, to devote to works of general utility or embellishment, and especially to the administration and to the army, almost all the resources of the treasury.

Every Emperor considered it a point of honor to adorn Rome with some monument on which posterity could read his name, to carry

out useful works in Italy, to relieve provincial cities ravaged by any scourge, or aid them by a grant in the completion of some enterprise.[1] Of this inscriptions furnish abundant proofs. One of them even gives us, in reference to a grant by Hadrian for the repairs of a road, the cost of the work as a hundred thousand sesterces per mile.[2] From time to time

TEMPLE OF ROME, ON A
COIN OF HADRIAN.
(BRONZE.)

the Emperors made donations of another sort: Hadrian on one occasion gave up arrears of taxes amounting to nine million sesterces.

Even if we knew the total of the pay and nearly the number of soldiers, yet too many items are wanting for it to be possible to say what was the whole cost of the army. In our estimates it is usual to allow about a million francs [$190,000] for a thousand men with the colors; it is probable that the proportion between these numbers was about the same in the Roman Empire.[3]

---

[1] Friedländer has collected (vol. iii. pp. 122–127) a good number of figures showing the considerable sacrifices made by the Emperors for this twofold form of aid. The Roman Republic had to pay for the transport of the corn, which it farmed out to companies of publicans; under the Empire, especially in the later centuries, it transferred this duty to corporations of carriers by water, whom it paid by a grant of privileges and exemption from taxes. The corn from Egypt and the Oriental provinces was also conveyed to Constantinople by possessores, who, in their native provinces, had not to furnish the *annonaria praestatio* (*Code Theod.* xiii. 5, 14). The state thus gained the cost of transport, and lost nothing by it on the *annona*, the fellow-citizens of those exempted paying for them.

[2] Mommsen, *Inscr. Neap.* No. 6,287.

[3] For regular pay alone we reach eighteen hundred thousand denarii a legion. To this expenditure must be added the unknown sum needed for the double pay of a large number of soldiers; the allowances of the officers, which rose rapidly (twenty-five thousand sesterces to a legionary tribune); the donations to the veterans; the allowances in kind made by the state, which will become daily more considerable (see Treb. Pollio, *Claudius*; Capitolinus, *Gordian III.* 28; and Vopiscus, *Aurelian*); the repairs of engines; the body of workmen; the medical service; the *donativa*, of a single one of which, that of Hadrian after the adoption of Verus,

The allowances or indemnities to the public functionaries of every class must have required considerable sums.[1] What did the court expend? Less under the good Emperors, more under the bad ones; but always a good deal, for the palace supported a whole population of servants and dependents, and we know that the physician of Claudius received five hundred thousand sesterces as fees, and the preceptor of the grandsons of Augustus one hundred thousand.

The Romans asserted, as we do, that to provide for public expenses the state had the right to impose a tax on anything that secured an advantage or a pleasure, and still more, that subjects owed the *tributum soli* for the ransom of the lands which victory had delivered up to their conquerors.[2] This was the theory of direct and indirect taxation. But while moderns derive their greater revenue from the latter, the Romans demanded it of the former. Especially they taxed landed property, which had to supply, besides these contributions in money and forced labor, enormous payments in kind for the wants of the palace, the administration, and the army. Thus were they led to concede to the land-owners privileges in exchange for the charges with which the latter were weighed down; so that the financial arrangements of this society became a new cause of separation between the classes of citizens.

1. *The Land-Tax.* — The lands were divided, according to their produce, into different classes, — lands of the first and second class, meadows, oak forests, ordinary forests, pasturage, pools, salt-works, etc. On the roll — which was renewed every ten years — were inscribed the name of the domain, the names of the canton and state in which it was situated, the number of acres of arable land; the number of trees, vines, and olive-trees which it contained; the extent of meadow and pasture land; the nation, the age, the employment of the slaves belonging to the property.[3]

The land-tax was payable at three dates, — on the first day of September, which was the beginning of the financial year, on the first of January, and the first of May.[4]

---

amounted to three hundred million sesterces, etc. I have already remarked that the *donativum* was a relic of the triumphal gold.

[1] See above, p. 221. [2] Dion, lii. 28. [3] Ulpian in the *Digest*, l. 15, 4.
[4] These were the dates on which, after Augustus, corn was distributed at Rome, and, after Domitian, the soldiers received their pay (Suet., *Oct.* 40).

The corn required for the civic *annona*, which supported Rome, and for the military *annona*, supplied to the army and state functionaries, was in reality only a part of the land-tax. It was the same also with the *cellaria*, or deliveries of wine, meat, oil, vinegar, wood, forage, and clothing.

The Romans settled in the provinces had to pay the *tributum soli*, which was fixed on the land, not on the person;[1] but Italy did not pay this.

2. *The Capitation-Tax.* — This, on the one hand, was levied upon merchants, manufacturers, bankers, and all those who, not being landed proprietors, possessed capital or personal property; and on the other hand, on those who helped these persons in preserving their goods or increasing them, as the wife, the child of full age, the peasant laborer, the slave. For the former the capitation-tax was proportional to their property; for the rest, it was only a personal payment. In Syria, according to a text in Ulpian, girls under twelve, boys under fourteen, and old men over sixty-five were exempt from this tax;[2] but if Dion is to be believed,[3] beggars had to deduct somewhat from their income for the fiscus. Doubtless the beggars referred to are those of whom Lucian speaks, in whose wallets were found gold pieces, mirrors, perfumes, and dice.[4]

3. *The Twentieth on Inheritances and Legacies.* — This contribution for Italy and for Roman citizens made up for the land-tax and capitation-charge levied elsewhere. Accordingly, when the property left by a citizen comprised a provincial domain, it is probable that his heirs were not liable for this part of the heritage to the tax of the twentieth, since it had already paid the *tributum soli*.

4. *The Revenues from the Domain Lands.* — The ancient *ager publicus* had been greatly reduced by sales and the foundation of colonies; yet the domains of the fiscus, which formed, as it were, the endowment of the crown, were still considerable, and these revenues were added to those which the Emperor's private fortune, increased by that which his predecessors had left, gave to him.[5]

---

[1] . . . *In vectigalibus ipsa praesidia, non personas conveniri* (Rescript of Antoninus and Verus in the *Digest*, xxxix. 4, 7). So the heritor of property was liable for the frauds committed by his predecessor. *Fraudati vectigalis crimen ad heredem . . . transmittitur* (ibid. 8).

[2] *Digest*, l. 15, 3, *proœm.*   [3] lxvi. 8.   [4] Lucian, *Piscat*. 45.

[5] Pliny (*Epist*. x. 75) transmits to Trajan a will made in favor of Claudius, and speaks of legacies left to this Emperor as belonging to his ninth successor. The sources whence the

Thus Augustus had taken in Egypt, as his share of the conquest.
the royal domain of the Ptolemies. Almost all the mines. quarries. and salt-works belonged to the Emperor. and his procurators
farmed out the working of them for 10 per cent of the produce.[1]
The treasury found a resource of some importance by the sale
of what remained in the warehouses of the corn paid as tribute.
after the regular distributions, and in the coinage of silver and
gold. which had become a profitable right. The Emperors had left
it to only a small number of Greek cities.[2] In the legislation of
the Early Empire there was never exemption for sacred things.
nor for the public domain of the Roman people or of the cities.[3]
and the claims of the treasury had the precedence over all others:
but we have seen on several occasions that these properties were
not inalienable. as the French royal domain professed to be.

5. *Indirect Taxes.* — These were derived from traffic. from the
transfer of certain properties. and from some acts of civil law.
The principal were: the customs, which were habitually levied
at the frontiers of the state and in certain groups of provinces.
both on entrance and exit, $2\frac{1}{2}$ per cent *ad valorem* on merchandise,[4] even on eunuchs and wild beasts intended for the combats in
the arena. 1 per cent on all merchandise except on articles of
food bought in the markets of Rome, 2 per cent on the price
for slaves, 5 per cent on that of freedmen; dues charged on
markets opened by the authorization of the Emperor or the
Senate.[5] and on bridges and roads;[6] a number of other taxes of
small importance which often varied: lastly. property lapsed or

treasury derived an increase of revenue were numerous. The *Digest* (xlix. 14, 1) enumerates
fourteen of them. and does not include them all.
  [1] Suet., *Tib.* 49; *Code Theod.* x. 19, 10, and 11.
  [2] Twenty-five cities are enumerated which coined silver money; only one. Caesarea in
Cappadocia, coining gold (Eckhel, *Doctr. num.* iii. 187). The Roman Senate had the right of
coining bronze money.
  [3] Gains in the *Digest*, xli. 3, 9. In 491 Anastasius admitted, for all public or private
property, a prescription of forty years.
  [4] . . . *Praeter instrumenta itineris omnes quadragesimam publicano debeant* (Quintilian,
Declamatio, cclix.). The three African provinces must have been subjected to much lower
rates of customs if the tariff of Zraia was that of the imperial customs. The *Digest* (xxxix. 4,
16, sect. 7) gives a list of the products of the East and Africa . . . *pertinentes ad vectigal*.
All the indirect taxes — that is, those levied on things or attaching to an act — were comprised
in the *vectigalia* (Cagnat, *Des Impôts indirects chez les Romains*, p. vi.).
  [5] Wilmanns. *Ephem. epigr.* ii. 271.
  [6] . . . *Vectigal quod in itinere praestari solet* (*Digest*, xxiv. 1, 21).

fallen into escheat, testamentary legacies, the product of penalties and confiscations, and of mines, quarries, and salt-works owned by the state or by individuals.[1]

6. *Coronary gold*, offered by the cities to the Emperor as a gift "of happy accession," or on the occasion of a victory, as under the Republic they offered such to the proconsuls. Often the good Emperors refused this; the bad, on the contrary, invented, like Caracalla, triumphs over the Barbarians to demand it several times.[2]

7. *Payments in kind*, or the corn for the *annonae* and the *cellaria*, which we have included in the *tributum soli*, the horses and carriages for the public post, the entertainment of soldiers and functionaries travelling at the Emperor's orders, the maintenance of highways, the repairs of aqueducts,[3] the cleansing of canals, the conveyance by land of supplies for the army, etc.

No one can say what all these imposts amounted to. But it is of little importance to know the exact total of the public

---

[1] . . . *Si salinas habeat pupillus* (*Digest*, xxvi. 9, 5). See in Hirschfeld, *Röm. Verwaltungsgesch.* pp. 72–91, and in Flach, *La Table de bronze d'Aljustrel* how wisely the working of the state mines was conducted in the Early Empire. The state, as proprietor of mines and quarries, worked them directly, as the quarries of Egypt and the mines of Carthagena, by convicts or slaves, who were guarded and kept in subjection by a large body of officers and soldiers. Or sometimes it relinquished the working of them to contractors, who drew together to the neighborhood of the works, for the wants of the workmen, traders and mechanics of every sort. But these mines and quarries were as a rule situated in desert and thinly populated places, and traders could only be attracted thither by granting them important advantages. Thus, as appears by the curious inscription of Aljustrel, discovered in 1876 in a mountainous region of the district of Beja, in Portugal, shoemakers, fullers, barbers, bathers, schoolmasters, etc., admitted within the jurisdiction of the mine had a monopoly of their calling, and were authorized to exact a penalty from every competing stranger, and even to confiscate the tools of his trade. This inscription belongs to the first century of the Christian era; the organization which it indicates, more profitable to the state than its own direct undertaking, must have existed in other grants. Now the mines and quarries, the property of the state, were very numerous. Monopoly, therefore, existed early in a great number of cases. We therefore need not be surprised when we see it later invading the whole world of labor, with its inseparable accompaniment of minute regulations, which will produce torpor, and then death, where free competition would have preserved life.

[2] Dion, lxxvii. 9.

[3] A senatus-consultum of the year A. U. C. 741, quoted by Frontinus, proves that dwellers near aqueducts were compelled to furnish, at the order of arbitrators, all that was required for the repairs of the aqueducts, and to permit, without compensation, roads to be made over their fields for the transport of the materials. The maintenance of highways was obligatory on the dwellers near them (*Code Theod.* xv. 3, 1, *ann.* 319), and this obligation is the origin of our forced labor and payments. The magistrates were armed with the necessary powers for carrying out these works (Ulpian in the *Digest*, xlviii. 8, sects. 8, 17, and 25). The powers of our town magistrates in the matter of public roads, etc., seem based on those of the Roman magistrate.

revenue, because this total, which has never any but a relative value, is very small among poor nations, and can be very high in a rich state. It is sufficient to affirm that in the two centuries which we are considering we find no serious complaint made;[1] and this means that the taxes were not out of proportion to the resources of the tax-payers, and that public wealth was developed under the

TI CAESA RI DIVI
AVGVSTIF DIVI
IVLIN AVGVSTO
PONTIF MAXIMOGOS IIII
IMP VIII YAIB POTESTAT XXXII
AVGVSTALES
RESPVBLICA
RESTITVIT

INSCRIPTION ON THE BASE OF A STATUE ERECTED TO TIBERIUS BY THE AUGUSTALES
OF PUTEOLI.

numberless forms which it can take in a great civilized state. Finally, we know that an economical Emperor could in a few years make considerable savings. At an interval of more than a century Tiberius and Antoninus left in the treasury nearly the same sum, —about a hundred and forty million dollars of our money.[2]

The financial system above explained, while it has bequeathed to us many usages. differs widely from our own. We find no taxes

[1] As proof to the contrary, mention has been made of the petition of the fishermen of Gyaros begging of Octavius a reduction of a third on their tribute of a hundred and fifty drachmas (Strabo. X. v. 3). But Antony had just overwhelmed Asia and Greece with imposts; therefore it is not astonishing that Gyaros should feel itself too heavily burdened. The peoples paid less than under their native rulers; thus the tribute of Cappadocia was reduced by one half at the death of its last king (Tac., Ann. ii. 42 and 56), and the same in Macedonia. Besides, the Romans having long kept to the terms of the ancient treaties. the debasement of the coin had of itself brought about a diminution of the tribute.
[2] Suet., Cal. 37.

self-imposed by those who are to pay them and strictly watched
over as to their apportionment, levying, and employment, by distinct and mutually independent powers. The taxes under the early
Empire continued to be what they had been under the Republic, — a
result of victory, a right of conquest. Accordingly, the Senate, and
afterwards the Emperor, had the free and absolute disposal of them
in the interest of the conquering people, who, in the midst of the
subject-nations, long constituted a privileged nation. In this we
find the explanation of the fact that the Republic bequeathed to
the Empire its system of double taxes — in money and in kind —
levied on the landed property of the provincials, who were finally
crushed under these intolerable burdens.

A further difference will also be remarked. The modern state,
while requiring only money from its subjects, with the revenue thus
obtained provides for all the public services, with but two exceptions;
namely, service as jurors, and military duty. The Roman state made
large exactions of money from its subjects; but besides this, following the general tradition of antiquity, it left as a personal charge on
its citizens a number of obligations in respect to the common weal,
from the filling of certain public offices which a man could not
decline, to those contributions of labor which were soon to increase
to a degree that will change the whole Empire into a vast workshop filled with indolent hereditary working men. This system
will seem to have simplified everything, by obliging each man to
do the work and to furnish the materials needed for the public
wants, and will be thought very economical. As a matter of fact,
however, it will produce extreme confusion, a frightful waste of
strength and of materials, a most unequal distribution of burdens,
and for many the forfeiture of individual liberty.

At the period of which we are now speaking, the financial system of the Empire had not as yet begun to have fatal results.
Means were found to satisfy all public needs by taxes whose burden
was not so heavy as to ruin the taxable material, the demands for
labor were not oppressive, and the personal liberty of the individual
was respected. In the provinces there were prosperous cities, on
the frontiers formidable armies; the conquered nations rendered
obedience willingly, and their worship of Rome and of the Augusti
was even more sincere than was, in the early French monarchy,

the veneration for royalty. Formed in the same manner. — by the substitution of one man's authority for the rule of many. — the two governments were alike formidable to the great. gentle towards the poor; with alternations, in the case of both. of good and bad rulers. In the case of the Empire. the good had now been ruling for nearly a century; but madmen or weaklings were soon to reappear, and assume that absolute power which is so dangerous in the hands of the violent. In a few generations the free institutions of the cities will have been destroyed: the admirable war-machine of the Antonines will be so deteriorated as to become powerless: the treasury will exhaust the sources of public wealth; and when days of misfortune arise, there will not be found in this terror-stricken crowd either a soldier or a man. Then. as we see this shattered colossus covering the world with its ruins. we shall be compelled to recognize the fact that peoples, like individuals, are the architects of their own destinies; that for the former as truly as for the latter, prosperity is the product of wisdom, and misfortune of improvidence.

CHAPTER LXXXVI

MANNERS.

I. — The Economical Revolution produced by the Conquest of the World : Period of the Greatest Roman Luxury.

WE have seen that, considered as a whole, this immense Roman Empire had many causes of prosperity : respect in the family, discipline in the city, industry and a relative wealth in the provinces ; moreover, in the second century, wise rulers and a skilful administration in the government, which for the time neutralized the disastrous effects of absolute power.

But did not these fair appearances conceal a fatal or hideous evil ? Was not this grandeur undermined by an insane extravagance which destroyed private fortunes, and by a depravity of manners which destroyed the human soul ?

Rome exercises over the human mind a sort of fascination which alters the proportions of men and things. Livy and Corneille have made the heroes of ancient days appear too great ; on the other hand, we now are apt to undervalue the Romans of the Empire. The fault arises from that scholastic rhetoric which took for the usual text of its declamations the advantages of poverty [1] and the dangers of riches, the virtues secured by the former and the vices resulting from the latter, — commonplaces which, for our misfortune, Rousseau took up again and the crowd has ever since repeated.

First of all, neither vice nor virtue is of necessity attached to poverty or to riches : for although want and prosperity may sometimes either of them be bad advisers, there are men who possess wealth, but are not held captive by it, as there are others whose poor abode has never sheltered an evil thought. Then, the manners

[1] This is the note which dominates in the whole of Latin literature, from Lucretius to Apuleius in his *Apology*. See the absurd letter of Seneca (No. 90) against the mechanical arts.

of early Rome were necessarily those of poverty, and by an inevitable change the manners of the Empire were those of wealth, or at least of competence. Again, if we except some glaring instances, such as always exist, this luxury was not more extravagant than our own, nor these fortunes greater than those which in our time give titles and orders to their fortunate owners. In our present study, we are not discussing a thesis of philosophy, but a question of social economy. We seek the truth and the political consequences of facts reduced from their legendary proportions to their real importance. When we have shown that this luxury among the Romans was confined to some cities, and this wealth to some families, and even to a certain period, we shall be led to think that follies to which a hundred millions of men remained strangers were not those which brought ruin upon the Empire.

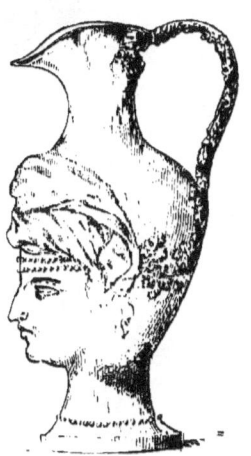

VASE IN THE SHAPE OF A HEAD BELONGING TO THE JEWEL-BOX OF A ROMAN LADY.

The censors declared that the rude manners of the early times were necessary to the Republic, and they would have been so had Rome continued a city of laborers, instead of becoming the capital of the world. They proscribed the growing luxury in dress and the table, the women's ornaments, the articles of gold, certain dishes, and even the fattening of poultry, which seemed to them a public danger.[1] Under Tiberius, again, the aediles sought to revive the edicts limiting the price to be spent on any one dish, and the number of dishes for each repast. At this news there was a great flutter in the city. "Apprehensions were excited," says Tacitus, "of some severe corrective from a prince who himself observed the ancient parsimony."[2] With his usual wisdom, Tiberius smiled gravely at the Spartan zeal of the aediles; he pointed out to them that Rome had need of the provinces in order to exist; that to destroy the established relations would be to upset the state; that, finally, it was dangerous to make laws which would so quickly be forgotten or despised.

[1] Pliny, *Hist. nat.* x. 71.
[2] *Ann.* iii. 51–54: . . . *Ne princeps antiquae parcimoniae durius adverteret.*

The commerce of the Romans had extended with their conquests. They had soon learned where to find the most precious marbles, the finest woods, the most supple textures, the most delicate viands;

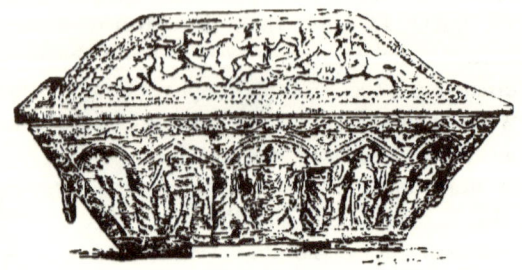

JEWEL-CASE OF A ROMAN LADY.[1]

and victory having given them the wealth accumulated for centuries by kings and peoples, they suddenly found themselves rich, like the Spaniards after the conquest of Peru. Then took place

ORNAMENTAL DETAILS OF THE BOX.

what has been seen under similar circumstances; namely, the desire to be better lodged, better clothed, and better fed. In the place of the stout tunic of coarse wool, the descendant of Cincinnatus wore a fine Milesian stuff dyed in Tyrian purple, and the daughter of the robust housewife who used to pound the corn and knead the bread for the family, covered her head, her neck, and her arms with precious pearls.[2] The small houses built of travertine were changed for marble edifices, wherein glittered all the luxury of Ephesus and Antioch. There were served up, on tables of Mauretanian cedar, turbot from Ravenna, oysters from Tarentum, the edible snails of Illyria or Africa and the sea-eel of Sicily, the wine of the Cyclades and the roe-deer of Ambracia, the pheasants of Colchis, the Persian

[1] Silver box found at Rome in 1793. Blacas collection. *Lettera di Visconti intorno ad una antica supellctile d' argento scoperta in Roma nell' anno 1793.* Roma, 1822, in 4to.

[2] See the toilette of Lollia Paulina in Pliny, *Hist. nat.* ix. 58.

peacock, the Egyptian flamingo, the Numidian guinea-fowl, and a thousand other articles of food, paid for dearly and brought from afar, yet not from so great a distance as that to which we send for Chinese tea and Arabian coffee, the sugar of America, the silk of Japan, and the diamonds of Brazil. Pliny complains of those who buy the mountain snow to mix with their wine.[1] It hardly becomes us to share in this virtuous indignation who, without self-reproach, bring ice from Norway and from Canada, and send it as far as India.

In a preceding chapter we have shown how rapidly the Mediterranean coasts became covered with flourishing cities, because of the facility with which the dwellers on the shores of that great Roman lake exchanged their products with one another, and everywhere found advantageous markets. In all directions vessels were furrowing that sea, no longer infested by pirates, while articles of daily consumption were on their way from the remotest countries along the great Roman roads; and from this easy communication resulted a general prosperity. That writers who themselves were freely enjoying the present should feign to regret the simplicity of earlier times, is not to be wondered at. It sounds well to praise the austere virtues, even when a man has no desire to practise them, and when the philosopher sits at his gilded table to write eulogiums upon poverty. How little sincerity there was in it all appears when we hear Apuleius, with the rough voice of Cato, taking to task his own times, and Martial celebrating the pleasures and the rustic virtues of the early days.

Let, therefore, the Epicurean Sallust and Varro and Seneca and Pliny complain because sea and land were scoured to bring some fresh gratification to the jaded voluptuary;[2] with the security that now prevailed everywhere, industry and commerce necessarily set in circulation a vast amount of products which it was no disgrace to enjoy. Many men used them well, some badly, — that is to say extravagantly, and wasted their wealth in idle display; like him, for instance, who in the time of Nero spent four million

---

[1] The ancients do not seem to have known our ices (Daremberg, *Oribase*, i. 625). [But probably the Italian *granita*, made with snow and flavored with fruit. — ED.]

[2] *Vescendi causa* (Sallust, *Cat.* 13); *Epulas quas toto orbe requirunt* (Seneca, *Ad Helv.* 10); *Insatiabilis gula* (*Id.*, *Epist.* 89), etc.

sesterces on the roses for a banquet, which money went. of course, to certain Campanian peasants who had learned the art of growing these flowers.[1] Is England no longer England because the descendant of those whose lives were so needy and hard in Queen Elizabeth's time now sails across the sea in a yacht more convenient and beautiful than Cleopatra's galley. or buys European pictures and statues of great price. or tranquilly loses twenty thousand pounds in betting at the Derby?[2] To bet is to use money badly. since it thus changes hands without doing the community any service on the way; but this Englishman. having probably as many vices and as many virtues as his ancestors had. has not the same manners, because his surroundings are different. Wealth, taking the place of poverty. has changed the conditions of his existence. it has not necessarily degraded his nature; and as his country has gained in political liberty what it has lost in rudeness of manners. England has grown greater by the change. The Roman Empire would have had the same fortune if it had possessed similar compensations.

Antiquity twice witnessed the economical phenomenon which has occurred twice also in Europe. in the sixteenth and nineteenth centuries, when enormous quantities of the precious metals were suddenly put into circulation. Alexander set free the treasure accumulated in bullion by the monarchs of Chaldaea. Assyria. and Persia, — more than four hundred million dollars in cash. Western Asia was inundated with this. and her commerce and manufactures received a powerful impetus. A good part of this wealth came to the Romans by the conquest of Macedonia. Pergamus. Syria, and Egypt. Add to this all that the proconsuls found to seize in Sicily. Carthage, Spain, Gaul,[3] and what Caesar flung to his legionaries when he had forced the doors of the *sanctius aerarium*

[1] Suet., *Nero*, 27. Roses blooming twice in the year were already known . . . *biferique rosaria Pasti* (Vergil, *Georg.* iv. 119, and Martial, *Epig.* xii. 31). They were imported from Egypt; but the trade declined when roses began to be cultivated in Italian greenhouses. Martial (*ib.* vi. 80, and xiii. 127): " The rose was formerly a spring flower, now a winter one."

[2] The Romans were also addicted to betting: *Quam spansia . . . de Scorpo fuerit et Incitato* (Martial, *Epig.* xi. 1). Scorpus was a groom of the circus, and the name of Caligula's horse Incitatus refers probably to the racehorses on which there was betting.

[3] The pillage of Carthage brought into the Roman treasury 726,000 pounds of gold and 867,000 pounds of silver (Pliny, *Hist. nat.* xxxii. 17). or 750,000,000 francs (about $150,000,000 of our money). Marius brought from Numidia nearly $7,000,000; Caesar from Gaul more than ten times as much, etc.

It was the product of the labor of ten centuries which the pillage of the civilized and barbaric world heaped up in the great capital in the hands of those families which divided among themselves the command.

The period of the greatest luxury at Rome extends from Lucullus to Nero; that is to say, from the conquest of Western Asia to the civil war which followed the extinction of the house of the Caesars. Then were exhibited all the extravagances of those nobles who in the intoxication of their prosperity knew how to govern neither the provinces nor their own wealth nor themselves. Lucullus and Caesar under the Republic, Caligula and Nero under the Empire, represent this new position of the patriciate. — the former with the lofty tastes of *grands seigneurs* fond of arts and letters, the two latter with the mad frenzy of tyrants who desired that nothing should appear impossible to them.[1]

The greatest fortunes which we know for those days and for the whole Roman epoch belonged to the augur Lentulus, under Tiberius, and the freedman Pallas, under Claudius, namely, 300,000,000 sesterces; while that of Narcissus, in Nero's reign, reached 400,000,000. This makes for the two former about $16,000,000, and for the third about $25,000,000. The property of the famous Apicius was only a quarter of what Narcissus possessed, that of Crassus only the half.[2] How many private individuals are there far richer than these in England, in the United States, and even in Russia! A French banker was ten times richer than this.[3] But the value of money being then much greater than

[1] We have seen (Vol. V. pp. 12, 13) Nero's Golden House; Vitellius found it to be unworthy of him (Dion, lxv. 4). Pompeius Paulinus, who had the command on the banks of the Rhine in 58, carried out a service of plate weighing twelve thousand pounds (Pliny, *Hist. nat.* xxxiii. 50). In 1868 there was found at Hildesheim, in Hanover, a treasure composed of sixty pieces of silver plate, some of which are very fine.

[2] Although a senatus-consultum had re-enacted the penalties of the *lex Cincia* against advocates who received money from their clients (Tac., *Ann.* xiii. 42), Eprius and Crispus had, from the time of Caligula to Vespasian, gained by their eloquence 300,000,000 sesterces (*Id., Orat.* 8); but there was included in their fortunes much of the wealth of proscribed persons.

[3] We have seen (Vol. V. p. 266, note 4) that the intrinsic value of the denarius and sestertius varied considerably under the Empire, but that their nominal value, instead of being represented by the quantity of silver which these pieces contained, was represented by the quantity of gold corresponding; a denarius and a sestertius meaning not so much a silver denarius and a silver sestertius as they meant respectively $\frac{1}{25}$ and $\frac{1}{100}$ of the aureus. Now the metallic value of the aureus varied but little in the two first centuries of the Christian era, averaging

now, while the mass of the population was much poorer, the distance between the condition of the crowd and of the few seemed much more considerable. Hence the wonder and the scandal. Yet the distance rapidly diminished. Born of pillage, this fortune of accident could not be renewed at the expense of subjects under a government which caused the property of the latter to be respected, nor at the expense of foreigners, because Rome in the time of the Republic having subjected all the rich nations, under the Empire had none but poor ones left to fight with. Instead of taking from these latter their gold, Rome gave them her own by commerce [1] and by the pensions paid to their chiefs.

The channels whence wealth was obtained being closed, and those by which it flowed out being widely opened, riches by degrees escaped from the hands in which victory had placed them. Some men were ruined by luxury and debauchery, others by confiscations. A part of the Senate had already been pensioned by Augustus, and we have seen Tiberius obliged, in spite of his parsimony, to come to the aid of several noble personages. The grandson of Hortensius,

about $4.90; and this makes the 300,000,000 sesterces, considering solely the metal employed, correspond to $14,700,000. The fortune of the Rothschild family certainly exceeds $190,000,000, and it is asserted that the Duke of Westminster has two or three times as much. It is known that the Duke of Buccleuch derives from his lands in Scotland an annual revenue of $875,000 (*Économiste franç.* of May 23, 1874). As to the exchangeable value, — that is to say, the purchasing power of money, — it is difficult to speak with certainty. Luxuries were very dear and articles of necessity were low in price, — which means that the purchasing power of money was weak in respect of the former, which were rare, and great as regards the latter, which abounded. In France a man can be fed and clothed and, outside of the great cities, be lodged at a cheap rate, while to live in luxury is very expensive; it must have been the same in the Empire. According to Martial (xii. 76), the amphora of wine cost 20 ases, and the modius of corn four; but these prices are absurd, which the poet employs to sharpen the epigram against the drunken laborer and the gourmand who eats and drinks his harvest instead of selling it. Yet we are authorized in concluding from a number of known facts that bread and wine were cheap. Varro says (*De R. R.* iii. 2) that the best meadows paid an annual rent, in Caesar's time, of 120 sesterces an acre, or about $5.88; this is still the price at which an acre of meadow land is let in France. Papinianus fixes the legal price of a slave at 20 aurei (*Digest.* iv. 31, and xl. 4, 17); it is now $140 in the bazaars of Constantinople and Cairo. The price of saddle-horses in Numidia was in the fourth century 400 denarii. For the price of houses in the cities, even in the neighborhood of Rome, and respecting what is understood as a small competency, see below, Sects. II. and III. of this chapter.

[1] On one occasion, says Pliny, Nero sent a Roman knight with a large sum of money to buy up all the amber that he could find on the coasts of the North Sea and the Baltic. The Germans also did a large trade with Rome in flaxen hair. Roman coins circulated among the Germans, and even in Scandinavia. There have been discovered in Scania 550 silver denarii, the series of which begins at Nero and ends at Septimius Severus (*Revue numism. belge*, series v. vol. iii. p. 335).

after obtaining 1,000,000 sesterces from the first Emperor, was still
a beggar under the second, who gave 200,000 sesterces to each of
his four children. The hand was outstretched without shame.
Verrucosus begs to have his debts paid ; others present to the Senate
a list of their creditors to gain the sympathy of the assembly for
their destitute condition. Some refuse magistracies because they
cannot meet the requisite expenses ; others are glad that Claudius
expels them from the Senate because of their poverty. Augustus

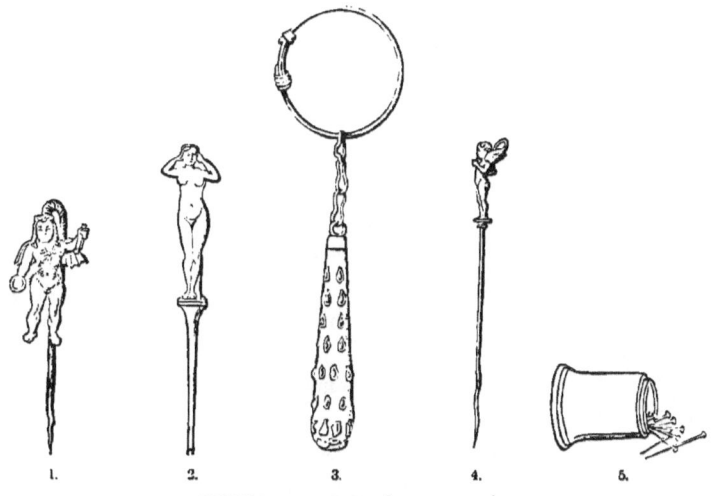

ARTICLES OF A WOMAN'S TOILETTE.[1]

and Tiberius had previously carried out a similar measure. There is
scarcely an Emperor who has not had to make up for many senators
the 1,200,000 sesterces required to be a member of the Senate.
When Vespasian ascended the throne, the first two orders had almost
ceased to exist, and he was obliged to form a new nobility out of
provincial families. Yet not all of these families could find means
to live creditably at Rome, if we may believe Juvenal, who shows
us praetors, tribunes, descendants of illustrious houses, begging for
the *sportula* at the gate of some rich freedman, and calculating at

[1] 1. Gold-headed pin found at Pompeii (Museum of Naples). 2. Ivory pin in the Museum
of Naples. 3. Case and gold bracelet (half-size) found at Panticapaea (Museum of St. Petersburg). 4. Gold pin surmounted by a Cupid playing a flute (Museum of the Louvre). 5. Pin-
box found at Pompeii (Museum of Naples).

the end of the year how much their scanty income has been augmented by this daily allowance.[1]

The Emperors themselves — and I refer to the best — were not always free from embarrassment. They were rich when the treasury was administered with the strictest economy, or when confiscations filled it. But those who confiscated were those also who squandered. We have seen that Caligula and Nero were at the end of their resources, and they deserved to be so. But Galba was economical from necessity as much as by nature; and yet on the accession of Vespasian the government was quite at a standstill. Nerva passed through a like crisis, and Marcus Aurelius was obliged to sell the jewels and furniture of the palace, and even the wardrobe of the Empresses.

A change then took place which has not been sufficiently noticed. From the time of Lucullus to that of Nero the wealth obtained from conquest has remained in the hands of a few, and all sorts of follies have therefore been possible; now it becomes divided and scattered, and by a natural tendency goes, following the requirements of luxury, to those who produce or import what luxury demands.

"When the kitchen is fat," says Franklin, "the will is lean." Whither did the millions of Apicius and the consular fortunes of the first period go? To those who had helped to devour them by furnishing the expensive objects. Octavius gives five thousand sesterces for a gray mullet; he commits an act of folly, at which Tiberius sneers; but it is a good thing for the fisherman, and for a whole year long gives comfort to his cabin. Let the poor man get the benefit of a few more follies of the kind, and he will at last have found a fortune in his nets; what at least formed then, as it does now, the competency of the small tradesman, — twenty thousand sesterces, or about eight hundred dollars of income.[2]

Not only is wealth displaced and divided among the mass of the population in proportion to the labor or skill of each, but it diminishes in quantity. The conversion of much gold and silver into objects of art, jewelry, and ornaments, keeps down to that extent the total of the quantity in circulation. Simply for the

---

[1] . . . *Ipsos Trojugenas* . . . *da praetori, da deinde tribuno* (i. 100, 101).

[2] One of Juvenal's characters (ix. 139) asks for this only, and a few small silver vases, with two strong slaves to shelter his old age from want and care (*quo sit mihi tuta senectus*).

gilding of the Capitol, Domitian used twelve thousand talents. Commerce with the East caused the disappearance of another part; fifty million sesterces went yearly to India, and probably as much to Arabia, whence they never came back;[1] lastly, the ocean kept what shipwrecks had given it, and the Barbarians restored no part of the pensions or presents made to their chiefs.[2]

Could the mines repair all these losses? Those of Spain, which were the richest,[3] yielded annually twenty thousand pounds weight of gold, — say four million three hundred thousand dollars. The silver mines, more numerous, but much more difficult to work, probably did not yield a much larger quantity, since all the silver ore at present produced by the whole of Europe, aided by the best processes, does not amount to a value of two million five hundred thousand dollars. The mines of Laurium were nearly abandoned, and those of Transylvania were just beginning to be productive. Therefore Spain continued to be the great workshop for the production of silver.[4] But the Carthaginians and the Roman Republic must have exhausted many of the veins; for in the time of Polybius forty thousand men were working in the mines of Carthagena alone, — which, however, yielded only twenty-five thousand denarii a day, or two and a half sesterces for each miner. The mines did not, therefore, return the Romans much more than the equivalent for what they lost yearly. Moreover, the specie was not abundant, as the rates of ordinary interest show; namely, 6 per cent in Italy, which had the most capital, 12 per cent and higher in the provinces. In the reign of Tiberius there was a monetary panic. Its disastrous

---

[1] Pliny (*Hist. nat.* vi. 26 and 32) says of the Arabs: "They are the richest people in the world, for the treasures of the Romans and Parthians flow to them. They sell the products of their seas (pearls from the Persian Gulf) and of their forests (scented woods, incense), and buy nothing." He also speaks of their gold mines, — doubtless the gold which they drew from Africa.

[2] We must also take account of the wear of coin, which obliged Trajan to withdraw all the consular coins from circulation, for the purpose of re-coinage. (See Vol. IV. p. 231. note 4.) M. de Laveleye estimates this loss at a quarter or a half per cent per annum, and at 280,000,000 francs [$13,200,000] yearly the manufacture of gold and silver bars into objects of luxury. These totals are exaggerated; probably they might be reduced by three-quarters for ancient times.

[3] Pliny, *Hist. nat.* xxxiii. 4.

[4] Gold was in proportion more common in the Empire than silver, for the ratio between the two metals was then as 1 to 12, and it has long been with us as 1 to 15. The Roman pound equals .32743 of a kilogramme; the kilogramme of gold is worth at present about $650. A Roman pound of gold was worth then, as metal, about $211.

results were only obviated by the Emperor's constituting from his own resources a fund of a hundred million sesterces. from which were made loans for three years without interest, on the condition of security being given for double the amount on landed property. This clause proves that the crisis especially affected the wealthy class. It had really been brought about by the rigorous application of a law of Caesar forbidding men to keep more than sixty thousand sesterces in specie. A similar law — which was never abolished, for in the next century Trajan and Marcus Aurelius applied it to the senators — obliged those who were unwilling to remain at the discretion of an informer to turn the larger part of their fortunes into real estate. From this it resulted that landed property gained daily in importance, in contrast with that which takes place in modern society, where personal and industrial wealth tends to take the precedence of territorial wealth. Now the latter does not fail, in societies where it dominates, to make an aristocracy of the proprietors of the soil; and to this the Empire finally came.

To conclude: with its small capital, its insufficient industrial implements,[1] and processes of labor which entailed an enormous expenditure of time, men, and money, the Roman world was poor, compared with our modern societies; and this relative poverty gave frightful proportions to isolated excesses. Besides, as it was surrounded by a Barbaric world which furnished it almost nothing, it was obliged to live from itself. Wealth, constantly destroyed by use, was not constantly renewed and increased by production. For the great Roman families the peace established by Augustus had been less profitable than war. In two or three generations they lost under the Empire what they had gained in the time of the Republic; and like two opposing forces which had spent themselves one against the other, the ancient patrician order disappeared at the same time with the family of the Caesars.

---

[1] The ancients had only the simplest machinery for manufacturing purposes; all was done by strength of arm. And how great a waste of force was occasioned by the faulty construction of the most ordinary machines employed by the Romans! According to a law of Constantine, the maximum burden of a four-wheeled cart was 326 kilogrammes for eight horses, — say 43 kilogrammes per horse; while two of our omnibus-horses draw at a trot loads of from 500 to 800 kilogrammes. The dead weight resulting from the bad construction of the vehicle must have been enormous, to which we add the difficulty arising from the very steep grade of the roads. Moreover, to judge from the horseshoes found in the excavations, the draught-horses must have been small and weak (Léger, *Les Travaux publics des Romains*, p. 173).

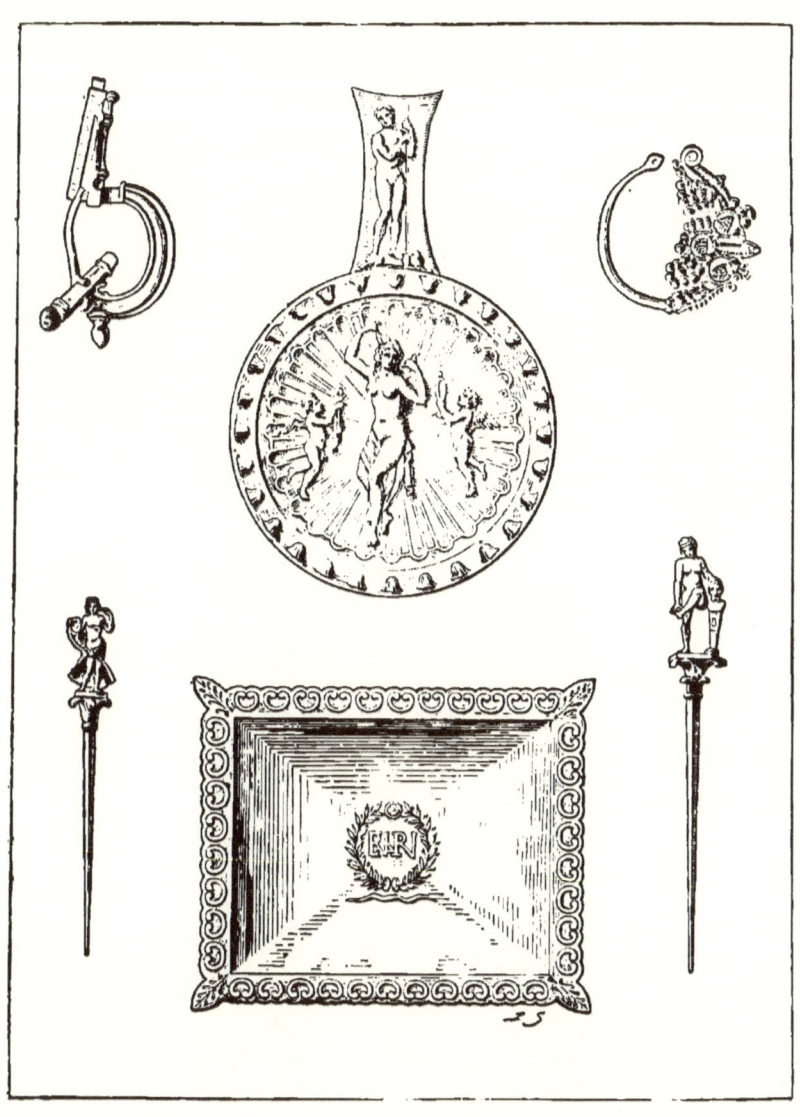

ARTICLES FROM THE JEWEL-CASE OF A ROMAN LADY, FOUND IN 1793.

Without perceiving that the gold obtained by conquest had returned to the conquered, whose commerce and agriculture it revived, Tacitus, at least, well observed the rapid impoverishment of the Roman nobility, and the change in habits of life which resulted therefrom. He even gives its date, — namely, the accession of Vespasian; that is, of the Emperor who was born in a moderate condition. "But when tyrants," he says, "shed the blood of their subjects, and the greatness of reputation formed a motive for destruction, those who escaped grew wiser. Besides, men of no family, frequently chosen senators from the municipal towns, brought with them the frugality they observed at home; and though, by good fortune or industry, many of them grew wealthy as they grew old, yet their former habits continued. But Vespasian was the great promoter of parsimonious living, himself a pattern of primitive strictness in his person and table; hence the compliance of the public with the manners of the Emperor, and the gratification of imitating him, operated more powerfully than the terrors of the law."[1]

The successors of Vespasian followed that Emperor's example Nerva, Trajan even, — notwithstanding some military tastes that he still retained beneath his purple, — Hadrian, and the two Antonines, strictly administered the public finances; and their only extravagance was in the construction of great edifices, which are the glory of a reign when it is art which builds them or public utility which calls for them. All the provincials holding office, who now formed the high society of Rome, readily modelled their mode of life after that of the new court.

We must, therefore, with Tacitus, distinguish two periods in speaking of the manners of the Early Empire, — that which ends at the death of Vitellius, and that which extends from Vespasian to Commodus.

The first of these periods is one of enormous follies. Then were seen those men, of whom there are always some in the world, who sought to dazzle by their conspicuous extravagance, and, having neither talents nor courage, to gain celebrity[2] by a fashionable

---

[1] *Ann.* iii. 55.

[2] . . . *Ut inter istos nomen invenias opus est non tantum luxuriosam rem, sed notabilem facere* . . . *In tam occupata civitate fabulas vulgaris nequitia non invenit* (Seneca, *Epist.* 122).

mistress, by high-bred horses. by banquets worthy of Lucullus.
Under the good Emperors want of occupation, and under the bad
ones the consciousness of danger. drove to these excesses the sons
of the great Roman families. Men took refuge from their idleness,
or their terror, in the profitless tumult of an existence which seemed
busy because it was one of excitement. The reign of Nero marks
the lowest point to which pagan morals fell, and the highest point
reached by the extravagance of the great.

But as, in respect to its political aspects. historians have been
too much disposed to merge the whole Empire in Rome, and take
note only of what went on in the palace or the curia, so in respect
to morals they have made Rome stand for the entire Empire, and
not even the whole of Rome. but the practices of its profligates and
fools. Doubtless elsewhere in the Empire than along the Via
Sacra or under the portico of Quirinus men could be found who
wasted their fortunes, men daily in quest of new pleasures, women
absorbed in the minute details of a costly toilette: but still it was
a very small minority, for it never ceased to excite public remark:
and these persons were dwellers in the great cities, or at the water-
ing-places, or around that Bay of Naples which has witnessed as
much folly as have certain points of the Norman sea-coast.

In respect to the masses of the population, they had gathered
up the crumbs from these too-well served tables. and by ministering
to this extravagance had gained a modest competence, — not enough,
however, to tempt them into cherishing desires beyond their means.

Some facts and figures concerning the table, clothing, and the
dwelling[1] will serve as proofs of these general observations.

II. — THE TABLE, DRESS, AND THE DWELLING.

"THE luxury of the table," says Tacitus, "was practised with
the most costly profusion. maintained for a hundred years. from the
battle of Actium to the revolution by which Galba obtained the

---

[1] On these questions see Friedländer, *Darstellung aus der Sittengeschichte Roms*, etc.
(who for the subjects treated by him supersedes the similar works previously published), and
the learned book by M. Baudrillart, *Histoire du luxe privé et public, depuis l'antiquité jusqu'à
nos jours.*

Empire." It had begun sooner; for celebrities of this class, as Lucullus, Hortensius, Philippus, and the culinary oddities are much earlier than Augustus. In Sylla's sumptuary law Macrobius found a multitude of dishes enumerated as being then very usual which in his time were no longer known. "Ye gods, what a list! To see so many sorts of fish and stews now unknown I cannot help believing that the dissoluteness of manners was extreme in that age." Roman gormandizing, like Roman extravagance, had diminished. Varro before the battle of Actium, and Pliny in Nero's time, show that the last republicans and the first senators of the Empire were rivals in gastronomic sensuality. Then were discovered new articles of food and new methods of preparing those already known. Then was practised what we claim to have invented, — piscienlture,[1] acclimatization, the transplantation of old trees, even of old vines.[2] They had greenhouses for flowers, fruits, the grape, and "the sterile winter is forced to give the products of autumn."[3] On the seacoast of Latium were naturalized fish from the Asiatic coast and many kinds of edible shell-fish ; and that the table of the *bon vivant* might never be without this course even on days when the sea was rough, there were fish-ponds where the best kinds were carefully preserved. These reservoirs were of such dimensions that the heirs of Lucullus derived forty million sesterces from those established by him, — a total which would seem impossible if a contemporary, Varro, had not said that one Hirrius from his obtained annually twelve million sesterces, and that he gave Caesar on one occasion six thousand lampreys.

Roman gluttony, critical and delicate, refused vulgar food such as mutton and beef,[4] it would have lighter dishes, and, in spite of the censor's edicts, the keeping of aviaries and parks became as lucrative as that of fishponds ; there were raised in them every sort of bird and animal, many which we no longer eat, such as the dormouse, peacock, crane, and flamingo. A matron belonging to a consular family sold yearly five thousand fattened thrushes at

---

[1] Pliny relates that a prefect of the fleet, a freedman of Claudius named Optatus, had propagated the *scarus* on the coasts of Latium. In the Lucrine lake, at Bordeaux, etc., there were beds of oysters (Marquardt, vol. v. pp. 2, 53, No. 477).

[2] Seneca, *Epist.* 86. [3] Martial, *Epigr.* viii. 68.

[4] Rome, like Paris, consumed a good deal of roast veal (Cic., *Ad. Fam.* ix. 20) ; instead of mutton, it still consumes an enormous quantity of lamb.

three denarii apiece, and even before the first triumvirate the raising
of peacocks brought Aufidius Lurco sixty thousand sesterces yearly.[1]
It was known how to fatten geese so as to give them an enormous
liver: a consul and a knight dispute the honor of this invention.[2]

The patricians found both pleasure and profit in these matters.
As the French nobility, after having lost political power, gave
themselves up to agricultural improvements, many governors imported plants and fruits from their Asiatic or African provinces,
and had them cultivated on their estates by slaves or freedmen
brought from those regions. From Lucullus, who forty years before
the battle of Actium had included in his share of spoil from Mith-
ridates the cherry-tree of Pontus, to the unknown traveller who in
Pliny's time introduced into the country adjacent to Naples the
melon, originally from the shores of the Oxus, there was a constant importation into Italy of new plants which were afterwards
improved. The Emperor Vitellius's father, for example, who governed Syria under Tiberius, made the attempt to naturalize in
his villa at Alba the greater part of the fruits of that province.
Thus Italy became the acclimatizing garden of the ancient world.[3]
Thence the most beautiful flowers, the most delicious fruits, were
introduced into the West, and those who most eloquently anathe-
matize the luxury of Rome to-day enjoy, without compunction, the
results of Rome's misdeeds.[4]

In speaking of the luxury at the Roman tables we must not
forget two men who mark its culminating point, — Apicius, with
a certain art; Vitellius, with gluttony. There were several Apicii,
of whom the most celebrated lived in the reigns of Augustus and
Tiberius. He invented some dishes, is believed to have composed
a treatise on cookery, and was reputed the greatest epicure living.
For a final honor he was taken as a model by the insane Elagabalus.[5]
He possessed a hundred million sesterces, and killed himself when

---

[1] Varro, *De re rust.* iii. 6, and Pliny, *Hist. nat.* x. 23.

[2] Pliny, *ib.* x. 21. A peacock cost fifty denarii, — dearer than a fat sheep (Varro, *De re
rust.* iii. 6). It was Hortensius who had the former served up at a banquet given to the
augurs.

[3] ... *Italia quae pene totius orbis fruges, adhibito studio colonorum, ferre didicerit*
(Columella, iii. 8).

[4] [On all this interesting subject the special book is Victor Hehn's *Hausthiere und Kultur
pflanzen*, now in its fifth edition. — Ed.]

[5] Histor. August., *Elag.* 18.

he had but ten million left, thinking, like Cardinal de Rohan, that a gentleman could not live on an income less than a hundred thousand dollars. Many moderns have had as capricious fancies without attaining his renown; in our own times many men give entertainments as sumptuous without surprising any one, while those of Apicius astonished some and scandalized others.

As for Vitellius, he was the worthy Emperor of those gormand-izing Romans who discovered a means of always eating, which we will not explain.[1] Yet it seems to have been less an effort of imag-ination than has usually been supposed when he invented his famous Minerva's shield, which held all the rarest eatables, if we judge by the banquets of Trimalchio, or by the feast which was given a cen-tury and a half earlier by the pontiffs and vestals of the Republic. The *menu* of this dinner was religiously preserved by the pontifex Metellus;[2] for sacerdotal feasts were famous at Rome, as they have been everywhere, for the dainty cheer which was provided.[3]

The list is a long one, and the Vatel of those days did his work well; but without doubt Carême, to whom the Czar Alexander gave the pay of a marshal of France, — thirty thousand francs a year, — and Chevet, who has prepared so many official banquets, were much greater *chefs*. And yet we are accustomed to rank Roman gluttony far above our own, wherein we certainly do the latter wrong.

In speaking of the Roman table we must not fail to mention a character who is thoroughly Roman, for in no other society is he found playing so distinct a part; I mean the parasite.

In the delicious climate of the Mediterranean countries, industry is fatiguing; hence men work as little as possible, while they pos-sess a great faculty for enjoyment. But pleasures are expensive, — how obtain them? By manual labor or by traffic? Certainly that is a way, but it seems a poor one; the clever adventurer will rather seek his fortune by his wits than by the work of his hands, espe-cially if he have no scruple in entering upon those evil ways where the informer's vocation, where servility, usury, legacy-hunting, find

---

[1] *Vomunt ut edant, edunt ut vomant* (Seneca, *Ad Helviam*, 10).

[2] *In indice Metelli pontificis maximi* (Macrobius, *Saturn.* III. xiii. 10).

[3] *Capitolinae pontificumque dapes* (Martial, *Epigr.* xii. 48). Cf. Hor., *Carm.* II. iv.; Val. Max., ii. 1, and Apuleius, *Metam. passim: Epulae vel cenae Saliares*.

rich spoil. The one great industry of this class is to live at the expense of others. There is always profit to be derived from the folly or the vanity of the rich, and if a man cannot snatch away an entire fortune, like the informer and the usurer, he can at least devour it piecemeal as a parasite.

He begins as a client: this is the first round of the ladder. "Come, come, Chaerestratus, it is daylight! Get up quickly!" Before sunrise he is on foot. He goes out in haste, his shabby toga on his shoulders, and completes his toilet as he hurries along. Is he on his way to his work? By no means. The true Roman citizen scorns all servile occupations. He is hastening to the house of Trimalchio, his patron. This man is an assiduous client. He must make his zeal noticeable, for that is all he has to live by. From morning till night he is at his patron's heels. What! Chaerestratus in the train of a freedman? Be not surprised; at his side and in the class with himself there are sons of patrician families. At noon he gets his pay. He brings his basket home full of fragments from the master's table. Ennius has said, and Juvenal repeats the words: *Oportet habere*, — a man must have. How he acquires, is of less consequence. An Emperor has said that money is always good, whencesoever it comes.

If Chaerestratus has a fund of humor, or if he has a hard skull, he will rise above the crowd. Instead of lingering around the door, reduced to snuffing the odor of the viands, as Jupiter lives on the smoke of the sacrifices, he will become the constant guest of the master; he is now the parasite. The trade is a good one, although it has its drawbacks; but what has not? Certain rich men enjoy having always at hand a butt, a laughing-stock. They have their slaves, it is true; but what pleasure is it to throw dirt at the head of a slave? That is an old joke, and has ceased to amuse. But a citizen, a Roman of ancient family, whom a freedman may make game of, — that is sport indeed! In an enumeration of the various categories of parasites, this one is called the *plagipatida*, or the *duricapito*. To be thrashed is his vocation. He recognizes his duty, and he bears all without a murmur. His shoulders or his head pay for his meal; and yet the pittance is often a meagre one.

"But what sort of a repast is it, after all!" says Juvenal to the parasite. "Wine such as wool just shorn would not imbibe,

and a mouldy fragment of crust that you cannot bite. . . . See
with how vast a body the lobster served to your patron fills the
dish, and with what fine asparagus it is garnished all around ; with
what a tail he seems to look down in scorn on the assembled guests
when he comes in raised on high by the hands of the tall slave.
But to you is served a common crab, scantily hedged in with half
an egg sliced. — a meal fit only for the dead, and in a dish too
small to hold it. . . . Wranglings prelude a fray, and soon you
begin to hurl cups as well, in retaliation ; . . . some day you will
present your head with shaven crown to be beaten, nor hesitate to
submit to the harsh lash."

Thus treated, — plenty of blows and little food, — the race of
the *duricapito* was dying out. The flatterer took his place. "I,"
said one of them, "attach myself to those men who, in spite
of their poor capacity, wish to be the first in everything. I smile
when they make a joke. They say · Yes,' so do I ; they say ‘No,' I
say ‘No' too. I must indeed be most unlucky for no one to say to
me : · Come and have supper with me.' " [1]

The highest class was the wit. But it is a hard business to
amuse a jaded pleasure-seeker and to be always ready with a *bon
mot !* The *derisor* — that is his name — is always on the watch for
news. He knows the subject of deliberation in the council of King
Pacorus, the number of ships which have left Africa, what has happened and what will never happen, even what Juno has whispered
in Jupiter's ear.

Unfortunately there is a dead season for the parasites when the
rich flee to the country. "Like the snails," says one of them,
" which during the dry season return into their shells and live on
their own juice, so the parasites live on their own means when
those whom they preyed upon are in the country." Happy the
parasite who has been able to put by something for this sad
time ! But he will be despised by his colleagues. "He is a
parasite of naught who has any money in his house." [2] The point
of honor in their profession is that a man must save nothing.
Thus vices make two victims, — the one who has them, and the
one who lives by them.

[1] Juvenal, *Sat.* v. ; Martial, *Epigr.* xii. 83.   [2] Plautus, *Capt.* i. 1, 12–16 ; *Pers.* I. iii. 46.

Yet the Empire was not entirely made up of Apicii or Trimalchios, and for two reasons, — first, the general mediocrity of fortunes permitted excesses only to the few: second, gluttons had a strong force against them in the climate of the country. It was not necessary that in the schools the disciples of Epicurus and Zeno alike should vie with one another in recommending sobriety : Nature, more imperious mistress, made it a law. Excess in alcoholic drinks, dangerous enough in the North, becomes in the South a vice which kills. There too strong a diet quickly brings on mortal diseases : an error as to food has made more victims in the French army in Algeria than the bullets of the Kabyles. The Syrian or African Arab lives on a few dates, and makes long journeys on a little flour mixed in the hollow of his hand with the water of a brook. The Greeks are as temperate now as ever, and the prohibition of wine to the believers in Islam is a salutary measure which Galen recommended in his time to the Romans. "Those who wish to be in good health," he says, "ought to water their wine."[1] In Italy, an intermediate zone between the warm and the damp countries, wine is made and drunk. At the Saturnalia, which was the feast of the lower classes, many drunkards were always to be seen. Some individuals had even aspired to the reputation of being great drinkers: such were Mark Antony the triumvir. Cicero's son, and Novellius Torquatus, who obtained the nickname of Tricongius, from emptying ten litres at a sitting.[2]

In general, sobriety prevailed. The elder Pliny ate very little. Seneca passed a whole year without a mouthful of meat; "he at last gave up wine and perfumes, and he partook of diet which he allowed himself with a moderation much resembling abstinence."

Seneca was fond of quoting from Epicurus: "With bread and water no man is poor, and every one can aspire to the sovereign happiness which Jupiter enjoys." We have seen the bill of fare of Lentulus; now let us examine one of the younger Pliny. A friend

[1] οἶνον ὑδατωμένον. In the East I have myself experienced very distinctly this effect of the climate. A glass of cold water or of coffee appears preferable there to all other drinks. Science, by calculating how much calorie a man loses daily by respiration, clearly explains the necessary sobriety of those living in the South. In cold countries there is a need of increasing the absorption of calorigenous matters, and in hot climates of restricting the amount.

[2] Pliny, Hist. nat. xiv. 28. Three congii equal 2 galls. 1 1/5 pt. Cibum levem et facilem (Pliny, Epist. iii. 5, 10). Seneca, Epist. 108; Id., Epist. 25.

whom he had invited to dinner having failed to accept the invitation, he enumerates, to cause regret to the delinquent, all the dainties which he had prepared, — " A lettuce for each, three snails, two eggs, sweet cake with mead and snow, olives, beet-root, gourds, onions, and many other things as delicate." [1] It was a dinner for a convent. Martial himself asked much less to be content, and the dinner he offers to Turanius is still more modest; although the *menu* is drawn up with the complacency of a poet who sought at the same time to write pleasing verses and to give a model of good taste in gastronomy. The demagogue Ganymede, who attempted to cause a riot at Crotona, claimed no more than thirty-five ases, and wine at discretion. The popular appetite did not then exceed a penny loaf daily; moreover, men submitted to earn it: [2] it is the portion of a *lazzarone*. But if these Southern people were satisfied with little food, they were fond of games, spectacles, fluent speech, and understood marvellously well how to make the most of spendthrifts or seekers after the municipal popularity. Hence so many festivals, public feasts, assemblies. brotherhoods, where, thanks to the Southern animation, the poverty of the spectacle was forgotten,[3] and the meagre entertainment provided at the expense of a vain and yet miserly donor.[4]

Dress. — Taken as a whole, the Roman world spent still less on dress than on food. It had, as we have, its *demi-monde*, who lived with great luxury, ruined young men of good family,[5] and sometimes old senators, and displayed the insolent extravagance which is peculiar to women of this class. Unhappily respectable matrons, or those who knew how to find means discreetly, wished to appear as fine as the courtesans, and expended even more on their toilet. Indeed the *mundus muliebris* was already an arsenal furnished with all the means of attack and preservation. I find belonging to it ointments which were used for painting the face. false teeth. false eyebrows, and even false hair, which was procured from Germany

---

[1] Pliny, *Epist.* i. 15.

[2] *Epigr.* i. 56; v. 78 and x. 48; xi. 52, where the feast is a little more complete. Juvenal sends also to Persicus (*Sat.* xi.) the *carte* of the dinner which he offers him. I do not give it, as it would be suspected of an affected frugality.

[3] See in Petronius, *Satyr.* 45, the "presents of the gladiators of the third quality at two sesterces apiece."

[4] Martial, *Epigr.* x. 74.

[5] See Vol. IV. p. 527. the decree of Claudius.

and India.[1]   The imperial courtesan Messalina, who was a bru-
nette, covered her head with blond hair. "You have your hair
curled, Galla, at a hair-dresser's in Suburra Street, and your eyebrows are brought to you every morning. At night you remove
your teeth as you do your dress. Your charms are inclosed in a
hundred different pots, and your
face does not go to bed with you."[2]

HEADDRESS OF JULIA, DAUGHTER OF
TITUS.[3]

In early times clothing was
made from the wool furnished by
the flock of the farm : by degrees
was introduced the use of Egyptian
linen, of Indian cottons, of China
silk ; there were muslins so transparent that they were called " woven
air." tunics figured with gold or
embroidered with pearls, precious
stones, and every kind of perfume.
At a plain betrothal festivity Pliny
saw Lollia Paulina covered with
pearls and emeralds from head to
foot, and quite ready to prove to
him, from the receipts in her hands,
that she had upon her person to
the value of forty million sesterces.

At an entertainment given by Claudius on Lake Fucinus, Agrippina
appeared in a chlamys woven of gold thread, and Nero, at the
funeral of Poppaea, burned more incense than Arabia Felix could
furnish in a year. "The extravagance of the women," said Pliny
bitterly, " costs us yearly a hundred million sesterces, which Arabia,
India, and Serica take from us."[4]   India alone took half this
amount. What would he say now that this same country takes
from Europe, one year with another, in coin or bars, forty or fifty
times more than in his days? Asiatic products were at that time
much dearer than now. Caesar gave a ring to Servilia which had

---

[1] This trade in hair was so considerable that the *Digest* (xxxix. 4, 16, sect. 7) enumerates
the *capilli indici* among the articles subject to custom-dues (Martial, *Epigr.* v. 68).

[2] Juvenal, *Sat.* vi. 120 ; Martial, *Epigr.* ix. 38.

[3] Capitoline Museum.

[4] *Hist. nat.* vi. 26 ; ix. 58 ; xii. 41.

cost him six million sesterces; Pliny values a pound of cinnamon
at fifteen hundred denarii: and in Aurelian's reign silk brought
its weight in gold.[1] Prices like these are unknown in our time.
But if the Eastern trade, which now exceeds seven milliards
[$1,330,000,000],[2] was represented by only a hundred million ses-
terces, and the commodities imported had the value which has been
assigned to them, we must admit that a very small amount of them
entered the Empire, and that a very few persons could have enjoyed
them. We are thus brought to the same conclusion, and we can
best express it by borrowing from Galen his own words: " In the
large cities rich women have silk, and for them are prepared at
Rome the perfumed essences."

Notwithstanding some extravagances of feminine luxury,[3] a comparison, if it were made, would not give the advantage of simplicity
to the moderns. We no longer live in the days when the gentlemen of Francis I. " wore their mills and their meadows on their
shoulders," when men's costume, made of gold, silver, silk, and
lace, cost, as did that of Bassompierre, more than forty thousand
livres; but our social life is still subjected to the most capricious
of sovereigns, — namely, fashion, — which every year changes the
cut and color of materials. The ancients were not subjected to this
servitude; and as for men, their dress covered the figure without
fitting it, one or two pieces of stuff thrown around the loins and
over the shoulders sufficing to clothe them. Any man could cut a
toga; and on holidays everybody, from the Emperor to the lowest
of the citizens, wore this garment. Between that of the rich and
that of the poor the difference was only in the whiteness and
fineness of the material; the man of fashion added the art of draping
himself well in it and making the folds fall gracefully. He moreover desired to have a well-stocked wardrobe, because the climate
compelled him to change his toga often, and his chief extravagance

---

[1] *Libra enim auri tunc libra serici fuit* (Vopiscus, *Aurel.* 41). Silk was sold at Rome (Martial, *Epigr.* xi. 27) and murrhine vases, which were imported from Parthia and Caramania. One
of these, bought by Nero, brought a price of three hundred talents [about $285,000] (Pliny,
Hist. nat. xxxvii. 7 and 8). Pliny mentions also a crystal cup sold at a hundred and fifty thousand sesterces, a Babylonian carpet bought by Nero for four million sesterces, some tables in
Mauretanian citron wood costing as much as one million four hundred thousand sesterces, etc.

[2] Neumann, *Uebersichten über Welthandel.*

[3] Tacitus (*Ann.* iii. 53) and Pliny (*Hist. nat.* xii. 41) speak, as regards dress, of the
luxury of women only.

was to have cloaks in different shades of purple. Caesar had forbidden these except for certain persons and on certain days; Augustus, Tiberius, even Nero, renewed these prohibitions without more
success, for in Domitian's reign Martial speaks of purple robes
publicly bought for ten thousand sesterces.[1]

The Dwelling Houses. — The favorite extravagance of the Romans
of the Empire was in the matter of buildings; they covered the
world with them. In the history of each reign we have seen the
numberless works undertaken by the Emperors, beginning with the
first. Augustus had built for the gods and the people; Caligula
and Nero built for themselves immense palaces which disappeared
with them. Of Nero's Golden House there remain only the descriptions by Suetonius and Pliny; but Livia's humble abode still exists.
Private individuals rivalled the Emperors. Already under the
Republic the nobility, driven from the city by the malaria, had
adopted the practice of passing the summer on the hills which over-
look the Roman Campagna,[2] or on the shores of the Bay of Naples.
When an imperial decree obliged the senators to invest a third of
their fortune in Italian landed property, the entire peninsula was
soon covered with country-houses, — and all the more quickly because
no country in the world is better adapted by its sites and climate
for pleasure residences of all kinds, whether on the shores of its two
seas or its many lakes, or on the slopes of its hills, which under a
burning sun keep their forests and their springs nourished by the
winter snows.[3] To these natural beauties the arts of Greece added
their charms. The most varied marbles,[4] stucco, glass, bronze, gold
and silver leaf, elegant paintings, fine arabesques which Raphael
did not disdain to imitate, decorated the walls, the ceilings, and,
that no space might be left unadorned, the floors bore mosaic

---

[1] *Epigr.* vi. 61; viii. 10.

[2] The villas of Pompey, Hortensius, Lucullus, and Cicero were famous. Yet the consuls
valued the villas of Cicero at Tusculum and Formiae, the former only at five hundred thousand
sesterces, and the latter at two hundred and fifty thousand (Cic., *Ad Att.* iv. 2). [But he
complains of this valuation bitterly. — ED.]

[3] The chalk-hills contain a number of caverns, which become filled at the time of rains,
and abundantly supply the springs during the summer. Thus it has been calculated that three
fourths of the quantity of the waters of the Tiber during low-water season are supplied from
subterranean lakes, and that its summer flow is never less than half the usual supply (Reclus,
Nouv. géog. univ. i. 460, 461).

[4] The most valuable marbles in Martial's time were those of Carystus in Euboea, Laconia,
Synnada in Phrygia, and Numidia. Cf. *Epigr.* ix. 75.

work, some of which were magnificent compositions, — as, for example, the battle between Darius and Alexander, found at Pompeii in the
"Faun's house," the figures in which are almost of natural size. In
the interior, columns of Numidian or Euboean marble, for which
in the next century Egyptian porphyry was substituted, supported
porticos where the air circulated freely, — in the summer protecting
from the sun, and in the winter concentrating its light and warmth.
At every step a statue, a costly vase, some object of art, some rich

BATTLE BETWEEN DARIUS AND ALEXANDER.[1]

hanging. Many rooms were decorated with special care, — the
atrium, where stood the *dii lares*, the images of ancestors, and
fragrant plants which purified the atmosphere; adjacent, were the
tablinum and the *cxedra* for visitors; farther away, the *triclinium*
for guests;[2] in a place apart, the women's room; elsewhere the
quarters for slaves. The courts were kept cool by "jets of water
received in marble basins bordered with flowers, as the rose,
the lily, violet, anemone, and the myrtle artistically trimmed," [3]
and, when space permitted it, some fine plane-tree, with smooth

---

[1] Mosaic of Pompeii.

[2] In the *tablinum* and the *triclinium* of Livia's house are found the Roman paintings which,
till quite lately, were the most ancient that had been discovered. Those of the tomb of the
Statilii Tauri (frontispiece to Vol. IV. Sect. II.) are anterior.

[3] *Lilia et violas et anemonas et fontes surgentes . . . tonsasque myrtos . . . habeant divites*
(Quintilian, viii. 3). Cf. Hor., *Carm.* ii. 15.

bark and elegant and vigorous form, afforded its shade.[1]   The
patio of the Spaniards calls to mind this charming taste.   Two
other buildings were never wanting to a complete habitation. — the
library, which was small, although all this society was literary, or
wished to appear such; and the baths, a complicated and expensive
structure,[2] consisting of several successive rooms of different temperature, ending with a palaestra, where gymnastic exercises restored
suppleness and strength to the limbs.   In the sanitary plans of the

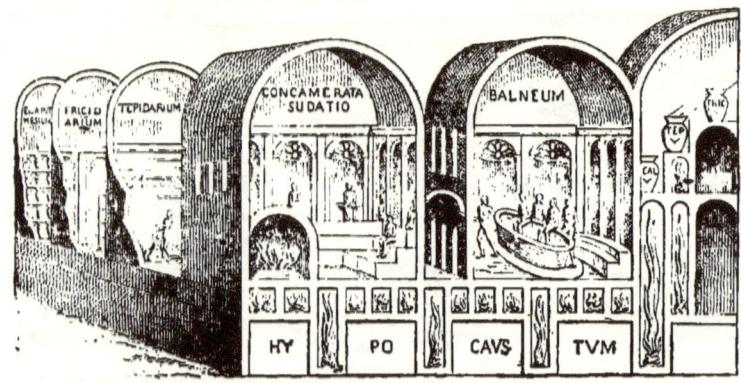

THE INTERIOR OF A BATH.[3]

Romans the bath with all its accessories played the principal part,
and no Roman passed the day without taking one.

At the same time, with all their grandeur and luxury, these
habitations were almost always arranged less with a view to comfort and home life than for ostentation.   Men prided themselves
upon their wealth now, as in earlier days upon their consulships,
and notoriety was sought by expensive buildings, since it could no
longer be obtained by triumphs.   The aristocracy of money had
succeeded the aristocracy of race.

The provincial cities imitated Rome, furnishing themselves, each
according to its resources, with temples and arenas, baths and

---

[1] *Areola quae quatuor platanis inumbratur* (Pliny, *Epist.* v. 6).

[2] Juvenal (*Sat.* vii. 178) speaks of private baths having cost six hundred thousand sesterces, and Horace of fish-ponds larger than Lake Lucrinus (*Carm.* ii. 15).   Respecting baths,
see Vol. IV. p. 354.

[3] A restoration made in the time of the Renaissance at the order of an architect, as a
theoretical plan of ancient baths.

FOUNTAIN IN MOSAIC DISCOVERED AT POMPEII IN 1881.

We are indebted to the kindness of M. Fiorelli, director-general of the excavations in Italy, for the drawing of this curious fountain, discovered in 1881.

theatres, basilicas and senate-houses. It was customary even to copy the names of streets: Antioch in Pisidia had a Velabrum and a Tuscan district; Lyons and the city of the Mattiaci, a Vatican; Toulouse and Cirta, a Capitol,[1] — a name which is still borne by the far from Roman town-house of the queen of Languedoc. Many cities had, like the capital, factions of the circus and distributions of corn. Their rich citizens had also, like the Roman senators, their house in town and their country-house each, and even several rural residences, to have variety of climate, and yet be always at home.[2] Accordingly, there was no lake or hot-spring, no hill-side well situated for the view or the sun, which had not its villa; when needful, Nature was forced to bend to the owner's taste. A rivulet flowed where a hill had once been; rocks once bare were covered with vineyards, and woods; men built out into the sea to have fish-ponds and baths which no tempest could disturb,[3] and "the azure wave retreated before the huge piers."[4] At Antium may still be seen remains of these submarine constructions. Were it not for the ocean tides from which the shores of Antium and Pozzuoli were exempt, our Norman sea would also be soon obliged to retreat before these costly constructions; but our modern rhetoricians would not find in them a subject for philosophical declamations.

Some of these dwellings were of great size: Seneca compares them to towns.[5] Still, all that we know of Roman antiquities leads us to suppose that the habitations of the majority were small and of little value. "At Sora, at Fabrateria, at Frusino," says Juvenal, "you can have a pretty house for the rent of a cellar at Rome."[6]

At Pompeii, which had some wealthy citizens, but two or three

---

[1] Henzen, *Index*, p. 168.

[2] The villas of the younger Pliny were in all parts of Italy, from the south to the foot of the Alps.

[3] See in Statius (*Silv.* ii. 2) his pretentious description of the villa of his friend Pollius Felix at Sorrento, and (*Silv.* i. 3) that of the villa of Vopiscus on the Anio. Cf. Seneca (*Epist.* 55) for the villa of Vatia at Baiae, and Philostratus (*Vit. Soph.* ii. 23) for that of the sophist Damianus at Ephesus.

[4] Ovid, *Am.* iii. 126.

[5] *Domos instar urbium* (Seneca, *Epist.* 90; *id.* 89). Tacitus speaks also somewhere of the *villarum infinita spatia.* Exaggerations so easily come to be habitual that a translator of Martial renders *non unius balnea solus habes* thus: "Thou possessest baths which might serve a whole people." Modern rhetoric, outdoing the ancient, has altered the true character of Roman history.

[6] *Sat.* iii. 223.

important dwellings have been found; the houses are small, the rooms low and dark, — our workmen would refuse to live in them, — and in the narrow streets, every few steps blocked by high crossing stones, only litters and hand-carriages could pass. At Athens the foundations of the old houses are still smaller, and Livia's house on the Palatine seems very unlike the abode of an empress. Pliny was rich, and possessed villas at the gates of Rome, in Tuscany, Beneventum, and near Como an estate belonging to him was let

PLINY'S VILLA.[1]

for more than four hundred thousand sesterces. He had besides, he tells us, some money employed in trade.[2] Accordingly, notwithstanding large benefactions to his native town and to his friends, he was still in a position to purchase a property worth three million sesterces in Latium. Lastly, he had a young wife whom he loved; he was a constant guest at the palace; he belonged by rank, relations, and fortune to the highest Roman society. Without doubt, therefore, his mode of life was that suited to one of the leading

---

[1] Restoration by Canina.

[2] *Epist.* v. 6.   *In Tusculano* (iv. 13) is put for *in Tuscano* (Henzen, *Tab. alim.* p. 63). *Epist.* x. 24; *Ib.* iii. 29.

persons of the Empire. Now he has left us a minute description
of his two villas at Laurentinum, on the sea-coast, and Tifernum, in
the upper valley of the Tiber. They contain every appliance for
comfort, but nothing for luxury, unless it be an object of beauty.
He does not tell us of his Corinthian bronzes, his paintings, his
statues, copies of Greek masterpieces; he speaks neither of the
rich tissues which he possesses, nor of Calpurnia's jewelry: but
he describes the judicious arrangement of the rooms, looking out
upon the sea or the mountains, where sunshine is found in the
autumn, coolness in the summer, and at all times calm and peace.[1]
We may say this was a wise man. Yes; but there were many
like him, who honorably enjoyed their wealth, who knew how to
use it well, and despised the vulgar pleasures of the prodigals, —
whose reign, moreover, had for the time passed away.

If we compare these dwellings with the *châteaux* of our rich
manufacturers, we shall probably find in the latter[2] less taste, but
more luxury; and there are houses belonging to English noblemen
which not even the most magnificent Roman villa ever equalled
in extent or in wealth of art treasures, furniture, plate, rare plants,
or in the efforts made to make use of the sun and brave the climate.
In all that relates to the delights of life we have received lessons
from Rome; but how greatly have the pupils surpassed their
masters![3]

The same is true of the passion for horses: some at Rome were
as celebrated as our winners at Longchamp, and they were sold as
dear. Caligula proposed to decorate his horse Incitatus with the
consular insignia, and Martial's popularity, in his best days of
public favor, was eclipsed by that of the racer Andremon. The

[1] It is probable that the description of Pliny's villa might be completed by borrowing from Martial that of the villa of Faustinus (iii. 58). The orator disdains to enter into details in which the poet, who is more simple, takes a delight.

[2] Yet in Pliny's villa at Tifernum there were many trifles of doubtful taste; and as there was affectation in his style, so we find it in his gardens, with their box-trees shaped as letters or in the figure of animals, their plants which design names, etc. If a meal is to be served here, the heavier dishes are arranged on the borders of the basin, and the lighter in vases in the form of ships and birds which float on the water.

[3] An economist has calculated that ten thousand English families possess plate to the value of at least five hundred pounds, and a hundred and fifty thousand to the value of a hundred pounds. The Romans had certainly much less. At Pompeii down to 1837 there had been discovered in the ruins only a hundred objects in silver (Becker, *Gallus*, ii. 322). It is true that many of the inhabitants returned to save their more precious property.

follies of the circus correspond to those of our race-courses; the latter are even greater than were the former, for betting is more general and higher at Longchamp and Epsom than it ever was at Rome or Antioch. In Apulia, Calabria, Sicily, and Cappadocia, vast pastures served for rearing horses, — which were always in demand, because travellers and merchants, rich men and those who sought to become rich, required them for pleasure or for business. The cross-bred horses of Spain and Africa were considered the best;

THE BIGA OF THE VATICAN.[1]

Antioch bought such, at great cost, on the banks of the Tagus and Guadalquivir. We import such from the Nedjed, — a still greater distance, and a more difficult journey. The Romans kept genealogies of the circus-winners; we have the stud-book, which is under the supervision of government. Putting aside betting-men and men of fashion, for whom the race-course is a place of business, we find that our hundred and twenty hippodromes are useful institutions. Why should we so sharply blame among the ancients what we

[1] An antique chariot of marble, decorated in relievo, with rosettes combined with foliage and corn-ears. Only one of the horses is antique. The sculptor Franzoni restored this beautiful monument, for which Pius VI. had constructed the rotunda in the Vatican called the Hall of the Biga.

approve among ourselves? Let us condemn on both sides the excesses, the scandals, and the money squandered, but let us accept the rest.

III. — The Smaller Industries and Fortunes.

On one point we are happily inferior to the ancients, — we require few domestic servants, while they had many. Thus the wife of Apuleius, whose fortune was not at all extraordinary, — four million sesterces, — possessed such a number that she was able to give each of her sons by her first marriage a wedding present of four hundred slaves.[1]

All the work of the house, and often that of the farm, was done by them. But industry having enlarged the field of labor, and the means of acquisition having increased in the same ratio with the wants that had been created, the owners of slaves had found it advantageous to interest them in increasing the produce of the earth and in rivalling free labor. Hence those *coloni* who had a right to a share in the crops, and those slaves engaged in industrial occupations and in traffic on equal shares with their masters.[2] The savings amassed in these forms of labor brought about numerous enfranchisements; and as the freedmen were the most intelligent of the slaves, after gaining freedom many attained to a competency, and some even to wealth. Doubtless they did not all go as far as Narcissus; but many gained enough to form in every city a class whose importance the treasury declared by imposing on it a special tax, — the *vectigal artium*.[3]

To the large fortunes corresponded the large estates, — another favorite subject of philosophic declamation. The ancients always

---

[1] This indicates that they were of inferior quality. Xenophon valued an ordinary slave at about $18.50 (1½ to 2 minae). The Roman soldiers were redeemed by the Achaeans at the rate of five minae, — about $87.50. Papinian, under Septimius Severus, fixed the usual price of a slave at 20 aurei. The indemnity granted by England in 1834 for the liberation of the slaves was at the rate of about $121. France gave in 1848 for the liberated slaves of Martinique $80.75, of Guadeloupe, $89.30, Senegal, $39.90, Nossibé, $13.30 apiece. These sums were much lower than the current rates. But we see that at both periods the price of human flesh was nearly the same.

[2] See above, p. 6 *et seq.*

[3] Suet., *Cal.* 40; Lampridius, *Alex. Sev.* 24.

made a boast of the seven acres of Curius and Fabricius, and
they were right; in the time when from the top of the Capitol
the enemy's frontier could be seen, the smallness of men's fortunes
was the guaranty of liberty and a means of safety. But when
Rome had become a world: when the class of small landowners
in Latium had been destroyed by war: when from the spoils of
victory and pillage the chiefs could form large domains; when
commerce and industry, developed by peace, in the heart of this
immense Empire opened new sources of wealth, — this economic
revolution, accomplished in a short space of time, produced political
and social perturbations which caused patriots and philosophers
to condemn wealth in all its forms. Then the elder Pliny exclaimed: "The *latifundia* have destroyed Italy, and they will soon
destroy the provinces." But Italian husbandry, which had long
employed irrigation,[1] was now seeking to appropriate the agricultural
improvements made in other climates. The rich alone possessed
the needful capital for running the risks and supporting the expense
of these experiments, so that large ownerships, — an evil at the
period when manners were simple, and later an inevitable consequence of the conquest of the world — had finally become a necessity
in the new social conditions. French agriculture would be im-
perilled if the profits of manufacturing industry did not build up
again the large estate in proportion as the civil code destroys it.
Besides, we find on this subject the usual exaggeration. Seneca,
who makes a sea out of a pond, does not hesitate to make a kingdom out of a farm.[2] Now the large estates were not more numerous than the large fortunes. The most extensive parks, inclosed
by walls, known to Varro, contained from twenty-five to thirty-
two acres; even in France there are many larger than this. In
Scotland, which within a century has increased tenfold in wealth,
the twelve largest landowners possess 4,339,722 acres.[3] At the
very gates of Rome the small proprietors were probably less rare

---

[1] Vergil speaks of it, —

Claudite jam rivos, pueri, sat prata biberunt.

[2] *Epist.* 89 and 90. Martial says also *Palestrina regna* of a little property at Praeneste
given by a patron to his client (xi. 71).

[3] The Duke of Sutherland alone has 1,207,190 acres, — the average extent of a French
department; and sixteen landowners in England hold 1,105,758, or an average of 69,110
apiece (*Enc. Brit.* 9th edit.).

than now.[1] In the territory of Caere a man who possessed fourteen *jugera* (not quite nine acres) is called by Martial the richest agriculturist in the district,[2] and he may well have appeared such to the poet, who, like many others, had an estate so small that he used to say: "My land bears only myself."[3] At Velleia forty-six landowners, probably the richest in the country, had estates of an average value of $13,000 to $15,000: these figures do not indicate extreme concentration of properties. Lastly, the *latifundia* were not always cultivated by servile labor; the younger Pliny used to let his lands to farmers,[4] and Columella advised the employment of free peasants (*coloni*).

We reason about the Empire, starting from the hypothesis that all was done by slave-labor. That had been nearly the case at the time when war encumbered Rome and Italy with captives, when Crassus had twenty thousand slaves whom he let out to contractors for all sorts of employments. But since the legions had restricted their duties to guarding the frontiers, war no longer supplied this trade, and the gaps made in the slave-population by mortality and manumissions were scarcely filled by servile births, slave-trading, the exposure, theft, and sale of children. There was left, therefore, for free artisans a large place in the field of labor, and this increased daily, in proportion as were developed the manufacturing industries of clothing, articles of food, building, objects of art, and the immense commerce which had to transport and sell the world's commodities. Saint Paul desired that the bishops and priests should follow an honest calling; and when Dion Chrysostom fled from Rome with no other property than Plato's *Phaedo* and an oration of Demosthenes, he was able to reach the extreme limits of the Empire by living on the road by the labor of his hands in the country farms or the city gardens.[5] Thus the foolish expenditure which dissipated patrician fortunes fell in golden rain on the workman and filled the strong-box of the merchant.

Even previous to the Empire, Varro pointed out to small proprietors the advantages they would secure by establishing "gardens

---

[1] Pliny (*Hist. nat.* xiv. 5) mentions several of them in a single chapter.
[2] *Epigr.* vi. 73.
[3] *Nil nostri, nisi me, ferunt agelli.*
Ibid. vii. 31.
[4] *Epist.* ix. 37.
[5] *Orat.* i.

in the neighborhood of cities, where flowers and fruit are sold for their weight in gold." [1]   As a proof of what could be done with small means and tact, he mentions the case of two of his old soldiers, brothers, the possessors of a small house with a half acre of land, which they had covered with plants loved by the bees, and who, from the honey of their hives, made yearly on the average

IRON STRONG-BOX FOUND AT POMPEII.[2]

ten thousand sesterces.[3] In the cities a multitude of trades needed by the rich, and requiring special workmen who were not to be found among their slaves, furnished work and bread to the poor. Juvenal's barber becomes possessor of fields and houses; Martial sees a shoemaker obtain a fortune which he himself never obtained.[4] Now of these people with small means, who by dint of economy, skill, and strokes of fortune were able to rise above their condition, there were then, as now, a very large number.[5] When Domitian

---

[1] *De Re rust.* i. 2 and 16.   [2] Museum of Naples.
[3] *Ibid.* iii. 16, 10.
[4] Juvenal, *Sat.* i. 24 ; he refers to it a second time (x. 224).   Martial, *Epigr.* ix. 74.
[5] On the countless number of small shopkeepers and small tradesmen at Rome, see Friedländer, i. 218 *et seq.*

had cleared the streets of the stalls which encumbered them. Martial exclaimed : "Rome is at last Rome again ; but lately the city was only one immense shop."[1] And the example of Pompeii proves that it was the same in the small cities.[2]

With its fifteen or eighteen hundred thousand inhabitants, Rôme presented the same social phenomena as our modern cities : above the small tradesfolk, the greater ones ; not far from the hovels where the former worked, the splendid establishments in which the latter carried on their business ; a rag-fair in all the narrow streets ; a Boulevard des Italiens along the Via Sacra, in the Septa of the Campus Martius, and in the Tuscan quarter ; here palaces, there stalls, — in a word, everywhere the hard struggle for life ; and then, as now, the small sometimes ended by consuming the great, the poor devouring the rich, industrious and skilful frugality getting the better of idle and prodigal wealth.

Official literature, — I mean the literature of high life, which is all that has come down to us, — living on the commonplaces of the past, saw nothing of all this industry, and continued to despise the laboring classes ; to this remark exception must be made in the case of Dion Chrysostom, who ranks the useful workman above the rhetorician with his gilded, empty speech.[3] But inscriptions, shop-signs, shapeless and yet significant fragments which were formerly neglected by history, attest this transformation, — the agricultural community of the elder Cato becoming the industrial community of the Empire. It was an economic and, of consequence, a social revolution, which, as we have shown,[4] made a very great change in the civil law. The same revolution was going on in all the provinces. Observe in the Museum at Saint-Germain the numerous sepulchral monuments to artisans which the excavations in Gaul alone have already brought to light. These monuments are evidence of two

---

[1] *Nunc Roma est, nuper magna taberna fuit.*

Epigr. vii. 61.

See also Mamurra's walk through the bazaars, *ubi Roma suas aurea vexat opes* (*ibid.* ix. 59).

[2] The inscription in Orelli, No. 4,323, where we read that a single proprietor at Pompeii had nine hundred shops to let, has another meaning (cf. *C. I. L.* iv. 1,136) ; but we still see in the ruins of this city a number of shops.

[3] *Orat.* vii. We do indeed find in Seneca, Statius, Lucian, etc., more than one passage in which labor is praised ; but it is only a passing reference. So long as slavery existed, the ideas of literary men would be opposed to the rehabilitation of labor.

[4] See, above, the chapter on The Family. The collections of inscriptions prove the large number of industrial colleges existing in the cities, and the great variety of industries.

facts. — the prosperity of these working men, who were rich enough
to prepare costly tombs for themselves. and the pride of these representatives of free labor. who. far from concealing their condition,
wished to be seen after death with the tool which they had used
during life. These men were evidently proud of their calling ; and
if this were so. their fellow-citizens must have considered their
pride legitimate.

Luxury is not in itself blamable ; when it is restricted and in
good taste. it reveals in those who show it a refinement suggesting
the existence of other virtues. Some of the charming paintings at
Pompeii give us no bad opinion of the men who ordered them,
and we are pleased to find in Livia's house those elegant decorations which suggest a well-regulated life. Plato has said: "The
beautiful is profitable." It is that luxury of a baser kind. which
leads into foolish. unproductive expenditure or addresses itself to
the sensual appetites, that should be proscribed. The latter filled
a large place in the Rome of the early Caesars. and we do not in-
tend to make its apology. It stimulated those passions which should
most carefully be restrained ; and were this the only form that
men could have. they would do better to dispense with it altogether.
Unfortunately the two forms are usually found together, and hence
philosophy condemns them both. History. which is better acquainted
with the true conditions of human societies. is satisfied with brand-
ing the abuse and showing that, by a just law of expiation. ill-
gotten wealth is rapidly scattered by the children of the spoliators.
The destitution of Hortalus. the despair of Apicius. the death of
so many personages who. like Vitellius. ended upon the Gemoniae
the orgies begun in palaces. inspire little pity. For these individual
disasters. history finds full compensation in the increased comfort
of the masses and in the substitution for an exhausted patriciate
of a new nobility having Tacitus and Pliny for its orators. Verginius
Rufus and Agricola for its generals, and Trajan and Hadrian for
its Emperors.

IV. — MAGNIFICENCE OF THE PUBLIC WORKS; THEATRES AND AMPHITHEATRES.

ANOTHER reservation is to be made when we speak of the enormous extravagance of the Romans; it is this: a part of the revenues of the state and the wealth of private individuals was employed in constructions not intended, like Versailles, to gratify the pride of the monarch, or, like the castles of the feudal lords of Mediæval Europe, to strengthen the insolence of a caste, but designed to promote the general interests of the Empire, — as highways, bridges, arsenals, and harbors, — or the beliefs, the pleasures, and the welfare of the masses. — like temples and basilicas, baths and porticos, circuses and theatres. The old words always in use at Rome and in the provincial cities, " the Republic and the sovereign people," compelled the Emperor on the banks of the Tiber, the rich in their municipium, to pay to the poor, in all sorts of gifts, the price of their power and their honors.

THE FLAVIAN AMPHITHEATRE.[1]

Of this Augustus set an example. It will be remembered that he boasted of having left Rome marble; and the most economical of the Emperors, Vespasian, did not hesitate to expend enormous sums in constructing the gigantic edifice called by the Romans the Colosseum. Even of the bad Emperors there were few who did not undertake some edifice intended for public utility. What modern capital has given to the masses buildings worthy of comparison with the theatre of Marcellus, the baths of Caracalla, the Colosseum of Vespasian, or those porticos where a man could walk in the open air, yet sheltered from sun and rain, for miles, with the masterpieces of Greek art before his eyes? If we except what has been done within the last few years in London and Paris, what are our aqueducts compared with those of the Romans for supplying water to the urban populations? In the countries of the South water is an object of prime necessity, since the bath is indispensable

---

[1] The Colosseum. The reverse of a large bronze of Titus representing in the centre the Colosseum, on the left a pyramid, and on the right a part of the Golden House.

for health. A gratuitous water-supply was, as we should say, a very democratic measure ; but the Romans knew how to make it everywhere accessible. Rome is still, notwithstanding the destruction of so many of the ancient aqueducts, the city best provided with public fountains in the world.[1] In the provincial cities the obtaining of a water-supply was the first important concern of the curia. We have seen, in Pliny's correspondence when governor of Bithynia, what vast sums were spent on these works. In modern times Lyons, between her two rivers, was long insufficiently supplied with water ; and the same was true in the case of Nîmes. In the former city the Romans had been able to raise water to the summit of Fourvières, and in the latter to bring it by the Pont du Gard from the pure springs of the Cevennes.[2]

A DANCER.[3]

Theatres and Amphitheatres. — That the Roman theatres were more harmful than useful to the public, was not the fault of those

[1] Water for drinking purposes per day per head: at Rome (1869), 0.944 m.; at Paris (1875), 0.2 m.; at London (1874), 0.125 m. (Reclus, *Nouv. géogr. univ.* p. 471).

[2] The aqueduct of Segovia is 216 feet high, the Pont du Gard 155 feet. The *Anio Vetus*, constructed B. C. 272, is 43,000 paces long; the *Aqua Marcia*, in 144, 62,000; the *Anio Novus*, in A. D. 52, 59,000. The total length of all the conduits which bring water to Rome was 263 miles, of which nearly twenty were on arches (Saglio's *Dict. des Antiq.: Aqueducs*).

[3] Statue from the Villa Albani.

www.ingramcontent.com/pod-product-compliance
Lightning Source LLC
Chambersburg PA
CBHW020941030726
47496CB00005B/1303